THE COLLECTED WORKS OF
G. K. CHESTERTON

XVIII

THE COLLECTED WORKS OF G. K. CHESTERTON
XVIII

THOMAS CARLYLE

LEO TOLSTOY

ROBERT LOUIS STEVENSON

CHAUCER

With Introduction and Notes by Russell Kirk

IGNATIUS PRESS   SAN FRANCISCO

© 1991 Ignatius Press, San Francisco
All rights reserved
ISBN 0-89870-373-5 (HB)
ISBN 0-89870-374-3 (PB)
Library of Congress catalogue number 85-81511
Printed in the United States of America

CONTENTS

General Editors' Introduction	7
A Note on the Texts	9
A Note on the Notes	11
Introduction by Russell Kirk	13
THOMAS CARLYLE	19
LEO TOLSTOY	33
ROBERT LOUIS STEVENSON	39
I 'The Myth of Stevenson'	41
II In the Country of Skelt	52
III Youth and Edinburgh	62
IV The Reaction to Romance	73
V The Scottish Stories	85
VI The Style of Stevenson	95
VII Experiment and Range	103
VIII The Limits of a Craft	114
IX The Philosophy of Gesture	123
X The Moral of Stevenson	132
CHAUCER	149
Introduction	151
I The Greatness of Chaucer	154
II The Age of Chaucer	174
III Public and Private Life	207
IV The Garden of Romance	235

CONTENTS

V	The Canterbury Tales	265
VI	Chaucer as an Englishman	291
VII	Chaucer and the Renaissance	315
VIII	The Religion of Chaucer	338
IX	The Moral of the Story	361

GENERAL EDITORS' INTRODUCTION

This volume contains several of Chesterton's finest commentaries on the lives and philosophical perspective of literary giants. Like his works on Saint Francis of Assisi and Saint Thomas Aquinas, G. K. Chesterton captures the soul of his subjects. *Robert Louis Stevenson*, for instance, generated this comment from Sir Edmond Gosse:

> I have just finished reading the book in which you smite the detractors of R. L. S. hip and thigh. I cannot express without a sort of hyperbole the sentiments which you have awakened of joy, of satisfaction, of relief, of malicious and vindictive pleasure. . . .
>
> It is and always since his death has been impossible for me to write anything which went below the surface of R. L. S. I loved him, and still love him, too tenderly to analyse him. But you, who have the privilege of not being dazzled by having known him, have taken the task into your strong competent hands. You could not have done it better.
>
> The latest survivor, the only survivor, of his little early circle of intimate friends thanks you from the bottom of his heart.

We are honored that Dr. Russell Kirk agreed to write the introduction to this volume. For more than forty years, Dr. Kirk has been in the thick of the intellectual controversies of our time. He has authored over twenty-five books that cover modern culture, political thought and practice, education theory and literary criticism. His 1953 work *The Conservative Mind*, revived the conservative intellectual movement in this country. President Ronald Reagan conferred upon Dr. Kirk the Presidential Citizens' Medal for distinguished service to the United States. He is the only man of letters to have received this award.

GEORGE J. MARLIN
RICHARD P. RABATIN
JOHN L. SWAN
General Editors

JOSEPH SOBRAN
Consulting Editor

PATRICIA AZAR
JOE MYSAK
REV. RANDALL PAINE, O.R.C.
Associate Editors

A NOTE ON THE TEXTS

Thomas Carlyle was published in 1902 by Hodder and Stoughton. It appeared in the series called "The Bookman Booklets", no. 1 December. J. F. Hodder Williams was listed as Co-Author. He contributed the biographical and portrait footnotes. Those footnotes are not included in this volume.

Leo Tolstoy was first published in 1903 by Hodder and Stoughton in "The Bookman Booklets", no. 3, March. The text from the 1904 edition, reissued as no. 4 in "The Bookman" series, is used in this volume.

The first British edition of *Robert Louis Stevenson* published in 1927 by Hodder and Stoughton is used in this volume.

Chaucer first appeared in 1932. The text found in this volume is from the British first edition published in 1932 by Faber and Faber.

A NOTE ON THE NOTES

Chesterton himself never used footnotes, and he would be surprised and amused that we are propping up some of his pages with these little annotations. We have decided, however, both in deference to G. K. and for the training of the reader, to let the vast majority of the pages stand on their own and leave a host of generally familiar names and references unannotated. As a rule, therefore, notes are furnished only for references clearly crucial to the context and of sufficient obscurity to send even the well-educated reader to the encyclopedia, lest the thread of narrative or argument be lost.

INTRODUCTION

This present volume's four studies in literary criticism and biography display Chesterton's talents at three stages in his life. His essays on Carlyle and Tolstoy, published respectively in 1902 and 1904 are the work of a rising young man of letters who, turning his back on nihilism, had come to profess Christian faith. *Robert Louis Stevenson*, published in 1927, shows us Chesterton at nearly the height of his influence, some two years after he had published *The Everlasting Man*. *Chaucer*, published in 1932, is the most important book of Chesterton's late years.

He was no biographer, Chesterton wrote of himself: he lacked the patience for seeking out details. Be that as it may, his studies of men of letters, like his studies of saints, are marked by interpretations and insights superior to those of the scholarly specialist. I have come upon no better defense and appreciation of Stevenson than Chesterton's; and his commentary upon Chaucer is highly illuminating.

Thomas Carlyle, a small monograph, was published by Hodder and Stoughton in 1902. With Carlyle, Chesterton shared a dislike for the shallowness of the Enlightenment of the eighteenth century—which, as Coleridge had put it, was "full of enlighteners but singularly deficient in light". Chesterton praises grim Carlyle for his irrationalism—the force "which makes men look at sunsets, laugh at jokes, go on crusades, write poems, enter monasteries, and jump over haycocks". Chesterton so wrote only twenty-one years after Carlyle's death.

Of Carlyle's *French Revolution*, Chesterton expresses his astonishment that the book "contrives to be as admirable and as accurate a history as it is, while from one end to the other there is hardly a suggestion that he comprehended the moral and political theories which were the guiding stars of the French Revolution". Some critics of Chesterton have been equally astonished that Chesterton himself could express some approbation for those revolutionary theories, which were so opposed to much that Chesterton, himself, believed.

This long essay, or little book, is full-blown Chesterton. Written as early as 1902 it is compact with paradoxes, aphorisms, asides, and apt analogies. Had Chesterton written nothing after 1902, his Carlyle essay ought to have guaranteed him a place in anthologies.

In 1904 Hodder and Stoughton brought out his essay on Tolstoy, together with other Tolstoy essays by G. H. Perris and Edward Garnett. Chesterton's contribution is an exercise in irony.

In a later story, "The Yellow Bird" (included in *The Poet and the Lunatics*, 1929), Chesterton presents us with a Russian psychologist who believes in emancipation, expansion, and the elimination of limits. The Russian theorist begins by liberating a caged canary (which is driven off immediately by other birds outside the country house), next he frees goldfish from their bowl to go down the drain, and lastly he ends by blowing up himself and the house where he had been a guest, thus defying the tyranny of the overarching sky. One may perceive the original of that anarchic psychologist in Chesterton's portrait of Tolstoy, drawn a quarter of a century earlier.

"A great modern writer who erases theology altogether", Chesterton comments,

> . . . denies the validity of the Scriptures and the Churches alike, forms a purely ethical theory that love should be the instrument of reform, and ends by maintaining that we have no right to strike a man if he is torturing a child before our eyes. He goes on, he develops a theory of the mind and the emotions, which might be held by the most rigid atheist, and he ends by maintaining that the sexual relation out of which all humanity has come, is not only not moral, but is positively not natural.

Such is Chesterton's judgment upon the mind of Tolstoy. Well written:

The ethical labor of Tolstoy, Chesterton remarked, was best exemplified by the decision of Russian Christian anarchists, in Canada, to turn loose all their animals, "on the ground that it is immoral to possess them or control them. . . . It is like a page from some fairy farce to imagine the Doukhabor solemnly escorting a hen to the door of the yard and bidding it a benevolent farewell as it sets out on its travels." The "Yellow Bird" in Chesterton's later story of madness is the counterpart of that liberated hen.

Deficient in poetry, Leo Tolstoy was not a mystic, Chesterton concluded; "and therefore he has a tendency to go mad." For mysticism keeps men sane; while logic drives them mad. (Here Chesterton doubtless had in mind Saint Ambrose's declaration that it has not pleased God to save men by logic.) One wishes that Chesterton had found time to enlarge his five-page witty essay into a book.

Chesterton's *Robert Louis Stevenson* is a work of gratitude: for reading Stevenson's romances during his formative years, had helped to redeem him from an artistic nihilism and from the peril of solipsism. Stevenson had set his face against the pessimism of Schopenhauer and all that school, and manliness ran through all of Stevenson's writings. Chesterton approved nearly everything in Stevenson's books,—except the vestiges of Calvinism.

In Stevenson, Chesterton found everywhere, "even in his mere diction and syntax, that theme that is the whole philosophy of fairytales, of the old romances and even of the absurd libretto of the little theatre—the conception that man is born with hope and courage indeed, but born outside that which he was meant to attain; that here is a quest, a test, a trial by combat or pilgrimage of discovery; or, in other words, that whatever else man is he is not sufficient to himself, either through peace or through despair."

This lengthy critical essay or commentary on Stevenson cannot be altogether understood unless the reader already is tolerably well acquainted with Stevenson's novels—as, in 1927, most literate people were; Chesterton does not provide synopses. Chesterton perceptively points out certain weaknesses of structure or background in one or another of Stevenson's books; for instance, *The Master of Ballantrae* would have been the better had Stevenson confined his setting to the Solway shore, rather than shifting the scene to a pirate vessel, to India, and to the wilderness of America. But with Stevenson's delineation of character, Chesterton finds no fault.

A large part of this book consists of Chesterton's asides, vastly ornamented with paradoxes and analogies. A modest specimen may suffice here:

> Just now we are incessantly asked to rejoice in the sight of youth enjoying itself; which I for one am very ready to do; but all the readier if

I can be quite certain that it is enjoying itself. And it is a curious fact that in characteristic contemporary literature there is an almost complete absence of joy. And I think it would be true to say, in a general fashion, that it is not childish enough to be cheerful.

That observation is even truer in *anno Domini* 1991 than it was in 1927. Chesterton complained of the gloominess of George Gissing's realism; nowadays the major book-review media puff the products of what T. S. Eliot labelled "the diabolical imagination".

Chaucer is more thoroughly biographical than is *Stevenson*, and is a work of considerable scholarship. Much of the book consists of a contrast between twentieth-century culture and medieval culture, to the disadvantage of the former. One thinks of Eliseo Vivas' remark that it is one of the marks of human decency to be ashamed of having been born into the twentieth century. Chesterton's assault on Calvinism, which runs through *Stevenson*, is renewed in this later study, however, his warm affection for Chaucer is communicated to the reader; this is a happy book.

Also it is on some themes a mordant book. They never will love where they ought to love, said Burke, who do not hate where they ought to hate. G. K. C. loved much and detested much.

Sometimes he was as contemptuous of the age preceding his own era as he was admiring of the fourteenth century. "The real vice of the Victorians", he wrote,

> was that they regarded history as a story that ended well—because it ended with the Victorians. They turned all human records into one three-volume novel; and were quite sure that they themselves were the third volume. History had come to an end; if not to a cessation, at least to a consummation. Therefore their doubts about the past were easily resolved, because they were not really troubled by doubts about the future. Whatever had obviously led to their own Constitutionalism or Commercialism was good. They did not really ask to what their Constitutionalism and Commercialism would lead. We, on the other hand, know where they have already led.

Chaucer's Pilgrims were diverse in station and much else, but shared a common purpose; nowadays it is otherwise.

It is very puzzling to look at the real society around us at this moment, and consider whether it has a purpose. For the present, at least, there is no Canterbury in sight for the Canterbury Pilgrims. The coloured cavalcade is halted somewhere in the suburbs, and suffering the bewilderment dating from that day, when sectarians and journalists and jerry-builders between them decided that every man should live in the same villa and every man in a different universe.

Polemical literary criticism flourishes at its most vigorous in Chesterton's *Chaucer*. The founder of great English literature still, nearly seven centuries after he wrote, instructs us that life is worth living. "Those strangely fanatical historians, who would darken the whole medieval landscape, have to give up Chaucer in despair; because he is obviously not despairing. His mere voice hailing us from a distance has the abruptness of a startling whistle or halloo; a blast blowing away all their artificially concocted atmosphere of gas and gloom." Chesterton knew that the end of humane letters is ethical, and so proclaimed to the naughty world of the twentieth century.

Chaucer, Stevenson, and Chesterton himself were endowed with what Gabriel Gale, in *The Poet and the Lunatics*, calls the centricities of genius; while Tolstoy was one of the terrible simplifiers. From the four studies within these covers, it is possible to learn much concerning the distinctions in literature and in life between normality and abnormity.

Russell Kirk
Mecosta, Michigan

THOMAS CARLYLE

1902

THOMAS CARLYLE

There are few cultivated people who do not pretend to have read Mr. Lecky's "History of Rationalism in Europe." That very able work covers the whole of one very important side of modern development. But the picture of the real progress, the real mental and moral improvement of our species during the last few centuries, will not be complete until Mr. Lecky publishes a companion volume entitled "The History of Irrationalism in Europe." The two tendencies, acting together, have been responsible for the whole advancement of the Western world. Rationalism is, of course, that power which makes people invent sewing machines, understand Euclid, reform vestries, pull out teeth, and number the fixed stars. Irrationalism is that other force, if possible more essential, which makes men look at sunsets, laugh at jokes, go on crusades, write poems, enter monasteries, and jump over hay-cocks. Rationalism is the beneficent attempt to make our institutions and theories fit the world we live in, as clothes fit the wearer. Irrationalism is the beneficent reminder that, at the best, they do not fit. Irrationalism exists to point out that that eccentric old gentleman, "The World," is such a curiously shaped old gentleman that the most perfect coats and waistcoats have an extraordinary way of leaving parts of him out, sometimes whole legs and arms, the existence of which the tailor had not suspected. And as surely as there arises a consistent theory of life which seems to give a whole plan of it, there will appear within a score or two of years a great Irrationalist to tell the world of strange seas and forests which are nowhere down on the map. The great movement of the eighteenth and nineteenth centuries, which rose to its height in the French Revolution and the Positivist philosophy, was the last great Rationalistic synthesis. The inevitable Irrationalist who followed it was Thomas Carlyle. This is the first and most essential view of his position.

In order to explain the matter more clearly, it is necessary to recur to our image of the old gentleman whom no tailor could fit. Not only do the tailors tend to think that clothes can be made to fit the old gentleman, but they tend very often to think that the whole question is a question of clothes. Thus, for instance, the Popes and Bolingbrokes of the earlier eighteenth century tried to make man a purer symbol of civilisation. They tried to pluck from him altogether his love of the savage and primeval, as they might have plucked off a shaggy wig from the old gentleman in order to put on a powdered one. A bystander of the name of Byron, who was indeed none other than the inevitable Irrationalist, startled them by pointing out that the shaggy object was not a wig at all, but the poor old gentleman's own hair; that, in other words, the love of the savage, the primeval, the lonely and unsociable, was a part of man, and it was their business to recognise it. Then arose the new fashion in cosmic clothes, which did recognise this natural element. Rousseau and Shelley took the old gentleman in hand, and provided him with spring-like garments, coloured like the clouds of morning. But one of their principles was the absolute principle of equality. Finding, therefore, that the old gentleman was wearing a curiously shaped hat, compounded of crown, coronet, and mitre, the great hat of Godhood, kinghood, and superiority, they proceeded, in order to make him more natural, to knock it off; and to them suddenly appeared the inevitable Irrationalist, a Scotch gentleman from Dunfriesshire, who, addressing them politely, said, "You believe that that regal object you are knocking off is his hat: believe me, gentlemen, it is his head. Such mistakes will occur after a hasty inspection, but that kingship is really a part of the old gentleman, and it is your business to recognise it." As Byron had come, just as the classic edifice of polite deism had been completed, to point out that the fact remained that he, Byron, did prefer walking by the seashore to taking tea in the garden, so Carlyle appeared, just as the austere temple of political equality was erected, to point out that the fact remained that he did think many people a great deal better than himself, and very many people a great deal worse. Thus, then, as the asserter of the natural character of kingship against the natural character of equality, it is that Thomas Carlyle primarily stands twenty-one years after his death.

Now I do not think, as I shall show later, that Carlyle ever really understood the true doctrine of equality: but it is certainly at least equally true that the egalitarians and the ordinary opponents of Carlyle have never done the least justice to Carlyle's doctrine of hero-worship. The usual theory is that he believed in a race of arrogant strong men, brutally self-sufficient and brazenly indifferent to ethical limits, and that he wanted these men to frighten and dominate the populace as a keeper or a doctor frightens and dominates the lunatic in a cell. It is not too much to say that there is scarcely a trace in Carlyle's works of this barbarous and ridiculous idea. If there be a trace of it here and there, it is mere explosion of personal ill-temper, and has nothing whatever in common with Carlyle's deliberate theory of the hero. His theory of the hero was that he was a man whom men followed, not because they could not help fearing, but because they could not help loving him. His theory, right or wrong, was that when a man was your superior you were acting naturally in looking up to him, and were therefore happy: that you were acting unnaturally in equalising yourself with him, and were therefore unhappy. Most people, except those solemn persons who are called with some humour free-thinkers, would agree, for instance, that the worship of God was a human function, and therefore gave pleasure to the performer of it, like eating or taking exercise. Now Carlyle held, rightly or wrongly, that the worship of man, of the great man, was also a human function, and therefore gave pleasure to the performer of it. It all depends upon whether we do take an egalitarian or an aristocratic view of the spiritual world. If the spiritual world is based upon equality, then, no doubt, to keep a man in an inferior position must spiritually depress and degrade him; but if beings in the spiritual world have higher and lower functions, it is obvious that it is equally depressing and degrading to a man to take him out of his position and make him either a citizen or an emperor.

Moreover, the real practical truth that underlay Carlyle's gospel of the hero has in other ways been misunderstood. The general idea is that Carlyle thought that, if a man were only able, everything was to be excused to him. If Carlyle, even at any moment, thought this, it can only be said that for that moment Carlyle was a fool, as many able men may happen to be. But, as a matter of fact, what Carlyle meant was something much sounder. To say that any man may tyrannise so long as he is able, is as ridiculous as saying that any man may knock people down so long as he is six feet high. But in urging this very obvious fact the opponents of Carlyle too often forget a simpler truth at the back of the Carlyle gospel. It is that, while in one sense the same moral test is to be applied to all men, there does remain in ordinary charitable practice a very great difference between the people who consider it necessary to see some definite thing done before they die, and the people who cheerfully admit that two hundred years will scarcely bring what they require, and that meanwhile they desire to do nothing. A Tolstoian anarchist who thinks that men should be morally persuaded for the next two or three centuries to give up every kind of physical compulsion may, it is quite conceivable, be more right than the English Home Secretary who finds himself responsible for the suppression of a riot in Manchester; but surely it is patently ridiculous to say that it is just as much to the anarchist's credit that he avoids shooting Manchester workmen as it would be to the Home Secretary's credit if he avoided shooting them. It would be equally ridiculous to say that, if the Home Secretary conceived it necessary to shoot them, from a sense of responsibility, his action, even if wrong, was really as wrong as the conduct of a Tolstoian who should shoot them without any reason at all. In this sense, therefore, there is really a different test, and a perfectly fair one, for men of action and for men of abstract theories and remote hopes.

Now, it must definitely be set to credit of men like Cromwell and Mirabeau, that they were undoubtedly opposed to and embarrassed by men whose projects, even in their own eyes, were scarcely a part of practical politics. These men exist in every country and in every age. They are wilfully and eternally in opposition. They do not agree sufficiently with the active powers even to argue with them with any profit. Their ideal is so far away that they do not even desire it with any immediate hunger. They count it a pleasant and natural thing to live and die in revolt. They are ready to be critics, they are ready to be martyrs, they are emphatically not ready to be rulers. In this way Cromwell, considering how he might make some English polity out of a chaos of English parties, had to argue for hours together with Fifth Monarchy men,[1] to whom the vital question was whether the children of malignants should not be slain, and whether a man who was caught swearing should not be stoned to death. In this way Mirabeau, striving to keep the Tradition of French civilisation intact amid a hundred essential reforms, found his way blocked by men who insisted on discussing whether in the ideal commonwealth men would believe in immortality, or go through a rite of marriage. Now, while fully granting that both types have an eternal value, it is certainly not just that precisely the same ethical test should be applied to Cromwell and the Fifth Monarchy men, to Mirabeau and the worshipper of pure reason. It is not just that we should judge in precisely the same way the pace of a butcher's cart which is obliged to get to Pimlico, and the pace of a butcher's cart which is designed at some time or other to reach the site of the Garden of Eden. It is not just that we should judge in the same way the man who is simply anxious to erect a parish pump, and the opponent of the pump, who looks forward to a day when there shall not only be no pump, but no parish. The man of action, then, really has in this sane and limited sense a claim to a peculiar kind of allowance, in that it is of vital necessity to him that a certain limited grievance should be removed. It is easy enough to be the man who lives in a contented impotence; the man who luxuriates in an endless and satisfied defeat. He does not desire to be effective; he only desires to be right. He does not desire passionately that something should be done; he only desires that it should be triumphantly proved to be necessary.

This is the real contribution of Carlyle to the philosophy of the man of action. He revealed, entirely justly, and entirely to the profit of us all, the pathos of the practical man. He made us feel, what is profoundly true, that the tragedy of the death of Mary, Queen of Scots, is nothing to the tragedy of the death of Elizabeth; that the tragedy of the death of Charles I. is nothing to the tragedy of the death of Cromwell. A man like Charles I. died triumphantly; he did not indeed die as a martyr, but he died as something which is much

[1] The Fifth Monarchy Men were Puritan radicals who flourished during the English Civil War of the 1640s. They believed that Christ would return soon to establish his reign on earth, the "Fifth Monarchy".

more awful and exceptional—a consistent man. He was worse than a tyrant; he was a logician. But a man like Cromwell is in a much harder case, for he does not wish to die and be a spectacle, but to live and be a force. He has to break altogether with the splendid logic of martyrdom. He has to eat his own words for breakfast, dinner, and supper. He has to outlive a hundred incarnations, and always reject the last; his progress is like that unnerving initiation in the wild tale of Tom Moore's,[2] in which the disciple had to climb up a stone stairway into the sky, every step of which fell away the moment his foot had left it. This is the only genuine truth that Carlyle brought from his study of strong men. If ever he said that we must blindly obey the strong man, he was merely angry and personal, and untrue to his essentially generous and humane spirit. When he said that we must reverence the strong man he sometimes expressed himself with a certain heated confusion, and left it doubtful whether he meant that we should reverence the strong man as we respect Christ, or merely as we respect Sandow. But we should all agree with him in his essential and eternal contribution—that we should pity the strong man more than an idiot or a cripple.

It may be said that there is a certain inconsistency between these two justifications of Carlyle's hero-worship; that we cannot at the same time respect a man because he is above us in a definite spiritual order, and because he is in what is popularly called a hole; that we cannot at once reverence Mirabeau because he was strong and because he was weak. This kind of inconsistency does exist in Carlyle; it is, I may say with all reverence and with all certainty, the eternal and inevitable inconsistency which characterises those who receive divine revelations. The larger world, which our systems attempt to explain and chiefly succeed in hiding, must, when it breaks through upon us, take forms which appear to be conflicting. The spiritual world is so rich that it is varied; so varied that it is inconsistent. That is why so many saints and great doctors of religion have

---

[2] Thomas Moore (1779–1852), regarded as the national poet of Ireland, wrote many poetical works such as *Epistles, Odes, and Other Poems* (1806), *Lalla Rookh* (1817), *Fables for the Holy Alliance* (1823), and *Legendary Ballads* (1830).

pinned their faith to paradoxes like the "Credo Quia Impossibile,"[3] the great theological paradoxes which are so much more dazzling and daring than the paradoxes of the modern *flâneur*.[4] The supreme glory of Carlyle was that he heard the veritable voices of the Cosmos. He left it to others to attune them into an orchestra. Sometimes the truth he heard was this truth, that some men are to be commanded and some obeyed; sometimes that deeper and more democratic truth that all men are above all things to be pitied.

It will be found relevant to what I have to say hereafter to remark at this point that I do not myself accept Carlyle's conception of the spiritual world as exhaustive. I believe in the essence of the old doctrine of equality, because it appears to me to result from all conceptions of the divinity of man. Of course there are inequalities, and obvious ones, but though they are not insignificant positively, they are insignificant comparatively. If men are all really the images of God, to talk about their differences has its significance, but only about the same significance which may be found in talking about the respective heights of twenty men, all of whom have received the Victoria Cross, or the respective length of the moustaches of twenty men, all of whom have died to save their fellow-creatures. In comparison with the point in which they are equal, the point in which they are unequal is not merely decidedly, but almost infinitely insignificant. But my reason for indicating my own opinion on the matter, at this point, is a definite one. Carlyle's view of equality does not happen to be mine; but it has an absolute right to be stated justly, and to be stated from Carlyle's point of view. It was not a brutal fear or a mean worship of force; it was a serious belief that some found blessedness in commanding, and some in obeying. Now this kind of intellectual justice was the one great quality which was lacking in Carlyle himself. He would not consent to listen to Rousseau's gospel, as I have suggested that we should listen to Carlyle's gospel. He would not put Rousseau's gospel from Rousseau's point of view. And consequently to the end of his days he never understood any gospel except Carlyle's gospel.

[3] *Credo Quia Impossibile* is Latin for "I believe that which is impossible."
[4] *Flâneur* is French for "lounger".

When a literary man is known to have been almost a monster of industry, when he has produced a colossal epic like "Frederick the Great" on the dullest of all earthly subjects—Germany in the eighteenth century—when he has piled up all the complicated material of the history of the French Revolution, lost it, and by a portent of heroism piled it all up again; when he has achieved such masterpieces of research as the discovery of sense in Cromwell's speeches, and good qualities in Frederick of Prussia; when an author has done all this, it may seem a singular comment upon him to say that his main characteristic was a lack of patience. But this was in reality the chief weakness, in fact the only real weakness, of Carlyle as a moralist. It is very much easier to have what may be called moral patience or mental patience than to have something which may best be described as spiritual patience. Carlyle was patient with facts, dates, documents, intolerably wearisome memoirs; but he was not patient with the soul of man. He was not patient with ideas, theories, tendencies, outside his own philosophy. He never understood, and therefore persistently undervalued, the real meaning of the idea of liberty, which is a faith in the growth and life of the human mind; vague indeed in its nature, but transcending in its magnitude even our faith in our own faiths. He was something of a Tory, something of a Sans-culotte, something of a Puritan, something of an Imperialist, something of a Socialist; but he was never, even for a single moment, a Liberal. He did not believe as the Liberal believes, first indeed in his own truth, which in his eyes is pure truth, but beyond that also in that mightier truth which is made up of a million lies.

And this spiritual impatience of Carlyle has left its peculiar mark in the only defect which can really be found in his historical works. Of the astonishing power and humour and poignancy of those historical works I think it scarcely necessary to speak. A man must have a very poor literary sense who can read one of Carlyle's slighter sketches, such as "The Diamond Necklace," and not feel that he has at the same time to deal with one of the greatest satirists, one of the greatest mystics, and incomparably one of the finest story-tellers in the world. No historian ever realised so strongly the recondite and ill-digested fact that history has consisted of human beings, each isolated, each vacillating, each living in an eternal present; or, in other words, that history has not consisted of crowds, or kings, or Acts of Parliament, or systems of government, or articles of belief. And Carlyle has, moreover, introduced into the philosophy of history one element which had been absent from it since the writing of the Old Testament — the element of something which can only be called humour in the just government of the universe. "He that sitteth in the heavens shall laugh them to scorn, the Lord shall have them in derision," is a note that is struck again in Carlyle for the first time after two thousand years. It is the note of the sarcasm of Providence. Any one who will read those admirable chapters of Carlyle on Chartism will realise that, while all other humanitarians were insisting upon the cruelty or the inconsistency or the barbarism of neglecting the problem of labour, Carlyle is rather filled with a kind of almost celestial astonishment at the absurdity of neglecting it.

But a definite defect there is, as I have suggested, in Carlyle, considered as an historian, and it flows directly from that real moral defect in his nature, an impatience with other men's ideas. In judging of men as men, he was not only quick and graphic and correct, but in the main essentially genial and magnanimous. Only a very superficial critic will think that Carlyle was misanthropic because he was surly. There is very much more real sympathy with human problems and temptations in a page of this shaggy old malcontent than in whole libraries of constitutional history by dapper and polite rationalists, who treat men as automata, and put their virtues and vices into separate pigeonholes. If I had made a mistake or committed a sin that had any sort of human character about it, I would very much rather fall into the hands of Carlyle than into the hands of Mr. Hallam[5] or Mr. James Mill.[6] But while Carlyle did realise the fact that every man carries about with him his own life and atmosphere, he did not realise that other truth, that every man carries

---

[5] Henry Hallam (1777–1859) was an English historian and the first member of the Historical School to write history without prejudice. He wrote *Europe during the Middle Ages* (1818) and the *Constitutional History of England*.

[6] James Mill (1773–1836) was a Scottish historian and economist who published *Elements of Political Economics* in 1821. He is the father of John Stuart Mill.

about with him his own theory of the world. Each one of us is living in a separate Cosmos. The theory of life held by one man never corresponds exactly to that held by another. The whole of man's opinions, morals, tastes, manners, hobbies, work back eventually to some picture of existence itself which, whether it be a paradise or a battle-field, or a school or a chaos, is not precisely the same picture of existence which lies at the back of any other brain. Carlyle had not fully realised that it was a case of one man, one Cosmos. Consequently, he devoted himself to asking what place any man, say Robespierre or Shelley, occupied in Carlyle's Cosmos. It never occurred to him sufficiently clearly to ask what place Shelley occupied in Shelley's Cosmos, or Robespierre in Robespierre's Cosmos. Not feeling the need of this, he never studied, he never really listened to, Shelley's philosophy or Robespierre's philosophy. Here, after a somewhat long circuit, we have arrived at the one serious deficiency in Carlyle's histories, a neglect to realise the importance of theory and of alternative theories in human affairs.

The standing example of this is the "History of the French Revolution." Carlyle's conception of the French Revolution is simply and absolutely that of an elemental outbreak, an explosion of nature in history, an earthquake in the moral world. Human nature, Carlyle seems to tell us, had been stifled more and more in the wrappings of artificiality, until, when its condition had just passed the tolerable, gagged, blinded, deaf, and ignorant of what it really wanted, by a gigantic muscular effort it burst its bonds.

So far as it goes, that is perfectly true of the French Revolution; but only so far as it goes. The French Revolution was a sudden starting from slumber of that terrible spirit of man which sleeps through the greater number of the centuries; and Carlyle appreciates this, and describes it more powerfully and fearfully than any human historian, because this idea of the spirit of man breaking through the formulae and building again on fundamentals was a part of his own philosophical theory, and therefore he understood it. But he never, as I have said, took any real trouble to understand other people's philosophical theories. And he did not realise the other fact about the French Revolution—the fact that it was not merely an elementary outbreak, but was also a great doctrinal movement. It is an astonishing thing that Carlyle's "French Revolution" contrives to be as admirable and as accurate a history as it is, while from one end to the other there is hardly a suggestion that he comprehended the moral and political theories which were the guiding stars of the French Revolutionists. It was not necessary that he should agree with them, but it was necessary that he should be interested in them; nay, in order that he should write a perfect history of their developments, it was necessary that he should admire them. The truly impartial historian is not he who is enthusiastic for neither side in a historic struggle: that method was adopted by the rationalistic historians of the Hallam type, and resulted in the dullest and thinnest and most essentially false chronicles that were ever compiled about mankind. The truly impartial historian is he who is enthusiastic for both sides. He holds in his heart a hundred fanaticisms. The truly philosophical historian does not patronise Cromwell and pat the King on the head, as Hallam does; the true philosophical historian could ride after Cromwell like an Ironside and adore the King like a Cavalier.

The only history that is worth knowing, or worth striving to know, is the history of the human head and the human heart, and of what great loves it has been enamoured: truth in the sense of the absolute justice is a thing for which fools look in history and wise men in the Day of Judgment. It is the glory of Carlyle that he did realise that the intellectual impartiality of the rationalist historian was merely emotional ignorance. It was his only defect that he extended his sympathy, in cases like that of the French Revolution, only to headlong men and impetuous actions, and not to great schools of revolutionary doctrine and faith. He made somewhat the same mistake with regard to the Middle Ages, touching which his contributions are unequalled in picturesqueness and potency. He conceived the mediaeval period in Europe as a barbaric verity, "a rude, stalwart age"; he did not realise what is more and more unfolding itself to all serious historians, that the mediaeval period in Europe was a civilisation based upon a certain scheme of moral science of almost unexampled multiplicity and stringency, a scheme in which the colours of a lacquey's coat could be traced back to a system of astronomy, and the smallest bye-law for a village green had some relation to great ecclesiastical and moral mysteries. It is remarkable that we always call a rival civilisation savage: the Chinese call us barbarians, and we call them barbarians. The Middle Ages were a rival civilisation, based upon moral science, to ours based upon physical science. Most modern historians have abused this great civilisation for being barbarous: Carlyle had made one great stride beyond them in so far that he admired it for being barbarous. But his fatal strain of intellectual impatience prevented him from getting on to the right side of Catholic dogmas, just as it prevented him from getting on to the right side of Jacobin dogmas. He never really discovered what other people meant by Apostolic Succession, or Liberty, or Equality, or Fraternity.

Probably his few mistakes arose from his unfortunate tendency to find "shams." Some have supposed this to be the essence and value of his message; it was in truth its worst pitfall and disaster. A man is almost always wrong when he sets about to prove the unreality and uselessness of anything: he is almost invariably right when he sets about to prove the reality and value of anything. I have a quite different and much more genuine right to say that bull's-eyes are nice than I have to say liquorice is nasty: I have found out the meaning of the first and not of the second. And if a man goes on a tearing hunt after shams, as Carlyle did, it is probable that he will find little or nothing real. He is tearing off the branches to find the tree.

I have said all that is to be said against Carlyle's work almost designedly: for he is one of those who are so great that we rather need to blame them for the sake of our own independence than praise them for the sake of their fame. He came and spoke a word, and the chatter of rationalism stopped, and the sums would no longer work out and be ended. He was a breath of Nature turning in her sleep under the load of civilisation, a stir in the very stillness of God to tell us he was still there.

LEO TOLSTOY

1903

TOLSTOY

If any one wishes to form the fullest estimate of the real character and influence of the great man whose name is prefixed to these remarks, he will not find it in his novels, splendid as they are, or in his ethical views, clearly and finely as they are conceived and expanded. He will find it best expressed in the news that has recently come from Canada, that a sect of Russian Christian anarchists has turned all its animals loose, on the ground that it is immoral to possess them or control them. About such an incident as this there is a quality altogether independent of the rightness or wrongness, the sanity or insanity, of the view. It is first and foremost a reminder that the world is still young. There are still theories of life as insanely reasonable as those which were disputed under the clear blue skies of Athens. There are still examples of a faith as fierce and practical as that of the Mahometans, who swept across Africa and Europe, shouting a single word. To the languid contemporary politician and philosopher it seems doubtless like something out of a dream, that in this iron-bound, homogeneous, and clockwork age, a company of European men in boots and waistcoats should begin to insist on taking the horse out of the shafts of the omnibus, and lift the pig out of his pig-sty, and the dog out of his kennel, because of a moral scruple or theory. It is like a page from some fairy farce to imagine the Doukhabor[1] solemnly escorting a hen to the door of the yard and bidding it a benevolent farewell as it sets out on it travels. All this, as I say, seems mere muddle-headed absurdity to the typical leader of

---

[1] The Doukhabors were a Russian-Canadian religious sect which arose in the mid-eighteenth century among the Kharkov peasants who preached the inherent goodness of man without the intercession of organized religion. Persecution in Russia led them to immigrate to Canada. Settling in Saskatchewan and British Columbia, they live communally as farmers. Their lifestyle resembles that of the Amish or Quakers.

human society in this decade, to a man like Mr. Balfour,[2] or Mr. Wyndham.[3] But there is nevertheless a further thing to be said, and that is that, if Mr. Balfour could be converted to a religion which taught him that he was morally bound to walk into the House of Commons on his hands, and he did walk on his hands, if Mr. Wyndham could accept a creed which taught that he ought to dye his hair blue, and he did dye his hair blue, they would both of them be, almost beyond description, better and happier men than they are. For there is only one happiness possible or conceivable under the sun, and that is enthusiasm — that strange and splendid word that has passed through so many vicissitudes, which meant, in the eighteenth century the condition of a lunatic, and in ancient Greece the presence of a god.

This great act of heroic consistency which has taken place in Canada is the best example of the work of Tolstoy. It is true (as I believe) that the Doukhabors have an origin quite independent of the great Russian moralist, but there can surely be little doubt that their emergence into importance and the growth and mental distinction of their sect, is due to his admirable summary and justification of their scheme of ethics. Tolstoy, besides being a magnificent novelist, is one of the very few men alive who have a real, solid, and serious view of life. He is a Catholic church, of which he is the only member, the somewhat arrogant Pope and the somewhat submissive layman. He is one of the two or three men in Europe, who have an attitude towards things so entirely their own, that we could supply their inevitable view on anything — a silk hat, a Home Rule Bill, an Indian poem, or a pound of tobacco. There are three men in existence who have such an attitude: Tolstoy, Mr. Bernard Shaw, and my friend Mr. Hilaire Belloc. They are all diametrically opposed to each other, but they all have this essential resemblance, that, given their basis of thought, their soil of conviction, their opinions on every earthly subject grow there naturally, like flowers in a field. There

---

[2] Arthur James, Earl of Balfour (1848–1930), British prime minister from 1902 to 1905, authored books on religion and philosophy. He also wrote the Balfour Declaration, giving the Jewish settlement in Palestine the assurance of protection by Britain (1917).

[3] Mr. Wyndham is likely a reference to George Wyndham (1863–1913), an English politician and writer.

are certain views of certain things that they must take; they do not form opinions, the opinions form themselves. Take, for instance, in the case of Tolstoy, the mere list of miscellaneous objects which I wrote down at random above, a silk hat, a Home Rule Bill, an Indian poem, and a pound of tobacco. Tolstoy would say: "I believe in the utmost possible simplification of life; therefore, this silk hat is a black abortion." He would say: "I believe in the utmost possible simplification of life; therefore, this Home Rule Bill is a mere peddling compromise; it is no good to break up a centralised empire into nations, you must break the nation up into individuals." He would say: "I believe in the utmost possible simplification of life; therefore, I am interested in this Indian poem, for Eastern ethics, under all their apparent gorgeousness, are far simpler and more Tolstoyan than Western." He would say: "I believe in the utmost possible simplification of life; therefore, this pound of tobacco is a thing of evil; take it away." Everything in the world, from the Bible to a bootjack, can be, and is, reduced by Tolstoy to this great fundamental Tolstoyan principle, the simplification of life. When we deal with a body of opinion like this we are dealing with an incident in the history of Europe infinitely more important than the appearance of Napoleon Buonaparte.

This emergence of Tolstoy, with his awful and simple ethics, is important in more ways than one. Among other things it is a very interesting commentary on an attitude which has been taken up for the matter of half a century by all the avowed opponents of religion. The secularist and the sceptic have denounced Christianity first and foremost, because of its encouragement of fanaticism; because religious excitement led men to burn their neighbours, and to dance naked down the street. How queer it all sounds now. Religion can be swept out of the matter altogether, and still there are philosophical and ethical theories which can produce fanaticism enough to fill the world. Fanaticism has nothing at all to do with religion. There are grave scientific theories which, if carried out logically, would result in the same fires in the market-place and the same nakedness in the street. There are modern aesthetes who would expose themselves like the Adamites if they could do it in elegant attitudes. There are modern scientific moralists who would burn their opponents alive, and would be quite contented if they were burnt by some new chemical process. And if any one doubts this proposition—that fanaticism has nothing to do with religion, but has only to do with human nature—let him take this case of Tolstoy and the Doukhabors. A sect of men start with no theology at all, but with the simple doctrine that we ought to love our neighbour and use no force against him, and they end in thinking it wicked to carry a leather hand-bag, or to ride in a cart. A great modern writer who erases theology altogether, denies the validity of the Scriptures and the Churches alike, forms a purely ethical theory that love should be the instrument of reform, and ends by maintaining that we have no right to strike a man if he is torturing a child before our eyes. He goes on, he develops a theory of the mind and the emotions, which might be held by the most rigid atheist, and he ends by maintaining that the sexual relation out of which all humanity has come, is not only not moral, but is positively not natural. This is fanaticism as it has been and as it will always be. Destroy that last copy of the Bible, and persecution and insane orgies will be founded on Mr. Herbert Spencer's "Synthetic Philosophy." Some of the broadest thinkers of the Middle Ages believed in faggots, and some of the broadest thinkers in the nineteenth century believe in dynamite.

The truth is that Tolstoy, with his immense genius, with his colossal faith, with his vast fearlessness and vast knowledge of life, is deficient in one faculty and one faculty alone. He is not a mystic: and therefore he has a tendency to go mad. Men talk of the extravagances and frenzies that have been produced by mysticism: they are a mere drop in the bucket. In the main, and from the beginning of time, mysticism has kept men sane. The thing that has driven them mad was logic. It is significant that, with all that has been said about the excitability of poets, only one English poet ever went mad, and he went mad from a logical system of theology. He was Cowper, and his poetry retarded his insanity for many years. So poetry, in which Tolstoy is deficient, has always been a tonic and sanative thing. The only thing that has kept the race of men from the mad extremes of the convent and the pirate-gallery, the night-club and the lethal chamber, has been mysticism—the belief that logic is misleading, and that things are not what they seem.

ROBERT LOUIS STEVENSON

1927

I

'THE MYTH OF STEVENSON'

In this brief study of Stevenson I propose to follow a somewhat unusual course; or to sketch what may be considered a rather eccentric outline. It can only be justified in practice; and I have a healthy fear that my practice will not justify it. Nevertheless, I have not adopted it without considerable thought, and even doubt, about the best way of dealing with a real and practical problem. So before it collapses completely in practice, I will give myself the triumph and the joy of justifying it in principle.

The difficulty arises thus. In the great days of Stevenson critics had begun to be ashamed of being critics, and of giving to their ancient function the name of criticism. It was the fashion to publish a book that was a bundle of reviews and to call it 'Appreciations.' But the world advances; and if that sort of book is published now, it might well bear the general title of 'Depreciations.' Stevenson has suffered more than most from this new fashion of minimising and finding fault; and some energetic and successful writers have thrown themselves into the business almost with the eagerness of stockbrokers, bent on making a slump instead of a boom in Stevenson Stock. It may be questioned whether we need welcome the bear any more than the bull in the china shop of elegant English letters. Others seem to make quite a hobby of proving a particular writer to be overrated. They write long and laborious articles, full of biographical detail and bitter commentary, in order to show that the subject is unworthy of attention; and write pages upon Stevenson to prove that he is not worth writing about. Neither their motives nor their methods are very clear or satisfactory. If it be true that all swans are geese to the discriminating eye of the scientific ornithologist, it hardly suffices to explain so long or so fatiguing a wild-goose chase.

But it is true that, in a sense more general than that of these rather irritable individuals, such a reaction does exist. And it is a reaction against Stevenson, or at least against Stevensonians. Perhaps it would be most correct to call it a reaction against Stevensoniana. And let me say at this early stage that I heartily agree that there has been far too much Stevensoniana. In one sense, indeed, everything about anybody so interesting as Stevenson is interesting. In one sense, everything about everybody is interesting. But not everybody can interest everybody else: and it is well to know an author is loved, but not to publish all the love-letters. Sometimes we only had to endure that most awful and appalling tragedy: a truth told once too often. Sometimes we heard Stevensonian sentiments repeated in violation of all Stevensonian rules. For of all things he hated dilution: and loved to take language neat, like a liqueur. In short, it was overdone; it was too noisy and yet all on one note; above all, it was too incessant and too prolonged. As I say, there were a variety of causes, which it would be unnecessary and sometimes unamiable to discuss. There was perhaps something in it of the very virtue of Stevenson; he was toler ant of many societies and interested in many men; and there was nothing to ward off the direst results of the men being interested in him. Especially after he was dead, one person after another turned up and wrote a book about meeting Stevenson on a steamboat or in a restaurant; and it is not surprising that such book-makers began to look as vulgar as bookies. There was perhaps something in it of the old joke of Johnson:[1] that the Scots are in a conspiracy to praise each other. It was often because the Scots are secret sentimentalists and cannot al ways keep the secret. Their interest in a story so brilliant and in some ways so pathetic was perfectly natural and human; but for all that, their interest was over-done. It was sometimes, I regret to say, because the interest might fairly be called a vested interest. Anyhow, any number of things happened to combine to vulgarise the thing; but vulgarising a thing does not really make it vulgar.

Now Stevenson's life was really what we call picturesque; partly because he saw everything in pictures; and partly because a chapter of accidents did really attach him to very picturesque places. He was born on the high terraces of the noblest of northern cities: in the family mansion in Edinburgh in 1850; he was the son of a house of highly respected architects of lighthouses; and nothing could be more really romantic than such a legend of men laboriously lifting the star-crowned towers of the sea. He failed to follow the family tradition, however, for various reasons; he was blighted with ill-health and a taste for art; the latter sent him to pick up picturesque tricks and poses in the art colony of Barbizon; the former very soon sent him southward into warmer and warmer

[1] Dr. Samuel Johnson (1709–1784) was an English poet, critic, lexicographer and essayist known for his wit and for his careful criticism of literature.

climates; and so it happens, as he himself remarked, that the countries to which we are sent when health deserts us have a magical and rather mocking beauty. At one time he had paid a sort of vagabond visit to America, crossing the ugly plains that lead to the abrupt beauty of California, that promised land. He described it in the studies called *Across the Plains*: a work vaguely unsatisfying both to writer and reader. I think it records the subconscious blank and sense of bewilderment felt by every true European on first seeing the very light and landscape of America. The shock of negation was in his case truly unnatural. He almost wrote a dull book. But there is another reason for noting this exception here.

This book makes no pretence of being even an outline of the life of Stevenson. In his particular case I deliberately omit such an outline, because I find that it has cut across and confused the very sharp and lucid outline of his art. But indeed in any case it would be very difficult to tell the tale with truth without telling it in detail, and in rather bewildering detail. The first thing that strikes us, on a rapid survey of his life and letters, is his innumerable changes of domicile, especially in his early days. If his friends followed the example he professes to set, in the matter of Mr. Michael Finsbury,[2] and refused to learn more than one address for one friend, he must have left his correspondence very far behind indeed. His wanderings in Western Europe would appear on the map as much wilder as well as wider than the 'probable course of David Balfour's[3] wanderings' in Western Scotland. If we started out to tell his story thus, we should have to note how he went first to Mentone and then back again to Edinburgh and then to Fontainebleau and then to the Highlands and then to Fontainebleau again and then to Davos in the mountains, and so on; a zigzag pilgrimage impossible to compress except in a larger biography. But all or most of it is covered by one generalisation. This navigation chart was really a hospital chart. Its jagged mountains represented temperatures; or at least climates. The whole story of Stevenson is conditioned by a certain complexity, which a tenderness for the English language will restrain us from calling a complex. It was a sort of paradox, by which he was at once more and less

[2] Mr. Michael Finsbury is a rowdy soliciter with shady clients in Stevenson's novel *The Wrong Box*.
[3] David Balfour is the hero of Stevenson's book *Kidnapped*.

protected than other men; like somebody travelling the wildest roads of the world in a covered waggon. He went where he did partly because he was an adventurer and partly because he was an invalid. By that sort of limping agility, he may be said to have seen at once too little and too much. He was perhaps a natural traveller; but he was not a normal traveller. Nobody ever did treat him as quite normal; which is the truth hidden in the falsehood of those who sneer at his childishness as that of a spoilt child. He was courageous; and yet he had to be shielded against two things at once, his weakness and his courage. But his picture of himself as a vagabond with blue fingers on the winter road is avowedly an ideal picture; it was exactly that sort of freedom that he could never have. He could only be carried from sight to sight; or even from adventure to adventure. Indeed there is here a curious aptness in the quaint simplicity of his childish rhyme that ran, 'My bed is like a little boat.' Through all his varied experiences his bed was a boat and his boat was a bed. Panoramas of tropic palm and Californian orange-grove passed over that moving couch like the long nightmare of the nursery walls. But his real courage was not so much turned outwards to the drama of the boat as inwards to the drama of the bed. Nobody knew better than he did that nothing is more terrible than a bed; since it is always waiting to be a deathbed.

Broadly speaking, therefore, his biography would consist of journeys hither and thither, with a donkey in the Cevennes, with a baronet on the French canals; on a sledge in Switzerland or in a bathchair at Bournemouth. But they were all, in one way or another related to the problem of his health as well as to the cheerfulness of his curiosity. Now of all human things the search for health is the most unhealthy. And it is truly a great glory to Stevenson that he, almost alone among men, could go on pursuing his bodily health without once losing his mental health. As soon as he came to any place, he lost no time in finding a new and better reason for having come there. It might be a child or a sonnet, a flirtation or the plan of a story; but he made that the real reason; and not the unhealthy reason of health. Nevertheless, there generally had been, somewhere in the background, some suggestion of the reason of health; as there was in that last great journey to his final home in the South Seas.

The one real break, I suspect, in this curious double process of protection and risk, was his break-away to America, which arose partly at least in connection with the matter of his marriage. It seemed to his friends and family, not so much like the conduct of an invalid who had done a bolt from the hospital, as the conduct of a lunatic unaccountably loose from the asylum. In truth, the voyage struck them as less mad than the marriage. As this is not a biographical study, I need not go deeply into the delicate disputes about that business; but it was admittedly at least unconventional. All that matters to the argument here is that, while there was much in it that was even noble, it was not normal. It was not love as it should come to youth: it is no disrespect to either to say that in both, psychologically speaking, there was an element of patching up as well as of binding together. Stevenson had met, first in Paris and later in America, an American lady married to a seemingly somewhat unsatisfactory American gentleman, against whom she took proceedings for divorce. Stevenson at the same time precipitately crossed the seas and in some sense pursued her to California; I suppose with some vague idea of being in at the death; and indeed he was very nearly in at his own. The escapade brought on him one of the worst and sharpest of his attacks of illness; the lady, being on the spot, naturally threw herself into nursing him; and as soon as he could stand on two rickety legs they were married. It caused consternation to his family, who were however really reconciled afterwards, it would seem by the personal magnetism of his foreign and almost exotic bride. Certainly in her society his literary work went with a renewed swing and even regularity; and the rest of his story is practically the story of his important works; varied by his, if possible, still more important friendships. There was illness, in which, it should be said, it was often a case of two invalids nursing each other. Then came the decision to fall back on the secure climate of the Pacific Islands; which led to his taking up his last station at Vailima on the island of Samoa: in a coloured archipelago which our cheerful forefathers might have described as the Cannibal Islands, but which Stevenson was more disposed to describe as the Islands of the Blest. There he lived as happily as can an exile who loves his country and his friends, free at least of all the daily dangers of his lung trouble; and there he died, very suddenly, at the age of forty-four, the beloved patriarch of a little white and brown community, to whom he was known as Tusitala or the Teller of Tales.

That is the main outline of the actual biography of Robert Louis Stevenson; and from the time when he clambered as a boy among the crags and castellations of the Painted Hill,[4] looking across the islets of the Forth, to the time when tall brown barbarians, crowned with red flowers, bore him on their spears to the peak of their sacred mountain, the spirit of this artist had been permitted to inhabit, and as it were to haunt, the beautiful places of the earth. To the last he had tasted that beauty with a burning sensibility; and it is no joke, in his case, to say that he would have enjoyed coming to his own funeral. Of course, even this generalisation is too much of a simplification. He was not, as we shall later have occasion to note, unacquainted with sombre nor, alas, with sordid surroundings. Oscar Wilde said with some truth that Stevenson might have produced yet richer and more purple romances if he had always lived in Gower Street; and he was certainly one of the very few who have managed to feel fierce and adventurous at Bournemouth. But broadly speaking, it is true that the outline of his life was romantic; and was therefore perhaps too easily turned into a romance. He himself deliberately turned it into a romance; but not all those romancing were such good romancers as he. So the romance tended to turn into mere repetition and gossip; and the romantic figure faded into journalism as the figure of Robin Hood faded into endless penny dreadfuls or schoolboy serials; as the figure of Micawber[5] was multiplied and cheapened into Ally Sloper.[6] Then came the reaction; reaction which I should call rather excusable than justifiable. But that reaction is the problem in any popular treatment of him to-day.

Now if I were to follow here the natural course of such a volume as this, I should have to begin by telling slowly and systematically

---

[4] "Painted Hill" is the ancient Pictish or Celtic name of the Castle of Edinburgh. Stevenson used it as the setting for *St. Ives*.

[5] Mr. Wilkins Micawber, a grandiloquent, broadly humorous character from Dickens' *David Copperfield*, lives in a state of perpetual financial embarrassment, but he is always expecting "something to turn up".

[6] Ally Sloper is the main character in Henry James' novel *Ally Sloper's Half-Holiday*.

the tale that I have just told rapidly and briefly. I should have to give a chapter to his childhood, to his favourite aunt and his yet more beloved nurse, and to all the things much more clearly recorded in *A Child's Garden of Verses*. I should have to give a chapter to his youth, his differences with his father, his struggles with his malady, his greater struggles about his marriage; working up slowly through the whole length of the book to the familiar picture of so many magazines and memoirs; the slender semi-tropical Tusitala with his long brown hair and long olive face and long strange slits of eyes, sitting clad in white or crowned with garlands and telling tales to all the tribes of men. Now the misfortune of all this would be that it would amount to saying, through a slow series of chapters, that there is nothing more to be said about Stevenson except what has been said a thousand times. It would be to suggest that Stevenson's serious fame does still really depend on this string of picturesque accidents; and that there is really nothing to be told of him, except that he wore long hair in the Savile Club or light clothes in the Samoan mountains. His life really was romantic; but to repeat that romance is like reprinting the *Scarlet Pimpernel* or offering the world an entirely new portrait of Rudolf Valentino. It is against this repetition that the reaction has set in; perhaps wrongly but certainly strongly. And to spin it out through the whole of this book would be to give the impression (which I should mildly resent) that this book is only the thousandth unnecessary volume of Stevensoniana. However I told his story in detail, though it were with all the sympathy I feel, I could not avoid that suggestion of a sort of jaded journalism. Stevenson's picturesque attitude and career are rather in his way at this moment; not for me, because I like the picturesque, but for this new pose which may be called the pose of the prosaic. To these unfortunate realists, to say that there were all these romantic things about him is only another way of saying that there was nothing in him. And there was a very great deal in him. I am driven to adopt some other method of bringing it out.

When I come to describing it, I find it is perhaps even more difficult to describe it than to do it. But something of this sort is what I propose to do. Loudon Dodd, in whom there is much of Louis Stevenson, says very truly in *The Wrecker*, that for the artist the external result is always a fizzle: his eyes are turned inward: 'he lives for a state of mind.' I mean to attempt the conjectural description of certain states of mind, with the books that were the 'external expression' of them. If for the artist his art is a fizzle, his life is often far more of a fizzle: it is even far more of a fiction. It is the one of his works in which he tells least of the truth. Stevenson's was more real than most, because more romantic than most. But I prefer the romances, which were still more real. I mean that I think the wanderings of Balfour more Stevensonian than the wanderings of Stevenson: that the duel of Jekyll and Hyde is more illuminating than the quarrel of Stevenson and Henley:[7] and that the true private life is to be sought not in Samoa but in Treasure Island; for where the treasure is there is the heart also.

In short, I propose to review his books with illustrations from his life; rather than to write his life with illustrations from his books. And I do it deliberately, not because his life was not as interesting as any book; but because the habit of talking too much about his life has already actually led to thinking far too little of his literature. His ideas are being underrated, precisely because they are not being studied separately and seriously as ideas. His art is being underrated, precisely because he is not accorded even the fair advantages of Art for Art's Sake. There is indeed a queer irony about the fate of the men of that age, who delighted in that axiom. They claimed judgement as artists, not men; and they are really remembered as men much more than they are remembered as artists. More men know the Whistlerian anecdotes than the Whistlerian etchings; and poor Wilde will live in history as immoral rather than unmoral. But there is a real reason for studying intrinsic intellectual values in the case of Stevenson; and it need not be said that exactly where the modern maxim would be useful, it is never used. The new criticism of Stevenson is still a criticism of Stevenson rather than of Stevenson's work; it is always a personal criticism, and often, I think, rather a spiteful criticism. It is simply nonsense, for instance, for a distinguished living novelist to suggest that Stevenson's correspondence is a thin

[7] William Ernest Henley (1849-1903), English poet and editor, was a revolutionary force in English literature. Henley, the author of the popular poem *Invictus*, collaborated with Stevenson on three plays.

stream of selfish soliloquy devoid of feeling for anybody but himself. It teems with lively expressions of longing for particular people and places; it breaks out everywhere with delight into that broad Scots idiom which, as Stevenson truly said elsewhere, gives a special freedom to all the terms of affection. Stevenson might be lying, of course, though I know not why a busy author should lie at such length for nothing. But I cannot see how any man could say any more to suggest his dependence on the society of friends. These are positive facts of personality that can never be proved or disproved. I never knew Stevenson; but I knew very many of his favourite friends and correspondents. I knew Henry James and William Archer; I have still the honour of knowing Sir James Barrie and Sir Edmund Gosse.[8] And anybody who knows them, even most slightly and superficially, must know they are not the men to be in confidential correspondence for years with a silly, greedy and exacting egoist without seeing through him; or to be bombarded with boring autobiographies without being bored. But it seems rather a pity that such critics should be called upon to hunt up Stevenson's letter-bag, when they might well think it time to form some conclusions about Stevenson's place in letters. Anyhow I propose on the present occasion to be so perverse as to interest myself in literature when dealing with a literary man; and to be especially interested not only in the literature left by the man but in the philosophy inhering in the literature. And I am especially interested in a certain story, which was indeed the story of his life, but not exactly the story in his biography. It was an internal and spiritual story; and the stages of it are to be found rather in his stories than in his external acts. It is told much better in the difference between *Treasure Island* and *The Story of a Lie*, or in the difference between *A Child's Garden of Verses* and *Markheim* or *Olalla*, than in any detailed account of his wrangles with his father or the fragmentary love-affairs of his youth. For it seems to me that there is a moral to the art of Stevenson (if the shades of Wilde and Whistler will endure the challenge), and that it is one with a real bearing on the future of European culture and the hope that is to guide our children.

---

[8] Sir Edmund Gosse (1849–1928) was an English poet, critic, essayist and biographer.

Whether I shall be able to draw out this moral and make it sufficiently large and clear, I know as little as the reader does.

Nevertheless, at this stage of the attempt I will say one thing. I have, in a sense, a sort of theory about Stevenson; a view of him which, right or wrong, concerns his life and work as a whole. But it is perhaps less exclusively personal than much of the interest that has been naturally taken in his personality. It is certainly the very contrary of the attacks which have commonly, and especially recently, been made on that personality. Thus the critics are fond of suggesting that he was nothing if not self-conscious; that the whole of his significance came from self-consciousness. I believe that the one really great and important work which he did for the world was done quite unconsciously. Many have blamed him for posing; some have blamed him for preaching. The matter which mainly interests me is not merely his pose, if it was a pose, but the large landscape or background against which he was posing; which he himself only partly realised, but which goes to make up a rather important historical picture. And though it is true that he sometimes preached, and preached very well, I am by no means certain that the thing which he preached was the same as the thing which he taught. Or, to put it another way the thing which he could teach was not quite so large as the thing which we can learn. Or again, many of them declare that he was only a nine days' wonder, a passing figure that happened to catch the eye and even affect the fashion; and that with that fashion he will be forgotten. I believe that the lesson of his life will only be seen after time has revealed the full meaning of all our present tendencies; I believe it will be seen from afar off like a vast plan or maze traced out on a hillside; perhaps traced by one who did not even see the plan while he was making the tracks. I believe that his travels and doublings and returns reveal an idea, and even a doctrine. Yet it was perhaps a doctrine in which he did not believe, or at any rate did not believe that he believed. In other words, I think his significance will stand out more strongly in relation to larger problems which are beginning to press once more upon the mind of man; but of which many men are still largely unaware in our time, and were almost entirely unaware in his. But any contribution to the solution of those problems will be remembered; and he made a very great contribution, probably greater than he knew. Lastly, these same critics do not hesitate, in many cases, to accuse him flatly of being insincere. I should say that nobody, so openly fond of play-acting as he was, could possibly be insincere. But it is more to my purpose now to say that his relation to the huge half-truth that he carried was in its very simplicity a mark of truthfulness. For he had the splendid and ringing sincerity to testify, in a voice like a trumpet, to a truth that he did not understand.

II

IN THE COUNTRY OF SKELT

Every now and then the eye is riveted, in reading current criticism, by some statement so astonishingly untrue, or even contrary to the fact, that it seems as if a man walking down the street were suddenly standing on his head. It is all the more noticeable when the critic really has a strong head to stand on. One of the ablest of the younger critics, whose studies in other subjects I have warmly admired, wrote in our invaluable *London Mercury* a study of Stevenson; or what purported to be a study of Stevenson. And the chief thing he said, indeed almost the only thing he said, was that the thought of Stevenson instantly throws us back to the greater example of Edgar Allan Poe; that both were pallid and graceful figures 'making wax flowers,' as somebody said; and of course the earlier and greater had the advantage of the later and the less. In fact, the critic treated Stevenson as the shadow of Poe; which may not unfairly be called the shadow of a shade. He almost hinted that, for those who had read Poe, it was hardly worth while to read Stevenson. And indeed I could almost suspect he had taken his own advice; and never read a line of Stevenson in his life.

If a man were to say that Maeterlinck[9] derives so directly from Dickens that it is difficult to draw the line between them, I should not at once seize the clue. But I should be momentarily at a loss to catch his meaning. If he were to say that Walt Whitman was so close a copyist of Pope that it is hardly worth while to read the copy, I should not at once seize the clue. But I should think these comparisons rather more close, if anything, than the comparison between Stevenson and Poe. Dickens did not confine himself to comic subjects so much as Poe did to tragic ones; and an Essay on Optimism might couple the names of Pope and Whitman. It might also include the name of Stevenson; but it would hardly beam and sparkle with the name of Poe. The contrast, however, is much deeper than labels or the commonplaces

---

[9] Comte Maurice Maeterlinck(1862–1949) was a Belgian Symbolist dramatist, essayist, and philosopher; winner of the Noble Prize for literature in 1911.

of controversy. It is much deeper than formal divisions between what is funny and what is serious. It is concerned with something which it is now fashionable in drawing-rooms to call psychological; but which those who would as soon talk Latin as Greek still prefer to call spiritual. It is not necessarily what the newspapers would call moral; but that is only because it is more moral than most modern morality.

When Stevenson was known as Stennis, by Parisian art students struggling with his name, it was the hour of Art for Art's Sake. Painting was to be impersonal, though painters (like Whistler) were sometimes perhaps a little personal. But they all insisted that every picture is as impersonal as a pattern. They ought to have insisted that every pattern is as personal as a picture. Whether or no we see faces in the carpet, we ought to see a mind in the carpet; and in fact there is a mind in every scheme of ornament. There is as emphatically a morality expressed in Babylonian architecture or Baroque architecture as if it were plastered all over with Biblical texts. Now in the same manner there is at the back of every artist's mind something like a pattern or a type of architecture. The original quality in any man of imagination is imagery. It is a thing like the landscapes of his dreams; the sort of world he would wish to make or in which he would wish to wander; the strange flora and fauna of his own secret planet; the *sort* of thing that he likes to think about. This general atmosphere, and pattern or structure of growth, governs all his creations however varied; and because he can in this sense create a world, he is in this sense a creator; the image of God. Now everybody knows what was in this sense the atmosphere and architecture of Poe. Dark wine, dying lamps, drugging odours, a sense of being stifled in curtains of black velvet, a substance which is at once utterly black and unfathomably soft, all carried with them a sense of indefinite and infinite decay. The word infinite is not itself used indefinitely. The point of Poe is that we feel that *everything* is decaying, including ourselves; faces are already growing featureless like those of lepers; roof-trees are rotting from root to roof; one great grey fungus as vast as a forest is sucking up life rather than giving it forth; mirrored in stagnant pools like lakes of poison which yet fade without line or frontier into the swamp. The stars are not clean in his sight; but are rather more worlds made for worms. And this corruption is increased, by an intense imaginative genius, with the addition of a satin surface of luxury and even a terrible sort of comfort. 'Purple cushions that the lamplight gloated o'er' is in the spirit of his brother Boudelaire who wrote of *divans profonds comme les tombeaux.*[10] This dark luxury has something almost liquid about it. Its laxity seems to be betraying more vividly how all these things are being sucked away from us, down a slow whirlpool more like a moving swamp. That is the atmosphere of Edgar Allan Poe; a sort of rich rottenness of decomposition, with something thick and narcotic in the very air. It is idle to describe what so darkly and magnificently describes itself. But perhaps the shortest and best way of describing that artistic talent is to say that Stevenson's is exactly the opposite.

The first fact about the imagery of Stevenson is that all his images stand out in very sharp outline; and are, as it were, all edges. It is something in him that afterwards attracted him to the abrupt and angular black and white of woodcuts. It is to be seen from the first, in the way in which his eighteenth-century figures stand up against the skyline, with their cutlasses and cocked hats. The very words carry the sound and the significance. It is as if they were cut out with cutlasses; as was that unforgettable chip or wedge that was hacked by the blade of Billy Bones out of the wooden sign of the 'Admiral Benbow.'[11] That sharp indentation of the wooden square remains as a sort of symbolic shape expressing Stevenson's type of literary attack; and if all the colours should fade from me and the scene of all that romance grow dark, I think that black wooden sign with a piece bitten out of it would be the last shape that I should see. It is no mere pun to say that it is the best of his woodcuts. Normally, anyhow, the scene is the very reverse of dark, and certainly the very reverse of indefinite. Just as all the form can best be described as clean-cut, so all the colour is conspicuously clear and bright. That is why such figures are so often seen standing against the sea. Everybody who has been at the seaside has noted how sharp and highly coloured, like painted caricatures, appear even the most ordinary

[10] *Divans profonds comme les tombeaux* is French for "low couches like tombs".

[11] In Stevenson's novels *Admiral Benbow* is a ship possibly named after the English admiral John Benbow (1653–1702).

figures as they pass in profile to and fro against the blue dado of the sea. There is something also of that hard light that falls full and pale upon ships and open shores; and even more, it need not be said, of a certain salt and acrid clearness in the air. But it is notably the case in the outlines of these maritime figures. They are all edges and they stand by the sea, that is the edge of the world.

This is but a rough experimental method; but it will be found useful to make the experiment, of calling up all the Stevensonian scenes that recur most readily to the memory; and noting this bright hard quality in shape and hue. It will make it seem all the stranger that any ornithologist could have confused the raven of Poe with the parrot of Long John Silver. The parrot was scarce more reputable; but he was a bird from the lands of bright plumage and blue skies, where the other bird was a mere shadow making darkness more dark. It is even worth noting that when the more modern pirates of *The Wrecker* carried away with them a caged bird, it had to be a canary. It is to be specially observed when Stevenson is dealing with things which many of his contemporaries made merely shadowy or unfathomably mysterious; such as the Highland hills and all the lost kingdoms of the Gael. His Highland tales have everything Scotch except Scotch mist. At that time, and even before, writers of the school of Fiona Macleod[12] were already treating such peoples entirely as the Children of the Mist. But there is very little mist on the mountains of Stevenson. There is no Celtic twilight about his Celts. Alan Breck Stewart[13] had no yearning for any delicate vapour to veil his bright silver buttons of his bright blue French coat. There was hardly a cloud in the sky upon that day of doom, when Glenure dropped dead in the sunshine; and he did not have red hair for nothing. Stevenson is even moved to mention that the servant behind him was laden with lemons; because lemons are bright yellow. This sort of making of a picture may not be conscious, but it is none the less characteristic. Of course I do not mean literally that all the scenes in any novel could have the same scheme of colour, or occur at the

---

[12] Fiona Macleod was the pseudonym of William Sharp (1855–1905), Scottish poet and man of letters.

[13] Alan Breck Stewart is one of the main characters in Stevenson's novel *Kidnapped*.

same time of day. There are exceptions to the rule; but even these will generally be found to be exceptions that prove the rule. The time of *A Lodging for the Night* is not unnaturally at night; but even in that nightmare of winter in mediaeval Paris the mind's eye is really filled rather with the whiteness of snow than the blackness of darkness. It is against the snow that we see the flaming mediaeval figures; and especially that memorable figure who (like Campbell of Glenure)[14] had no right to have red hair when he was dead. The hair is like a scarlet splash of blood crying for vengeance; but I doubt whether the doomed gentleman in Poe's poetry would have been allowed to have red hair even when he was alive. In the same way, it would be easy to answer in detail, by finding some description of night in the works of Stevenson; but it would never be the night that broods eternally on the works of Poe. It might be said, for instance, that there are few more vivid or typical scenes in the Stevensonian tales than that of the duel at midnight in *The Master of Ballantrae*. But there again the exception proves the rule; the description insists not on the darkness of night but on the hardness of winter, the 'windless stricture of the frost'; the candles that stand as straight as the swords; the candle-flames that seem almost as cold as the stars. I have spoken of the double meaning of a woodcut; this was surely, in the same double sense, a steel engraving. A steely cold stiffens and steadies that tingling play of steel; and that not only materially but morally. The House of Durrisdeer does not fall after the fashion of The House of Usher. There is in that murderous scene I know not what that is clean and salt and sane; and, in spite of all, the white frost gives to the candles a sort of cold purification as of candlemas. But the point is, at the moment, that when we say this deed was done at night, we do not mean that it was done in the dark. There is a sense of exactitude and emphatic detail that belongs entirely to the day. Here indeed the two authors so strangely compared might almost have conspired in advance against the critic who compared them: as when Poe's ideal detective prefers to think in the dark, and therefore puts up the shutters even during the day.

[14] Glenure, a reference to Campbell of Glenure, is a character in Stevenson's *A Lodging for the Night*.

Dupin[15] brings the outer darkness into the parlour, while Durie[16] carries the candlelight into the forest.

These images are not fancies or accidents: their spirit runs through the whole scene. The same incident, for instance, shows all the author's love of sharp edges and cutting or piercing action. It is supremely typical that he made Mrs. Durie thrust the sword up to the hilt into the frozen ground. It is true that afterwards (perhaps under the sad eye of Mr. Archer and the sensitive realists) he consented to withdraw this, as 'an exaggeration to stagger Hugo.' But it is much more significant that it did not originally stagger Stevenson. It was the very vital gesture of all his works that that sharp blade should cleave that stiff clay. It was true in many other senses, touching mortal clay and the sword of the spirit. But I am speaking now of the gesture of the craftsman, like that of a man cutting wood. This man had an appetite for cutting it clean. He never committed a murder without making a clean job of it.

Whence did that spirit come; and how did the story of it begin? That is the right and real way of beginning the story of Stevenson. If I say that it began with cutting figures out of cardboard, it might sound like a parody of the pedantic fancies about juvenile psychology and early education. But perhaps it will be better even to run the horrid risk of being mistaken for a modern educationist, rather than to repeat the too familiar phrases by which the admirer of Stevenson has got himself described as a sentimentalist. Too much has been talked in this connection about the Soul of the Child or the Peter Pan of Samoa; not because it is untrue, but because it is a mistake to tell a truth too often, so that it loses its freshness; especially when it is the truth about how to remain fresh. Many are perhaps rather tired of hearing about it; though they would never be tired of having it. I have therefore deliberately approached the matter by another road; and even by a road running backwards. Instead of talking first about Cummy and the nursery anecdotes of Master Louis (at the risk of making a really graceful figure grow ridiculous

---

[15] Dupin is a reference to C. Auguste Dupin, an amateur detective character created by Edgar Allan Poe.

[16] Chesterton is referring to James Durie, Stevenson's amateur detective.

by mere repetition, in the eyes of multitudes of greatly inferior people) I have tried to take the stock and normal of his work first, and then note that it really does date in a special sense from his childhood; and that it is not sentimental and not senseless and not irrelevant to say so.

If therefore we ask, 'Where does the story of Stevenson really start; where does his special style or spirit begin and where do they come from; how did he get, or begin to get, the thing that made him different from the man next-door?' I have no doubt about the answer. He got them from the mysterious Mr. Skelt[17] of the Juvenile Drama, otherwise the toy theatre, which of all toys has most of the effect of magic on the mind. Or rather, of course, he got it from the way in which his own individual temper and talent grasped the nature of the game. He has written it all in an excellent essay and at least in one very real sentence of autobiography. 'What is the world, what is man and life but what my Skelt has made them?' The psychological interest is rather more special than is conveyed by the common generalisation about the imagination of infancy. It is not merely a question of children's toys; it is a question of a particular kind of toy, as of a particular kind of talent. It was not quite the same thing, for instance, to buy toy theatres in Edinburgh as it would have been to go to real theatres in London. In that little pasteboard play there might be something of the pantomime; but there was nothing of the dissolving view. The positive outline of everything, so well sketched in his own essay, the hard favour of the heroine, the clumps of vegetation, the clouds rolled up stiff as bolsters—these things meant something to the soul of Stevenson by their very swollen solidity or angular swagger. And it is hardly an exaggeration to say that he spent his life in teaching the world what he had learnt from them. What he learnt from them was very much more than anybody else had ever learnt from them; and that is his teaching and his qualification to teach. But to the last he presented his morality in a series of Moral Emblems which had something in common with those definite outlines and defiant attitudes; and there was never any name for it but his own name of Skeltery.

[17] Mr. Skelt is a character of Stevenson's invention which represented life to him as a toy theatre. His term "skeltery" represented Stevenson's "philosophy".

It was because he loved to see on those lines, and to think in those terms, that all his instinctive images are clear and not cloudy; that he liked a gay patchwork of colour combined with a zigzag energy of action, as quick as the crooked lightning. He loved things to stand out; we might say he loved them to stick out; as does the hilt of a sabre or the feather in a cap. He loved the pattern of crossed swords; he almost loved the pattern of the gallows because it is a clear shape like the cross. And the point is that this pattern still runs through or underneath all his more mature or complex writing; and is never lost even at the moments when he is really tragic or, what is worse, realistic. Even when he mourns as a man, he still rejoices as a child. The men in divers' helmets like the monsters, in the sordid misery of *The Ebb-Tide*, are still like masks of pantomime goblins against the glowing azure. And James Durie is quite as clear, we might say quite as bright, in his black coat as Alan Breck in his blue one.

Taking such a toy as a type or symbol, we may well say that Stevenson lived inside his toy theatre. It is certain that he lived in an exceptional sense inside his own home; and often, I imagine, inside his own bedroom. It is here that there appears, thus early in his life, that other element that was destined to darken it, often with something like the shadow of death. I know not how far that shadow could sometimes be traced upon the nursery wall. But it is certain that he was at least relatively a delicate or sickly child; and was therefore more thrown back upon that inner imaginative life than if he had been more robust in boyhood. The world inside that home was largely a world of his own; yes, even a world of his own imagining, a thing not so much of firelight as of pictures in the fire. The world outside his home was very different, even for those who shared his home life; and that is a contrast that I shall have occasion to emphasise, when we come to the crisis of his youth. It is enough to note here the paradox that he was to some extent protected by family life even from the heavier traditions of his family. As it did not build lighthouses in the garden pond, so it did not always bring the Kirk into the nursery. He has described how his stern Calvinistic grandfather tolerated in the nursery the wild Arabian fables that he might well have denounced in the pulpit. As even that Edinburgh house defended him from the winter winds of Edinburgh, so it protected him in some degree from the full icy blasts of Puritanism which blew so high in public life. It may have been that he was a sick child; it may have been that he was a spoilt child; but this fact that he was largely left alone with his daydreams, dwelling in that house within a house which is typified by the toy theatre, is a thing to be remembered; for it means much at a later stage.

In this matter of what has been called the Child in R. L. S., I have admitted that there has been far too much talking; but there has been far too little thinking. The thing is a reality; and it does remain as a very considerable problem for the reason, as yet quite unsolved by the modern world, even when most is said about it. We have a mass of testimony from men of every description, from Treherne to Hazlitt,[18] or from Wordsworth to Thackeray, to the psychological fact that the child experiences joys which glow like jewels even in retrospect. None of the normal naturalistic explanations explain that natural fact; and some have suggested that it is indeed a supernatural fact. In the ordinary sense of mental growth, there is no more reason for the child being better than the man than for the tadpole being better than the frog. And the attempts to explain it by physical growth are even weaker. There is a good example of the weakness in one of the essays of Stevenson, who found himself, of course, at the particular modern moment to catch the first fashion and excitement of Darwinism. Speaking of the old Calvinist minister who confessed the gorgeous spell of the *Arabian Nights*, he suggests that in the brain of the theologian there is still the gambolling ape; the ancestor of man; 'probably arboreal.' It marks the security of such science, I may remark, that anthropologists are now saying that he was probably not arboreal. But anyhow, it is a little difficult to see why a man should love the complexity of labyrinthine cities, or wish to ride with the jewelled cohorts of the high princes of Arabia, merely because his relative had once been a hairy beast clambering like a bear on the top of a branching pole. It reminds one of the glorious apology which Stevenson made for having

---

[18] Chesterton is referring to William Hazlitt (1788-1830), English critic and writer of miscellany.

expected that a wealthy man would know a Governor of Christ's Hospital: 'A man with a cold in his head does not necessarily know a rat-catcher; and the connection, as it appears to my humbled and awakened sense, is equally close.'

The connection between the expanding energy of the young monkey and the secret daydreams of the young child is equally close. As a matter of fact, the time when the boy is most full of the energy of a monkey is emphatically not the time when the child is most full of the imaginative pleasures of a poet. These always come at a less vigorous period; they very often come to a less vigorous person. They especially and notably did so in the case of Stevenson; and it is absurd to explain the intensity of an infant who is an invalid by the bodily exuberance of a lad at the time when he is often rather a lout. Stevenson, with all the advantage of his disadvantages, may have lived through the period when everybody has a touch of loutishness. But that uncomfortable period of youth was not the period when the coloured pictures in his mind were most clear; they were much clearer later in the age of self-control and earlier in the age of innocence. The main point to be seized here is that they were coloured pictures of a particular kind. The colours faded, but in a certain sense the forms remained fixed; that is, that though they were slowly discoloured by the light of common day, yet when the lantern was again lit from within, the same magic-lantern slides glowed upon the blank screen. They were still pictures of pirates and red gold and bright blue sea, as they were in his childhood. And this fact is very important in the story of his mind; as we shall see when his mind reverted to them. For the time was to come when he was truly, like Jim Hawkins, to be rescued by a leering criminal with crutch and cutlass from destiny worse than death and men worse than Long John Silver—from the last phase of the enlightened ninteenth century and the leading thinkers of the age.

III

YOUTH AND EDINBURGH

It is the suggestion of this chapter that when Stevenson first stepped out of his early Edinburgh home, he slipped upon the step. It may have been nothing worse, to begin with, than the ordinary butter-slide of the buffoonery of youth; such buffoonery as makes up the typical Edinburgh tale called *The Misadventures of John Nicholson*. But that tale alone would suggest that there was something a little greasy or even grimy about the butter. It is an odd story for Stevenson to have written; and no Stevensonian has any particular desire to dwell on those few of his works that might almost have been written by somebody else. But it has a biographical importance that has hardly been properly estimated, even in connection with this rather overworked biography. It is a curiously unlovely and uncomfortable comedy, not even uncomfortable enough to be a tragedy. The hero is not only not heroic, but he is hardly more amusing than attractive; and the fun that is made of him is not only not genial, but is not particularly funny. It is strange that such misadventures should come from the mind that gave us the radiant harlequinade of *The Wrong Box*. But I mention it here because it is full of a certain atmosphere, into which Stevenson was plunged too abruptly, as I believe, when he passed from boyhood into youth. It is true to call it the atmosphere, or one of the atmospheres, of Edinburgh; yet it is the very reverse of so much that we rightly associate with the arid dignity of the Modern Athens. There is something very specially sordid and squalid in the glimpses of low life given in the dissipations of John Nicholson; and something of the same kind comes to us like a gust of gas from the medical students of *The Body Snatcher*. When I say that this first step of Stevenson led him rather abruptly astray, I do not mean that he did anything half so bad as multitudes of polite persons have done in the most polished centres of civilisation. But I do mean that his city was not, in that particular aspect, very polite or polished or even particularly civilized. And I notice it because

YOUTH AND EDINBURGH

it has been noticed too little; and some other things have been noticed too much.

It is an obvious truth that Stevenson was born of a Puritan tradition, in a Presbyterian country, where still rolled the echoes, at least, of the theological thunders of Knox;[19] and where the Sabbath was sometimes more like a day of death than a day of rest. It is easy, only too easy, to apply this by representing Stevenson's father as a stern old Covenanter who frowned down the gay talents of his son; and such a simplification stands out boldly in black and white. But like many other black and white statements, it is not true; it is not even fair. Old Mr. Stevenson was a Presbyterian and presumably a Puritan, but he was not a Pharisee; and he certainly did not need to be a Pharisee in order to condemn some parts of the conduct of his son. It is probably true that almost any other son might have offended equally; but it is also true that almost any other father would have been equally offended. The son would have been the last to pretend that the faults were all on one side; the only thing that can concern posterity in the matter is in certain social conditions which gave to those faults a particular savour, which counted for something even when the faults themselves have been long left behind. And while people have written rather too much about the shadow of the Kirk and the restrictions of a Puritan society, there is something that has not been seen about what may be called the under-side of such a Puritan city. There is something strangely ugly and ungracious not merely about the virtues but about the vices and especially the pleasures, of such a place. It can be felt, as I say, in Stevenson's own stories and in many other stories about Edinburgh. Blasts of raw whisky come to us on that raw wind: there is sometimes something shrill, like the skirl of the pipes, about Scottish laughter; occasionally something very nearly insane about Scottish intoxication. I will not connect it, as did a friend of mine, with the hypothesis that the heathen Scots originally worshipped demons; but it is probably connected with the same rather savage intensity which gave them their theological thoroughness. Anyhow, it is true that in such a world

---

[19] Chesterton is referring to John Knox (1505–1572), the Scottish religious reformer.

even temptation itself has something terrifying as well as tempting; and yet something at the same time undignified and flat. It was this that cut across the natural poetic adventure or ambition of a young poet; and gave to the early part of his story a quality of frustration, if not of aberration.

What was the matter with Stevenson, I fancy, in so far as there was ever anything much the matter with him, was that there was too sharp a contrast between the shelter and delicate fancies of his childhood and the sort of world which met him like the wind on the front doorstep. It was not merely the contrast between poetry and Puritanism; it was also the contrast between poetry and prose; and prose that was almost repulsively prosaic. He did not believe enough in Puritanism to cling to it; but he did believe very much in a potential poetry of life, and he was bewildered by its apparently impossible position in the world of real living. And his national religion, even if he had believed in his religion as ardently as he believed in his nation, would never have met that particular point at issue.

Puritanism had no idea of purity. We might almost say that there is every other virtue in Puritanism except purity; often including continence, which is quite a different thing from purity. But it has not many images of positive innocence; of the things that are at once white and solid, like the white chalk or white wood which children love. This does not detract at all from the noble Puritan qualities: the republican simplicity, the fighting spirit, the thrift, the logic, the renunciation of luxuries, the resistance to tyrants, the energy and enterprise which have helped to give the Scot his adventurous advantage all over the world. But it is none the less true that there has been in his creed, at best, negative rather than positive purity: the difference between the blank white window and the ivory tower. I know that a Victorian prejudice still regards this interpretation of history by theology as a piece of most distressing bad taste. I also know that this taboo on the main topic of mankind is becoming an intolerable nuisance; and preventing anybody, from the Papist to the atheist, from saying what he really thinks about the most real themes in the world. And I will take the liberty of stating, in spite of the taboo, that it is really relevant here to remember this Puritan defect. It is as much a fact that the Kirk of Stevenson's country had no cult of the Holy Child, no feast of the Holy Innocents, no tradition of the Little Brothers of St. Francis, nothing that could in anyway *carry on* the childish enthusiasm for simple things, and link it up with a lifelong rule of life — this is as much a fact as that the Quakers are not a good military school or the good Moslem a good wine-taster. Hence it followed that when Stevenson left his home, he shut the door on a house lined with fairy gold, but he came out on a frightful contrast; on temptations at once attractive and repulsive, and terrors that were still depressing even when they were disregarded. The boy in such surroundings is torn by something worse than the dilemma of Tannhäuser. He wonders why he is attracted by repellent things.

I will here make what is a mere guess in the dark; and in a very dark matter of the mind. But I suspect that it was originally out of this chasm of ugly division that there rose that two-headed monster, the mystery of Jekyll and Hyde. There is indeed one peculiarity about that grim grotesque which I have never seen noted anywhere; though I dare say it may have been noted more than once. It will be realised that I am not, alas, so close a student of Stevensoniana as many who seem to think much less of Stevenson. But it seems to me that the story of Jekyll and Hyde, which is presumably presented as happening in London, is all the time very unmistakably happening in Edinburgh. More than one of the characters seem to be pure Scots. Mr. Utterson, the lawyer, is a most unmistakably Scottish lawyer, strictly occupied with Scots Law. No modern English lawyer ever read a book of dry divinity in the evening merely because it was Sunday. Mr. Hyde indeed possesses the cosmopolitan charm that unites all nations; but there is something decidedly Caledonian about Dr. Jekyll; and especially something that calls up that quality in Edinburgh that led an unkind observer (probably from Glasgow) to describe it as 'an east-windy, west-endy place.' The particular tone about his respectability, and the horror of mixing his reputation with mortal frailty, belongs to the upper middle classes in solid Puritan communities. But what is especially to the point of the present argument, there is sense in which that Puritanism is expressed even more in Mr. Hyde than in Dr. Jekyll. The sense of the sudden stink of evil, the immediate invitation to step into stark filth, the abruptness of the alternative between that prim and proper pavement and that black and reeking gutter — all this, though doubtless involved in the logic of the tale, is far too frankly and familiarly offered not to have had some basis in observation and reality. It is not thus that the ordinary young pagan, of warmer climes, conceives the alternative of Christ and Aphrodite. His imagination and half his mind are involved in defending the beauty and dignity of the joy of gods and men. It is not so that Stevenson himself came to talk of such things, when he had felt the shadow of old Athens fall on the pagan side of Paris. I allow for all the necessary horror of the conception of Hyde. But this dingy quality does not belong only to the demon antics of Hyde. It is implied, somehow, in every word about the furtive and embarassed vices of Jekyll. It is the tragedy of a Puritan town; every bit as much as that black legend which Stevenson loved, in which the walking-stick of Major Weir[20] went walking down the street all by itself. I hope to say something in a moment about the very deep and indeed very just and wise morality that is really involved in that ugly tale. I am only remarking here that the atmosphere and setting of it are those of some tale of stiff hypocrisy in a rigid sect or provincial village; it might be a tale of the Middle West savagely dissected in the Spoon River Anthology. But the point about it is that the human beauty which makes sin most dangerous hardly appears by a hint; this Belial[21] is never graceful or humane; and in this there seems to me to be something suggestive of the inverted order and ugly contrast with which licence presents itself in a world that has frowned on liberty. It is the utterance of somebody who, in the words of Kipling, knew the worst too young; not necessarily in his own act or by his own fault, but by the nature of a system which saw no difference between the worst and the moderately bad. But whatever form the shock of evil might take, I think it jerked him out of the right development of his romantic nature; and was responsible for much that seemed random or belated in his life.

I do not mean to imply that the morality of the story itself has anything of weakness or morbidity; my opinion is very much the

---

[20] Major Weir was a character in Stevenson's unfinished novel *Weir of Hermiston*.
[21] Belial is used in the Scriptures to mean "worthlessness" or wickedness and is often personified in the Old Testament as a biblical name of the devil.

other way. Though the fable may seem mad, the moral is very sane; indeed, the moral is strictly orthodox. The trouble is that most of those who mention it do not know the moral, possibly because they have never read the fable. From time to time those anonymous authorities in the newspapers, who dismiss Stevenson with such languid grace, will say that there is something quite cheap and obvious about the idea that one man is really two men and can be divided into the evil and the good. Unfortunately for them, that does not happen to be the idea. The real stab of the story is not in the discovery that the one man is two men; but in the discovery that the two men are one man. After all the diverse wandering and warring of those two incompatible beings, there was still only one man born and only one man buried. Jekyll and Hyde have become a proverb and a joke; only it is a proverb read backwards and a joke that nobody really sees. But it might have occurred to the languid critics, as a part of the joke, that the tale is a tragedy; and that this is only another way of saying that the experiment was a failure. The point of the story is not that a man *can* cut himself off from his conscience, but that he cannot. The surgical operation is fatal in the story. It is an amputation of which both the parts die. Jekyll, even in dying, declares the conclusion of the matter; that the load of man's moral struggle is bound upon him and cannot be thus escaped. The reason is that there can never be equality between the evil and the good. Jekyll and Hyde are not twin brothers. They are rather, as one of them truly remarks, like father and son. After all, Jekyll created Hyde; Hyde would never have created Jekyll; he only destroyed Jekyll. The notion is not so hackneyed as the critics find it, after Stevenson has found it for them thirty years ago. But Jekyll's claim is not that it is the first of such experiments in duality; but rather that it must be the last.

Nor do I necessarily admit the technical clumsiness which some have alleged against the tale, merely because I believe that many of its emotions were first experienced in the crude pain of youth. Some have gone into particular detail in order to pick it to pieces; and Mr. E. F. Benson[22] has made the (to me) strange remark that the structure of

---

[22] E. F. Benson (1867–1940), the son of an Archbishop of Canterbury, was an English novelist, essayist and biographer. He was the author of *Colin* (1923).

the story breaks down when Jekyll discovers that his chemical combination was partly accidental and is therefore unrecoverable. The critic says scornfully that it would have done just as well if Jekyll had taken a blue pill. It seems to me odd that any one who seems to know so much about the devil as the author of *Colin* should fail to recognise the cloven hoof in the cloven spirit called up by the Jekyll experiment. That moment in which Jekyll finds his own formula fail him, through an accident he had never foreseen, is simply the supreme moment in every story of a man buying power from hell; the moment when he finds the flaw in the deed. Such a moment comes to Macbeth and Faustus and a hundred others; and the whole point of it is that nothing is really secure, least of all a Satanist security. The moral is that the devil is a liar, and more especially a traitor; that he is more dangerous to his friends than his foes; and, with all deference to Mr. Benson, it is not a shallow or unimportant moral. But although the story ultimately emerged as a gargoyle very carefully graven by a mature master-craftsman, and was moreover a gargoyle of the greatest spiritual edification, eminently suited to be stuck on to the most sacred edifice, my point for the moment is that the stone of which it was made was originally found, I think, by Stevenson as a boy, kicking about the street, not to mention the gutter. In other words, he did not need to leave the respectable metropolis of the north to find the weaknesses of Jekyll and the crimes of Hyde.

I deal with these things in general terms, not merely out of delicacy, but partly out of something that I might almost call impatience or contempt. For the quarrels between the Victorian whitewashers and the Post-Victorian mudslingers seem to me deficient in the ordinary decent comprehension of the difficulties of human nature. Both the scandalised and the scandalmonger seem to me to look very silly beside the sensible person in the Bible, who confined himself to saying that there are things that no man knows, such as the way of a bird in the air and the way of a man in his youth. That Stevenson was in the mature and sane sense a good man is certain, without any Victorian apologetics; that he never did anything that he thought wrong is improbable, even without any elaborate cloacan[23]

---

[23] Cloacan means a sewer or a channel for moral filth and corruption.

researches; and the whole thing is further falsified by the fact that, outside a certain religious tradition, very few either of the whitewashers or the mudslingers really believe in the morality involved. The former seek to save nothing better than respectability; the latter even when they slander can hardly condemn. Stevenson was not a Catholic; he did not pretend to have remained a Puritan; but he was a highly honourable, responsible and chivalrous Pagan, in a world of Pagans who were most of them considerably less conspicuous for chivalry and honour. I for one, if I may say so, am ready to defend my own standards or to judge other men by theirs. But the Victorian pretence that every well-dressed hero of romance with over five hundred a year is born immune from the temptations which the mightiest saints have rolled themselves in brambles to control — that does not concern me and I shall not discuss it again.

But what does concern me, at this particular stage of the story, is not the question of what Stevenson thought right or wrong when he had become consciously and consistently a Pagan, but the particular way in which right and wrong appeared to him at this crude and groping age when he was still by tradition a Puritan. And I do think there was something tail-foremost, to use one of his own favourite words, in the way in which evil crept into his existence, as it does into everybody else's. He saw the tail of the devil before he saw his horns. Puritanism gave him the key rather to the cellars than the halls of Babylon; and something thus subterranean, suffocating and debased rolls like a smoke over the story of Jekyll and Hyde. But I only mention these matters as part of a general unfolding of his mind and moral nature, which seems to me to have had a great deal to do with the later development of his destiny. The normal, or at least the ideal, development of a man's destiny is from the coloured chamber of childhood to an even more romantic garden of the faith and tryst of youth. It is from the child's garden of verses to the man's garden of vows. I do not think that time of transition went right with Stevenson; I think that something thwarted or misled him; I think it was then that the east wind of Edinburgh Puritanism blew him out of his course, so that he returned only long after to anything like a secure loyalty and a right human relation. In a word, I think that in his childhood he had the best luck in the world, and in his youth the worst luck in the world; and that this explains most of his story.

Anyhow, he found no foothold on those steep streets of his beautiful and precipitous city; and as he looked forth over the litter of little islands in the large and shining estuary, he may have had some foreshadowing of that almost vagabond destiny which ended in the ends of the earth. There seemed in one sense no social reason why it should not end in Edinburgh as it had begun in Edinburgh. There seemed nothing against a normal successful career for one so brilliant, so graceful and essentially so humane; his story might have been as comfortable as a Victorian three-volume novel. He might have had the luck to marry an Edinburgh lady as delightful and satisfactory as Barbara Grant. He might have presided over the revels of a new bunch of Stevensons, coming home from Leith Walk laden with the gay portfolios of Skelt. They also might have bought Penny Pickwicks or gone about girt with lanterns; and his own view of these thing might have altered, though not necessarily weakened, with the responsibility of one who sees them reproduced in others. But among these early Edinburgh pranks, which he has left on record, was one which is something of a symbol. He speaks somewhere of a special sort of apples which he gathered by the seashore, which were such as might well be gathered from the salted and crooked trees that grow by the sea. I do not know what it was; or what form it took; or whether it ever took any definable form at all. But somehow or other, in thought or word or deed, in that bleak place he ate the apple of knowledge; and it was a crab apple.

I think it was partly the pains of youth that afterwards made so vivid to him the pleasures of childhood. The break in his life was of course partly due to the break in his health. But it was also due, I think, to something ragged and unseemly in the edge of life he laid hold of when he touched the hem of her garment; to something unsatisfactory in all that side of existence as it appears accidentally to the child of Puritan conventions. The effect on him was that, during those years, he grew up too much out of touch with his domestic and civic, if not his national traditions; knowing at once too much and too little. He was never denationalised; for he was a Scotsman; and a Scotsman never is, even when he is in theory internationalised. But he did begin to become internationalised, in the sense that he gained a sort of indiscriminate intimacy with the culture of the world, especially the rather cynical sort of culture which was then current. The local and domestic conventions, which were in many ways wrong, lost their power to control him even when they were right. And in all that retrospect nothing remained so real as the unreal romances of the first days. In the Puritan creeds there was nothing that he could believe, even as much as he had believed in make-believe. There was nothing to call him back half so clearly as the call of that childish rhyme of which he afterwards wrote, in the touching dedication that has the burden, 'How far is it to Babylon?' Unfortunately it is not very far to Babylon. That cosmopolitan market of the arts, which is in his story perhaps best represented by Paris, called to him more and more to live the life of the complete artist, which in those days had something like a touch of the complete anarchist. He passed into it, ultimately in person and already in spirit; there was nothing to call him back but the thin and tiny cry of a tin trumpet; that sounded once and was mute.

I say there was nothing to call him back; and very little to restrain him; and to any one who really understands the psychology and philosophy of that time of transition, it is really rather a wonder that he was so restrained. All his after adventures will be misunderstood if we do not realize that he left behind him a dead religion. Men are misled by the fact that he often used the old national creed as a subject; which really means rather that it had become an object. It was a subject that had ceased to be subjective; he worked upon it and not with it. He and the inheritors of his admirable tradition, like Barrie and Buchan;[24] treated that national secret genially and even tenderly; but their very tenderness was the first soft signal that the thing was dead. At least they would never have so fondled the tiger-cat of Calvinism until, for them, its teeth were drawn. Indeed this was the irony and the pathos of the position of Scottish Calvinism: to be

[24] Chesterton is referring to Sir John Buchan (1875–1940), Scottish writer and governor general of Canada from 1935 to 1940.

rammed down people's throats for three hundred years as an unanswerable argument and then to be inherited at the last as an almost indefensible affection; to be expounded to boys with a scowl and remembered by men with a smile; to crush down all human sentiments and to linger at last in the sentimental comedy of Thrums.[25] All that long agony of lucidity and masterful logic ended at last suddenly with a laugh; and the laugh was Robert Louis Stevenson. With him the break had come; and it follows that something in himself was broken. The whaups were crying round the graves of the martyrs, and his heart remembered, but not his mind; great Knox blew thrice upon the trumpet, and what thrilled him were no words but a noise; Old Mortality seemed still to be tinkering on his eternal round to preserve the memorials of the Covenant, but a bell had already tolled to announce that even Old Mortality was mortal. When Stevenson stepped into the wider world of the Continent, with its more graceful logic and even its more graceful vice, he went as one emptied of all the ethics and metaphysics of his home, and open to all the views and vices of a rationalistic civilisation. All the deeper lessons of his early life must have seemed to him to be dead within him; nor did he himself know what thing within him was yet alive.

[25] Thrums is the setting for many of Sir James Barrie's stories; it represents Barrie's birthplace which was known as Kirriemuir.

IV

THE REACTION TO ROMANCE

When a man walks down the street with a very long feather stuck in his hat and streaming behind him, or carrying a gold-hilted rapier cocked at a gallant angle, there are some among the typists and clerks of Clapham Junction shrewd enough to perceive that there is something faintly ostentatious about him. And when a man walks down Piccadilly or the parade at Bournemouth with long hair streaming behind him and surmounted by an embroidered smoking-cap, there are not wanting critics so acute as to deduce (with all the detailed shrewdness of Sherlock Holmes) that such a man is not entirely averse from being looked at. Many long and laborious studies of Stevenson have been published lately, to fortify and establish this remarkable result; and I need not devote myself to proving it further. Let us record with all due solemnity that Robert Louis Stevenson has been convicted by the court of being very vain, if 'dressin up' in the manner of a child, and not resenting the consequent conspicuous position, be the marks of vanity. But there is one aspect of this truth which seems to me to have been strangely and even astonishingly overlooked. Everybody talks as if Stevenson had been not only conspicuous but quite unique in this sort of vanity. Everybody seems to assume that among the artists of his time he was entirely alone in his affectation. Contrasting in this respect with the humdrum respectability of Oscar Wilde, notable as the very reverse of the evangelical meekness of Jimmy Whistler, standing out as he does against the stodgy chapel-going piety of Max Beerbohm,[26] having none of the cheery commonplaces of Aubrey Beardsley[27] or the prosaic self-effacement of Richard Le Gallienne,[28] he naturally aroused attention by the

[26] Max Beerbohm (1872–1956) was an English satirist and caricaturist famous for his irreverent parodies.
[27] Aubrey Beardsley (1872–1898) was an English artist known for black and white sketches on erotic subjects.
[28] Richard Le Gallienne (1866–1947) was an English poet and essayist.

slightest deviation into oddity or dandyism; things notoriously so unpopular among the decadents of the 'nineties. Among other things, everybody seems to have forgotten that Stevenson lived for some time among the Parisian art students; who have never been remarkable for the bourgeois regularity of their coats and hats. Yet he actually mentions the offensive smoking-cap himself as originating in the Bohemian masquerade of the Quartier Latin. There he was not so much being eccentric as being conventional; for the convention was unconventionality. A mob of men in that place, and at that age, would have played the same sort of tricks and worn the same kind of clothes; nor was Stevenson, as I have said, the only one of them who carried these attitudes and antics through life. Any one of them might have worn a smoking-cap; none of them would have objected to any variety of fool's cap, though they hardly wished it identified with a dunce's cap. Many of them, still alive, would cheerfully admit that the cap fits. But poor Stevenson is to be remembered as a fool, because all the fools are forgotten except Stevenson.

It was not that sort of oddity that was really odd. The costume for which he is now conspicuous was really part of a carnival. The attitude in which he stands, to the astonishment and grief of the critics, was really the fashion of a crowd. But what was really individual and interesting about him was the way in which he did actually react against the surroundings; the point at which he refused to run with the crowd or follow the fashion. No insanity in that cheerful lunatic asylum is so interesting to the psychologist as the shock of Stevenson going sane. No romantic ruffianism in which he may or may not have indulged is so curious as the real spirit of his revolt into respectability.

Treasure Island, if hardly a historical novel, was essentially a historical event. The rise or revolt of R. L. S. must be taken in relation to history, to the history of the whole European mind and mood. It was, first and last, a reaction against pessimism. There was thrown across all that earth and sky the gigantic shadow of Schopenhauer. At least it seemed gigantic then, though some of us may already have suspected that the shadow was larger than the man. Anyhow, in that period we might almost say that pessimism was another name for culture. Cheerfulness was associated with the Philistine, like the broad grin with the bumpkin. Pessimism could be read between the lines of the lightest triolet or most elegant essay. Any one who really remembers that time will admit that the world was much more hopeful after the worst of its wars than it was not long before. Mr. H. G. Wells, whose genius had just been discovered by Henley was very much older than he is now. He was prophesying that the outline of history would end, not in communism, but in cannibalism. He was prophesying the end of the world: a crack of doom not even cheerful enough to be a day of judgement. Oscar Wilde, who perhaps filled up more room, both in mind and body, than anybody else on that stage at that moment, expressed his philosophy in that bitter parable in which Christ seeks to comfort a man weeping and is answered, 'Lord, I was dead and you raised me to life; what else can I do but weep?'

This was the spirit that was behind all that levity; a levity that was like fireworks in more ways than one. We talk of some Whistlerian satire as a squib; but squibs can only shine in the dark. It is all the difference between the colours of fireworks that have their backs to the vault of night and the colours of church windows that have their backs to the sun. For these people all the light of life was in the foreground; there was nothing in the background but an abyss. They were rather nihilists than atheists; for there is a difference between worshipping Nothing and not worshipping anything. Now the interest of the next stage of Stevenson is that he stood up suddenly amid all these things and shook himself with a sort of impatient sanity; a shrug of scepticism about scepticism. His real distinction is that he had the sense to see that there is nothing to be done with Nothing. He saw that in that staggering universe it was absolutely necessary to stand somehow on something; and instead of falling about anyhow with all the other lunatics, he did seek for a ledge on which he could really stand. He did definitely and even dramatically refuse to go mad; or, what is very much worse, to remain futile. But the whole turning-point of the tale is now missed; partly by the too concentrated idolatry of the sentimentalists, and partly by the too concentrated spite of the iconoclasts. They miss the *historic* relation of the man to his time and school. It was one of the crowd of artists who showed mutinous signs of deserting art for life. It was even one of the decadents who refused to decay.

Now what really remains interesting in this story of Stevenson, in spite of all the vain repetitions, is the authority to which he appealed. It was rather an odd one; and many would have said that his sanity was madder than madness. He did not appeal to any ideal of the sort usually pursued by idealists; he did not try to construct an optimist philososphy like Spinoza or Emerson; he did not preach a good time coming like William Morris[29] or Wells; he did not appeal to Imperialism or Socialism or Scotland: he appealed to Skelt.

Familiarity had dulled the divine paradox that we should learn morality from little children. He advanced the more disturbing paradox that we should learn morality from little boys. The young child who should lead us was the common (or garden) little boy: the boy of the catapult and the toy pistol—and the toy theatre. Stevenson seemed to say to the semi-suicides drooping round him at the café tables; drinking absinthe and discussing atheism: 'Hang it all, the hero of a penny-dreadful play was a better man than you are! A Penny Plain and Twopence Coloured was an art more worthy of living men than the art that you are all professing. Painting pasteboard figures of pirates and admirals was better worth doing than all this; it was fun; it was fighting; it was a life and a lark; and if I can't do anything else, dang me but I will try to do that again!' So was presented to the world this entertaining spectacle of the art student surrounded by easels on which other artists were debating the fine shades of Corot[30] and Renoir, while he himself was gravely painting mariners a bright prussian blue out of a shilling paint-box and shedding their blood in streams of unmistakable crimson lake. That is the primary paradox about Stevenson's early manhood; or, if you will, the real joke about Stevenson. Of all the intellectualism in Bohemia the result was the return to Skelt. Of all that wallowing in Balzac the remarkable outcome was *Treasure Island*. But it is no

---

[29] William Morris (1834–96) was an English artist, poet and prominent advocate of socialism.

[30] Chesterton is referring to Jean Baptiste Camille Corot (1796–1875), a French landscape painter.

exaggeration to say that it had still more to do with toys than treasures. Stevenson was not really looking forward or outward to a world of larger things, but backward and inward into a world of smaller ones: in the peepshow of Skelt, which was still the true window of the world.

Thus, Skelt and his puppets seemed made for a repartee to the favourite phrases of the pessimists. Also that world was haunted as with a melody by the hedonist despair of Fitzgerald's Omar: one of the great historical documents of this history. No image could make them bow their heads with more hopelessness and helplessness of despair than that famous one:

> 'We are none other than a moving row
> Of magic shadow-shapes that come and go
> Around the sun-illumined lantern held
> At midnight by the Master of the show.'

And no image could make the infant Stevenson kick his little legs with keener joy. His answer, in effect, to the philosophy of the magic shadow-shapes, was that the shadow-shapes really were magic. At any rate, they really did seem to the children to be magic: and it was not false but true psychology to call the thing 'a magic lantern.' He was capable of feeling passionate delight in being such a Lantern-Bearer. He was capable even of feeling passionate delight in being such a shadow. And any one who has seen a shadow pantomime as a child, as I have, and who has retained any living link with his own childhood, will realise that Omar was as unlucky in his commentary on the lantern-show as the delightful curate in *Voces Populi* who talked about Valentine and Orson.[31] He was teaching optimism as an illustration to pessimism. Later we may make a guess at the nature of this glamour about such tricks or toys; the point for the moment is that they were associated with gloom in philosophy, while they were associated with pleasure in psychology. The same applies to more common examples of the fancies of the fatalist. When the sage said that men are 'only puppets,' it must have seemed

[31] Valentine and Orson are the two heroes from the French romance of the same name.

to the young Louis almost like the blasphemy of saying they were 'only pirates.' It might well seem to any child like saying that they were only fairies. There was something weak about bewailing drearily the fate of the puppets of destiny to an audience that was eagerly awaiting the joyful apocalypse of a puppet-show. The Stevensonian reaction might be roughly represented by the suggestion—if we are as futile as puppets, is there anything particular to prevent our being as entertaining as Punch? And there is, as I say, a real spiritual mystery behind this mystical ecstasy of mimicry. If living dolls were so dull and dead, why in the world were dead dolls so very much alive? And if being a puppet is so depressing how is it that the puppet of a puppet can be so enthralling?

It is to be noted that this sort of romanticism, as compared with realism, is *not* more superficial, but on the contrary more fundamental. It is an appeal from what is experienced to what is felt. When people are avowedly talking about happiness and unhappiness, as the pessimists were, it is futile to say that shadows and sham pasteboard figures *ought* not to make people happy. It was futile to tell the young Stevenson that the toy-theatre shop was a dingy booth stocked with dusty rolls of paper, covered with ill-drawn and ungainly figures; and to insist that these were the only facts. He naturally answered: 'My facts were my feelings; and what do you make of those facts? Either there is something in Skelt; which you do not admit. Or else there is something in Life; which you also do not admit.' Hence arose that answer to the realists which is best expressed in the essay called *The Lantern-Bearers*. The realists, who overlook so many details, have never quite noticed where lay the falsity of their method; it lay in the fact that so long as it was materialistic, it could not really be realistic. For it could not be psychological. If toys and trifles can make people happy, that happiness is not a trifle and certainly cannot be a trick.

This is the point that has been missed in all the talk about posing. Those who repeat for the hundredth time that he posed have not got as far as the obvious question, 'Posed as what?' All the other poets and artists posed; but they posed as the members of the Suicide Club. He posed as Prince Florizel[32] with a sword, challenging the

[32] Prince Florizel, the Prince of Bohemia, was the romantic hero of Shakespeare's *Winter's Tale* whom Stevenson characterized in *The New Arabian Nights*.

THE REACTION TO ROMANCE

President of the Suicide Club. He was, if you will, the foolish masker I have imagined, tricked out with a feather and a sword or dagger; but not tricked out more extravagantly than those who appeared as fantastic figures at their own funeral. If he had a feather, it was not a white feather; if he had a dagger, it was not a poisoned dagger or the pessimist dagger that is turned inwards; in short, if he had a posture it was a posture of defence and even of defiance. And it was, after all, the fashionable posture of his time which he set himself to defy. And it is here that it is really relevant to remember that he was not altogether posturing when he said he was defying death. Death was much nearer to him than it was to the pessimists; and he knew it whenever he coughed and found blood on his handkerchief. He was not pretending to defy it half so much as they were pretending to seek it. It is no very unreasonable claim for him that he made a better use of his bad health than Oscar Wilde made of his good health; and nothing affected in the externals of either can alter the contrast. The dagger may have been theatrical; but the blood was real. As Cyrano said of his friend, '*Le sang, c'est le sien.*'[33] And it really was the absence of courage in the current culture that awoke his protest or pose. In any case, the intellectual fine shades were morally more than a little shady. But he hated chiefly the loss of what soldiers call morale rather than what parsons call morality. All that world cowered under the shadow of death. All alike were travelling under the flag of the skull and crossbones. But he alone could call it the Jolly Roger.

What is really not appreciated about Stevenson is the abruptness of this breakaway. We talk of looking back with gratitude to innovators or the introducers of new ideas; but in fact nothing is more difficult to do, since for us they are now necessarily old ideas. There is only one moment, at most, of triumph for the original thinker; while his thought is an originality and before it becomes merely an orgin. News spreads quickly; that is, it grows stale quickly; and though we may call a work wonderful, we cannot easily put ourselves in the position of those for whom it was a cause of wonder, in the sense of surprise. Between the first fashion of talking too much

---

[33] *Le sang, c'est le sien* is French for "the blood, it is his".

in praise of Stevenson, and the newer fashion of talking nonsense in disparagement of Stevenson, we have become quite familiar with the association of certain ideas; of extreme stylistic polish applied to rough schoolboy adventure of the Penny Plain figure tinted as carefully as a minature. But these ideas were not always associated in the way in which Stevenson associated them. We may tear the combination to pieces, but it was he who wove it together; and—as many would have thought—of very incongruous threads. It really did seem preposterous to many that a serious literary artist of the age of Pater[34] should devote himself to rewriting Penny Dreadfuls. It was just as if George Meredith[35] had chosen to put all his fine feminine psychology into writing the sort of twopenny novelettes that were read by housemaids, and called 'Pansy's Elopement' or 'Winnie's Wedding Bells.' It was as if Henry James had been heard to say or, so to speak, to suggest, that there was, after all, and in a way quite annoyingly overlooked, *something*—something that really should have been better evaluated and re-expressed, as it were, in all that really unquestionable productiveness of *Ally Sloper's Half-Holiday*. It was as if Paderewski[36] had insisted on only going round with a barrel-organ; or Whistler had confined himself solely to painting public-house signs. A distinguished dramatist, who is old enough to remember in his youth the first successes of Stevenson's manhood, told me how absurd it seemed at the time that anyone should take seriously such gutter literature of the *gamin*. A book written only for boys generally meant a book written only for errand-boys. It seemed a strange association of ideas that it should be written carefully as a book for men, and even for literary men. It does not seem so strange now; because Stevenson has done it quite a long time ago. But it is important to realise that not everybody thought it natural to expend the style of *Pulvis Et Umbra* on the equivalent of 'Dick Deadshot Among the Pirates.' It was the very last sort of enthusiasm that would

[34] Walter Pater (1839-94), English essayist and critic, was known as a Renaissance revivalist as well as a humanist.

[35] George Meredith (1828-1909) was an English poet and novelist, best known for the novel *The Egoist* (1879). He believed in the intellectual equality of the sexes.

[36] Ignace Jan Paderewski (1860-1941) was a Polish pianist, composer and statesman.

have easily carried any of his cultivated contemporaries off their feet. The typical literary man, with the outlook and philosophy of that generation, would have been about as likely to pass his life in throwing paper darts or chalking caricatures of his publisher on a blackboard.

Thus, there is one of those phrases quoted too much, as against so many quoted too little, that he and his artistic friends bore with them bulky yellow volumes 'quite impudently French.' But, by the tests of that artistic world, *Treasure Island* is quite impudently English. By the conventions of that world, there was nothing unconventional about studying Balzac or being Bohemian. It was much more unconventional to study Captain Marryat[37] and to write about the good captain who flew the Union Jack over the stockade, in defiance of the bad buccaneers. From the standpoint of Art in those days even that flag was a much too Moral Emblem. It is only when we understand what there was that seemed quaint and even undignified in his adventurous antic, that we can clearly understand the unconscious truths that lay behind it. For, as against the black flag of pessimism, his flag was a Moral Emblem. There was a morality in his reaction into adventure; his appeal to the spirit of the highway—though it were sometimes the spirit of the highwayman.

In other words, he appealed to his own childhood. A tale is told of it: that when some one chaffed him about a toy sword he replied solemnly, 'The hilt is of gold and the scabbard of silver and the child is well content.' It was to that moment that he suddenly returned. Groping for something that would satisfy, he found nothing so solid as that fancy. That had not been Nothing; that had not been pessimistic; that was not a life over which Lazarus could do nothing but weep. That was as positive as the paints in the paint-box and the difference between vermilion and crome yellow. Its pleasures had been as solid as the taste of sweets; and it was nonsense to say that there had been nothing in them worth living for. Play at least is always serious. So long as we can say, 'Let us pretend,' we must be sincere. Therefore he appealed across the void or valley of his somewhat sterile

---

[37] Captain Frederick Marryat (1792–1848), English author of nautical novels, is best known for *Peter Simple* (1834).

youth to that garden of childhood, which he had once known and which was his nearest notion of paradise. There were no shrines in the faith or in the city of his fathers; there were no channels of consecration or confession; there was no imagery save in the faceless images left behind by the image-breakers. A man in his mood of reaction towards happiness might almost as well have prayed to the Black Man who figured as the Scottish provincial devil as to the God behind the black cloud that sent out such stiff horrific rays in the Calvinist family Bible. But in all that waste of Scottish moorland, the sun still glowed on that square of garden like a patch of gold. The lessons were lost, but the toys were eternal; the men had been harsh, but the child had been well content; if there were nothing better, he would return.

In the elementary philosophy of the thing, of course, what moved Stevenson was what moved Wordsworth; the unanswerable fact of that first vividness in the vision of life. But he had it in his own quaint way; and it was hardly the vision of meadow, grove and stream. It was rather the vision of coffin, gallows and gory sabre that were apparelled in celestial light, the glory and the freshness of a dream. But he was appealing to a sort of sanguinary innocence against a sort of silent and secretive perversion. Here, as everywhere in this rude outline, I am taking a thing like *Treasure Island*, in a spirit of simplification and symbol. I do not mean, of course, that he wrote *Treasure Island* sitting in a café on the boulevards; any more than I mean that he wrote *Jekyll and Hyde* in the cellar or a garret in the lands of the Cowgate. Both these books were developed by stages of the greatest literary care in later life; and pursued with the characteristic consistency of his art through all the equally characteristic mutability of his domicile. When I say that a certain book came out of a certain experience, I mean that he drew on that experience to write it, or that is was the ultimate result of the reaction which that experience produced in his mind. And I mean in this case that what shaped and sharpened Stevenson's memory of the mere nonsense of Skeltery was his growing sense of the need of some escape from the suffocating cynicims of the mass of men and artists in his time. He wished to go back to that nonsense; for it seemed, by comparison, quite sensible.

Treasure Island was written as a boy's book; perhaps it is not always read as a boy's book. I sometimes fancy that a real boy could read it better if he could read it backwards. The end, which is full of skeletons and ancient crime, is in the fullest sense beautiful; it is even idealistic. For it is the realisation of an ideal, that which is promised in its provocative and beckoning map; a vision not only of white skeletons but also green palm trees and sapphire seas. But the beginning of the book, considered as a boy's book, can hardly be called idealistic; and is found in practice to be rather too realistic. I may make an egotistical confession here, which I think is not unique and not without its universal inference about the spirit of youth. When I read the book as a child, I was not horrified by what are called the horrors. Something did indeed shock me, just a little more than a child should be shocked; for of course he would have no fun if he were never shocked at all. But what shook me was not the dead man's chest or the live man's crimes or the information that 'Drink and the devil have done for the rest'; all that seemed to me quite cheery and comforting. What did seem to me ugly was exactly what might happen in any inn-parlour, if there were no pirates in the world. It was that business about apoplexy; or some sort of alcoholic poisoning. It was the sailor having a mysterious thing called a stroke; so much more terrifying than any sabre-stroke. I was ready to wade in seas of gore; for all that gore was crimson lake; and indeed I always imagined it as a lake of crimson. Exactly what I was not ready for were those few drops of blood drawn from the arm of the insensible sailor, when he was bled by the surgeon. That blood is not crimson lake. Thus we have the paradox that I was horrified by the act of healing; while all the rowdy business of hitting and hurting did not hurt me at all. I was disgusted with an act of mercy, because it took the form of medicine. I will not pause to draw the many morals of this paradox; especially in relation to a common fallacy of pacifism. I will content myself with saying, whether I make my meaning clear or no, that a child is not wicked enough to disapprove of war.

But whatever be the case with most boys, there was certainly one boy who enjoyed *Treasure Island*; and his name was Robert Louis

Stevenson. He really had very much of the feeling of one who had got away to great waters and outlandish lands; perhaps even more vividly than he had it later, when he made that voyage not metaphorically but materially, and found his own Treasure Island in the South Seas. But just as in the second case he was fleeing to clear skies from unhealthy climates, so he was in reviving the adventure story escaping from an exceedingly unhealthy climate. The microbe of morbidity may have been within him, as well as the germ of phthisis; but in the cities he had left behind pessimism was raging like a pestilence. Multitudes of pale-faced poets, formless and forgotten, sat crowded at those café tables like ghosts in Hades, worshipping 'la sorcière glauque,'[38] like that one of them whose mortality has been immortalised by Max. It is too often forgotten that if Stevenson had really been only a pale young man making wax flowers, he would have found plenty of pale young men to make them with him; and the flowers and flower-makers would long have withered together. But he alone escaped, as from a city of the dead; he cut the painter as Jim Hawkins stole the boat, and went on his own voyage, following the sun. Drink and the devil have done for the rest, especially the devil; but then they were drinking absinthe and not with 'Yo ho ho'; consuming it without the most feeble attempt at any 'Yo ho ho'—a defect which was, of course, the most serious and important part of the affair. For 'Yo ho ho' was precisely what Stevenson, with his exact choice of words, particularly desired to say just then. It was for the present his most articulate message to mankind.

[38] *La sorcière glaugue* is French for "sea-green sorceress or witch".

V

THE SCOTTISH STORIES

Proverbs are generally true, when they are the proverbs of the people; so long as they are not proverbs about another people. It was unwise to search Sussex to discover if Kentish men had tails, or England to learn if French husbands had horns. And obviously there is much that is misleading in the traditional type of the practical Puritanical Scotsman, with his dry thrift and bleak respectability. A figure of such severe decorum is not very vividly evoked either by the title of Rab the Ranter[39] or the Wizard of the North. And few of our own generation are yet convinced of it, even by the scientific severity that has given us *Peter Pan* or the sober responsibility that stiffens the narrative of *The New Arabian Nights*. The readers of the latter work will be much interested to realise that a Scotsman is incapable of seeing a joke, since he seems so eminently capable of making one; and the reader of the former will be disposed to suggest that the national jesting is not too sober but rather too extravagant. *Peter Pan* carries on by lineal tradition the cult of the child, beginning with *Treasure Island*; but if there be anything to criticise in Sir James Barrie's beautiful fantasia, it is that wilder things happen to Wendy in a London nursery than ever happened to Jim in a tropical island. The only objection to living in a nursery where the dog is the nurse, or the father lives in the dog-kennel, is that there seems no necessity to go to the Never-Never Land to look for the things that never happen. Whatever else we say of the Scottish genius, it is certainly not merely dry or prosaic; and indeed the real mixture of the Scottish genius is as full of contradictions as that pattern of crosses in the Scottish plaid. And even here there is subtlety as well as cross-purposes; and the tartan may be an old tribal form of camouflage.

There is an aspect of a Scottish hill or moor, which for the moment will look grey and at the least change of light look purple; which is in itself an image of Scotland. A passing from the most

---

[39] Chesterton is possibly referring to a dog story by Dr. John Brown titled *Rab and His Friends* (1859).

dispassionate to the most passionate tint, which seems to be no more than a new shade, might well represent the mixture of restraint and violence that runs through the national history and the national character. Stevenson stands for one of those moments in the national history when the grey turned to purple; and yet in his purple there is still a great deal of grey. There is a great deal of restraint, artistic even more than moral; there is a certain coolness in the commentary even on picturesque objects; there is even a certain absence of the common conception of passion. There are shades even in purple; there are differences between the purple orchid and the purple heather; and his often seems to be like white heather, for luck. In other words, his idea of happiness is still of the breezy and boyish sort; and though he described the happiness of lovers very happily in *Catriona* and began to foreshadow their unhappiness in *Weir of Hermiston*, he attacked the theme relatively late in life; and it counted for little in that original idea of a return to simplicity, which had come upon him like a wind from a playground. Imagine how annoyed Jim Hawkins would have been, if a lot of girls had been allowed to muck up the business of going after treasure! So brilliant is this resurrection of boyhood, that we almost believe for the moment that Stevenson must have been as young and callous as Jim. Only I suspect, as I say, that in some ways he had even made himself a little callous in those matters. There his adventures had been misadventures. He did not recall for mere pleasure the memory of youth, as he did the memory of boyhood.

The two novels about David Balfour are very notable examples of what I have mentioned generally as the Stevensonian note; the brisk and bright treatment, the short speeches, the sharp gestures and the pointed profile of energy, as of a man following his nose very rapidly along the open road. The great scenes in *Kidnapped*, the defence of the Round House or the confrontation of Uncle Ebenezer and Alan Breck, are full of those snapping phrases that seem to pick things off like pistol shots. A whole essay on the style of Stevenson, such as I shall attempt forlornly and ineffectually on another page, might be written by a real critic on the phrase, 'His sword flashed like quicksilver into the huddle of our fleeing enemies.' The fact that the name of a certain metal happens to combine the word 'silver' with the word 'quick' is simply a rather recondite accident; but the art of Stevenson consisted in taking advantage of such accidents. To those who say that such tricks are easy to play or such words easy to find, the only answer is, 'Go and find them.' An author cannot create words, unless he be the happy author of *Jaberwocky* or *The Land Where the Jumblies Live*; but the nearest he can come to creating them is finding them in such a fashion and for such a use. The characters in the story are excellent, though perhaps there are really only two of them. There are more in the sequel called *Catriona*; and the study of the Lord Advocate Prestongrange is a highly interesting attempt to do a very difficult thing; to describe a politician who has not altogether ceased to be a man. The dialogue is spirited and full of fine Scottish humours, but all these things are almost as secondary in *Kidnapped* and *Catriona* as they are in *Treasure Island* itself. The thing is still simply an adventure story, and especially a boy's adventure story; such as is fitted to describe the adventures of a boy. And there are moments when it is the same boy; and his name is neither Hawkins nor Balfour, but Stevenson.

But though the thing is to be criticised (and admired) strictly as an adventure story, there are sidelights of interest about it considered as a historical novel. It carries on a rather curiously balanced critical attitude, partly inherited from the attitude of Sir Walter Scott; the paradox of being intellectually on the side of the Whigs and morally on the side of the Jacobites. There is enough moral material, in the story of the long legal murder of James of the Glens, to raise a whole clan of Jacobites and roll them red-hot down the pass of Killiecrankie.[40] But there still stands over against it the large legal assumption that in some sort of way all these things will be for the best, which is the inheritance of the providential view of the Presbyterian settlement. Similarly, it is obvious in the earlier story that David Balfour does not really differ very much from Alan Breck, in his view of the oppression of the Highland crofters and their pathetic loyalty to the past. In the ethical balance of the Appin Murder, if he does not palliate tyrannicide, he certainly says nothing calculated to palliate

---

[40] Killiecrankie is a pass located in the Grampions, Scotland.

tyranny. It is obvious that he is moved and impressed with the spectacle of a whole peasantry loyal to their ideal and defying a more civilised but a much more cynical pressure. But, curiously enough, when Stevenson saw exactly the same story acted before his eyes in the tragedy of the peasants of Ireland, he was carried away by some newspaper nonsense about the wickedness of the Land League (prodded perhaps by the rather absurd Jingoism of Henley) and, with all his native courage and much less than his native sense, wanted to plant himself on an eviction farm belonging to a family named Curtin, whom he seemed to regard as the sole victims of the social situation. It did not seem to occur to him that he was merely assisting the Master of Lovat to bully David Balfour. He seemed really to suppose that, in those social conditions, the Irish peasants could look for justice to imperial governments which abolished all local rights and carried away every Irish patriot to be tried before a packed jury of foreigners and foes. 'Justice, David! The same justice, by all the world, that Glenure found by the roadside.'

But this curious and sometimes inconsistent mingling of the grey Whiggery with the purple Jacobite romance, in the traditional sentiment of such Scots as Stevenson, is connected with much deeper things touching the hold that their history had upon them. It is necessary to state at this stage that there is really and seriously an influence of Scottish Puritanism upon Stevenson; though I think it rather a philosophy partially accepted by his intellect than the special ideal that was the secret of his heart. But every philosopher is affected by philosophy; even if, as in the immortal instance in Boswell, cheerfulness is always breaking out. And there was a part of Stevenson's mind that was not cheerful; which I think, in some manifestations, was not even healthy. And yet the tribute of truth is due to that special Scottish element; that even when we say it was not healthy, we can hardly venture to say it was not strong. It was the shadow of that ancient heathen fatalism, which in the seventeenth century had taken the hardly less heathen form of Calvinism; and which had sounded in so many Scottish tragedies with a note of doom. We appreciate it sharply when we turn from his two Scottish comedies of adventure to his third Scottish romance, which is a tragedy of character. It is true, as may be noted later, that even into this concentrated drama of sin and sorrow there enters a curious and rather incongruous element of the adventure story; like a fragment of the former adventures of David or Jim. But leaving that aside for the moment, we must do justice to the dignity which is given to the story itself by its more sombre scenery and its sterner creed. Stevenson showed his perfect instinct when he called it *A Winter's Tale*. It is his one story in black and white, and I cannot recall one word that is a patch of colour.

In touching on the rather neglected point of the nastier side of Puritan sociology, the raw and barbarous flavour about its evil and excess, I may have seemed to underrate the higher though harsher aspects of Scottish Puritanism. I do not mean to do so; and certainly nobody can afford to do so in attempting an adequate study of Stevenson. He remained to the day of his death in some ways particularly loyal to the Presbyterian tradition; I might say to the Presbyterian prejudices; and at least in one or two cases to the Presbyterian antipathies. But I think it was mostly rather a case of the modern religion of patriotism, as against the larger patriotism of religion. Like many other men of frank, tart and humorous prejudices (which are the sort of prejudices that need never prejudice us against a man) he was apt to see in some foreign things the evils to which he had grown accustomed in native things; and to start again the great international dispute of the pot and the kettle. It is amusing, for instance, to find the young Scotsman in *Olalla* gravely disapproving of the grim Spanish crucifix, with its tortured and grimacing art; and presumably leaving that land of religious gloom, to go back and enjoy the charm and gaiety of Thrawn Janet. If there was ever grim and grimacing art, one would think it was in that twisted figure; and even Stevenson admitted that Olalla got more comfort from the crucifix than Janet from the minister; or, I will add, the minister from the ministry. Indeed, stories of this kind are told by Stevenson with a deliberate darkening of the Scottish landscape and exultation in the ferocity of the Scottish creed. But it would be quite a mistake to miss in this a certain genuine national pride running through all the abnormal artistry; and a sense that the strength of the tribal tragedy testifies in a manner to the strength of the tribe.

It might be maintained that the best effect of the Scotsman's religious training was teaching him to do without his religion. It enabled him to survive as a certain sort of freethinker; one who, unlike his more familiar fellows, is not so intoxicated with freedom as to forget to think. It might be said that among the Scots, so far from a sentimental religiosity taking the place of dogmatic religion (as is generally the case among the English), something like the very opposite had occurred. When the religion was dead, the theology remained: at any rate, the taste for theology remained. It remained because, whatever else it is, theology is at least a form of thought. Stevenson certainly retained this turn of mind long after his beliefs, like those of most of his generation, had been simplified to vanishing point. He was, as Henley said, something of the Shorter Catechist; even when his own Catechism had become shorter still. All this, however, was indubitably a strength to him and his nation; and a real reason for gratitude to their old religious tradition. Those dry Deists and hard-headed Utilitarians who stalked the streets of Glasgow and Edinburgh in the eighteenth and early nineteenth centuries were very obviously the products of the national religious spirit. The Scottish atheists were unmistakable children of the Kirk. And though they often seemed absurdly detached and dehumanised, the world is now rather suffering for want of such dull lucidity. To put it shortly, by being theological they had at least learnt to be logical; and in dropping the Greek prefix as a superfluous trifle they still have the sympathy of many moderns much less logical than themselves. The influence of all this sort of clarity on Stevenson is very clear. It did not happen to be his mission to figure as the metaphysical Scotsman; or draw out his deductions along the lines of logic. But he did always by instinct draw lines that were as hard and clear as those of a mathematical diagram. He himself has made a very luminous and valuable comparison between a geometrical theorem and a work of art. I have had cause to remark again and again, in the course of this sketch, on a certain almost arid decision in the strokes of Stevenson's style. I believe it was due in no small degree to that inheritance of definition, that goes with an inheritance of dogma. What he wrote was not written, as he said scornfully of some literary performance, in sand with a salt-spoon; it was at least in the tradition of scriptures cut with steel into stone. This was among the many good things that he got from the spiritual atmosphere of his ancestry. But he got other things as well; though they are less easy to describe and far less easy to commend.

From time to time I have insensibly and inevitably fallen into a tone of defending Stevenson, as if he needed defence. And indeed I do think that he needs some defence; though not upon the points in which it is now considered necessary to defend him. I do feel a certain impatience with the petty depreciation of our own time, which seems much more frivolous and far less generous than the boom of a best-seller. I do feel a certain contempt for those who call every phrase affected that happens to be effective; or who charge a man with talking for effect, as if there were anything else to talk for. But I should think it very unfair to revile the revilers of Stevenson, without taking the risk of saying where I think he is, if not to be reviled, at least to be rebuked. There was, I think, a weaker strain in Stevenson; but it is the very opposite of the weakness now generally alleged by critics; indeed it is the very opposite of what they would probably regard as weak. The excuse for it, in so far as it existed to be excused, was in the very direction of that sharp turn which he took in early life, when he turned his back upon the decadents. I have already said, and it can hardly be said too often, that the story of Stevenson was a reaction against an age of pessimism. Now the real objection to being a reactionary is that a reactionary, as such, hardly ever avoids reacting into evil and exaggerational. The opposite of the heresy of pessimism was the twin heresy of optimism. Stevenson was not at all attracted to a placid and pacific optimism. But he did begin to be too much attracted to a sort of insolent and oppressive optimism. The reaction from the idea that what is good is always unsuccessful is the idea that what is good is always victorious. And from that many slide into the worse delusion; that what is victorious is always good.

In the days when Stevenson's ancestors the Covenanters were fighting with the Cavaliers,[41] a fine old Cavalier of the Episcopalian

---

[41] The Cavaliers were supporters of the Stuarts against the Puritans at the time of Charles I.

persuasion made a rather interesting remark; that the change he really hated was represented by saying 'The Lord' instead of 'Our Lord.' The latter implied affection, the former only fear; indeed he described the former succinctly as the talk of devils. And this is so far true that the very eloquent language in which the name of 'The Lord' has figured has generally been the language of might and majesty and even terror. And there really was implied in it in varying degrees the idea of glorifying God for His greatness rather than His goodness. And again there occurred the natural inversion of ideas. Since the Puritan was content to cry with the Moslem: 'God is great,' so the descendant of the Puritan is always a little inclined to cry with the Nietzschean: 'Greatness is God.' In some of the really evil extremes, this sentiment shaded darkly into a sort of diabolism. In Stevenson it was very faintly present; but it is occasionally felt; and by me (I must confess) felt as a fault. It is faintly felt, for instance, in the next great Scottish romance, *The Master of Ballantrae*; it is felt more definitely, I think, in the Scottish romance of *Weir of Hermiston*. In the first case, Stevenson said in his correspondence, in a tone that was humorous and healthy enough, that The Master was all he knew of The Devil. I do not in the least object to The Master being The Devil. But I do object to a subtle subconscious something, which every now and then seems almost to suggest that he is The Lord. I mean The Lord in the vague sense of a certain authority in aristocracy, or even in mere mastery. Perhaps I even dimly feel that there is the distant thunder of The Lord in the very title of The Master.

This thing, however we define it and in whatever degree we admit it, had advanced in several degrees when he wrote the later story. Perhaps it was partly the influence of Henley; who, with all his many generous virtues, certainly had this weakness to the point of hysteria. I mean the loss of the natural reaction of a man against a tyrant. It sometimes takes the form of the least masculine of all vices, the admiration for brutality. It has been much debated whether bullies are always cowards; I am content to remark that the admirers of bullies are always, by the very nature of things, trying to be cowards. If they do not always succeed, it is because they have unconscious virtues restraining that obscene worship: and this was true even of Henley; and far truer of Stevenson. Stevenson had always a training in real courage; for he fought when he was weak. But it cannot be denied that, by a combination of causes, his own revolt against spineless pessimism, the reactionary violence of Henley, but chiefly I think the vague Scottish tradition of a God of mere power and terror, he grew too familiar in his later works with the sort of swaggering cult of fear. I feel it in the character of Weir of Hermiston, or rather in the attitude of everybody else, including the author, towards that character. I do not mind the judge exulting over the game of insulting and hanging somebody; for I know the judge can be baser than the man he hangs. But I do mind the author exulting over it, when I know he is not base at all. The same fine shade of unpleasantness can be found in the last pages of *The Ebb-Tide*. My point might be put crudely by saying that I do not object to the author creating such a loathsome person as Mr. Attwater; but I do rather object to his creating him and not loathing him. It would be truer to put the point in another form; that there would be no objection if he loathed and admired Attwater exactly as he loathed and admired Huish. In a sense he obviously did admire Huish; as it was the very passion of his life to admire courage. But he did not expect anybody to look up to Huish; and there are moments when he seems to think it natural that people should look up to Attwater. This secret idolatry of what a feminine sentiment calls 'strength,' this was the only lesion in Stevenson's perfect sanity, the only running sore in the normal health of his soul; and even that had come from too violent an effort to be healthy. So he might, poor fellow, have started a haemorrhage by moving too vigorously on his pillow.

For I am not blaming him for having any such evil, in the sense of having any excess of it. I blame him, being what he was, for having even a touch of it. But I think it is unfortunately certain that he did have a touch of it. There is something almost cruel in thus tracing the innocent springs of cruelty. But, as has been said so often and so foolishly and so truly, Robert Louis Stevenson was a child. It is the moral of these chapters about his nation, his city and his home, that he was also something more than a child. He was a lost child. There was nothing to guide him in the mad movements and reactions of modernity; neither his nation nor his religion nor his irreligion were equal to the task. He had no chart for that gallant voyage; he was hardly to blame if he thought he had to choose between the savage rock of the pride of Scylla and the suicidal whirlpool of the despair of Charybdis. Only, like Ulysses, for all his adventurousness, he was always trying to get home. To vary the metaphor, his face was for ever turning like the sunflower towards the sun, even if it were behind a cloud; and perhaps after all there is nothing truer than the too familiar phrase from the diary of the doctor or the nurse; that he was a sick child, who passed his life in trying to get well.

VI

THE STYLE OF STEVENSON

Before writing this chapter I ought to explain that I am quite incapable of writing it; at least as many serious literary authorities think it ought to be written. I am one of those humble characters for whom the main matter of style is concerned with making a statement; and generally, in the case of Stevenson, with telling a story. Style takes its own most living and therefore most fitting form from within; as the narrative quickens and leaps, or the statement becomes warm or weighty, by being either authoritative or argumentative. The sentence takes its shape from motion; as it takes its motion from motive. And the motive (for us outcasts) is what the man has to say. But there is a technical treatment of style for which I have a profound respect, but it is a respect for the unknown, not to say the unintelligible. I will not say it is Greek to me, for I know the Greek alphabet and I do not know the alphabet of these grammars of cadence and sequence; I can still even read the Greek Testament, but the gospel of pure and abstract English brings me no news. I salute it from afar as I do musical harmony or the higher mathematics; but I shall not introduce into this book a chapter on any of these three topics. When I speak of the style of Stevenson I mean the manner in which he could express himself in plain English, even if it were in some ways peculiar English; and I have nothing but the most elementary English with which to criticise it. I cannot use the terms of any science of language, or even any science of literature.

Mr. Max Beerbohm, whose fine and classic criticism is full of those shining depths that many mistake for shallowness, has remarked truly enough on the rather wearisome repetitions in the newspapers, which did great harm to the Stevensonian fame at the time of the Stevensonian fashion. He notices especially that a certain phrase used by Stevenson about his early experiments in writing, that he has 'played the sedulous ape' to Hazlitt or to Lamb, must be permanently kept in type in the journalistic offices, so frequently do the journalists quote it. There are about a thousand things in Stevenson much more worth quoting, and much more really enlightening about his education in letters. Every young writer, however original, does begin by imitating other people, consciously or unconsciously, and nearly every old writer should be quite as willing to admit it. The real irony in the incident seems never to have been noticed. The real reason why this confession of plagiarism, out of a hundred such confessions, is always quoted, is because the confession itself has the stamp not of plagiarism but of personal originality. In the very act of claiming to have copied other styles, Stevenson writes most unmistakably in his own style. I think I could have guessed amid a hundred authors who had used the expression 'played the sedulous ape.' I do not think that Hazlitt would have added that word 'sedulous.' Some might say he was the better because the simpler without it; some would say that the word is in the strict sense too *recherché*; some might say it can be recognised because it is strained or affected. All that is matter for argument; but it is rather a joke when so individual a trick is made a proof of being merely imitative. Anyhow, that sort of trick, the rather curious combination of two such words, is the thing I mean by the style of Stevenson.

In the case of Stevenson, criticism has always tended to be hypercriticism. It is as if the critic were strung up to be as strict with the artist as the artist was with himself. But they are not very consistent or considerate in the matter. They blame him for being fastidious; and so become more fastidious themselves. They condemn him for wasting time in trying to find the right word; and then waste more time in not very successful attempts to prove it is the wrong word. I remember that Mr. George Moore[42] (who at least led the attack when Stevenson was alive and at the height of his popularity) professed in a somewhat mysterious manner to have exposed or exploded the whole trick of Stevenson, by dwelling at length on the word 'interjected': in the passage which describes a man stopping a clock with interjected finger. There seemed to be some notion that because the word is unusual in that use, it showed that there was nothing but artificial verbalism in the whole tragedy of *Jekyll and Hyde* or the fun

---

[42] George Moore (1852–1933) was an Irish novelist and critic.

of *The Wrong Box*. I think it is time that this sort of fastidiousness about fastidiousness should be corrected with a little common sense. The obvious question to ask Mr. Moore, if he objects to the word 'interjected,' is, 'what word would you use?' He would immediately discover that any word would be much weaker and even much less exact. To say 'interposed finger' would suggest by its very sound a much clumsier and less precise action; 'interjected' suggests by its very sound a sort of jerk of neatness; a mechanical neatness correcting mechanism. In other words, it suggests what it was meant to suggest. Stevenson used the word because it was the right word. Nobody else used it, because nobody else thought of it. And that is the whole story of Stevensonian style.

Literature is but a language; it is only a rare and amazing miracle by which a man really says what he means. It is inevitable that most conversation should be convention; as when we cover a myriad beautiful contrasts or comedies of opposites by calling any number of different people 'nice.' Some writers, including Stevenson, desired (in the old and proper sense) to be more nice in their discrimination of niceness. Now whether we like such fastidious felicities or no, whether we are individually soothed or irritated by a style like that of Stevenson, whether we have any personal or impersonal reason for impatience with the style or the man, we ought really to have enough critical impartiality and justice to see what is the literary test. The test is whether the words are well or ill chosen, not for the pupose of fitting our own taste in words, but for the pupose of satisfying everybody's sense of the realities of things. Now it is nonsense for anybody who pretends to like literature not to see the excellence of Stevenson's expression in this way. He does pick the words that make that picture that he particularly wants to make. They do fix a particular thing, and not some general thing of the same sort; yet the thing is often one very difficult to distinguish from other things of the same sort. That is the craft of letters; and the craftsman made a vast multitude of such images in all sorts of materials. In this matter we may say of Stevenson very much what he said of Burns. He remarked that Burns surprised the polite world, with its aesthetes and antiquarians, by never writing poems on waterfalls, ruined castles or other recognised places of interest; the very fact, of course, which showed Burns to be a poet and not a tourist. It is always the prosaic person who demands poetic subjects. They are the only subjects about which he can possibly be poetic. But Burns, as Stevenson said, had a natural gift of lively and flexible comment that could play as easily upon one thing as another; a kirk or a tavern or a group going to market or a pair of dogs in the street. This gift must be judged by its aptness, its vividness and its range; and anybody who suggests that Stevenson's talent was only one piece of thin silver polished perpetually in its napkin does not, in the most exact and emphatic sense, know what he is talking about. Stevenson had exactly the talent he attributes to Burns of touching nothing that he did not animate. And so far from hiding one talent in one napkin, it would be truer to say that he became ruler over ten cities; set in the ends of the earth. Indeed the last phrase alone suggests an example or a text.

I will take the case of one of his books; I deliberately refrain from taking one of his best books. I will take *The Wrecker*, a book which many would call a failure and which nobody would call a faultless artistic success, least of all the artist. The picture breaks out of the frame; indeed it is rather a panorama than a picture. The story sprawls over three continents; and the climax has too much the air of being only the last of a long string of disconnected passages. It has the look of a scrap-book; indeed it is very exactly a sketch-book. It is merely the sketch-book of Loudon Dodd, the wandering art student never allowed to be fully an artist; just as his story is never allowed to be fully a work of art. He sketches people with the pen as he does with the pencil, in four or five incongruous societies, in the commercial school of Muskegon or the art school of Paris, in the east wind of Edinburgh or the black squall of the South Seas; just as he sketched the four fugitive murderers gesticulating and lying in the Californian saloon. The point is (on the strict principles of *l'art pour l'art*, so dear to Mr. Dodd) that he sketched devilish well. We can take the portraits of twenty social types in turn, taken from six social worlds utterly shut out from each other, and find in every case that the strokes are at once few and final; that is, that the word is well chosen out of a hundred words and that one word does the work of twenty. The story starts: 'The beginning of this yarn is my poor father's character'; and the character is compact in one paragraph. When Jim Pinkerton first strides into the story and is described as a young man 'with cordial, agitated manners,' we walk through the rest of the narrative with a living man; and listen not merely to words, but to a voice. No other two adjectives could have done the trick. When the shabby and shady lawyer, with his cockney culture and underbred refinement, is first introduced as handling a big piece of business beyond his *metier*, he bears himself 'with a sort of shrinking assumption.' The reader, especially if he is not a writer, may imagine that such words matter little; but if he supposes that it might just as well have been 'flinching pride' or 'quailing arrogance' he knows nothing about writing and perhaps not much about reading. The whole point is in that hitting of the right nail on the head; and rather more so when the nail is such a very battered little tintack as Mr. Harry D. Bellairs of San Francisco. When Loudon Dodd merely has to meet a naval officer and record that he got next to nothing out of him, that very negation has a touch of chilly life like a fish. 'I judged he was suffering torments of alarm lest I should prove an undesirable acquaintance; diagnosed him for a shy, dull, vain, unamiable animal, without adequate defence—a sort of dishoused snail.' The visit to an English village, under the shadow of an English country house, is equally aptly appreciated; from the green framework of the little town, 'a domino of tiled houses and walled gardens,' to the reminiscences of the ex-butler about the exiled younger son; 'near four generations of Carthews were touched upon without eliciting one point of interest; and we had killed Mr. Henry in the hunting field with a vast elaboration of painful circumstance and buried him in the midst of a whole sorrowing county, before I could so much as manage to bring upon the stage my intimate friend, Mr. Norris. . . . He was the only person of the whole featureless series who seemed to have accomplished anything worth mentioning; and his achievements, poor dog, seemed to have been confined to going to the devil and leaving some regrets. . . . He had no pride about him, I was told; he would sit down with any man;

and it was somewhat woundingly implied that I was indebted to this peculiarity for my own acquaintance with the hero.' But I must not be led away by the large temptation of quoting examples of the cool and collected and sustained irony, with which Loudon Dodd tells his whole story. I am only giving random examples of his rapid sketches of very different sorts of societies and personalities; and the point is that he can describe them rapidly and yet describe them rightly. In other words the author does possess a quite exceptional power of putting what he really means into the words that really convey it. And to show that this was a matter of genius in the man, and not (as some of his critics would imply) a matter of laborious technical treatment applied to two or three prize specimens, I have taken all these examples from one of the less known works, one of the least admired and perhaps of the least admirable. Whole tracts of it run almost as casually as his private correspondence; and his private correspondence is full of the same lively and animated neatness. In this one neglected volume of *The Wrecker* there are thousands of such things; and everything to show that he could have written twenty more volumes, equally full of these felicities. A man who does this is not only an artist doing what most men cannot do, but he is certainly doing what most novelists do not do. Even very good novelists have not this particular knack of putting a whole human figure together with a few unforgettable words. By the end of a novel by Mr. Arnold Bennett or Mr. E. F. Benson I have the sense that Lord Raingo or Lord Chesham is a real man, very rightly understood; but I never have at the beginning that feeling of magic; that a man has been brought to life by three words of an incantation.

This was the genius of Stevenson; and it is simply silly to complain of it because it was Stevensonian. I do not blame either of the other two novelists for not being somebody else. But I do venture to blame them a little for grumbling because Stevenson was himself. I do not quite see why he should be covered with cold depreciation merely because he could put into a line what other men put into a page; why he should be regarded as superficial because he saw more in a man's walk or profile than the moderns can dig out of his complexes and his subconsciousness; why he should be called artificial because he sought (and found) the right word for a real object; why he should be thought shallow because he went straight for what was significant, without wading towards it through wordy seas of insignificance; or why he should be treated as a liar because he was not ashamed to be a story-teller.

Of course there are many other vivid marks of Stevenson's style, besides this particular element of picked and pointed phrase, or rather especially the combination of picked and pointed phrases. I might make much more than I have made out of something in his rapidly stepping sentences, especially in narrative, which corresponds to his philosophy of the militant attitude and the active virtues. That word angular, which I have been driven to use too often, belongs to the sharpness of his verbal gestures as much as to the cutlasses and choppers of his pasteboard pirates. Those early theatrical figures, from the sketch-book of Skelt, were all of them in their nature like snapshots of people in swift action. Three-Fingered Jack could not have remained permanently with the cudgel or the sabre swung about his head nor Robin Hood with the arrow drawn to his ear; and the descriptions of Stevenson's characters are seldom static but rather dynamic descriptions; and deal rather with how a man did or said something than with what he was like. The sharp and shrewd Scottish style of Ephraim Mackellar or David Balfour seems by its very sound exactly fitted to describe a man snapping his fingers or rapping with his stick. Doubtless so careful an artist as Stevenson varied his style to suit the subject and the speaker; we should not look for these dry or abrupt brevities in the dilettante deliberations of Loudon Dodd; but I know very few of the writer's works in which there are not, at the crisis, phrases as short and sharp as the knife that Captain Wicks rammed through his own hand. Something should also have been said, of course, of the passages in which Stevenson deliberately plays on a somewhat different musical instrument; as when he exercised upon Pan's Pipes in respectful imitation of Meredith upon a penny whistle. Something should have been said of the style of his poems; which are perhaps more successful in their phraseology than their poetry. But these again teem with these taut and trenchant separate phrases; the description of the interlacing branches like crossed sword in battle; the men upholding the falling skies like unfrowning caryatids; the loud stairs of honour and the bright eyes of danger. But I have already explained that I profess no scientific thoroughness about these problems of execution; and can only speak of the style of Stevenson as it specially affects my own taste and fancy. And the thing that strikes me most is still this sense of somebody being pinked with a rapier in a particular button; of a sort of fastidiousness that has still something of the fighting spirit; that aims at a mark and makes a point, and is certainly not merely an idle trifling with words for the sake of their external elegance or intrinsic melody. As a part of the present criticism, such a statement is only another way of saying, in the old phrase, that the style is the man; and that the man was certainly a man and not only a man of letters. I find everywhere, even in his mere diction and syntax, that theme that is the whole philosophy of fairy-tales, of the old romances and even of the absurd libretto of the little theatre — the conception that man is born with hope and courage indeed, but born outside that which he was meant to attain; that there is a quest, a test, a trial by combat or pilgrimage of discovery; or, in other words, that whatever else man is he is not sufficient to himself, either through peace or through despair. The very movement of the sentence is the movement of a man going somewhere and generally fighting something; and that is where optimism and pessimism are alike opposed to that ultimate or potential peace, which the violent take by storm.

VII

EXPERIMENT AND RANGE

In any generalisation about Stevenson, it is of course easy to forget that his work was very varied, in the sense of being very versatile. In one sense, he tried very different styles; and was always very careful only to try one style at a time. The unity of each accentuates the diversity of all. The very fact that he was careful to keep each several study in its own tone or tint, makes the range of his work look more like a patch work than it really is. It is always a sharp contrast between complete and homogeneous things; when these things are broken up in subdivisions, the whole falls back into a more mixed but a more general pattern. In one sense this is merely a platitude. It would hardly be difficult to point out that the style of *Prince Otto* is very different from the style of *The Wrong Box*. It is different with the whole difference between a man working in wax or cardboard or ivory or ebony. *Prince Otto* is a sort of china shepherdess group, practising arcadian courtliness in an eighteenth-century park; the other is a sort of Aunt Sally pelted with comic misfortunes as if with cocoanuts. Nobody is likely to confuse these forms of art; nobody sets up a china shepherdess to be pelted with cocoanuts; few are so chivalrous as to approach their Aunt Sally with the deferential bows of a courtier. But when we get past this obvious contrast, which nobody could possibly miss, we find that (in a queer manner) there is versatility without variety. What makes those two stories stand out in our memory is a certain spirit with which they are told; yes, and even a certain style as well as spirit. It is not exactly the stories themselves; still less is it any real immersion of the author in the subjects of the stories themselves. We feel, even as we read, that Stevenson would be the last man really to wish to be imprisoned for life in a petty German court or poised for ever amid such very fragile china. We know it, just as we know that Stevenson does not really intend to turn his attention to the leather-business, or even (though here we may fancy the temptation stronger) to become a rowdy solicitor with shady clients, in the manner of the priceless Mr. Michael Finsbury. We remember the treatment more than the subject; because the treatment is really much more alive than the subject. Long after the ghosts in that ornamental garden have faded, and we have completely forgotten Who was Who at the court of Prince Otto, we hear and remember in the depths of that valley, 'the solid plunge of the cataract.' And long after the details of the Tontine System[43] have become blurred and all the far less interesting details of our own daily life along with them, when all lesser things have diminished and life itself is fading from my eyes — I shall still see before me the Form called up by that inspired paragraph: 'His costume was of a mercantile brilliancy best described as stylish; nor could anything be said against him, except that he was a little too like a wedding guest to be quite a gentleman.'

Even through these wide divergences of subject, therefore, there runs something which is not only the genius but decidedly the method of Stevenson. In one sense he is careful to vary the style; in another sense the style is never varied. We might say, so to speak, that it is the style within the style that is never varied. But subject to this general understanding, it is only just to him to insist on the wide range that he managed to cover in his short and very much hampered literary life. He once reproached himself with not having enlarged his life by building lighthouses as well as writing books. But the firm of Stevenson and Son might have been mildly convulsed if there had risen on every side lighthouses in seven styles of architecture; a Gothic lighthouse, an ancient Egyptian lighthouse, and a lighthouse like a Chinese pagoda. And that is what he did with the towers of imagination and the light of reason.

There are indeed, as I have hinted, one or two places where it may be maintained that Stevenson let his style stray; and wandered into other tracks, sometimes older tracks, away from the immediate track of travel. Personally, I have this feeling about the wanderings of the Master of Ballantrae and the Chevalier Burke. They are a sort

---

[43] The "Tontine System" invented by Italian banker Lorenzo Tonti, is a joint financial arrangement where an annuity is shared by the number of people who have contributed equally to the prize. The prize is awarded to the only remaining beneficiary.

of adventure story in the wrong place; and though Mr. James Durie was certainly an adventurer in the bad sense, it is imposible to make him one in the good. It is impossible to turn a villain into a hero for the purposes of pure romance; Jim Hawkins could not have gone on his adventures permanently arm-in-arm with Long John Silver. The episode of Blackbeard is a sort of fizzling anti-climax, spluttering like the blue matches in that fool's hat. Such a shoddy person had no claim to be so much as mentioned in that spiritual tragedy of the terrible twin spirits; the brothers of Durrisdeer. It is almost as if pirates were really a private mania with the author; and he could not keep them out of the tale if he tried; though pirates have really no more business in this tale than pirates in *The Wrong Box*. But it is curious to note how completely they are discoloured by the white death-ray that shines on that winter's tale. Their blood and gold were not really red; their seas were not even really blue. This was no occasion for Two-pence Coloured. The very style of Mackellar's narrative might be shrewdly summed up indeed under the title of A Penny Plain. But this is not only because that worthy steward was addicted to plainness and not averse to pennies. It is also because he is addicted to home and habit and averse to adventure; and the notion of the Master dragging him across half the world has something about it ungainly and grotesque and unworthy of the intensity of their intellectual and spiritual relations. The truth is that the Master of Ballantrae is not only a family demon but also a family ghost; and ought not to haunt any house except his own. Ghosts do not travel like tourists; even for the pleasure of visiting their relatives in the colonies. The story of the Duries is emphatically domestic; like those very domestic stories of home life in which Oedipus butchered his father or Orestes trampled on the body of his mother. These incidents were regrettable, and even painful; but they were all kept in the family. Something tells us that most of them happened behind high barred doors or in terrible unrecorded interviews. They did not wash their bloody linen in public; least of all did they wash it in all the seven seas of the British Empire. But the appearance of the Master first in India and then in America has almost the suggestion of the Prince of Wales on an imperial tour. Now those scenes in *The Master of Ballantrae* which do take place in the dark house of his fathers, or in the dim and wintry plantations without, do have an indefinable grandeur and even hugeness of outline that recalls the Greek tragedies. Nay, they have even that hint of long wanderings and remote places, which is lost when the wanderings and the places are too elaborately followed out. At that unforgotten moment when the stranger first stands up, long and black and slender on the point of rock, and makes a motion with his cane that is like a spoken word of mockery, we do feel that he might have come from the ends of the earth, that he might have strolled from the empire of the Mogul[44] or fallen from the moon. But the irony of the story is in that hateful love, or that pure love of hatred, that is the link between him and his; and makes him as domestic as the roof-tree even when he is as destructive as the battering-ram. It is curious, and perhaps over-curious, to find this rare fault in the work which is in its principal parts so faultless. It may seem still more pedantic to pick another very small hole in it; but it seems to me that Stevenson missed one great chance, in a way he rarely did, when he made even Mackellar such a prig as to write for the last line of the epitaph a phrase like, 'With his fraternal enemy.' Surely the words would have stood out with a much more sinister and significant finality, if he had merely written, 'And sleeps in the same grave with his brother.'

But this mixture of two types of tale in one is the very reverse of characteristic. I know not where else in his works it can be found; unless perhaps we might take exception to the slight element of political irritation that makes itself felt, of all places in the world, in the amiable nightmare of *The Dynamiter*. It is really impossible to use a story in which everything is ridiculous to prove that certain particular Fenians[45] or anarchist agitators are ridiculous. Nor indeed is it tenable that men who risk their lives to commit such crimes are quite so ridiculous as that. But broadly speaking, the characteristic

---

[44] Chesterton is referring to an Indian Muslim of or descended from Mongol, Turkish or Persian origins during the Muslim-Tartar Empire in India (1526–1707).

[45] Chesterton is referring to the Fenians, one of the legendary bands of warriors in ancient Ireland.

of this writer's conscientious artistry is that he is very careful to keep the different forms of art in water-tight compartments. It was, of course, a sentiment about technique and material which was very fashionable in the age of Whistler and the world where Stevenson had studied art. And the artist would as soon have stuck a lump of marble into the middle of a bas-relief in terracotta, or applied a coat of paint to a tracery he was making out of ivory, as put a piece of tragedy into the middle of a tea-table comedy or a burst of righteous indignation into a farce. In all this part of Stevenson's mind, especially as revealed in his letters, most of the critics have missed the very lasting effect of the chatter of craftsmanship, and all the jargon of tricks of the trade, which he heard among the French art students. He had reversed almost the whole philosophy of everything that they wanted to do; but he still retained the dialect in which they talked about how it was done. But he talked it much better than they did; and he had his own knack of using the right word even for the search for the right word. It is typical that he said that a story must have one general tendency; and that in the whole book there must not be a single word 'that looks the other way.' There is not a single word that looks the other way in the whole of *Prince Otto* or in the whole of *The Wrong Box*.

But now and then he did something more than this. He created a form of art. He invented a *genre* which does not really exist outside his work. It may seem a paradox to say that his most original work was a parody. But certainly the notion of *The New Arabian Nights* is quite as unique in the world as the old *Arabian Nights*; and it does not owe its real ingenuity to the model which it mocks. Stevenson here wove a singular sort of texture, or mixed a singular sort of atmosphere, which is not like anything else; a medium in which many incongruous things may find a comic congruity. It is partly like the atmosphere of a dream; in which so many incongruous things cause no surprise. It is partly the real atmosphere of London at night; it is partly the unreal atmosphere of Baghdad. The broad and placid presence of Prince Florizel of Bohemia, that mysterious semireigning sovereign, is treated with a sort of vast and vague diplomatic reserve; which is like the confused nightmare of an old cosmopolitan courtier. The Prince himself seems to have palaces in every country; and yet the humorous reader suspects, with half his mind, that the man is really only a pompous tobacconist, whom Stevenson happened to find in Rupert Street and chose to make the hero of a standing joke. This double mentality, like that of the true dreamer, is suggested with extraordinary skill without loading with a single question the inimitable lightness of the narrative. The humour of Florizel's colossal condescension constitutes not only a new character, but a new sort of character. He stands in a new relation to reality and unreality; he is a sort of solid impossibility. Since that time many writers have written such fanciful extravagances about the lights of London; for Stevenson suffered much more than Tennyson from that of which the latter complained when 'all had got the seed.' But few of them have really struck those ironical semitones or made the same thing so completely a cockney conspiracy and an Arabian fairytale. We have heard much of making the life of the modern town romantic; and many of the attempts in modern poetry seem only to make it more ugly than it really is. We have at the present moment a considerable cult of the fantastic; with the result that the fantastic has become rather a fixed type. It is picked out in crying colours of crome yellow or magenta; with the result that it is perhaps too obviously a puppet. But Prince Florizel of Bohemia is not a puppet. He is a presence; a person who seems to fill the room and yet to be such stuff as dreams are made of; not simply a thing made of stuffing. The rigid and unreal dolls may fall into dust when the mood changes; but we do not easily imagine anybody kicking the stuffing out of Florizel. I will not say that the *New Arabian Nights* is the greatest of Stevenson's works; though a considerable case might be made for the challenge. But I will say that it is probably the most unique; there was nothing like it before, and I think, nothing equal to it since.

But it is worth while to remark that even here, where the atmosphere might be expected to be more hazy, the generalisation stands about edges and the exact extravagance of Skelt. However delicate is the air of mockery or mystery, there is very little change in the staccato style. The quarrel with the Suicide Club is 'put to the touch of swords' and the phrase tingles like the twin blades of Durisdeer. Nothing could be more angular than Mr. Malthus, the horrible paralysed man who plays on the brink of the precipice of suicide; he is as hard as a huge beetle. There is all the jerk of the old energetic puppets when he jumps from his seat, losing his disease for an instant at the sight of death. There is more movement in that one paralytic than in crowds of softly moving society figures, in milder or more meditative fiction. The very clatter of his broken bones down the stone steps of Trafalgar Square, of which we hear but an echo, has that almost metallic quality. Jack Vandeleur's 'brutalities of gesture,' his pantomime of opening and shutting the hand, are surely somewhat piratical; he had been Dictator of Paraguay; but I think he had sailed there on the *Hispaniola*. In short we have here once more the continuity of a style within a style. And the inner thread within the silk is as thin and hard as wire.

Again, it illustrates this variety of experiment that Stevenson also wrote a detective story; or as he characteristically called it (in a sort of pedantic plain English) a police novel. He wrote it in collaboration with Mr. Lloyd Osbourne; and I have considered another aspect of it already, in the local colour of *The Wrecker*. But *The Wrecker* is ultimately a police novel; and the best sort of police novel, in which the police are never called in. Stevenson explained his reasons for leading up to the problem with studies of social life; and certainly it says much for the liveliness of that life that we do not grow so impatient as to offer the obvious comment. Otherwise we should certainly make one reasonable criticism. The writer may be pardoned if he is a long time getting to the solution, but not when he is such a long time getting to the mystery. It must be confessed that we have to wait for the question to be asked, as well as for it to be answered. Personally I am very glad to wait in the waiting-room of Pinkerton and Dodd. But anyhow when the question is asked, it is with great animation; and the excitement of beginning to piece together a puzzle, which is the essence of a detective story, has seldom been more lively and lifelike than in the cross questions and crooked answers of Captain Nares and his supercargo. Here, however, the detective story merely illustrates the fact of his having almost as many irons in the fire as Jim Pinkerton. It illustrates the general fact that he tried a great many different styles; and yet his style was not different.

If there were experiments in which his touch was less happy they were, strangely enough perhaps, those connected with the simple or semi-savage world in which he found so much happiness. *The Island Nights' Entertainments* are not quite so entertaining as the Arabian Nights' Entertainments, whether New or Old. The explanation may be found, perhaps, in that casual phrase with which he swept the South Seas and swept away a good many imperial or international illusions, probably without knowing it; when he said of all those regions, 'It is a large ocean but a narrow world.' He did not really find new types, at least among the white men; he rather found new countries full of old and battered types, white men who no longer looked very conspicuously white. One exception must be allowed; the story of *The Ebb-Tide* has a very great deal of kick in it; even though we hardly have the full satisfaction of seeing all the characters kicked. Anyhow, it is quite certain that whatever was the cause of the relative ineffectiveness of some of the work done at Vailima, it was not due to his having written himself out or experienced any weakening of power. For the very last days of all were spent in producing what was, or would have been, his most powerful piece of work. I have said something elsewhere, in connection with the Scottish romances, of his last great story, which is unfortunately a great fragment. Actually (I am tempted to say fortunately) the story named after Weir of Hermiston is not mainly about Weir of Hermiston. At least it is not about the first and most famous person of that name; and the best chapters of the book now in existence are concerned with the most sensitive and passionate shades of the Scottish temperament; richer shades of passion than he had ever yet attempted to touch. If ever the grey moor turned purple, it did at the moment when the girl lifted her voice to sing the song of the Elliots. He never forgets his abrupt gesture; and it was never so arresting as when her psalm-book page was rent across.

When Stevenson drew the long bow for the last time, like Robin Hood, he had two strings to his bow; and they both broke; but one was much stronger than the other. In other words he had two stories in his head, both of which broke off short; and perhaps it is not surprising that the weaker was rather neglected in favour of the stronger. The story of *St. Ives* contains excellent things, as does everything that he ever wrote, down to the most casual private letter. But it may be called disappointing, with rather more exactitude than is usual in the use of that word. *St. Ives* can hardly avoid being a sort of historical novel; and yet it is a rather unhistorical novel. By which I do not mean that there may be mistakes about dates or details; which matter nothing in fiction and are made too much fuss of even in history. I mean it is unhistorical in showing a strange lack of historical imagination and the sense of historical opportunity. It is the story of a soldier of Napoleon imprisoned on Edinburgh Rock and escaping from it. But indeed we might fancy it was Stevenson and not St. Ives who was imprisoned on Edinburgh Rock. And Stevenson does not escape from it. Such a subject demanded a sort of international interpreter; but it is in truth the most strangely insular of all his books. St. Ives is not a Frenchman; he is the less and not the more French because he is given all the foppery and swagger which spinsters in Edinburgh in 1813 doubtless did associate with a Frenchman. He is no more a French soldier than Bonaparte was Boney. He has neither the French realism nor the French idealism. He does not look at England as a Frenchman of the revolutionary wars would have looked at it. This story is simply France seen from Britain; it is not, as it should be, Britain seen from France. Unless St. Ives were a very bitter Royalist (which he evidently was not, but a moderate Bonapartist) he would quite certainly have conceived himself as carrying not mere military glory but the light of reason and philosophy and social justice to the aristocratic and autocratic states. He would have been impatient with the illogical resistance to rational things; not merely annoyed at not being shaved or provided with a looking-glass. But St. Ives is not a French soldier. He is a man in a French uniform; but so was Alan Breck Stewart. And that blessed and beloved name may perhaps recall to us that vanity and a love of fine coats can occasionally be found, even in the British Isles.

But perhaps in this very insularity there is something like a return to earlier things, and a rounding off of his life. In that sense the story of Stevenson, like the story of St. Ives, began on the crag and castle of Edinburgh; and it may be right that it should in a fashion end there, and not really get any further. The most really Stevensonian scenes, in their spirit and spitfire animation, are those which occur first in the prison. It seems almost as if St. Ives was more free before he escaped. The business of the duel with sticks turned into spears, by the addition of scissor-blades, has all the hilarity of his old dance of death. That alone serves as an excellent symbol of that magnifying of the sharp and the metallic; and the way in which steel was always a sort of magnet to his mind. Perhaps he was the first quiet householder to whom it ever occurred to see even scissors as swords.

But the book offers a yet better example of this return to an almost narrowly national romance, like the flight of a homing bird. It occurs almost in the first few lines of the book; yet it might stand in a fashion for a title to all his books. It occurs in connection with the highly characteristic passage, typical of his love of gay pictorial colouring, in which he instantly lights up the prison hill with flames; saying that the yellow convict coats and the red uniforms made up together 'a lively picture of hell.' And with reference to this he remarks, as if in passing, that the ancient Pictish or Celtic name of that castle of Edinburgh was 'The painted hill,' or, as I have seen it somewhere in another version, 'The painted rock.' That might stand as a symbol of many things here less sufficiently suggested; of a Scotsman dressed, or almost disguised, as an artist; of a style that could be at once abrupt and austere, and yet was always vivid with colour; but above all of that combination of colour with a solemn and childish caricature which we have seen in the background of his boyhood; for the landscape of Skelt consisted entirely of painted rocks. Stevenson had a passion of compression. With all his output, he had a strange ambition to be a man of few words. It seems to me that he was always seeking in words for a combination that should be also a compression; for two words that should instantly give birth to the third thing that he really wanted to say. It may be questioned, of him as of any other artist, whether he ever really succeeded in saying it. But we might amuse ourselves with the fancy that such a system of brilliant abbreviations might be more and more rapidly, like signals, uttered and understood; that some day a symbol of two words might stand for a thesis as a cryptic Chinese character stands for a word; and that all men could easily write and read such compact hieroglyphics. If that were so, it were hardly an exaggeration to say that the great mission given by God to Robert Louis Stevenson was to say the words 'painted rock' and perish.

Anyhow, it was in the midst of these new experiments that he did perish; fulfilling the very terms of his challenge in *Aes Triplex*; of the happy man whom death finds flushed with hope and planning vast foundations. And indeed his death may well come also at the end of this chapter of experiment, as the last of his experiments. I was a lad when the news came to England; and I remember that some of his friends doubted at first, because the telegram said that he died making a salad; and they 'had never heard of his doing such a thing.' And I remember fancying, with a secret arrogance, that I knew one thing about him better than they did, though I never saw him with these mortal eyes; for it seemed to me that if there were something that Stevenson had never been known to do before, it would be the very thing that he would do. So indeed he died mixing new salads of many sorts; and the image is not inappropriate or irreverent; but only touched with a certain lightness and resilience as of a coiled spring that belonged to him from first to last; and is that quality which Dr. Sarolea has truly called the French spirit of Stevenson. He died swiftly as if struck with an arrow and even over his grave something of a higher frivolity hovers upon wings like a bird; 'Glad did I live and gladly die,' has a lilt that no repetition can make quite unreal, light as the lifted spires of Spy-glass Hill and translucent as the dancing waves; types of a tenuous but tenacious levity and the legend that has made his graveyard a mountain-peak and his epitaph a song.

VIII

THE LIMITS OF A CRAFT

The truest adverse criticism of Stevenson was written by Stevenson. It was also very Stevensonian; for it took the form of saying, about his own fictitious characters, that his temptation was always 'to cut the flesh off the bones.' Even here we may note his peculiar cutting or hacking accent; it sounds like some horrid crime of Barbecue or Billy Bones. Indeed that word is sufficiently symbolic of Stevenson. His name might have been Bones, like the seafaring man at the 'Admiral Benbow'; nor was this only because his eternal boyhood was as full of skeletons as the school life of Traddles.[46] It was also because of a certain bony structure in his whole taste and turn of mind; something that was angular though slender like his own slim and brittle frame and long Quixotic face. Nevertheless the words were uttered as a condemnation; and they were a just condemnation.

The real defect of Stevenson as a writer, so far from being a sort of silken trifling and superficial or superfluous embroidery, was that he simplified so much that he lost some of the comfortable complexity or real life. He treated everything with an economy of detail and a suppression of irrelevance which had at last something about it stark and unnatural. He is to be commended among authors for sticking to the point; but real people do not stick quite so stubbornly to the point as that. We can here best realise his real error, as well as his real originality, by comparing his with the great Victorian novelists in whose vast shadow he grew up. I shall have occasion to note afterwards that his collision was not with these in the matter of morals or philosophy; for on that side he was looking forward and not back. But there is a strong contrast, and a striking new departure, in the passage from the very best of Thackeray or Trollope to the first sketches, I had almost said scratches, of Stevenson. Those sketches were in a few lines, and only of the necessary lines; it was the whole

---

[46] Tommie Traddles, who was an attorney admitted on the roll at Gray's Inn, is a reference to a character in Dickins' *David Copperfield*.

point that one unnecessary line was a loss and not a gain. Compared with this, the very best of the old Victorian novels were full of padding. But there was something to be said for the Victorian padding; as there was for the Victorian upholstery. Comfort is not always a contemptible thing, when its other name is hospitality; and Dickens and Thackeray and Trollope had a huge hospitality for their own characters. They were heartily and unaffectedly glad to see them; and especially glad to see them again. Hence their taste for sequels and continuous family histories; and all the positively last appearances of Mr. Pendennis or Mrs. Proudie. And this repetition, this rambling, even this padding, did in a curious confused fashion confirm the reality of the characters. As the padded Victorian furniture did really make people feel at home, so the padded Victorian novels made the reader feel at home with the characters. Now the reader never does feel quite at home with Stevenson's characters. He cannot get rid of an impression that he knows too little about them; though he knows that he knows all that is important about them. His tragedy is that he knows only what is important. Alan Breck Stewart is not only a very lively but a very loveable character. And yet there is too little of him to love; though he might well draw his claymore upon us, if we made so dangerous an allusion. We are not quite at ease with him, as we are at ease with Pickwick or Pendennis. We know the vital things about him; and they are very vital. But we do not know *thousands* of things about him; as we do about a man with whom we have lived through a long Early Victorian novel. Stevenson has in fact done exactly what he accused himself of doing; it is he who wields the claymore and he has cut the flesh off the bones.

An illustration of the difference, of course, could be found in the presentation of the externals of a character. The dark vivacity of the face of Alan Breck, the eyes with their 'dancing madness, at once engaging and alarming,' springs up before us as clearly as a coloured photograph in the first few words of description; and the same few words have already set strutting the whole brisk little figure in the blue coat and silver buttons and the swagger of the big sword. But the whole operation is so rapid and complete as to have something about it almost unconvincing, like a conjuring trick. It is like seeing something by a single flash of lightning; there is in that illumination a sort of illusion. For in the heart of anything that partakes of magic there is also something of mockery. It is not so that we 'get to know' the personal appearance of somebody in Thackeray or Trollope. It is by a multitude of apparently accidental or even unnecessary allusions that we gradually gain the impression that Warrington was dark and moody with a blue shaven chin. The appearance of Lord Steyne is scattered all over *Vanity Fair* in scraps; his red whiskers in one chapter, his bandy legs in another, his bald head in a third. But this is so like the way in which we really do talk about real people, that in comparison there is something almost unreal about Stevenson's rapid realism. Perhaps the story-teller ought to remember more often that he is a man telling a story. Perhaps he even forgets that it is supposed to sound like a true story. And after all a man does not say to his wife at dinner, in real life, 'A stranger came to my office this morning; he was of an elegant, strenuous figure, with a fine falcon profile, the eyebrows and the corners of the mouth touched with temper; and a general appearance which, though not without distinction, was thrown up in a somewhat theatrical fashion by his dashing cutaway coat and white spats and the magenta-coloured orchid in his buttonhole.' Such a soliloquy seldom resounds in the suburban home; and if the stranger's appearance comes to count for anything, it comes out bit by bit; as in saying, 'I wasn't altogether surprised when he threw the inkstand; for I saw by his eyebrows he had a beast of a temper,' or, 'The office-boy was taken out incapacitated with laughter at the first sight of the spats.' In the same way, nobody does actually say, as Mackellar does in the Stevensonian romance, 'I was now near enough to see him, a very handsome figure and countenance, swarthy, lean, long, with a quick, alert, black look, as of one who was a fighter and accustomed to command; upon one cheek he had a mole, not unbecoming; a large diamond sparkled on his hand; his clothes, although of the one hue, were of a French and foppish design; his ruffles, which he wore longer than common, of exquisite lace.' Men do not really describe things like that; would that they described anything so well! These facts about the Master of Ballantrae would have come out in a more fragmentary fashion in the real record of a real Mackellar. The diamond would have been mentioned in connection with a rumour of thieves; the lace in connection with the laundry. And that is more or less how the older Victorian novelists did often describe or mention these things; and I think it really does give an impression of reality. Compared with it, the very completeness of Stevenson seems incomplete. But it is also true that the older Victorians could not have achieved this familiar realism except by being a little more formless than Stevenson and lacking his beautiful and piercing sense of the clarity of form. Though he may seem to describe his subject in detail, he describes it to be done with it; and he does not return to the subject. He never says anything needlessly; above all he never says anything twice. Few will venture to say that Thackeray never says anything twice; or that he was incapable in some cases of saying twenty times. Yet in some ways this repetition, though sometimes boring, is somehow convincing; I might almost say comforting. It comes from that comfortable sense of social ease, which was a mark of the England of that brief period of mercantile success; or at least of that part of England which consisted of the merchants who had succeeded. And it exhibited, along with its other virtues and vices, that rather coarse benevolence that was at once a virtue and a vice. 'The British merchant's son shan't want, sir,' said old Mr. Osborne; and neither should the spiritual child of Mr. William Makepeace Thackeray. Words shall be poured out on him like wine; pages shall open for him like parks, in which he may wander. He shall be allowed to hang about as long as he likes and the poorest relations of the story shall be asked again and again to dinner. In short, the reader shall 'get to know him' and discuss all sorts of little details about him at leisure; they shall not all be disposed of once and for all in one closely packed paragraph. We return to the word hospitality; and the chatter of a hundred friends and relations at an English Christmas party. In comparison the verbal economy of the Scottish romancer suggests something of the old joke against the Scot. He is so very thrifty that his characters are almost thin.

The loftiest things of this world have their weakness or defect;

and with that word 'thin' we come to the limit of the glory of Skelt and discover that even the maker of toy theatres is human. Just as Stevenson gained in that school of boyish bravado his admirable sense of symbolic attitude and action, his deep joy in gay colour and gallant carriage, his fine feeling for life as a story and honour as a fight; his response to the challenge of the open door or the drag of the road over the hill — as he gained all these great virtues and values under the symbol of A Penny Plain and Twopence Coloured, so he betrayed also even in his best work something of the technical limitation of such an instrument. And it cannot be more clearly stated than by saying that these flat figures could only be seen from one side. They are aspects or attitudes of men rather than men; though the aspects and attitudes are of great importance considered as symbols, like the flat haloes of saints or the flat blazonry of shields. In that sense only they are not deep enough; and lack another measurement. They are deep enough in the sense in which any beautiful picture is deep; in the sense that anything beautiful always means more than it says; possibly means more than it means to mean. In that sense there can be depth enough even in the shallow scenery of Skelt, when the child's eye plunges into it. But there is not depth in the sense of a great familiarity with the other side of the scenery or the implied life behind the scenes. When all is said and done, the splendid and inspiring figure of Three-Fingered Jack is a figure and not a statue. You cannot walk round him; and if he has no more than three fingers, he has much less than three dimensions. But the important paradox is that in this the imperfection of the work is actually due to the perfection of the art. It is exactly because Balfour or Ballantrae only do what they are meant to do, and do it so swiftly and well, that we have a vague feeling that we do not know them as we know more loitering, more rambling or more sprawling characters. This is, if you will, a weakness in the author's work; but it is even more emphatically a weakness in the critics who call him weak. For they accuse him of the very opposite of his real fault; of a sort of self-indulgent delicacy or a luxury of mere words. The evil arises from his very passion of economy and severity; from the fact that he pruned too much, so as almost to kill the plant: from the fact that he went too straight to the point, so that the movement was too quick to be clear, let alone familiar; above all from the fact that such hardness of technique had about it something almost inhuman. He does sometimes simplify the puppet so much as to show the wire. But even in that relation between wire and wood there is a queer sort of realism.

Stevenson was a man who believed in craftsmanship; that is, in creation. He had not the smallest natural sympathy with all those hazy pagan and pantheistic notions often covered by the name of inspiration. He might not have expressed it in the phrase that man is an image of the Creator; but he did very definitely regard man as a maker of images. There is, and has long been pouring upon the world, mostly in an immediate sense from the Germans and the Slavs, probably in an ultimate sense from the dark philosophies of Asia, a sort of doctrine of mystical helplessness that takes a hundred forms; and that recognises everything in the world except will. It denies the will of God and it does not believe even in the will of man. It does not believe in one of the most glorious manifestations of the will of man, which is the act of creative choice essential to art. The tendency has been admirably treated in the work of M. Henri Massis in his book on the Defence of the West; and another French writer of the same school, M. Maritain, has remarked on the important part which the word *artifex*, as the title of an artist, played in mediaeval philosophy as well as mediaeval craftsmanship. As we shall see later, it is the paradox of Stevenson that he would have cared nothing for such mediaeval metaphysics; and yet he carried out in practice precisely what these writers are now maintaining in principle. He was, if every there was one, an *artifex*; not a mere mouthpiece of elemental powers or destinies, but a man making something by the force of will and in the light of reason. It was a sort of craftsmanship characteristic of mediaeval work in literature as well as sculpture. It was strikingly present in those mediaeval poets whom Stevenson himself admired; and perhaps admired more than he understood. It is supremely typical of the close and finely carved ballades of Villon.[47] Indeed the name of Stevenson will always, I suppose, be picturesquely associated with the name of Villon; if only because of

---

[47] François Villon (1431-?) was a Frenchman considered to have been the finest poet of the late Middle Ages.

the fine macabre nocturn of *A Lodging for the Night*. And yet if there was one thing in the world about which Stevenson was entirely wrong, it was about François Villon. He was even, on that subject guilty of a very unusual lapse of logic and error of fact. In his essay on Villon, while showing all the enthusiasm of a fine critic for a fine poet, he insists with almost rabid emphasis that the mind of the man was rotten with mere bestial cynicism and base materialism. 'His eyes were sealed with their own filth'; and he could see nothing noble or beautiful in heaven or earth. And to this he adds the rather curious remark that even in that France of the fifteenth century Villon might have learnt something better; since a few years before Joan of Arc had lived one of the noblest lives in history. It seems rather hard on poor Villon to attribute to him a contented ignorance of all such people as Joan of Arc; since he actually goes out of his way to mention her in the most famous of his ballades; 'The good lady of Lorraine whom the English burnt at Rouen.' But the criticism is far more false according to the spirit than according to the letter. It is founded on a sort of modern fashionable fallacy, compounded of sentimentalism and optimism, to the effect that a man who is rather bitter about this world cannot have any ideals; whereas the bitterness does sometimes come from the intensity of his ideals. Anyhow, there is no doubt, to anybody who can read poetry without prejudice, that Villon had ideals and high ideals; only they happened to be highly Catholic ideals. The devotional poem that he wrote for his old mother, which describes her gazing at the glowing medieaval window, itself glows with sincerity. And he wrote at least one line that would be sufficient to destroy the accusation; one of those lines that are too simple to be adequately translated, 'Offrit à la mort sa très claire jeunesse'; which is something like, 'Offered his clear and shining youth to death.' He wrote it of Jesus Christ; but what better thing could be written of Joan of Arc?

I have paused upon this parenthesis; because it foreshadows the general view to which all these rather rambling criticisms ultimately tend; that Stevenson stood for the truth and did not quite understand the truth he stood for. If he had understood it he would have known that the virile craftsmanship which he was only too eager to admire in Villon, was really connected with certain virtues, which were none the less the virtues of a craftsman because they happened to be the virtues of a thief. Nobody pretends that Villon was a saint; but the socially disreputable externals of his sin do not (for those of his faith) make him a specially or supremely hopeless sinner. If he was a thief, nobody can prove that he was not a penitent thief; and the moral system to which he was attached had raised such a man to its altars under the somewhat paradoxical title of The Good Thief. He was probably the last man to expect in his own person to be that night in paradise; but he was not any further off from heaven merely because he was likely to be hanged high on a gallows. Here we have once more, I fancy, a touch of Calvinism with its finger of fear. There is also that grim and stony optimism attributed to the Old Testament, with its divine favouritism for the fortunate. But though the surface of this rather superficial criticism was alien to that free will which is the creed of craftsmanship, the personal creative spirit underneath the criticism was still that of the genuine Christian craftsman. When Stevenson set about to describe Villon and his gang of ragamuffins, under the snow and gargoyles of mediaeval Paris, he carved his grotesque as carefully as a gargoyle and balanced his story as beautifully as a French ballade. He did not take opium and absinthe and then sit down to wait for nameless cosmic energies to pour into his soul from nowhere. His spirit was a spirit utterly different from the mystical scepticism common in his time. He was responsible; he was deliberate; he was thrifty; he thoroughly deserved the dignified title of a working man.

The point here is that even his chief fault as an artist was typically the fault of a craftsman. He worked too narrowly, perhaps, producing only a thing perfect of its kind out of certain materials, by a certain method and under the limitations of a certain style. The same sort of criticism that feels a French ballade to be too fixed and artificial a form, the same sort of criticism that feels a fourteenth-century Virgin to be too stiff or affected in its posture, does doubtless feel a story of Stevenson to be too meagre in its materials or too strict in its stylistic unity. As I have explained above, I do not mean to suggest that such criticism is entirely unjust or unreasonable. Stevenson's work has its faults, like other good work; and its chief deficiency does appear in a certain defect of thinness, which is produced by this instinct for hard simplification. But nobody could adequately write a history of nineteenth-century literature without noting this important departure in the direction of a closer and more vigilant verbal choice, as compared either with the cheerful laxity that went before it or the more gloomy laxity that has come since. Whatever else Stevenson stands for, he certainly stands for the idea that literature is not mere sensation or mere self-expression or mere record; but is sensation appealing to certain senses, self-expression in a certain material and record in a certain style. And in this he was certainly asserting the rights of the soul of man, as against various formless forces which some regarded as the soul of nature; the *anima mundi*[48] of the pantheists. In this way Stevenson represented the same deep, ancient, hieratic and traditional truth that was taught to that generation by William Morris; and neither of them had the least idea what it was.

[48] *Anima mundi* is Latin for "soul of the world".

IX

THE PHILOSOPHY OF GESTURE

Something has been said, from time to time, in these pages about the justice or injustice of the alleged reaction against Stevenson. Little or nothing will be said about its final success or failure, and that for at least two reasons. First, that such guesses about the fashions of the future are generally quite wide of the mark, because they are founded on a very obvious fallacy. They always imply that public taste will continue to progress in its present direction; which is, in truth, the only thing we know that it will not do. A thing that wanders away in great winding curves may end anywhere; but to turn each curve into a straight line striking out into the void will be wrong in any case. This is obvious even in the tolerably short history of the modern novel. Victorians had a sort of parlour game of comparing Dickens and Thackeray; but they would have been amazed to hear modern young people declaring that Thackeray is much more sentimental than Dickens. They would have been astounded by the revival of Trollope, accompanied by the comparative neglect of Thackeray. For to the more earnest Victorians of that world, Trollope was another name for triviality. They would have felt as we should feel if we were told that Charles Garvice would outlive John Galsworthy.[49] For a great genius may appear in almost any disguise; even in the disguise of a successful novelist. The second reason for which I wave away from me the prophet's mantle, and decline to decide the question of the future, is that I do not think it very much matters. There are fine writers of the past as well as the present, who are read only by few; and I do not admit that the many know all about them, merely because they never knew them. I do not see why we should so blindly distrust popularity and so blindly trust posterity. But some of the conditions of survival may perhaps be generally considered.

The fame of Stevenson in the future will stand or fall with the

[49] John Galsworthy, (1867–1933), English novelist and playwright, noted for his portrayals of the English upper class.

strength or weakness of a particular argument. It was perhaps most compactly expressed by a critic who accused him of 'externality.' What he called the fault of externality I should be inclined to ascribe to the fallacy of internalism. Perhaps it will be recognised better if I call it the fallacy of 'psychology.' It is the notion that a serious novelist should confine himself to the inside of the human skull. Now Stevenson's fiction if full of pantomime; in the strict sense of animated action or gesture. And it really seems as if the critics, by a sort of pun or perversion of meaning, associated it with a children's pantomime; though Stevenson would have been the last to object even to that. Anyhow, this idea that intellectual fiction should concern the solitary and uncommunicative intellect is a very obvious fallacy indeed. It is sound enough to say that we can see below the surface; but not that we cannot see what is on the surface. Least of all is it sensible to say that we cannot believe in it because it has come to the surface; though it were as enormous as a spouting whale. Indeed the tone rather recalls that of some sceptics who implied that sailors ought not to think they saw the Great Sea Serpent, because it was a quarter of a mile long when they saw it. So we may well urge that psychological things are not less psychological because they come to the surface in pantomime. The argument amounts to saying that a really delicate piece of clockwork only exists when the clock stops. And indeed I suppose these critics would consider the action of a clock, in whirling its hands about, a very offensive piece of foreign gesticulation. It is like saying that a locomotive steam-engine is only a steam-engine when it is standing still; or that a building blowing up with a loud bang offers a final proof that it was not a powder-magazine.

Indeed in this respect the psychological critics are rather backward even in psychology. It generally distresses such people more to be behind the times than to be against the truth; and in this case it seems possible that they are both. The objection to their fallacy of internalism is that it is nonsense to think only of thoughts and not of words or deeds, since words are only spoken thoughts and deeds are only acted words. They are in fact the most dominant words and the most triumphant thoughts; the thoughts that emerge. But, according

THE PHILOSOPHY OF GESTURE 125

to 'the latest modern psychology' (that infallible and immutable authority), it is even more of a mistake to treat the surface so superficially. Acts are not only the swiftest thoughts; they are even too swift to be called thoughts. They come from something more fundamental than common or conscious thinking. It is exactly our subconsciousness that appears in acts more than in words, or even thoughts. It is precisely our subconsciousness that bites its nails or twirls its moustaches, that kicks its heels or grinds its teeth. According to some, it is even our subconsciousness (that jolly companion) that occasionally cuts our mother's throat or picks our father's pocket. I do not take the latest modern psychology quite so seriously; but what element of truth there is in it is all against the tone of the latest Stevensonian, or Anti-Stevensonian, criticism. The test of fine fiction, by this or any other standard, is not whether it follows out threads of thought in silence; not whether it is subjective rather than objective or avoids any violent issue in events. It is simply whether it is right; whether the psychology is right and whether the act represents it rightly. In psychology, as in any other science, one cannot be more than right. And the most embittered critic will find it very difficult to show that Stevenson was very often wrong. What the embittered critic can show, and what will make him still more embittered, is that Stevenson expressed everything by some dramatic act. And, according to such critics, anything that is dramatic is melodramatic. The boyish brooding and smarting sentimental self-importance of David Balfour during his one quarrel with Alan Breck Stewart are described so delicately and exactly as to be worthy of George Meredith, who was so excellent with boys; they might easily be the broodings of Evan Harrington or Harry Richmond.[50] Only in Stevenson's story they end (alas!) in the crossing of blades and Alan tossing away his sword; and that, of course, is dreadfully melodramatic. One cannot be psychological inside a sword-belt; and cerebral processes must not take place under a three-cornered hat. The interlude of Henry Durie's crippled and almost half-witted happiness, when the shadow

[50] Evan Harrington and Harry Richmond were two characters created by author George Meredith and used in the novels *Evan Harrington* and *The Adventures of Harry Richmond*.

of his brother is withdrawn for a season and his child is growing in the sun, is as pathetic and as true as any lucid interval (if such there be) in the suburban depression of the school of Gissing. Only when the fool's paradise is lost, by a random word about the possible perversion of the child, it is not to be denied that Henry Durie falls to the earth like a stone. And the thoughtful critic explains that such a man cannot have had any really internal feelings; because his internal feelings were strong enough to knock him down. The dark, drudging and almost automatic altruism of poor Herrick, amid all his tangle of treasons in *The Ebb-Tide*, is as sad and true as the most miserable modern could wish it to be. But then Herrick jumps into the sea with a great splash; though he ought to endear himself to the modern critic by not actually doing anything after all, even for the fruitful cult of suicide. The girl Kirstie's 'gabble' of recollection and daydream and imaginary lovers' quarrels, as she goes home from church' is quite as true to the actual inner workings of the young sentimental mind as any feminine fine shade in Henry James. But then the critic cannot be expected to forgive her for giving two or three little skips as she walks along the road. No lady in Henry James ever skipped. It is because in each of these cases some outward motion makes memorable the inward mood that these critics feel that it cannot really be so very inward. It is to be noted that they do not commit themselves to a positive negation; they do not affirm that the characters in question would *not* feel as they are described as feeling; they do not even say that they would not act as they are described as acting; that David would not fight or Durie fall or Kirstie leap upon the road. They simply have a refined and delicate feeling that psychological fiction ought to deal only, or mostly, with unspoken words or uncompleted thoughts. That is a very interesting point of view; and it is just as well to have it clearly stated and understood. If Stevenson had only served as an excuse for expounding this interesting critical thesis, they might so far thank him and even constrain themselves to be reasonably polite to him. Anyhow, that seems to be their principle; and I have paused long enough upon it to show that I do not wish to ignore it. Only I would respectfully submit that their quarrel is not with Stevenson; certainly their quarrel is not merely with Stevenson. It is with Homer and the bending of the bow; it is with Hamlet and the leap into the grave; it is with Francesca dropping the book or Quixote driving at the windmill; it is with Henry putting on his crown or Anthony putting off his helmet; it is with Roland in Roncesvaux, blowing the horn and breaking the sword and holding up his glove to God. It is in all those epic energies which gave to the last story and its sequel the noble title of Songs of Action—*Chansons de Geste*.

Among the many unreasonable objections to the Stevensonian romance, I admit that there is a reasonable objection that may be advanced here. It may be said that he was guilty of externality in this sense; that he sometimes began with externals, in so far as he saw in some scene or other setting the suggestion or rather the provocation of romance. 'Certain dank gardens cry aloud for a murder,' he very truly observed; and he was often moved to commit the murder in a vicarious literary manner. He wished sometimes, he said, to fit every such place with its appropriate legend. Superficially there is sense in this objection; but in a deeper and more sympathetic sense I do not admit that it contradicts what I have said of the deep spring of gesture or the deliberation of craftsmanship. It merely means that there was from the first, in any such work of art, the unity of mood that there always ought to be. It means that he had decided what sort of novel he would write, before he had decided what novel he would write; and this is right and inevitable. The dank garden cannot cry aloud immediately, in so many words, 'In this place the sinister tutor with one eye larger than the other buried the old sailor's cutlass with which he had killed the horribly but secretly wicked admiral who was really his brother.' No dank garden ever expressed itself with such accuracy when crying aloud to anybody; but it is none the less true that the exact shade of gloom and the exact outline of disorder may have suggested, not merely a vulgar murder, but a murder having certain special qualities of the unnatural or the strange. This does not prove that they were not *deep* feelings which thus rose up at the sight of the strange landscape and groped to find their appropriate images of doom. It only proves that the origin of the story was of the same sort as the origin of a poem. We can call Stevenson a prose poet, if we like; but we cannot call him a superficial writer, unless all poets are superficial.

I shall have occasion to remark elsewhere that there is one strictly technical sense in which Stevenson's treatment can be called a thin or a flat treatment. It is a sense in which we might say that a certain style in decorative ironwork is light and slender, in which we might say that Whistler's way of laying on monochrome washes was merely flat. It has its defects, even considered as a technical treatment; there is an artistic aversion to filigree; and many have maintained that Whistler's washes were too washy. But it is essential that this criticism should not be confused with the suggestion I have just answered; the suggestion that the spiritual significance of the pattern or the picture is shallow and not deep. That is another matter and has nothing whatever to do with the question of our favourite form; and though Stevenson's favourite form was sometimes picturesque to excess, there was nothing platitudinous or merely sentimental about the moral of the picture. On the contrary, he was very much drawn towards difficult and perplexing moral themes and liked to put puzzles to himself in the possible relations of human souls. Only, as we have seen, he liked to make the human soul come to a conclusion in some fashion and announce its conclusion in some way. Hence all the abrupt signals and bodily departures which the sensitive so much lament; hence the coin hurled through the windowpane at Durrisdeer; the banjo flung into the fire on Midway Island; the knife sticking in the mast or the diamond tossed into the river. In short, Stevenson's stories were often problem stories, in the style of what were called problem plays. But by one crime he disqualified himself for the company of the really realistic and earnest authors of problem plays or problem novels. He had a weakness for solving the problem.

There is in this merit the other side of a fault; and a fault of which he has often been accused. He was called self-conscious; and in his work he was perhaps a little too self-conscious, as compared with some writers whose fundamental and even almost forgotten impulses were allowed to flow forth more freely, and perhaps more naturally. But these things are a matter of degree and balance; and some may hold that it is the opposite type that has now become unbalanced. Walking the world to-day, I am not sure that I do not prefer the self-conscious to the subconscious. Stevenson felt a responsibility in art which was like his vivid and almost morbid sense of responsibility in conduct. His problems of conduct were indeed sometimes a little anarchical; and his ethical decision in them perhaps a little amateurish. Like Ibsen and Bernard Shaw and many men of his time, he had not quite discovered the pressing practical necessity of having a general rule, in the absence of which the world becomes a welter of exceptions. But he was intensely interested in the right moral solution whatever it might be; even if it seemed to involve the inversion of a moral rule. And this sense of social responsibility was thoroughly sincere; even when the special pleading had to be, perhaps, a little too individual to be social. It was natural for a novelist, perhaps, to feel most fiercely and keenly the particular personal case. Anyhow, I think he generally did so; as did Loudon Dodd in *The Wrecker*, when he balanced opium and Jim. He was certainly vastly intrigued by that sort of problem. Henley called him a Catechist; but he should have said Casuist.[51] He professed to have a defective sympathy with Catholicism; and he was still probably provincial enough to have had a horror of Jesuitry; but as a matter of fact he was more casuistical than any Jesuit. He was much less clear about the original universal dogmas of a catechism, whether it were the Shorter Catechism or the Penny Catechism. But he was much more closely concerned about the special occasion when the general sense of those doctrines seemed challenged by a special necessity. We may say, therefore, that, in life and in literature, he was essentially a conscientious person. And a conscientious person is presumably a conscious person; and sometimes perhaps a self-conscious person. He committed a great many crimes vicariously in his books; and delivered batches of corpses to his publishers in the style required of all writers of sensational romance. But his deaths had the delicacy and fine distinction of murder; and nothing of the vulgar communism

---

[51] Chesterton is referring to casuistry which is the study of cases of conscience or the science dealing with moral matters.

of massacre. In the one episode in his stories that might be called a massacre, the butchery of the old crew of *The Flying Scud* by Wicks and his men, the whole horror of the incident is in its intense individualism. It is in the fact that the men have to be slain one by one; in the fact that the massacre is not a massacre but a series of murders. He went so far, in his correspondence, as to say cheerfully of Henry Durie's bloody trap for his brother that it is 'a perfectly cold-blooded murder of which I expect and intend the reader to approve.' But even here it will be noted that he intended something, and said so; seeming almost as cold-blooded as the murderer. But at least he did not commit murders without knowing it, in the manner of our more subconscious criminals and maniacs in modern fiction. He was not in sympathy with those more recent heroes who seem to seduce and betray and even stab in a sort of prolonged fit of absence of mind. There had not been established, for him or for his characters, that convenient back-stairs of unconscious mind or automatic motion, by which something that is not ourselves (and makes for unrighteousness) may escape from the cellar into the street. It was perhaps a defect; but in the whole of his life and work there is a complete absence of absence of mind.

And with this matter of responsibility, and the reliance on the will in moral matters, we come to that larger question to be considered in the last chapter. It will be in a sense a summary of what has already been said; and yet it will be necessary to say it somewhat more plainly, and in relation to large matters about which many modern people are rather too confused or too timid to talk plain. For the moment it need only be said that the importance of Stevenson largely consists in his relation with the tendency of his age. That tendency was towards a certain mysticism of materialism, of which the most dogmatic expression is what is called monism; but which can be more lightly expressed in a hundred forms, as that all life is one, or that everything is heredity and environment, or that the impersonal is higher than the personal, or that men live by the herd instinct or the soul of the hive. Our fathers called the general atmosphere fatalism; but it has now any number of more idealistic names. Stevenson felt all this, without exactly defining it; he felt it in the realism of nineteenth-century literature, in the pessimism of contemporary poetry, in the timidity of hygienic precaution, in the smugness of middle-class uniformity. And while he was entirely of that time and society, while he read all the realists, knew all the artists, doubted with the doubters and even denied with the deniers, he had that within him which could not but break out in a sort of passionate protest for more personal and poetical things. He flung out his arms with a wide and blind gesture, as one who would find wings at the moment when the world sank beneath him.

X

THE MORAL OF STEVENSON

Even those unfortunates for whom the tale of *Treasure Island*, and the tradition continued in the pirates of *Peter Pan*, form an episode that is ended, may still be asked to consider it as an episode; to consider it, or perhaps to reconsider it. Even those who hardly feel it as a piece of literature will be forced at least to accept it as a piece of history. I am not one of these dismal and disinherited persons, as the reader has perhaps by this time darkly suspected; but I am quite content for the moment to put aside the question of whether their lack of appreciation is due to the advance of literary experiment or the decline of literary taste. I ask them for the moment to consider it not as a literary masterpiece, but merely as a curiosity of literature. I ask them to pause upon the episode of the Stevensonian Buccaneers, much as they might pause upon the episode of the real Buccaneers; upon some quaint old volume about the real lives of Blackbeard and Henry Morgan.[52] Just as there would always be some historical interest in considering how the pirate sack of Panama was related to the great affairs of the Spanish Empire or the English Navy, so there is always some philosophical interest in considering how Stevenson's romanticism was related to realism and rationalism and all the great movements of the nineteenth century. In short, I am content for the moment if all that wonderful library of books is lumped together under the name of one of the least of them; and considered as a Footnote to History.

What was the historical meaning then of that strange splash of crimson lake on the drab age of Gissing and Howells;[53] like a burlesque bloodstain in a detective story? To begin with, I foresee that

---

[52] Henry Morgan (1635?–1688), Welsh buccaneer, was Commander-in-chief of the naval force of Jamaica. He was responsible for the capture of Panama City in 1671.

[53] George Gissing(1857–1903) was an English novelist, critic and essayist. William Dean Howells (1837–1920) was an American novelist, critic and poet. Both were writers who extolled the drab lifestyle and virtues of the end-of-the-century middle class.

THE MORAL OF STEVENSON

in having stated the matter thus historically, I have laid myself open to some criticisms of the strictly historical sort. It may be said that the dates and details of Stevenson's life and time do not correspond with such a comparison; that he came too early in the Victorian progress to be really a type of the 'nineties; and that his real rivals or models were the Victorian Philistines. I do not admit this as a truth, even where I might admit part of it as a fact. An anachronism is often simply an ellipsis; and an ellipsis is often simply a necessity. The thing that a living intelligence like that of Stevenson feels is not the stale and static conventions of his world, but the way the world is going. We talk familiarly of time and tide; and, in a case like this, it is idle to remember a time without realising that it was a tide. The author of *The Ebb-Tide* knew well enough what tide was at that moment ebbing. It was the tide of what many regarded as Victorian virtue and all the happiness described in the three-volume novel. Stevenson knew very well that this stuffy sort of stuff was not the strong menace or promise of the coming time. He sometimes pokes fun at the Philistines; but he thrusts with furious energy at the Aesthetes.[54] Compare for instance the way in which he speaks of Walter Besant[55] with the way in which he speaks of Henry James, when he has to differ from them both, in that admirable letter about 'art competing with life.' He dismisses the successful novelist as representing something that had already failed; but he takes seriously the serious novelist, and is obviously afraid that in the long run his more subtle methods may succeed. Those more subtle methods, of the impressionists and realists and the rest, were obviously for him the real danger because they were the rising tide. In short, it may be complained that I have represented Stevenson as reacting against decadence before it existed. And I answer that this is the only real way in which a fighting man ever does successfully attack a movement; when he attacks later, he attacks too late.

Or again, it may be said that I exaggerate the novelty of work like

[54] Aesthetes were followers of a movement in the 1880's in which the adoption of sentimental anarchism was carried to extravagant lengths and often accompanied by affectation of speech and manner and with eccentricity of dress.
[55] Walter Besant (1836–1901) was an English novelist.

that of *Treasure Island*; and that it was but a natural continuation of the historical novel of Scott or the nautical novel of Marryat. Here again I think the critic will not only miss a fine distinction, but a very sharp point. The old novels were novels; they were not boys' stories, but simply stories. The comedy of the Oldbucks and Osbaldistones[56] is as much a solid comedy of character as that of Mr. Bennett[57] or Miss Bates.[58] It is only Scott's incurable and almost unconscious sense of romance that sends the comedy characters to the dangerous cliff or to the Clachan of Aberfoyle. There was no deliberate and defiant return to juvenile art out of season, such as that which is flaunted in Stevenson's letters as well as in Stevenson's story. The point can be best illustrated once more by the memory of Skelt's Juvenile Drama. It is one thing to say that a painter like Maclise or an actor like Macready may have had a style that would strike us as stagey and pompous. Maclise and Macready did not themselves think that they were stagey and pompous. It would be quite another thing to revive the actual figures of the old toy theatre, almost (in a sense) *because* they were stagey and pompous. Stevenson obviously resurrected all this romance, not because it was the fashion of his time, like the historical painting of Maclise, but because it was *against* the growing fashion of his time; and had to be fought for as a new fashion because it was really an old fashion. He glorified an antiquated Skeltery, when he knew it was antiquated. He concentrated on a certain type of book for boys, when he knew it had long been abandoned to boys. He is often called self-conscious; and in this sense he was very self-conscious. He was as self-consciously copying an old piratical penny dreadful as the Pre-Raphaelites were self-consciously copying an old mediaeval religious picture. As they were carefully inlaying it with jewels of childlike colour, he was carefully resetting the lost jewel of his own childhood. But he knew he was not merely fashionable, just as he knew that he was not really five years old.

[56] Oldbucks and Osbaldistones were characters in Sir Walter Scott's novel *Antiquary*.

[57] Mr. Bennett is a reference to the father given to witty cynicisms in Jane Austen's *Pride and Prejudice*.

[58] Miss Bates is a comical, chatty character in Jane Austen's *Emma*.

What then exactly did he mean? What, so to speak, did *it* mean; even if in a sense he did not mean it; or at least, did not mean to mean it? First of all it was, I think, a sort of dash for liberty; and especially a dash for happiness. It was a defence of the possibility of happiness; and a kind of answer to the question, 'Can a man be happy?' But it was an answer of a curious kind, defiantly delivered in rather curious circumstances. It was the escape of a prisoner as he was led in chains from the prison of Puritanism to the prison of Pessimism. Few have understood that passage in the history of the manufacturing civilisation of northwest Europe and America. Few have realised that the gloomier sort of modern materialism often came upon a class that was only just escaping from an equally gloomy sort of spirituality. They had hardly come out of the shadow of Calvin when they came into the shadow of Schopenhauer. From the world of the worm that dieth not, they passed into a world of men dying like worms; and in the case of some of the decadents, almost exulting in being devoured by worms like Herod. Puritanism and pessimism, in short, were prisons that stood near together; and none have ever counted how many left one only for the other; or under what a covered way they passed. Stevenson's escapade was an escape; a sort of runaway romantic evasion for the purpose of escaping both. And as a fugitive has often fled and hidden in his mother's house, this outlaw took refuge in his old home; barricaded himself in the nursery and almost tried to creep into the dolls'-house. And he did it upon a kind of instinct, that here had dwelt definite pleasures which the Puritan could not forbid nor the pessimist deny. But it was a strange story. He had his answer to the question 'Can a man be happy?'; and it was, 'Yes, before he grows to be a man.'

It is only the obvious things that are never seen; and a thing is often counted stale merely because men have been staring at it so long without seeing it. There is nothing harder to bring within a small and clear compass than generalisations about history, or even about humanity. But there is one especially evident and yet elusive in this matter of happiness. When men pause in the pursuit of happiness, seriously to picture happiness, they have always made what may be called a 'primitive' picture. Men rush towards complexity; but they yearn towards simplicity. They try to be kings; but they dream of being shepherds. This is equally true whether they look back to a Golden Age or look forward to the most modern Utopia. The Golden Age is always imagined as an age free from the curse of gold. The perfect civilisation of the future is always something which many would call the higher savagery; and is conceived in the spirit that spoke of 'Civilisation, its Cause and Cure.' Whether it is Arcadia of the past or Utopia of the future, it is always something simpler than the present. From the Greek or Roman poet yearning for the peace of pastoral life to the last sociologist explaining the ideal social life, this sense of a return and a resolution into elemental things is apparent. The pipe of the shepherd is always something rather plainer than the lyre of the poet; and the ideal social life is some more or less subtle form of the simple life. Of this tendency there is yet a third and perhaps a truer expression. It may be remarked that these daydreams of happiness concern rather the dawn than the day. The reactionary wishes to return to what he would call 'the morning of the world.' But the revolutionist is quite equally prone to talk about waiting for the daybreak, about songs before sunrise, and about the dawn of a happier day. He does not seem to think so much about the noon of that day. And one mode in which this morning spirit is expressed is the return to the child.

Stevenson might have been asking his question a hundred years before, at the time of the first humanitarian revolt against the Puritans; when the same city of Geneva, that had seen Calvin found the religion of pessimism, saw Rousseau found the religion of optimism. If he had been in that first liberal or naturalistic movement, he would probably have felt that the best expression of the romantic movement was in the fulfilment of romantic love. Paul and Virginia, instead of Poll and Robinson Crusoe (not to mention Long John Silver), would have been the happy inhabitants of the desert island. In that honeymoon of humanity, it would have seemed quite enough that Edwin and Angelina united at last (by a dignified civil marriage by the Registrar of the Republic) would populate the world with pure and happy republicans. But that eighteenth-century Arcadia had clouded over long before Stevenson's time; and indeed he was prone to be a little too cloudy even about those of its principles which are really clear. And while the more Bohemian artists of the later time continued to claim all the liberties and more than the laxities of such a theory, they had left off pretending that it led to such felicity in practice. Indeed there has been a curious irony in this respect about the modern artists, especially the literary artists. Half the outcry against them arose, rightly or wrongly, because they insisted that their books must be repulsive in order to be realistic or sordid in order to be true. They insisted on a free hand in describing sex; and seemed to assume, in their own apologia, that to describe sex is to describe sin—and sorrow. They insisted that anything pretty must be a pretence; and never saw how sharply they were reflecting on the end of that very dance of pretty nymphs and cupids, which had brought them the licence that they liked best. In short, they seemed to make two claims; first to be free to find the perfect happiness of passion; and second, to be free to describe how exceedingly unhappy it is. In life one might do anything to follow love, because it was so very beautiful; and in art one must do anything to describe love, because it was so abominably ugly. Their own anarchical doctrines were really contradicted by their own anarchical descriptions. The house of love, in which it was necessary to take out such hospital licences for amputation and vivisection, could hardly be (as the poet said) the house of fulfilment of craving. It was certainly not the house that Rousseau and the old romantic liberals had craved. Anyhow, it was not possible for a man of Stevenson's generation to look for this light and lucid happiness in sex, or in that sense even in sentiment. It was not possible for a romantic who, perhaps born out of his due time, was living not in the age of Rousseau but in the age of Zola. Thus we find in Stevenson something like an actual avoidance of those themes of passion, that were throbbing in the new fiction all around him; and avoidance even of that normal romantic love, which is not touched at all in *Kidnapped* and touched gracefully but still lightly even in *Catriona*. It was not only that girls interfere with adventures. It was not only that he could not be one of those for whom a girl is the only adventure. It was also because a man living under the harsh challenge of the new realism could no longer pretend that it was an adventure which always ended well. He wished to escape into a world of more secure pleasure and perhaps of less potential pain. And this is connected with very profound truths of psychology, which have not yet been properly explored. But most men know that there is a difference between the intense momentary emotion called up by memory of the loves of youth, and the yet more instantaneous but more perfect pleasure of the memory of childhood. The former is always narrow and individual, piercing the heart like a rapier; but the latter is like a flash of lightning, for one split second revealing a whole varied landscape; it is not the memory of a particular pleasure any more than of a particular pain, but of a whole world that shone with wonder. The first is only a lover remembering love; the second is like a dead man remembering life.

I once heard in a railway-train a farmer's family of the Puritan sort discussing with a Nonconformist minister the action of a boy, at the front in the Great War, who had occupied himself in hospital with carving a wooden cross and sent it home to his family. His family was pained but apologetic. Their remarks had a continual chorus of, 'He didn't mean anything by it.' This extraordinary state of mind intrigued me so much that I listened to the rest of the conversation; at intervals of which the minister repeated firmly that we didn't want that sort of thing; what we wanted was a living Christ. And it never seemed to occur to this reverend gentleman that he was at that moment at war with every living as well as every Christian thing; with the creative instinct, with the desire for form, with the love of family, with the impulse to send signals and messages, with humour, with pathos, with the virility of martyrdom and the vividness of exile. It was in truth the carver of the cross who was bearing witness to a living Christ and the partisan of a living Christ who was repeating a dead form. It was none the less so, because it was not a fixed shape in wood. This curious incident has always remained in my memory, however, if only for its fresh and superficial humour. The image of the unconscious youth who didn't mean anything by it, who merely whittled a stick until it came by sheer ill-luck into the form of a cross, will always be a source of fruitful entertainment to the mind. The idea of the young man hacking wood about right and left in a reckless manner, and seeing theological symbols spring up on every side in spite of his most earnest efforts, has something in it of the fairy tale. And the idea that if he had only known what was coming, nothing would have induced him to touch anything so improper and shocking, is a matter of deep indwelling joy.

And yet, strangely enough, I must in a manner apologise to the poor minister and admit that something like that fantastic suggestion may really occur. After all, there is in the world a great crowd of unconscious cross-builders of unintentional crosses. There is, running through the very framework of our houses and our furniture, a sort of pattern of crosses. There are a great many honest carpenters and joiners who make wooden crosses and don't mean anything by it. But the figure means something for all that; precisely because it is a fundamental figure, based on basic principles of balance and conflict and support. All our chairs and tables are full of crosses, of cross-bars and cross-beams; and it is probable that most of us use the furniture without feeling the significance; do not think of a table as the condition of a communion table and can sit on a chair without immediately speaking *ex cathedra*. And in the same fashion, the more we study active and artistic history, the more often we shall see men making thrones when they meant only to make chairs or building churches when they meant only to build houses. And in the retrospect of religious history, it seems to me that most excursions and even aberrations have only served to scrawl on a larger scale the truth of certain ancient doctrines near and necessary to man; and illustrate orthodoxy if only with awful examples. Milton was himself an example; for he told more truth than he intended, when he said that new Presbyter was but old Priest writ large. It was indeed the human need of a priest written large; and it was written very large indeed.

Now the men of Stevenson's generation, and especially the men who were as intelligent as he was, were perhaps more unconscious of the real case for these old ideas than any men who have lived before or since. Nothing was further from their thoughts than the suggestion that their artistic fancies could refer back to those antiquated and sombre dogmas about the Fall or obscuration of the divine light by sin. Wordsworth, though he is sometimes called pantheistic, saw in the vivid pleasures of childhood what he called intimations of immortality. Stevenson admitted that he often found it difficult to get any intimations of immortality. And yet, if he could bear no witness to the Resurrection, he was continually bearing witness to the Fall. We say lightly enough of a good man that he is a Christian without knowing it. But Stevenson was a Christian theologian without knowing it. Nothing, as I say, would have surprised him or his generation more than to discover it; and it may be that some even of a younger generation are so traditional as to have missed the gradual unfolding of the truth. He would have been the first to say that such dogmas were dead and that we cannot put back the clock to the fifth century. Yet he did not explain why he was so often trying to put back his own clock to his fifth year. For the truth is that there really is no sense or meaning, in this continuous tribute of the poets to the poetry of early childhood, unless it be, as Treherne says, that the world of sin comes between us and something more beautiful or, as Wordsworth says, that we came first from God who is our home. I will not pause to distinguish here between the true doctrine of the Fall and the doctrine of depravity which the Calvinists had probably taught to Stevenson, which would alone be enough to explain his not knowing how orthodox he was. Nor will I here expound the distinction between original and acted sin, apart from the ideal of infant baptism; or the already bewildered modern sceptic would probably think I was mad. He must accept my benevolent assurance that it is rather he that is mad; or rather, through no fault of his own, mentally defective. The point is that there really is no explanation of this intense imaginative concentration on babies except a mystical explanation. The whole point of Stevenson's story is that of a man haunted by a tune, always seeking for the broken notes of a lost melody; which he himself called the note of the time-devouring nightingale. 'But only children hear it right.' Why?

Moreover, as I have already noted, this principle of the beatific vision of innocence was even more proved in the breach than in the observance. The rationalists and realists who were praising the adult pursuit of happiness, or ought to have been praising such a pursuit of happiness, were (and still are) mainly occupied with describing unhappiness. They only prove that free life and free love are really worse than any ascetic had ever represented them. The naturalistic philosophies did not only contradict Christianity. The naturalistic philosophies also contradicted the naturalistic novels. Their own exercise of their own right of expression was quite enough to show that the mere combination of the maturity of reason with the pleasures of passion does not in fact produce a Utopia. We need not debate here whether the Zolaists were justified in so laboriously describing horrors. If mere liberty had really led to happiness, they would have been describing happiness. It would not have been necessary for a grown man with a library of modern literature to hide himself in a twopenny toy theatre in order to be happy.

This very simple truth is probably too simple to be seen; because, like many such things, it is too large to be seen. But certainly it is still there to be seen, if any of the moderns could enlarge their minds enough to see it. The type of realism has changed since the days of Zola, just as the type of romance has changed since the days of Stevenson. But it has not answered this unanswerable distiction between the cheerful songs of innocence and the meloncholy songs of experience. Of the recent literature of the rising generation, there is much that is frivolous, but uncommonly little that is joyous. Just now we are incessantly asked to rejoice in the sight of youth enjoying itself; which I for one am very ready to do; but all the readier if I can be quite certain that it is enjoying itself. And it is a curious fact that in its characteristic contemporary literature there is an almost complete absence of joy. And I think it would be true to say, in a general fashion, that it is not childish enough to be cheerful. In this connection I may be allowed once more to be at once anecdotal and allegorical. When I first saw the title of *The Green Hat* I pictured it as the top-hat of an gentleman who had a fancy for that colour. I imagined him a strutting symbolic figure of springtime, with hair like the hawthorn and a hat like the new leaves; my mind lost itself amid tree-tops and all the antics of the April wind; I imagined him chasing his hat to elfland and the end of the world, or climbing trees to find the blue bird nesting in the green headgear. The mere idea of a green hat gave me a glimpse into that elusive element of which the blue bird was made the emblem. When I opened the book and found that the green hat was only a lady's hat, and that the book was full of sentiments about sex, I was as blankly disappointed as a boy who has been given a dictionary instead of a book. My feelings towards the intrusive females were those of Jim Hawkins; much what he would have felt if a fashionable lady had disuaded Squire Trelawney from going to sea. It is true that the people in the book professed to be enjoying themselves, in what appeared to be their own fashion; but they could not help me to enjoy myself, as I should have done with the only true, real and original story of the green hat. I recognised that there was wit in the work, but no fun in it; there was no stir of that deep gale of spring; but rather an accepted air of autumn; of things dancing as dead leaves dance; like the Falling Leaves in the joyful revelation of Mr. Aldous Huxley. I know all about the defence of this gloomy realism on the ground that it is real. I have known it ever since the time of Stevenson writing on Zola. But I am not talking about whether this literature is reasonable or justifiable; I am talking about whether it does in fact call up, or even try to call up, the passion of positive joy.

That is why this episode is worth noting and recalling if only as an episode; and all the more so, if it is in sharp contrast with the episodes that went before. I have admitted that some part of Stevenson's deliberate choice of childishness was a reaction from ill-chosen surroundings and courses of conduct in the period of passion and of youth. But the younger writers, who boast of choosing for themselves, seem just as unsuccessful in making passion identical with pleasure; and just as unsuccessful in preserving the youthful spirit of youth. I have admitted that when he made his dash for liberty and happiness, it may have appeared that there was no alternative but that of Puritanism or pessimism. But the new writers who are not threatened with Puritanism seem to be just as much moved to pessimism. There seems no explanation of the two tempers; except that the apostle of childhood was at least seeking pleasure where it could be found, while the apostles of youth are seeking it where it cannot be found. What awaits us after all these episodes I will not pretend to prophesy; I will only profess to hope that it may be the reuilding of the great and neglected Christian philosophy, to which all contributions will be thankfully received, especially those of atheists and anarchists. And that is really the chief importance, both of the man who can show human nature happy in the nursery and the man who can only show it unhappy in the night-club. Both of them may be, and generally are, of the sort that would smile scornfully at the thought of calling up the old pious fables about heaven and hell. But in fact Stevenson was describing the kingdom of heaven and calling it Skelt; while Zola was describing all the kingdoms of hell and calling it real life. Neither of them get outside the iron ring of the real truth of the matter; that the one thing, however babyish, really is a picture of contentment, while in the other the only decent element is discontent.

It may be that the world will forget Stevenson, a century or so after it has forgotten all the present distinguished detractors of Stevenson. It may be quite the other way, as the poet said; it may be the world will remember Stevenson; will remember him with a start, so to speak, when everybody else has forgotten that there ever was any story in a novel. The dissolution hinted at by Sir Edmund Gosse, whereby fiction which was always a rather vague form shall become utterly formless, may have by that time dropped out of the novel all its original notion of a narrative. Mr. H. G. Wells, if he lives to delight the world so long, will be able to deliver the goods in the form of great masses of admirable analyses of economics and social conditions, without the embarrasment of having to remember at every two hundred pages or so that he has somewhere left a hero in a motor-car or a heroine in a lodging-house. Miss Dorothy Richardson[59] may pour out those vivid inventories of the furniture and family crockery, which her subconscious self notes with the accuracy of an inventory clerk, without being pestered to tell us who owned these objects, or what was the object of owning them. The psychologists may present us with a series of subtle and fascinating

---

[59] Dorothy Richardson (1833–1957) was an novelist and great pioneer of the stream-of-consciousness school of writing.

states of mind, without our being morbidly curious to inquire whose mind. They in turn may yield to some other school; such as those bright and breezy Americans who call themselves Behaviourists. They declare with some warmth that there is really nothing in their minds and that they only think with their muscles; which, in the case of some thinking, we might well believe. At present the Behaviourists are on their best behaviour. But there seems no reason why this new sort of muscular Christianity should not eventually invade the novel, just as psychoanalysis did; and we shall all be able to rejoice in a new type of fiction in which a bright thought flashes through Edwin's biceps or a vivid memory rises unbidden in the deltoid of Angelina. For it is the habit of modern psychological science to make quite sure of its fiction a long time before it is sure of its facts. But the trouble about such fiction will be that it is very much of a novelty, but not much of a novel. The passion for making patterns of loops and spirals, like a chart of currents at sea, has so far dissolved the outline of individuality that we lose all sense of what a man is, let alone what a man wants. Nameless universal forces streaming through the subconsciousness, run very truly like that dark and sacred river that wound its way through caverns measureless to man. When this process of shapelessness is complete, it is always possible that men may come upon a shape with something of a sharp surprise; like a geologist finding in featureless rocks the fossil of some wild creature, looking as if petrified in the last wild leap or on the wing. Or it is as if an antiquary, passing through halls and temples of some iconoclastic city, covered with dizzy patterns of merely mathematical beauty, were to come upon the heaving limb or lifted shoulder of some broken statue of the Greeks. In that condition it may be that the novel will again be novel. And in that condition, in that reaction, certainly no novel will serve its purpose so forcibly, or make its point so plainly, as a novel by Stevenson. The story, the first of childish and the oldest of human pleasures, will nowhere reveal its structure and its end so swiftly and simply as in the tales of Tusitala. The world's great age will in that degree begin anew; the childhood of the earth be rediscovered; for the story-teller will once more have spread his carpet in the dust; and it will really be a magic carpet.

But whether or no the world returns thus to Stevenson, whether or no it returns thus to stories, it will certainly return to something; and to something of this kind. The only thing which we can safely prophesy is the one thing which is always called impossible. Again and again we are told, by all sorts of priggish and progressive persons, that mankind cannot go back. The answer is that if mankind cannot go back, it cannot go anywhere. Every important change in history has been founded on something historic: and if the world had not again and again tried to renew its youth, it would have been dead long ago. As the poet makes his songs out of memories of first love, or the writer of fairy-tailes has to play at being a child as the child plays at being a man, so every republican has looked back to the remote republics of antiquity and even the Communist talks about a primitive community of goods. The sharp return to simplicity, as the expression of the fiery thirst for happiness—that is the one recurring fact of all history; and that is the importance of Stevenson's place in literary history. Nor is there the smallest reason to suppose that the literary history of the future will in this respect be any different from the literary history of the past. On the contrary, the two or three examples of extreme change, with which the most recent days have challenged us, have very curiously confirmed this old truth in a new way. Of that it is indeed true to say that the more it changes, the more it is the same thing; and a jolly good thing too.

Fashions change; but this return to the nursery is not a fashion and it does not change. If we turn to the very latest, and we might say loudest of literary innovators, we still find that in so far as they are saying anything, they are saying that. Let us suppose that the Stevensonian way of doing it is altogether dated and out of date; let us leave Stevenson behind in the dead past, along with such lumber as Cervantes and Balzac and Charles Dickens. If we shoot forward into the most fashionable fads and fancies, if we rush to the newest salons or listen to the most advanced lectures, we do not escape the challenge of our childhood. There is already a group, we might say a family group, of poets who consider themselves, and are generally considered, the last word in experiment and in extravagance; and who are not without real qualities of deep atmosphere and suggestion.

Yet all that is really deep in the best of their work comes out of those depths of garden perspective and large rooms as seen by little children, white with the windows of the morning. The best poetry of Miss Sitwell[60] is after all a sort of parody of *A Child's Garden of Verses*, decked with slightly altered adjectives that would mildly surprise the child. But the poet is as certainly groping after her own lost shadow as the child who 'rose and found the shining dew on every buttercup'; and is even more ready to idealize the moving cloud of the crinoline than he who was content to say, 'Whenever Aunty moves around, her dresses make a curious sound.' In Miss Sitwell's version they would make a still more curious sound, the nature of which I have not the courage to conjecture. The shining dew might become the shrieking dew, or on a more moderate estimate the sniggering dew; but it would still be a long-lost child who stood bewildered in those grey meadows before the dawn. Many have complained, and perhaps justly, of the almost American modernity of the artistic ambition of these artists. They announce their message through a megaphone; they shout it through pantomime masks; they hustle and push and pick quarrels; but there is someting in them, for all their efforts to advertise—or to hide it. And that something is the new form of the reaction of Stevenson; exactly as Stevenson was the new form of the reaction of Rousseau. Many have speculated on what they are really after; but what they are really after is still the same: those lost children who are themselves; lost in the deep gardens at dusk.

That is why the real story of Stevenson must end where it began; because it was to that end that he himself perpetually wandered and strove. I said at the beginning that the key to his career was put early into his hands; it was well symbolised by the paint-brush dipped in purple or prussian blue, with which he started to colour the stiff caricatures upon the cardboard of Skelt. But that paint-brush has been in other hands besides his; I remarked elsewhere that, dipped in somewhat paler hues, it has brightened the lives of many of those vague Victorian aunts whose cloudy crinolines float through the

---

[60] Chesterton is referring to Dame Edith Sitwell (1887–1964), English poet and prose writer.

gardens of the new 'Early Victorian' poetry. Neither perhaps know that, even in lingering on such things, they do but illustrate a more ancient parable and the mystery of a child set in the midst. Here, however, we may take the matter more lightly and leave it to tell its own story; but at least it is amusing to reflect that the old story of the unconsciously comic tombstone, the epitaph that was the butt of a hundred jests, is not really so far wrong after all; that there is a sort of truth concealed in that remarkable inscription, and that (leaving on one side a somewhat needless allusion to the Earl of Cork) we may repeat the epitaph with truth and even with profundity: 'He also painted in watercolours. For of such is the kingdom of heaven.'

CHAUCER
1932

INTRODUCTION

If I were writing this in French, as I should be if Chaucer had not chosen to write in English, I might be able to head this preliminary note with something like *Avis au Lecteur*; which, with a French fine shade, would suggest without exaggeration the note of warning. As it is, I feel tempted to write, 'Beware!' or some such melodramatic phrase, in large letters across the frontispiece. For I do really desire to warn the reader, or the critic, of some possible mistakes in or about this book: touching its real purpose and its inevitable pitfalls.

It were perhaps too sanguine a simplicity to say that this book is intended to be popular; but at least it is intended to be simple. It describes only the effect of a particular poet on a particular person; but it also expresses a personal conviction that the poet could be an extremely popular poet; that is, could produce the same effect on many other normal or unpretentious persons. It makes no claim to specialism of any sort in the field of Chaucerian scholarship. It is written for people who know even less about Chaucer than I do. It does not in any of the disputed details, dictate to those who know much more about Chaucer than I do. It is primarily concerned with the fact that Chaucer was a poet. Or, in other words, that it is possible to know him, without knowing anything about him. A distinguished French critic said of my sketch of an English novelist that it might well bear the simple title, 'The Praise of Dickens'; and I should be quite content if this tribute only bore the title of 'The Praise of Chaucer'. The whole point, so far as I am concerned, is that it is as easy for an ordinary Englishman to enjoy Chaucer as to enjoy Dickens. Dickensians always quote Dickens; from which it follows that they often misquote Dickens. Having long depended on memory, I might be quite capable of misquotation; but I fear I have fallen into something that may seem even more shocking: a sort of irregular popular translation. I do incline to think that it is necessary to take some such liberties, when first bringing Chaucer to the attention of fresh and casual readers. However that may be, all this part of the explanation is relatively easy; and the intention of the book is tolerably obvious.

Unfortunately this plan of simplification and popularity is interrupted by two problems, which can hardly be prevented from presenting a greater complexity. In the second chapter, I plunged rather rashly into the wider historical elements of Chaucer's age; and soon found myself among deep tides that might well have carried me far out of my course. And yet I cannot altogether regret the course that I actually followed; for there grew upon me, while writing this chapter, a very vivid realization which the chapter itself does not very clearly explain. I fear that the reader will only pause to wonder, with not unjust irritation, why I sometimes seem to be writing about modern politics instead of about medieval history. I can only say that the actual experience, of trying to tell such truths as I know about the matter, left me with an overwhelming conviction that it is because we miss the point of the medieval history that we make a mess of the modern politics. I felt suddenly the fierce and glaring *relevancy* of all the walking social symbols of the Chaucerian scene to the dissolving views of our own social doubts and speculations today. There came upon me a conviction I can hardly explain, in these few lines, that the great Types, the heroic or humorous figures that make the pageant of past literature, are now fading into something formless; because we do not understand the old civilized order which gave them form, and can hardly even construct any alternative form. The presence of the Guilds or the grades of Chivalry, the presence of the particular details of that day, are not of course necessary to all human beings. But the absence of the Guilds and the grades of Chivalry and the absence of any positive substitute for them, is now a great gap that is none the less a fact because it is a negative fact. Feeling this so strongly, at the moment, I simply could not force myself to the usual stiff official attitude of dealing with all such things as dead; of talking of Heraldry as if it were Hieroglyphics or dealing with the friars as if they had disappeared like the Druids. But I apologize for the disproportion of the second chapter, which spoils the simplicity of the opening and the general intention. Perhaps I might put up my notice of warning, and warn the reader not to read the second chapter. Now I come to think of it, I might warn him not to read the book at all; but in this, perhaps, there would be a tinge of inconsistency. Nevertheless, the book would have served its purpose if anyone had learned, even by getting as far as this page, that what matters is not books on Chaucer, but Chaucer.

Lastly, it would be affectation on my part to deny that the very subject forces me to face (or as ostentatiously to avoid) a subject on which I am in a sense expected to be controversial; on which I could not really be expected to be non-controversial. But this problem is all the more practical, because of the particular summary, or main truth about Chaucer, which is most borne in upon my mind, on rereading and reconsidering his work. Chaucer was a poet who came at the end of the medieval age and order; which certainly contained fanaticism, ferocity, wild asceticism and the rest. There are some who really suggest that it contained only fanaticism, ferocity and the rest. Anyhow, I was faced with the fact that Chaucer was the final fruit and inheritor of that order. And I was also confronted with the fact, which seems to me quite as certain a fact, that he was much *more* sane and cheerful and normal than most of the later writers. He was less delirious than Shakespeare, less harsh than Milton, less fanatical than Bunyan, less embittered than Swift. I had in any case to construct some sort of theory in connexion with this practical problem and this practical fact. Therefore in this book I advance the general thesis; that, in spite of everything, there was a balanced philosophy in medieval times; and some very unbalanced philosophies in later times.

I am sorry; I could easily have ended differently; it would be much more simple and sociable to treat Chaucer only as a charming companion and sit down with him at the Tabard without further questioning about whence he came. But something is due to conviction; my book was bound to make some attempt to explain Chaucer; and this is the only way I can explain him.

G. K. C.

I

THE GREATNESS OF CHAUCER

It is beginning to be realized that the English are the eccentrics of the earth. They have produced an unusually large proportion of what they used to call Humorists and would now perhaps rather call Characters. And nothing is more curious about them than the contradiction of their consciousness and unconsciousness of their own merits. It is nonsense, I regret to say, to claim that they are incapable of boasting. Sometimes they boast most magnificently of their weaknesses and deficiencies. Sometimes they boast of the more striking and outstanding virtues they do not possess. Sometimes (I say it with groans and grovelings before the just wrath of heaven) they sink so low as to boast of not boasting. But it is perfectly true that they seem to be entirely unaware of the very existence of some of their most extraordinary claims to glory and distinction. One example among many is the fact that they have never realized the nature; let alone the scale, of the genius of Geoffrey Chaucer.

I say advisedly the scale; for what seems to me altogether missed is the *greatness* of Chaucer. Men say the obvious things about him; they call him the Father of English Poetry, but only in the sense in which the same title has been given to an obscure Anglo-Saxon like Caedmon. He also has been called the Father of English Poetry, though what he wrote is not in that sense poetry and not in any sense English. They say that Chaucer marks the moment when our language began to be formed out of French and Saxon elements; but they see nothing elemental about the man who did so much to form it. They say (probably falsely) that Chaucer borrowed from Boccaccio the notion of a framework of stories; and they admit that he brightened it a little by giving more personality to the tellers of the *Canterbury Tales.* They admit (sometimes with a faint air of surprise) that this fourteenth-century man was acquainted with the nature of a joke; they concede a certain courtesy and urbanity, and then generally turn with relief to digging up the old original dull stories which

Chaucer made interesting. In short, there has been perceptible, in greater or less degree, an indescribable disposition to *patronize* Chaucer. Sometimes he is patted on the head like a child, because all our other poets are his children. Sometimes he is treated as the Oldest Inhabitant, partially demented and practically dead, because he was alive before anybody else in Europe to certain revolutions of the European mind. Sometimes he is treated as entirely dead; a bag of dry bones to be dissected by antiquarians, interested only in matters of detail. But in no common English ears, as yet, does his name actually sound as a thunderclap or a trumpet-peal, like the name of Dante or of Shakespeare. It may seem fanciful to say so, but the name of Chaucer has not yet completely achieved the sound of a *serious* thing. It is partly the popular sense that Early English is a sort of Pidgin English. It is partly the pedantic prejudice that medieval civilization was not civilized. It is partly a sheer incapacity to thank those who have given us everything, because we cannot imagine anything else.

The medieval word for a Poet was a Maker, which indeed is the original meaning of a Poet. It is one of the points, more numerous than some suppose, in which Greek and medieval simplicity nearly touch. There was never a man who was more of a Maker than Chaucer. He made a national language; he came very near to making a nation. At least without him it would probably never have been either so fine a language or so great a nation. Shakespeare and Milton were the greatest sons of their country; but Chaucer was the Father of his Country, rather in the style of George Washington. And apart from that, he made something that has altered all Europe more than the Newspaper: the Novel. He was a novelist when there were no novels. I mean by the novel the narrative that is not primarily an anecdote or an allegory, but is valued because of the almost accidental variety of actual human characters. The Prologue of *The Canterbury Tales* is the Prologue of Modern Fiction. It is the preface to *Don Quixote* and the preface to *Gil Blas*. The astonishing thing is not so much that an Englishman did this as that Englishmen hardly ever brag about it. Nobody waves a Union Jack and cries, 'England made jolly stories for the whole earth.' It is not too much to say that

Chaucer made not only a new nation but a new world; and was none the less its real maker because it is an unreal world. And he did it in a language that was hardly usable until he used it; and to the glory of a nation that had hardly existed till he made it glorious.

I know not why the people who are so silent about this go about glorying in the fact of having painted Tasmania red in an atlas or in-troduced the golf of Tooting to the upper classes of Turkey. But it is certain that, while some of them have (if it were possible) over-rated the greatness of Shakespeare, most of them have unaccountably underrated the greatness of Chaucer. Yet most of the things that are hinted in depreciation of Chaucer could be said as easily in depreciation of Shakespeare. If Chaucer borrowed from Boccaccio and other writers, Shakespeare borrowed from anybody or anything, and often from the same French or Italian sources as his forerunner. The answer indeed is obvious and tremendous; that if Shakespeare borrowed, he jolly well paid back. But so did Chaucer, as in that very central instance I have named; when he turned the decorative picture-frame of the Decameron into the moving portrait-gallery of the ride to Canterbury.

It is worth noting, touching that patronizing tone towards the childishness of Chaucer, that there is very much the same patronizing tone in many of the earlier compliments to Shakespeare. In the case of Shakespeare, as of Chaucer, his contemporaries and immediate successors seem to have been struck by something sweet or kindly about him, which they felt as too natural to be great in the grand style. He is chiefly praised, and occasionally rebuked, for freshness and spontaneity. Is it unfair to find a touch of that patronizing spirit even in the greatest among those who were less great?

> Or sweetest Shakespeare, fancy's child,
> Warble his native wood-notes wild.

I suspect Milton of meaning that his own organ-notes would be of a deeper and grander sort than wood-notes so innocently warbling. Yet somehow, as a summary of Shakespeare, the description does not strike one as comprehensive. Hung be the heavens with black . . . have lighted fools the way to dusty death . . . the multitudinous seas incarnadine . . . let the high gods, who keep this dreadful pother o'er our heads, find out their enemies now—these do not strike us exclusively as warblings. But neither, it may respectfully be submitted, are all the woodnotes of Chaucer to be regarded as warblings. There are things in Chaucer that are both austere and exalted, such as certain lines in his religious poems, especially his addresses to the Blessed Virgin; there are things in Chaucer that are both grim and violent, such as the description of the death-blow that broke the neck of the accuser of Constance.[1] And if he only occasionally rises to the grand or descends to the grotesque, it is not obvious that he is the less like life for that.

These examples, I may say in passing, afford an opportunity to say a word of explanation, even at this stage, about the spelling and diction of Chaucer and how I have decided to deal with it. In this also Chaucer suffers from a somewhat unfair disadvantage as compared with Shakespeare. Much of Shakespeare, as a matter of fact, was actually printed in an old spelling which would make many familiar lines look fantastic or awkward. Shakespeare's old English was near enough to be easily modernized; Chaucer's old English was just remote enough to make it hard to do so while preserving the accent and melody. Nobody can read it, indeed, without wishing that some of its antiquated words were in modern use. The wretched scribe, starving for descriptive terms, will find many which he will envy the scribe of the fourteenth century. Indeed, the two examples I have given themselves illustrate the point. There is no nobler image of the ideal, in the ideal sense of that vulgarized term, than that single glimpse in Chaucer:

> Virgin, that art so noble of apparail
> That leadest us unto the highë tower
> Of Paradise . . .

nor can I ever read it without a sort of vision, of a garden tilted on a remote turret and a woman in trailing raiment, splendiferous like a comet, going up a winding stair. But, incidentally, what a pity that we cannot say 'apparail', instead of being dismally reduced to saying

---

[1] Constance is a character in Chaucer's "The Man of Law's Tale", one of the *Canterbury Tales.* She is an allegorical figure, a personification of the *Constantia*, which means "steadfastness". She may also represent the Church. Also used by John Gower in *Confessio Amantis;* both writers took this figure from Nicholas Trivet's *Anglo-Norman Chronicles (1355).*

'apparel'. And, oddly enough, there is a similar detail in the other instance I took at random; for when the slanderer of Constance was 'strook' so as to break his neck-bone, we have the pleasing further fact that his eyes 'brast out of his head'; which is going about as far as grotesque violence will go. But will not the envious man of letters think pensively and tenderly about the possibilities of the word 'brast'? When the sensational novelist makes the hero burst the bonds knotted by the atrocious Chinaman, how much better if he brast them! When the comic novelist says that Mr. Pobbles burst his collar, how much more forcible if he brast his collar! For this reason there is every argument for leaving Chaucer's language as it stands, and even admitting its superiority for some of Chaucer's purposes. Nevertheless, for reasons which I shall explain more fully elsewhere, I propose in many cases boldly to modernize the Chaucerian language, and especially for the purpose that is immediate here: that of showing that Chaucer was great in the sense in which Matthew Arnold connected greatness with what he called 'high seriousness' and the grand style.

Let anyone knowing only the popular and patronizing impression of a merry gossip or warbling court minstrel, suppose that he has presented to him without context or criticism merely such a verse as this, printed as I have printed it:

> Such end hath, lo, this Troilus for love:
> Such end hath all his greatë worthiness,
> Such end hath all his royal estate above,
> Such end his lust, such end his nobleness,
> Such end hath all the false world's brittleness:
> And thus began his loving of Creseid
> As I have told; and in this wise he died.

Nobody who knows what English is will say that that verse is not dignified. Nobody who knows what tragedy is will say it is unworthy of a tragic poet. The words and spelling are not exactly as Chaucer wrote them, but they represent with some reasonable worthiness what Chaucer meant us to read. Now if anybody is so excruciatingly fond of the expression 'swich fin' that he desires to mingle it with his daily talk, as I have desired to use 'brast' and 'apparail', it will be easy for him (by the laborious literary research involved in looking at the book) to discover that 'swich fin' is Chaucerian for 'such end' and to convict me of having poisoned the well of English undefiled. But I will modestly yet obstinately repeat that it does not give the modern reader an idea of the dignity, that was in Chaucer's mind and gesture, to repeat 'swich fin' five times; especially as we do not know how Chaucer pronounced it and are almost certainly pronouncing it wrong.

Here, however, I have introduced this quotation in a quotable form, in order to emphasize the fact that Chaucer was capable of greatness even in the sense of gravity. We all know that Matthew Arnold denied that the medieval poet possessed this 'high seriousness'; but Matthew Arnold's version of high seriousness was often only high and dry solemnity. That Chaucer was, in that passage about Troilus, speaking with complete conviction and a sense of the greatness of the subject (which seem to me the only essentials of the real grand style) nobody can doubt who reads the following verses, in which he turns with terrible and realistic scorn on the Pagan gods with whom he had so often played. I have mentioned these matters first to show that Chaucer was capable of high seriousness, even in the sense of those who feel that only what is serious can be high. But for my part I dispute the identification. I think there are other things that can be high as well as high seriousness. I think, for instance, that there can be such things as high spirits; and that these also can be spiritual.

Now even if we consider Chaucer only as a humorist, he was in this very exact sense a great humorist. And by this I do not only mean a very good humorist. I mean a humorist in the grand style; a humorist whose broad outlook embraced the world as a whole, and saw even great humanity against a background of greater things. This quality of grandeur in a joke is one which I can only explain by an example. The example also illustrates that clinging curse of all the criticism of Chaucer; the fact that while the poet is always large and humorous, the critics are often small and serious. They not only get hold of the wrong end of the stick, but of the diminishing end of the telescope; and take in a detail when they should be taking in a design. The Chaucerian irony is sometimes so large that it is too large to be seen. I know no more striking example than the business of his own contribution to the tales of the Canterbury Pilgrims. A thousand times have I heard men tell (as Chaucer himself would put it) that the poet wrote *The Rime of Sir Topas* as a parody of certain bad romantic verse of his own time. And the learned would be willing to fill their notes with examples of this bad poetry, with the addition of not a little bad prose. It is all very scholarly, and it is all perfectly true; but it entirely misses the point. The joke is not that Chaucer is joking at bad ballad-mongers; the joke is much larger than that. To see the scope of this gigantic jest we must take in the whole position of the poet and the whole conception of the poem.

The Poet is the Maker; he is the creator of a cosmos; and Chaucer is the creator of the whole world of his creatures. He made the pilgrimage; he made the pilgrims. He made all the tales that are told by the pilgrims. Out of him is all the golden pageantry and chivalry of the Knight's Tale; all the rank and rowdy farce of the Miller's; he told through the mouth of the Prioress the pathetic legend of the Child Martyr and through the mouth of the Squire the wild, almost Arabian romance of Cambuscan. And he told them all in sustained melodious verse, seldom so continuously prolonged in literature; in a style that sings from start to finish. Then in due course, as the poet is also a pilgrim among the other pilgrims, he is asked for his contribution. He is at first struck dumb with embarrassment; and then suddenly starts a gabble of the worst doggerel in the book. It is so bad that, after a page or two of it, the tolerant innkeeper breaks in with the desperate protest of one who can bear no more, in words that could be best translated as 'Gorlumme!' or 'This is a bit too thick!' The poet is shouted down by a righteous revolt of his hearers, and can only defend himself by saying sadly that this is the only poem he knows. Then, by way of a final climax or anticlimax of the same satire, he solemnly proceeds to tell a rather dull story *in prose*.

Now a joke of that scale goes a great deal beyond the particular point, or pointlessness, of the *The Rime of Sir Topas*. Chaucer is mocking not merely bad poets but good poets; the best poet he knows; 'the best in this kind are but shadows'. Chaucer, having to represent himself as reciting bad verse, did very probably take the opportunity of parodying somebody else's bad verse. But the parody is not the point. The point is in the admirable irony of the whole conception of the dumb or doggerel ryhmer who is nevertheless the author of all the other rhymes; nay, even the author of their authors. Among all the types and trades, the coarse miller, the hard-fisted reeve, the clerk, the cook, the shipman, the poet is the only man who knows no poetry. But the irony is wider and even deeper than that. There is in it some hint of those huge and abysmal ideas of which the poets are half-conscious when they write; the primal and elemental ideas connected with the very nature of creation and reality. It has in it something of the philosophy of a phenomenal world, and all that was meant by those sages, by no means pessimists, who have said that we are in a world of shadows. Chaucer has made a world of his own shadows, and, when he is on a certain plane, finds himself equally shadowy. It has in it all the mystery of the relation of the maker with things made. There falls on it from afar even some dark ray of the irony of God, who was mocked when He entered His own world, and killed when He came among His creatures.

That is laughter in the grand style, *pace*[2] Matthew Arnold; and Arnold, with all his merits, did not laugh but only smiled—not to say smirked. It is the presence of such things, behind the seeming simplicity of the fourteenth-century poet, which constitutes what I mean here by the greatness of Chaucer. He was a man much less commonplace than he appeared; I think than he deliberately appeared. He had so great a faith in common sense that he seems to have accepted with a smile the suggestions of the commonplace. But he was not commonplace. He was not superficial. His judgments are sufficient to show that he was not superficial. There is perhaps no better example of it than his journey to Italy and probable friendship with Petrarch, who was crowned with universal acclamation in the Eternal City as the one and only supreme and universal poet of the age; nor indeed was the admiration of the age undeserved. Petrarch was a poet, a prophet, a patriot, almost everything except what he was called, the greatest genius alive. It is typical of the neglected side of Chaucer that he admired Dante more than Petrarch.

---

[2] *Pace* means "by the leave of. . . ."

It may be questioned in passing, whether this understanding is understood. Dante was very different from Chaucer; but he was not so utterly different as the sound of the two names would now generally imply. It must be remembered that people began to talk patronizingly of a cheerful or almost chirpy Chaucer, at the very time when they talked about a merely Byronic or melodramatic Dante. Those who see Dante as something to be illustrated by Doré[3] might well be content that Chaucer should be illustrated by Stothard.[4] But there was another Chaucer who was illustrated by Blake. There was an element in Chaucer that was symbolic to the eye of a serious mystic. A medieval writer actually said that Chaucer's *House of Fame* had put Dante into English. And though this is an extravagant exaggeration, it is not (as some would think) an extravagant contrast. There is much more of Dante in the description of Chaucer, as he is whirled aloft by the golden eagle of the gods, feeling that Thought can lift us to the last heaven with 'the feathers of philosophy', than there is in the ordinary nineteenth-century notion that Dante was a dark and lowering Dago who was really only at home in Hell. Chaucer caught sight of the eagle; his tale is not always 'of a cock'. Yet he is greatest perhaps with the cock and not the eagle. He is not a great Latin epic poet; he is a great English humorist and humanist; but he is great. The very case of the cock in the Nun's Priest's Tale is concerned with richer and deeper things than a mere fable about animals. It is not enough to talk, as some critics do, about Reynard the Fox or the Babrian origins. Just as they mainly insist that 'Sir Topas' is a parody, so they are chiefly struck by the fact that the fable is a fable. Curiously enough, in actual fact, it is either much more or much less than a fable. The interpretation is full of that curious rich native humour, which is at once riotous and secretive. It is extraordinarily English, especially in this, that is does not aim at being neat, as wit and logic are neat. It rather delights in being clumsy; as if clumsiness were part of the fun. Chaucer is not accepting a convention; he is enjoying a contradiction. Hundreds of years

[3] Paul Gustave Dore (1833–83), a French illustrator and painter, is known for his engraved book illustrations. He illustrated, among others, Dante's *Inferno* (1861 edition).
[4] Thomas Stothard was a nineteenth century painter. One of his paintings depicted the Biblical tale "Joseph Interprets Dreams in Prison".

afterwards, a French poet was struck by the strutting parody of humanity in the poultry yard, and elaborated the same medieval jest, giving the cock the same medievel name. But the Chantecler of Rostand, with its many beautiful and rational epigrams in the French manner, has about it a sort of exact coincidence of mimicry, which fits it to the province of an actor. Rostand is pleased, as a stage manager, with the aptness of making a man act like a cock. Chaucer is pleased with the absurdity of making a cock act like a man. These are aesthetic and psychological impressions, about which nobody can prove anything; but I am pretty certain that Chaucer revelled, I might say wallowed, in the wild disproportion of making his little farmyard fowl talk like a philosopher and even a scholar. The chicken in question is hatched from the works of Aristotle and Virgil; the Song of Roland, or at least the Carolingian legend;[5] and was also (it is reassuring to know) very properly instructed in the Gospels. In a speech of great eloquence, the fox is compared to Ganelon[6] and Judas Iscariot and to the Greek who betrayed Troy to its downfall. The cock's oration involves a deep dissertation on the reliability of Dreams, and their relation to the problem of freewill, fate and the foreknowledge of heaven; all considered with a sensitive profundity of which any chicken-run may well be proud. In other words, in one sense the very sense of all this is its nonsense; at least its aptitude is its ineptitude. It is always difficult to make the fable, or even the four-footed animal, go on all fours. In this case Chaucer does not care if his two-footed animal has a leg to stand on. It has to limp as well as strut; the whole fun of the fable is in its being lopsided; and he only partially disguises his biped in feathers. Then, when the imposture is quite obvious, he delights in asserting it again, allowing, as it were, his cock to hide hurriedly behind the one feather it has left. I can imagine nothing more English, or more amusing, than this exasperating evasion. He launches a denunciation of Woman as the destroyer of Paradise, and then explains to the ladies, as with a bow and a beaming smile:

[5] The Carolingian legend refers to romances of Medieval and Renaissance Europe, relating stories of Charlemagne's paladins.
[6] Ganelon is one of the traitors among Charlemagne's paladins.

> If I the counsel of woman woldë blame
> Pass over, for I said it in my game ...
> These be the cockë's wordës and not mine,
> I can none harm of no woman divine.

There is something intensely individual in this playing in and out of the curtain, and putting on and off of the feathered mask. It is all the more subtle because nobody who reads Chaucer as a whole will doubt that, despite his occasional and probably personal grumblings against some faithless or scornful woman, he did really have a respect for women, which was not merely a bow to ladies. But if there is something here of subtlety, there is also something here of scope or scale. There is a largeness and liberty in the humorist who gets such huge enjoyment out of the metaphysical chicken, and expands so large a world of fancy out of the little opportunity of the fable. That is the quality in Chaucer which I would here emphasize first, because it should be realized before we go on to the secondary matters of origins and parallels and interpretations of particular points. The mind of Chaucer was capacious; there was room for ideas to play about in it. He could see the connexion, and still more the disconnexion, of different parts of his own scheme, or of any scheme. In the first example of 'Sir Topas', he completes his own scheme with his own incompleteness. In the second example we find him taking the tiny opening of a trivial farmyard fable, to expand it into an almost cosmic comedy. He seems to see himself as a small featherless fowl talking about the riddle of Destiny and Deity. Both have the same quality, not very easy to describe, the quality by which a very great artist sometimes allows his art to become semi-transparent, and a light to shine through the shadow pantomime which makes it confess itself a shadowy thing. So Shakespeare, at the highest moment of two of his happiest comedies, utters those deep and not unhappy sayings, that the best in this kind are but shadows, and that we are such stuff as dreams are made of, and our little life is rounded with a sleep. I say that this deeper note does exist in Chaucer, for those who will start with sufficient sympathy to listen for it, and not be content with some crabbed inquisition into whether he stole something from Petrarch or wrote something to please John of Gaunt.

THE GREATNESS OF CHAUCER

For one thing is quite certain; nobody who takes Chaucer quite so literally, I might say quite so seriously, will ever understand him. There is a sort of penumbra of playfulness round everything he ever said or sang; a halo of humour. Much of his work is marked by what can only be called a quiet exaggeration, even a quiet extravagance. It is said, in the description of him, that there was something elvish about his face; and there was something elvish about his mind. He did not object to playing a kind of delicate practical joke on the reader, or on the plan of the book; and all this may be summed up here, for convenience, under the example I have given. He did not mind making his fable something more than fabulous. He enjoyed giving a touch or two to the story of cock and hen; that made it look like the story of a cock and bull.

We shall see more of this double outlook when we come to the conjectures about his private life, and especially about his personal religion. For the moment the matter to be established is a matter of scale or size; the fact that we are not here dealing with a mind to be merely patronized for its simplicity, but with a mind that has already baffled many commentators with its complexity. In one sense he is taken too seriously and in the other sense not seriously enough. But in both senses, almost as many men have lost themselves in Chaucer's mind as have lost themselves in Shakespeare's. But in the latter case they are like children wondering what their father means; in the former, like beaming uncles, wondering what the child means.

I mean that in the popular attitude towards Chaucer, and to some extent even in the more cultured criticism of him, there is a curious and rather comic suggestion of 'drawing him out'. I have said elsewhere that to many modern Englishmen a fourteenth-century Englishman would be like a foreigner. These modern Englishmen do really treat Geoffrey Chaucer as a foreigner. Some of them treat him very much as Mr. Podsnap treated the foreign gentleman. It will be remembered that that worthy merchant not only talked to the alien as if he must necessarily be slightly deaf, but as if he was in every other way defective, and had to have things put very plainly to him in words of one syllable. Yet Mr. Podsnap was really encouraging the foreign gentleman; he was drawing him out. Only there was a general feeling of pleased surprise that there was anything there to be drawn out. Chaucer is treated as a child, just as the foreign gentleman was treated as a child; but I am sure that Chaucer was quite sufficiently subtle to be as much amused at it as the foreign gentleman. Hence it will be generally found, even now, that anything like a problem or puzzle in Chaucer is approached quite differently from a problem or puzzle in Shakespeare. When somebody finds one of the Sonnets as dark as the Dark Lady,[7] he admits that it is just possible that Shakespeare's mind may have been slightly superior to his own. But he has made up his mind that Chaucer's mind must have been more simple than his own, merely because Chaucer lived at the most complicated and entangled transitional time in European history, and drew on the traditions of about four European literatures instead of one. We shall get no further till we allow for this central and civilized character in the medieval poet; for the fact that he knew his philosophy; that he thought about his theology; and for the still more surprising fact that he saw the joke of the jokes he made, and made a good many more jokes than his critics have ever seen.

There is indeed one character, which Chaucer shares with all the great ancient poets, which may in some quarters weaken his position as a great modern poet. There are many moderns who say that man is not a thinker, when they mean he is not a freethinker. Or they say he is not a freethinker, when they mean that his thinking is not tied tight and fast to some special system of materialism. But the point I mean is much deeper than these mere quarrels about secularism and sectarianism. The greatest poets of the world have a certain serenity, because they have not bothered to invent a small philosophy, but have rather inherited a large philosophy. It is, nine times out of ten, a philosophy which very great men share with very ordinary men. It is therefore not a theory which attracts attention as a theory. In these days, when Mr. Bernard Shaw is becoming gradually, amid general applause, the Grand Old Man of English letters, it is perhaps ungracious to record that he did once say there was nobody, with

[7] In Shakespeare's Sonnets 127–152, the poet tells of his love for the "Dark Lady" despite her unworthiness.

the possible exception of Homer, whose intellect he despised so much as Shakespeare's. He has since said almost enough sensible things to outweigh even anything so silly as that. But I quote it because it exactly embodies the nineteenth-century notion of which I speak. Mr. Shaw had probably never read Homer; and there were passages in his Shakespearean criticism that might well raise a doubt about whether he ever read Shakespeare. But the point was that he could not, in all sincerity, see what the world saw in Homer and Shakespeare, because what the world saw was not what G. B. S. was then looking for. He was looking for that ghastly thing which Nonconformists call a Message, and continue to call a Message, even when they have become atheists and do not know who the Message is from. He was looking for a system; one of the very little systems that do very truly have their day. The system of Kant; the system of Hegel; the system of Schopenhauer and Nietzsche and Marx and all the rest. In each of these examples a man sprang up and pretended to have a thought that nobody had ever had. But the great poet only professes to express the thought that everybody has always had. The greatness of Homer does not consist in proving, by the death of Hector,[8] that the Will to Live is a delusion and a snare; because it is not a delusion and a snare. It does not consist in proving, by the victory of Achilles, that the Will to Power must express itself in a Superman; for Achilles is not a Superman, but, on the contrary, a hero. The greatness of Homer consists in the fact that he could make men feel, what they were already quite ready to think, that life is a strange mystery in which a hero may err and another hero may fail. The poet makes men realize how great are the great emotions which they, in a smaller way, have already experienced. Every man who has tried to keep any good thing going, though it were a little club or paper or political protest, sounds the depths of his own soul when he hears that rolling line, which can only be rendered so feebly: 'For truly in my heart and soul I know that Troy will fall.' Every man who looks back on old days, for himself and others, and realizes the changes that vex something within us that is unchangeable, realizes better the immensity of his own meaning

---

[8] Hector is the most magnanimous and noble of all the Trojan chieftains in Homer's *Iliad*.

in the mere sound of the Greek words, which only mean, 'For, as we have heard, you too, old man, were at one time happy.' These words are in poetry, and therefore they have never been translated. But there are perhaps some people to whom even the words of Shakespeare need to be translated. Anyhow, what a man learns from *Romeo and Juliet* is not a new theory of Sex; it is the mystery of something much more than what sensualists call Sex, and what cads call Sex Appeal. What he learns from *Romeo and Juliet* is not to call first love 'calf-love'; not to call even fleeting love a flirtation; but to understand that these things which a million vulgarians have vulgarized, are not vulgar. The great poet exists to show the small man how great he is. A man does not learn from Hamlet a new method of Psychoanalysis, or the proper treatment of lunatics. What he learns is not to despise the soul as small; even when rather feminine critics say that the will is weak. As if the will were ever strong enough for the tasks that confront it in this world! The great poet is alone strong enough to measure that broken strength we call the weakness of man.

It has only been for a short time, a recent and disturbed time of transition, that each writer has been expected to write a new theory of all things, or draw a new wild map of the world. The old writers were content to write of the old world, but to write of it with an imaginative freshness which made it in each case look like a new world. Before the time of Shakespeare, men had grown used to the Ptolemaic astronomy, and since the time of Shakespeare men have grown used to the Copernican astronomy. But poets have never grown used to stars; and it is their business to prevent anybody else ever growing used to them. And any man who reads for the first time the words, 'Night's candles are burnt out,' catches his breath and almost curses himself for having neglected to look rightly or sufficiently frequently, at the grand and mysterious revolutions of night and day. Theories soon grow stale; but things continue to be fresh. And, according to the ancient conception of his function, the poet was concerned with things; with the tears of things, as in the great lament of Virgil; with the delight in the number of things, as in the lighthearted rhyme of Stevenson; with thanks for things as in the Franciscan Canticle of the sun or the *Benedicite Omnia Opera*.

That behind these things there are certain great truths is true; and those so unhappy as not to believe in these truths may of course call them theories. But the old poets did not consider that they had to compete and bid against each other in the production of counter-theories. The coming of the Christian cosmic conception made a vast difference; the Christian poet had a more vivid hope than the Pagan poet. Even when he was sometimes more stern, he was always less sad. But, allowing for that more than human change, the poets taught in a continuous tradition, and were not in the least ashamed of being traditional. Each taught in an individual way; 'with a perpetual slight novelty' as Aristotle said; but they were not a series of separate lunatics looking at separate worlds. One poet did not provide a pair of spectacles by which it appered that the grass was blue; or another poet lecture on optics to teach people to say that the grass was orange; they both had the far harder and more heroic task of teaching people to feel that the grass is green. And because they continue their heroic task, the world, after every epoch of doubt and despair, always grows green again.

Now Chaucer is a particularly easy mark for the morbid intellectual or the mere innovator. He is very easily pelted by the pedants, who demand that every eternal poet should be an ephemeral philosopher. For there is no nonsense about Chaucer; there is no deception, as the conjurers say. There is no pretence of being a prophet instead of a poet. There is no shadow of shame in being a traditionalist or, as some would say a plagiarist. One of the most attractive elements in the curiously attractive personality of Chaucer is exactly that; that he is not only negatively without pretentiousness, but he is positively full of warm acknowledgement and admiration of his models. He is as awakening as a cool wind on a hot day, because he breathes forth something that has fallen into great neglect in our time, something that very seldom stirs the stuffy atmosphere of self-satisfaction or self-worship. And that is gratitude, or the theory of thanks. He was a great poet of gratitude; he was grateful to God; but he was also grateful to Gower.[9]

---

[9] Chesterton is referring to John Gower (1325?–1408), English poet and friend of Chaucer.

He was grateful to the everlasting Romance of the Rose; he was still more gratefull to Ovid and grateful to Virgil and grateful to Petrarch and Boccaccio. He is always eager to show us over his little library and to tell us where all his tales come from. He is prouder of having read the books than of having written the poems. This easy and natrual traditionalism had become a little more constrained and doubtful even by the time of the Renaissance. There is no question of Shakespeare concealing or diguising his borrowed plots; but we do feel that he dealt with them as mere dead material, of no interest until he made it interesting. He did in a sense destroy the originals by making the infinitely more mighty and magnficent parodies. Even great originals sink under him; he comes to bury Plutarch not to praise him. But Chaucer would want to praise him; he always confesses a literary pleasure which may well conceal his literary power. He seems the less original, because he is concerned to praise and not merely to parody. There is nothing he likes better than telling the reader to read books that are not his own books; as when the Nun's Priest expansively refers the company to the numerous works dealing with the subject of Woman, which excuse him from justifying the sentiments of a cock or further analysing the defects of a hen. Perhaps, by the way, there is a Chaucerian joke, of the sort that is called sly, in making the Confessor of the Nuns (of all men) say that he, for his part, knows no harm about any woman. It is the same in any number of passages, as in that admirably cheerful passage that begins:

> A thousand timës have heard men tell
> That there is joy in heaven and pain in hell,
> And I accord right well that it is so,
> And yet indeed full well myself I know
> That there is not a man in this countrie
> That either has in heaven or hell y'be,

and which goes on to explain that these things rest on Authority; and that we must depend on Authority for many things, especially the things of which we can only read in books. It is typical of the obtusity of some partisans that this passage has been quoted as evidence of scepticism, when it is in perfectly plain words a justification of faith. But the point is that Chaucer talks in that cheerful voice, or writes in that almost jaunty style, because he is not in the least ashamed of depending on 'oldë bookës', but exceedingly proud of it, and, above all, exceedingly pleased to testify to his own pleasure. This is a temper which will always seem 'unoriginal' to the sensational sectarian; or the quack with a new nostrum; or the monomaniac with one idea. Yet, as a fact of literary history, Chaucer was one of the most original men who ever lived. There had never been anything like the lively realism of the ride to Canterbury done or dreamed of in our literature before. He is not only the father of all our poets, but the grandfather of all our hundred million novelists. It is rather a responsibility for him. But anyhow, nothing can be more original than an origin.

When we have this actual originality, and then added to it this graceful tone of gratitude and even humility, we have the presence of something which I will venture to call great. There is in the medieval poet something that can only be conveyed by the medieval word Largesse; that he is too hearty and expansive to conceal the connexion between himself and his masters or models. He would not stoop to ignore a book in order to borrow from it; and it does not occur to him to be always trying to secure the copyright of a copy. This is the sort of cool and contented character that looks much less original than it is. A man must have a balance of rather extraordinary talents, and even rather extraordinary virtues, in order to seem so ordinary. As they say of St. Peter's at Rome, it is so well proportioned that it looks almost small. To the eyes of sensational innovators, with their skyscraper religions toppling and tumbling, and conspicuous by their crazy disproportion, it does look very small. But it is in fact very large; and there is nothing larger in its way than the spirit of Chaucer, with its confession of pleasure and its unconsciousness of power.

May I be pardoned if I insert a sort of personal parenthesis here? All this does not mean, what I should be the last man in the world to mean, that revolutionists should be ashamed of being revolutionists or (still more disgusting thoughts) that artists should be content with being artists. I have been mixed up more or less all my life in such mild revolutions as my country could provide; and have been rather more extreme, for instance, in my criticism of Capitalism than many who are accused of Communism. That, I think, is being a good citizen; but it is not being a great poet; and I should never set up to be a great poet on any ground, but least of all on that ground. A great poet as such deals with eternal things; and it would indeed be a filthy notion to suppose that the present industrial and economic system is an eternal thing. Nor, on the other hand, should the idea of the poet dealing with things more permanent than politics be confounded with the dirty talk of the 'nineties, about the poet being indifferent to morals. Morals are eternal things, though the particular political immorality of the moment is not eternal. Here again I can modestly claim to have cleared myself long ago of the horrid charge of being a True Artist. I have been mixed up in politics, but never in aesthetics; and I was an enthusiast for the Wearing of the Green, but never for the Wearing of the Green Carnation. In those days I even had something like a prejudice against pure Beauty; there seemed to be very much the wrong sort of betrothal between Beauty and the Beast. But, for all that, it is true that the true poet is ultimately dedicated to Beauty, in a world where it is cleansed of beastliness, and it is not either a new scheme or theory on the one hand, nor a narrow taste or technique on the other. It is concerned with ideas; but with ideas that are never new in the sense of neat, as they are never old in the sense of exhausted. They lie a little too deep to find perfect expression in any age; and great poets can give great hints of them in any. I would say no more of Chaucer than that the hints that he gave were great.

There is at the back of all our lives an abyss of light, more blinding and unfathomable than any abyss of darkness; and it is the abyss of actuality, of existence, of the fact that things truly are, and that we ourselves are incredibly and sometimes almost incredulously real. It is the fundamental fact of being, as against not being; it is unthinkable, yet we cannot unthink it, though we may sometimes be unthinking about it; unthinking and especially unthanking. For he who has realized this reality knows that it does outweigh, literally to infinity, all lesser regrets or arguments for negation, and that under all our grumblings there is a subconscious substance of gratitude. That light of the positive is the business of the poets, because they see all things in the light of it more than do other men. Chaucer was a child of light and not merely of twilight, the mere red twilight of one passing dawn of revolution, or the grey twilight of one dying day of social decline. He was the immediate heir of something like what Catholics call the Primitive Revelation; that glimpse that was given of the world when God saw that it was good; and so long as the artist gives us glimpses of that, it matters nothing that they are fragmentary or even trivial; whether it be in the mere fact that a medieval Court poet could appreciate a daisy, or that he could write, in a sort of flash of blinding moonshine, of the lover who 'slept no more than does the nightingale'. These things belong to the same world of wonder as the primary wonder at the very existence of the world; higher than any common pros and cons, or likes and dislikes, however legitimate. Creation was the greatest of all Revolutions. It was for that, as the ancient poet said, that the morning stars sang together; and the most modern poets, like the medieval poets, may descend very far from that height of realization and stray and stumble and seem distraught; but we shall know them for the Sons of God, when they are still shouting for joy. This is something much more mystical and absolute than any modern thing that is called optimism; for it is only rarely that we realize, like a vision of the heavens filled with a chorus of giants, the primeval duty of Praise.

II

THE AGE OF CHAUCER

One of the most necessary and most neglected points, about the story called history, is the fact that the story is not finished. Generally speaking, we do not realize a problem of the past till we realize it as a problem of the present, and even of the future. This is what was really the matter with the 'liberal' historians of the nineteenth century. No men talked more about the future, as something different from the past. No men thought less about the future, as something different from the present. The Victorians are somewhat excessively derided to-day, because their notion of a novel was a story that ended well. The real vice of the Victorians was that they regarded history as a story that ended well—because it ended with the Victorians. They turned all human records into one three-volume novel; and were quite sure that they themselves were the third volume. History had come to an end; if not to a cessation, at least to a consummation. Therefore their doubts about the past were easily resolved, because they were not really troubled by doubts about the future. Whatever had obviously led to their own Constitutionalism or Commercialism was good. They did not really ask to what their Constitutionalism and Commercialism would lead. We, on the other hand, know where they have already led. They have led us to where we are at present; and where that is, the Lord only knows.

There are four facts about Chaucer, which are the four corners of the world he lived in; the four conditions of Christendom at the end of the fourteenth century. In themselves they can be stated very simply. Chaucer was English; at a time when the full national identity was still near its beginning. Chaucer was Catholic; at a time when the full Catholic unity of Europe was near the beginning of its end. Chaucer was chivalric, in the sense that he belonged, if only by adoption, to the world of chivalry and armorial blazonry, broadly French, when that world was in its gorgeous autumn, glorious with decay. Finally, Chaucer was non the less *bourgeois,* as our dear comrades say, in the sense that he himself was born and bred of burgesses, of tradesmen working under the old Guild system, also already rather too grand for its own good, but fresher and stonger than the fading feudal system. His figure bestrides the gap between these two last systems. It is as if he had the Trade Guild for a mother and the Order of Knighthood for a father.

Now we cannot understand any of these things by dismissing them as dead things, as the nineteenth century did, and never thinking of their application to our own present or future. We cannot, like the Victorians, talk about them as if they were stone hatchets or wattle houses; things obviously left behind in the past. They are no longer only in the past but also in the future; if not as possibilities at least as comparisons. Take the first two together; for they were parts of one problem. If we think (and rightly) that Rome did not adequately realize the growth of national life in the north, we must still follow the idea further; at least as far as the time when patriotism turned into Prussianism.[10] Quite apart from religion, we must realize that there was a case, and may again be a case for Europe having a centre. And we must anticipate, in the future, many pathetic attempts of Europe to be centralized without a centre. It is the same with the two last as with the two first of the four conditions. We may reasonably or even rightly think that society was fettered by feudal heraldry; but we must understand exactly what we lost by losing it. Similarly, we may think that trade was fettered by Guilds; but our own trade is not so happy just now that we can forget the Guild, without understanding exactly what we lost by losing it. Touching all these things, we must try to imagine, not so much merely what is to be said for them, as what is to be said against the absence of them.

I have therefore decided, after some doubt and reflexion, to dwell a little further on each of these four conditions; to dwell at what some may think disproportionate length on the real reason for their presence in those days, and the real problem of their absence in these days. All are subject to one formula. We have not seen the last of any of them, but if they are really lost in the future, it may yet turn

---

[10] Prussianism is the policy of advocating strong militarism, authoritarian or rigid control, typical of the practices and policies of Prussia.

out to be through losing the forms they had in the past. I will preface these four brief sketches by two generalizations. The great medieval civilization had already been wounded, perhaps mortally wounded, by two great griefs; the first material and the other moral. The first was the Black Death, which turned Christendom into a house of mourning, and had dreadful results of every kind; the worst being that priests became so few, and bad priests had so easily become priests, that the whole great Christian philosophy and morality was brought into contempt. The second fatality, I think was the failure of the Crusades which remained as a sort of hopeless taunt or challenge never accepted. Half the men of Chaucer's time were haunted by the Crusade that never happened. His friend Froissart tells how Bruce[11] sent his heart to Palestine, whither he had failed to go; his patron Henry of Bolingbroke consoled himself by dying in the Jerusalem Chamber after his failure to go to Jerusalem. As will be seen in a moment, in more ways than one, the Crusade was a sort of dark background of judgement to all the bright and brittle triumphs and scandals of that day.

First, the special spirit of Chaucer as an Englishman I have dealt with at length in the chapter under that name. It is only necessary to note here one fact that was really peculiar to England, which, unlike the Church and Chivalric Orders and the Guilds, was not common to all Europe. This was the particular break in the history of the Plantagenents. By the time England had ceased to be a King and his people, and had become a group of gentlemen and their servants. It is but a bitter consolation to call them the best gentlemen and the best servants. Everywhere else, whatever was lost by the Pope was gained by the King. Sometimes it happened even though the King were a Catholic King. The French King had already made a monopoly of the Papacy; the Spanish King was later to attempt to make a sort of monopoly of the Church; and even the English King did, for a brief and brazen hour of triumph, become Head of the Church. But whatever happened to the English King, this was not what happened to the English nation. There another and special force was already at work, which was destined to make the triumph of the King

---

[11] Robert I the Bruce was King of Scotland from 1306 to 1329. He raised arms against England for Scottish independence. After much fighting England finally recognized Scotland's sovereignty in the Treaty of Northampton (1328).

THE AGE OF CHAUCER

as brief as it was brazen. That fact was the evolution of the Aristocratic State, which begins far back in Chaucer's time and before; chiefly by an alliance between the Barons and the great merchants of the City of London. It thus touches the life of Chaucer at two points, since his people were London traders and his patrons were, at least partly, of the baronial party. It was also mixed up with the problem of the peasants, or those who regarded themselves as peasant proprietors, while the lawyers still regarded them as serfs. They therefore rose in the famous Peasant Rising and killed the lawyers; a comprehensible and (relatively) even commendable course; though they also showed some disposition to hang anybody who could read or write; which is perhaps carrying the distrust of professionalism too far. But with all this Chaucer had less to do, being a Londoner and, on his more popular side, a son of the Guilds and not the peasantry. Nevertheless, it was at the Court, where he counted for a good deal, that the whole quarrel of kings, barons, merchants and peasants came to a crisis and a crash.

The life and death of Richard the Second constitute a tragedy which was perhaps the tragedy of English history, and was certainly the tragedy of English monarchy. It is seldom seen with any clearness; because of two prejudices that prevent men letting in on it the disinterested daylight of their minds. The first is the fact that, though it happened more than five hundred years ago, it is still dimly felt to be a Party Question. Shakespeare, in the time of the Tudors, saw it as an opportunity for exalting a sort of Divine Right; later writers, in the time of the Georges, have seen in it an opportunity for depreciating Divine Right. What is much more curious is the fact that neither ever noticed that the unfortunate Richard did not by any means merely stand for Divine Right; that in his earliest days he stood for what we are accustomed to consider much later rights, and for some which were, at least relatively speaking, the rights of democracy. The origin of this oblivion is in the second of the two modern prejudices. It is the extraordinary prejudice, sometimes identified with progress, to the effect that the world has always been growing more and more liberal, and that therefore there could be no popular ideals present in earlier times and forgotten in later times. The case of Richard the Second might have been specially staged in order to destroy this delusion. He was very far from being a faultless sovereign; he did various things which permit modern Parliamentarians to represent him as a despotic sovereign; but he was, by comparison with many contemporaries and most successors, a democratic sovereign. He did definitely attempt to help the democratic movement of his day, and he was definitely restrained from doing so. Shakespeare is full of sympathy for him, but Shakespeare was not full of sympathy for what most modern people would find sympathetic. He does not even mention the fact that the prince, whom he represents as bewailing the insult to his crown, and appealing to the sacred immunity of his chrism, had in his youth faced a rabble of roaring insurgent serfs, had declared that he himself would be their leader, the true demagogue of their new democracy, had promised to grant their demands, had disputed desperately with his nobles to get those demands granted, and had finally been overruled and forced to abandon the popular cause by that very baronial insolence which soon forced him to abandon the throne. If we ask why the greatest of dramatists was blind to the most dramatic of historic scenes, the young king claiming the leadership of the oppressed people, the explanation is perfectly simple. The explanation is that the whole theory, that 'the thoughts of men are widen'd with the process of the suns', is all ignorant rubbish.

How could the suns widen anybody's thoughts? The explanation is that the men of Shakespeare's time understood far less of the democratic ideal than the men of Chaucer's time. The Tudors were occupied in their own time, as Shakespeare is occupied in his great play, with the sixteenth-century mystical worship of The Prince. There was much more chance in the fourteenth century of having a mystical feeling about The People. Shakepeare's Richard is religious, to the extent of always calling himself The Lord's Anointed. The real Richard would also, very probably, have referred to the people as God's Flock. Ideas were mixed and misused in both periods, as in all periods; but in the time of Chaucer and Langland there was much more vague and general moral pressure upon the mind of the presence of problems of mere wealth and poverty, of the status of a peasant or the standards of a Christian, than there was in the time of Shakespeare and Spenser; of the splendour of Gloriana[12] and the

---

[12] Gloriana, representing Elizabeth I, was the Queen of Faeryland in Spenser's *The Faerie Queene*.

Imperial Votaress[13] in the West. Therefore Shakespeare, great and human as he was, sees in Richard only the insulted king; and seems to think almost as little about the subjects of Richard as about the subjects of Lear.

But Richard had thought about the subjects of Richard. He had, in his early days and in his own way, tried to be a popular king in the sense of a popular leader. And though the popular ideas failed, and in some cases were bound to fail, they would have been much more present to the mind of a great writer of that time, than they were to the mind of one of the Queen's Servants under the last of the Tudors. In other words, even when there really is progress, as there certainly is growth, the progress is not a progress in everything, perfectly simple and universal and all of a piece. Civilizations go forward in some things, while they go backward in others. Men had better looms and steam hammers in 1850 than in 1750, but not handsomer hats and breeches or more dignified manners and oratory. And in the same way a man in the position of Shakespeare had more subtle and many-coloured arts, but not more simple and popular sympathies, than a man in the position of Langland. The Renaissance exalted the Poet, but even more it exalted the Prince; it was not primarily thinking about the Peasant. Therefore the greatest of all the great sons of the Renaissance, rolling out thousands of thunderous and intoxicant lines upon the single subject of the reign of King Richard the Second, does not trouble himself about The Peasants' War.

The real stories of this world are not melodramas or fables with a moral, and we seldom see simple retribution for a simple crime or even simple martyrdom for a simple idea. Nobody maintains that Richard was dethroned on the direct issue of the frustrated popular sympathies of his youth; he was dethroned for the somewhat simpler reason that he had an unscrupulous relative who wanted his throne. Nor need anyone maintain that there were no other excuses for the dethronement; though almost certainly there was no other motive. But the fact remains that there did disappear, with the last true Plantagenet, the last true attempt of the monarch to take the side of the mob against the governing class; and it is certain that since that day,

---

[13] The Imperial Votaress of the West is a reference to Queen Elizabeth I.

and for centuries increasingly, the mob in England has been impotent and the governing class has governed. A profound instinct told our modern historians that with the quarrel of Richard and Bolingbroke the true Party System had begun. They might be more or less indifferent to York and Lancaster, and admit that the tangle and thicket of the Wars of the Roses mostly consisted of thorns. But the long quarrel of English history was not between the Lancastrians and the Yorkists, but between the Lords and the King. Long before we were born the Lords had completely conquered; and the historian could at least see that the first blow was struck at Pomfret, three hundred years before the last blow was struck at Whitehall.

Here is the first typical instance; showing that medieval history is useless unless it is modern history. The problem has remained; anyhow it has returned. The general view of government by a gentry, even in its best sense, must be affected by the present problem of whether it ought to continue; whether it can continue; whether a thing so undefined and atmospheric can be restored. It is not at all impossible that the age following Maurras and Mussolini may want Monarchy restored. It is one thing to tolerate the rich because they are gentlemen; and another to tolerate the bounders because they are rich. The lastest phase of the thing may be seen in what is called the Public School tradition; the final outcome of the fact that medieval schools dedicated to poverty or pure learning were turned, after the Reformation, into the fenced training-camps of a governing class. The paradox of such a system, at this moment, is that it might really be easier to revive it as a medieval Public School than as a modern Public School. Anyhow, anybody can see that such associations are at the very instant of transition. The finest of Public School songs unconsciously confesses that even gazing at the past involves gazing at the future; and few will claim to know what will happen to that tradition, twenty or thirty or forty years on.

Next, as to the religious position: put these four facts together. Chaucer was a perfectly orthodox Catholic, and the English had hitherto been little interested in the old medieval heresies. But to them the Pope had begun to seem faintly foreign; *not* on the theory that he was an Italian priest in Rome, but, on the contrary, on the theory that he was a French priest at Avignon. The French King had carried the Papacy there; challenging the Schism and almost dragging it into the French Wars. The Papacy stood, of course, for the international ideal; but it stood for two other things, good or bad. First, for the Friars and such international movements which depended *only* on the Papacy. Second, for more dubious 'drives' of the Charity Bazaar sort; not always producing (or receiving) perfect charity. Lastly, there was a general discontent with the *practical* Christianity of the time; producing Lollards,[14] the most practical (and therefore the most stupid) of heretics. But most men were Reformers without being Lollards.

Most wanted what was called 'a reform of the Head and Members'. Unfortunately too many, even at the later reforming councils of Basle and Constance, confined themselves rather to reforming the Head; because of the special horror of the two-headed monster of the Schism. It is by no means certain, however, that the Head was worse than the Members.

It is the paradox of history that the Pope was really more important after the Reformation than before it. He was always important to Catholics, of course, as the tribunal of truth in disputed matters; but as a political and social figure, he really bulks bigger in the modern world than he did in the medieval world; at least in the later medieval world. The reason for this is really very reasonable. His personal position had been diminished by division and rivalry. But his doctrinal position was rather more clearly defined after it had been defied. In the scandal of the Schism there had been two or even three Popes; whom various nations accepted. But in the supreme struggle of the Reformation there was only one Pope; even if he was one whom nations renounced. The proceedings of the Protestant nations who renounced him made it quite clear, for the first time, why the earlier nations had accepted him. Whoever was right or wrong in the quarrel, it became perfectly clear that those who quarrelled with

---

[14] The Lollards were members of a fourteenth century English movement associated with John Wycliff. They demanded ecclesiastical reform. Lollards travelled preaching that the Bible was the primary source of belief. Many of their ideas were influential as a basis for the Protestant Reformation.

the Pope began to quarrel with the Creed. There had been no hint of that sort of thing in the rather squalid squabble of the rival Popes of the Middle Ages. The Popes might make each other look foolish, or denounce each other as fools; but they did not denounce the Faith as folly. Nobody who attacked the Pope attacked the Papacy. Still less did anybody attack the Papacy in the sense of attacking the Church. Thousands of Christians were shocked and pained at the mere fact that a false Pope could put himself up against a real Pope. But they would not have been shocked, but startled out of their wits, if one of the Popes had stood up and said there was no such thing as Purgatory. They would not have felt pain, they would have felt mortal terror at a world gone mad, if a Pope had told another Pope to leave off talking nonsense about prayers for the dead or praise of the Blessed Virgin. When the nations that had broken away from the Papacy did begin to say things like this, an entirely new sort of importance began to attach to the Papacy from which they had broken away. Even the people who said these things could see that fact. They could see that the Pope was now the power who held a whole moral and metaphysical system together; as they themselves had proved, by parting with him in order to found a new moral and metaphysical system. But in the later Middle Ages, before the break had come in actual ecclesiastical government, the whole situation was much more vague and dim. People knew that the Pope was a part of the system; but the system was so solid and universal that they hardly thought that anything was needed to be the protector of the system. We must not look therefore to men in the age of Chaucer for any of that sharp partisanship, any more than that sharp antagonism, which afterwards came to clash over the position of the Roman Pontiff. A man like Chaucer would most certainly have been a furious Papist, if he had thought that the alternative was to be a Puritan. But he lived in a world which had not yet even seen a real Puritan. In that world, in that sense, and in that sense alone, we may say that such a man felt himself rather as a Catholic than as a Papist. He had no notion of what results would follow a real split in Christendom; for since the beginnings of such a split had been stopped by St. Dominic, in the Albigensian affair, there had never been anything to suggest such a catastrophe to such a Catholic layman. But the Catholic layman, especially the good Catholic layman, was very far from happy. He knew that things were going wrong; he knew that the Church ought to put them right; but he did not look at the Pope to put them right precisely as a Catholic would look to-day: and that all the less, in Chaucer's case, because the Pope was a prisoner of the French King — as Chaucer had been; the prisoner of an enemy.

Meanwhile, however, the Pope had long appeared to Europe in another aspect that had nothing to do with his theological authority, but which was destined more than any other accident to precipitate the disaster. He wanted to collect money for various objects; many of them normal, some of them rather of the Renaissance type of ambition; like that which was destined later on to bring about the break in Germany: the building of St. Peter's. The trouble was not so much what he was doing as the way in which the thing was done. The shortest way of describing it is to say, in modern language, that the Papacy condescended to employ up-to-date methods of Advertisement. It put its trust in people who professed to be a sort of Publicity Experts. In the religious atmosphere of the time, it took the form of going about delivering ranting sermons about the Indulgences attached to works of piety and charity; and then sending round the hat in the usual rather vulgar fashion. But the trouble with these men, as with many Publicity Experts, was that there was nothing pious or charitable about *them*. They were only expert — and vulgar. It constantly happens, even now, when good people are so silly as to trust merely capable people. These hustling advertising agents dragged religion in the mire; but they got the money. But the root of the whole evil was there. It was that they had not been chosen as priests or preachers, not even as fanatical priests or preachers, but as what the Americans would call live wires and go-getters. These in turn doubtless produced a rabble of imitators of yet more ragged reputation, touts and cheapjacks entirely irresponsible, but familiarizing everybody with the idea of making the Faith a stunt or (worse still) a business proposition. The contempt that normal Catholics felt for all this is written in red-hot letters in Chaucer's account of the Pardoner.

When Chaucer says, in his vivid way, that the Pardoner had pardon 'brought from Rome all hot', he means what moderns call Hustle. But during part of this period, there was another problem. Rome was not always situated in Rome. The Pope of Avignon was rather unfairly regarded as a Frenchman because he was a prisoner of the French. Often, of course, he was a Frenchman—for the same reason. Chaucer's great contemporary Petrarch felt the scandal, though not from the English standpoint, like Chaucer. Petrarch also had his quarrel with the 'French' Popes. He was perhaps most famous, after his love for Laura,[15] for his lamentations over Babylon; which was his polite name for the city of Avignon, the French exile of the Roman Pontiffs. Critics are beginning to be rather more reasonable in discriminating, if not discrediting, the religious denunciations of particular partisans in the Middle Ages. We should allow for the fact that Petrarch was a little partial to Laura; and we may well allow that he was not entirely impartial about Avignon. The time has gone by when any poet denouncing any Pope was assumed to have the gift of Infallibility. Something may be discounted in the invectives of Dante; more in the invectives of Petrarch; and something (which concerns us more closely here) in the invectives of Chaucer, not indeed against any Pope or Anti-Pope, but against certain religious groups or parties which were really, though only relatively, connected with the Papacy.

It is a commonplace that Chaucer makes fun of the Friar. Chaucer makes fun of so many people, that I always doubted whether we could lean so heavily as the learned do on the political or partisan significance of his satire. Still it may well be that, like Langland, he was of the party opposed to the Friars, probably because his sympathies were with the ordinary village priests. What is not so fully understood is that this question also was indirectly connected with the undercurrent of quarrel about the Popes. Men criticized the Roman officialism in many matters in which it was really wrong. But it is typical of its history that it was even then criticized, more severely, for an attitude in which it was right. It is impracticable to discuss

---

[15] Laura was the love of Petrarch and the subject of his collection of sonnets called *Rimes* or *Canzoniere*.

fully here the merits of the quarrel about the Friars. There is a merely traditional anecdote that Chaucer, in early youth, was fined for fighting with a friar and knocking him about in Fleet Street. There is no historical proof of it; but, if it were true, it would be possible that his aversion to the friar in the story was as personal and accidental as his aversion to the friar in the street. Shakespeare is admitted to have been very fond of friars, even by those who regard him as an emancipated Englishman of the Elizabethan settlement. Chaucer is recognized as having uttered very violent and outspoken criticism of friars, even by those who regard him as the slave of a superstition that silences every criticism. It is perfectly possible that there were merely personal affections or aversions in both cases; and it is as likely that Chaucer was wrong as that Shakespeare was right. But many of the learned have thrown themselves into the quarrel with all the fury of Chaucer attacking the friar in Fleet Street; and have done their best to reproduce the edifying quarrel of the Frere and the Sompnour, in the interests of England or of Rome. As I say, these large historical matters cannot be adequately considered here. But in so far as we do consider them, it had better be upon principles that are really historical and really large.

The Sompnour, or Summoner, is an official of the ecclesiastical court, and he stands in this story for the ecclesiastical authorities actually ruling England, from the Archbishop of Canterbury downwards. The Frere, or Friar, stands for the Dominican and Franciscan Orders, of preaching and begging brethren, who claimed freedom from local jurisdictions and appealed direct to the Pope. It is always assumed that Chaucer was entirely on the side of the former, mainly because he makes a more or less amusing figure of the Friar. The argument might well be turned the other way; for he makes a most horrifying and revolting figure of the Summoner. Many a man would prefer to be satirized as the Friar, with his popularity and athletic prowess, his strong white neck and eyes twinkling like frosty stars, rather than to be championed in the person of the Summoner with his red eruptive visage, and pimples and rank onion-laden breath. If Chaucer really was championing the Church authorities of England against foreign friars, he seems to have chosen a queer sort of champion. But I have myself a dark suspicion that Chaucer was writing a poem, and especially telling a story; and that to him as an artist the vivid and coloured figures of the Summoner and the Friar were of much more importance than the interests they represented in ecclesiastical law. Nevertheless, as I have said, it is well to see the ecclesiastical and social situation in the large, if we see it at all. There were two sides to the dispute between the Friars and the national or parochial clergy, and there is one side that is almost entirely neglected and never certainly emphasized.

It will be found again and again, in ecclesiastical history, that the new departure, the daring innovation, the progressive party, depended directly on the Pope. It was naturally more or less negatively resisted by the bishops, the canons, the clergy in possession under political and patriotic settlements. Official oligarchies of that sort generally do resist reform and experiment, either rightly or wrongly. It is no more peculiar to Catholics than to an Anglican Archdeacon talking about Bolshevism or a Baptist in Tennessee talking about Negro Education. But whenever there appeared, in Catholic history, a new and promising experiment, bolder or broader or more enlightened than existing routine, that movement always came to be identified with the Papacy; because the Papacy alone upheld it against the resisting social medium which it rent asunder. So, in the present case, it was really the Pope who upheld St. Francis and the popular movement of the Friars. So, in the sixteenth century, it was really the Pope who upheld St. Ignatius Loyola and the great educational movement of the Jesuits. The Pope, being the ultimate court of appeal, cannot for shame be a mere expression of any local prejudice; this may easily be strong among local ecclesiastics, without any evil intention; but the remote arbiter at Rome must make some attempt to keep himself clear of it. Thus arises the situation of which Chaucer very possibly complained, of which many in Chaucer's time certainly complained; that a particular set of men, more recent or less rooted than the parish clergy, talked as if they were the Pope's pet children, and need take no notice of anybody but him. Anybody can see that this could be an irritating attitude; but there were two sides to the question. The Friars or the Jesuits were partly irritating because they were innovating, and in many matters, especially at the beginning, improving. And the Pope often supported the improvement, because he alone was independent and strong enough to do so. The Pope was often very much in advance of the Church, as the Encyclical on Labour of Pope Leo XIII would have been very much in advance of many reactionary bishops and priests of his time. Protestants will not damage their Protestantism by understanding that for Catholics, in history, the Pope is a *leader* as well as a ruler.

By the time of Chaucer, indeed, it is likely enough that the movement of Dominic and Francis had passed its best period; and that the popular Friars were sometimes unpopular, with the people as well as the priests. It is quite probable; but the poet's personal jokes against friars do not prove it. Chaucer was no more certainly justified in abusing the friars in poetry than in belabouring the friar in Fleet Street; in both cases we should need to know a little more of the facts; a little more about the friars—and the friar. But it is worth while to note that Rome had originally supported an innovation in supporting the Friar; as later a less worthy innovation in supporting the Pardoner. Both came from Rome being in the centre of civilization and readier for new notions than the provinces were. If this was so about ideas that really were new, like those of St. Francis, it is the more obvious about ideas like the unity of nations, that never were new—except to very new people.

The international ideal, which seems so very modern to the moderns, was of course very ancient to the Popes. They had originally risen in a cosmopolitan community, covering the civilized world, and their real mistake was that they thought the world was more international than it was. But this is not a mistake of barbaric bigotry; it rather amounted to thinking the world more enlightened than it was. Anyhow, the misunderstanding between the national and international ideas had begun long before; even in the time of the English discontent about Peter's Pence. France, the first of the entirely national nations, had been responsible for the prolonged insult of Avignon. The monstrous progeny of Anti-Popes had been born largely out of the readiness of rival kingdoms to back rival Pontiffs. The nations, for good or evil, were becoming themselves;

and it would doubtless have been better if the Popes had understood the process. But it is far from self-evident that the process was entirely what we now call a progress.

In any case, we have seen that the Church was heavily weakened by these three calamities. The Black Death which decimated the priesthood, leaving hardly enough priests to go round and admitting a good many who had much better not have gone round. The captivity of the Pope, who seemed to be in the pocket of the French King, and was defied by other Popes supported by other kings. And the uneasy conscience and general depression following on the failure of the Crusade. In this spiritual desert it was natural that there should appear prophets, whether we call them fanatics or reformers; and to some extent at least they were supported by a general discontent. It is very difficult to be fair to them to-day; because their ghosts have been set to lead armies that they never led, and would probably have refused to lead. Anybody who was born within three hundred years either way, of the one great crack or explosion of the sixteenth century, is dragged out of his grave to demonstrate as a Protestant or Papist, and carry a banner in a triumph of St. Bartholomew or the Boyne[16]. Men like Wycliffe, living in Chaucer's time, had no notion of such things. They probably began by feeling a quite comprehensible sympathy with the hard-worked village priests, as against the monks, whose life should mean contemplation, and often did mean contemplation, but obviously might mean idleness. Whenever it really meant contemplation, it meant incessant activity. Generations before, the Friars had thus rebelled against the Monks; now a new school of Simple Preachers was rebelling against the Friars. But for events utterly different in origin, the Simple Preachers might have been absorbed by Christendom like the Friars—and later had the honour of being denounced as decadent like the Friars. But there was another difference: and it did arise partly from the operation of a very ordinary human weakness.

Some historical critics seem to express a faint surprise that a number of people were sympathetic with Wycliffe up to a certain point,

[16] The Boyne was a battle in 1690 in Ireland in which King William III defeated the forces supporting the deposed James II.

and then lost their sympathy with him. There is supposed to be a vague savour of this in a whole group, which included a gentleman named Chaucer (with whom we are more immediately concerned); another literary man like Langland; a great lord like John of Gaunt; possibly even a King like Richard the Second. Various explanations have been offered of this change or chill in their relations to the reformers. John of Gaunt was one of those rather dangerous aristocrats who have too much activity for their intelligence; and, being rather stupid, probably prided himself on being broadminded. It is said that he felt a faint coolness creeping over his sympathy with the New Movement, when the peasants in revolt took particular care to burn down his own palace. Reasons far less reasonable have been alleged for the fine distinction which others drew between Wycliffe the reformer and Wycliffe the theologian. Many explanations are indeed possible; but I would timidly suggest this possibility; that men like Chaucer and Langland may have supported Wycliffe to some extent in practice, and then repudiated him more completely in theory, for a particular reason of their own. The reason was (odd as it will sound in modern ears) that they supported him when he was right and repudiated him when he was wrong.

Wycliffe was only one example of a man who yeilds to a temptation, which few reformers have been sufficiently clear-headed to resist. He became so irritated with the fact that the Idea was badly carried out in practice, that at last he was weak enough to turn and attack the Idea in theory. The Idea that God gives Himself to mankind in the Blessed Sacrament has nothing to do with the fact that some particular priests are fools or knaves or ignorant or incompetent for their office. Wycliffe began by objecting to the latter condition, to which Chaucer and Langland, and probably John of Gaunt, equally and rightly objected. But there is here some haunting temptation which perpetually betrays reformers. It betrays the reformers of modern as of medieval times. It is as applicable to the idea of property as to the idea of priesthood; to the Married State as to the Mass. In a dark hour, poor Wycliffe seems to have tried, though vaguely, to apply it to the Mass. Therefore we find him splitting hairs about Transubstantiation, which was much less logical than splitting heads with bills and axis, like the sane though savage peasants. The logical, or rather illogical, process is perfectly simple and perfectly familiar. A man sets out to distribute Milk to mothers or families or the whole community. He very soon discovers that distribution is not so easy as it looks. Before long he is perfectly familiar with the fact of people intercepting milk, stealing milk, making a corner in milk, adulterating milk, poisoning milk. He is very naturally in a rage, which verges on a revolutionary rage; nor is he wrong in proposing even precipitate and violent action against those who swindle about milk or poison milk. But there always comes a time when he is tempted to turn, in a towering passion and say, 'There shall be no Milk.' That is what happened at the Reformation. That is what happens in nearly every revolution. That is why modern revolutionists want to destroy the household because of the housing shortage; or abolish private property because most people have not got enough of it.

There is therefore nothing to be deduced from the fact, if it be a fact, that Chaucer sympathized with the Wycliffites in matters of discipline, but abjured them in matters of doctrine, except the fact (otherwise already familiar) that Chaucer had a clear head. But it has some relation to the general thesis of this book; that he also had a clear philosophy. That philosophy was a Christian philosophy, and all the more so because it had been mixed in the original Christian fashion with many Pagan influences. What is not sufficiently realized is that this Christian philosophy, even in the Middle Ages, could be and was a cool and well-balanced philosophy. The true meaning of the importance of Boethius has not been seen. There is a truth, perhaps unconscious, in Chaucer's use of the phrase about 'the feathers of philosophy'. His own touch was as light as a feather; but the feather came truly from an angel's wing.

It is the same with Chivalry: the long shadow falling on the fourteenth century from the Crusade. What we call militarism was almost unknown to medievalism. But that is partly because what we call militarism depends on most people being unmilitary. Medieval kings seldom possessed what was afterwards called a standing army; in the sense of a professional specialist army. Nevertheless, away at the back of all that was medieval was a sort of half-forgotten foundation which was military. This arose from two facts, far back in the beginning; first, that when Rome itself collapsed it left a number of garrisons and military outposts, to be the nuclei of national and local recovery; and second, that this world, when it began to recover, was suddenly invaded and almost vanquished by Islam; so that it could think of nothing but swords and spears for nearly a thousand years. One result was that the social *formation* remained military. The standing army soon became very standing-at-ease army, and later, so to speak, a sitting army or even a sleeping army. But the system of subordination and obedience had been originally military. European aristocracy was a military hierarchy; just as Indian aristocracy was a religious hierarchy. The Duke is the Commander-in-Chief; the Marquis is the Warden of the Marches; the Knight is the Cavalry soldier; the Squire is the shield-bearer, and so on. These local commands, mixed with the Pagan legacy of slavery and modified by the family sentiment of Christianity, had produced what we call the feudal system. As a whole, these local commands tended to gather round certain central commands, some eight or ten of them in Western Europe, which were called monarchies. But even in France, where the monarchy was most centralized, there had been a time when the great Dukes had been too strong for it; and in England the great Dukes overthrew it. Apart from this, however, a change had passed over all that chivalry and aristocracy; a change vividly visible in Chaucer's time, as compared with the time of its original beginnings in the Roman Camp or the early medieval Crusade.

The crucial phrase 'bearing arms' had begun to shift its emphasis from the notion of carrying weapons to the notion of carrying coats of arms. This is far from meaning that men did not fight. They fought in the wars between England and France in Chaucer's time. They fought even more in the wars between England and England just after Chaucer's time. But it might fairly be said that, where the first medieval men had fought for a cross or a creed, the later medieval men actually fought for a coat of arms. The French Wars were heraldic wars; fought upon a point of pedigree; ending in the quartering of the Leopards and the Lilies. The Wars of the Roses were heraldic wars; also fought upon a point of pedigree; ending characteristically in the Tudor Rose particoloured, parti-per-pale. But there was a collateral effect of all this, of which a word must be said, if we are to realize the peculiar rich autumnal atmosphere of the Chaucerian epoch. There went side by side with the exaggeration of heraldry, an exaggeration of costume; a fantasy in coats as well as in coats of arms. The figures of the lords standing round the long sunset of the splendour of Edward the Third, the lords who were to rebel against his heir, have indeed something of the burning but decaying colour of the sunset clouds. There is doubtless something ominous and unnatural, especially in the lurid light of later disasters, about those toppling headdresses, those sleeves slashed into points like plumes, those crazily curling shoes; like the outlines of prehistoric birds of fabulous beasts rather than men. Nevertheless, there was another side to the matter, and if we are to understand Chaucer, we must try to sympathize with something that is behind such heraldry, and even such fantasy; something that was universally taken for granted in the fourteenth century; something that has been almost entirely forgotten by the twentieth.

I have remarked elsewhere on a common saying; supposed to be shrewd and realistic and rational; actually shallow and ignorant and totally false. I mean the statement that modern people think modern dress ugly, only because all people have always thought contemporary dress ugly. If I find less than perfect loveliness in a billy cock hat, it is insisted that Garrick[17] thought the same about a three-cornered hat; that Van Dyck[18] thought the same about a Van Dyck hat; and Chaucer the same about a hood. It is enough to answer that Garrick did not think it odd to act Roman or Romantic heroes in his own clothes; that Van Dyck *did* think the Van Dyck costume beautiful, as anybody can tell to whom paint is plain like print; and that there is not a line or a word to suggest that Chaucer as a poet thought that there was anything particularly unpoetical about his own clothes. The truth is (as I have shown in another place) that nobody until the nineteenth century, and the ugly industrial revolution, ever *did* think that there was anything particularly unpoetical about his own clothes. All of them, without exception, would paint

---

[17] David Garrick (1717-79) was an English actor and manager of the Drury Lane Theatre.

[18] Sir Anthony Van Dyck (1599-1641) was a Flemish portrait painter.

the Twelve Apostles, or even the Greek gods, in what were for them modern clothes. We have thought our modern clothes ugly, simply because our modern clothes have been ugly; and it does credit to our taste. But the real point to grasp about the costume of another period, such as that of the later Middle Ages, is not so much aesthetic as moral. The ultimate justification of heraldry, even in its extravagant decline, lay in the fact that it was a sort of pattern or standard of significance, by which even slighter and more trivial things tended to be significant. And this fact was not a little helpful, to a humane and humorous writer, in the matter of really enjoying the costumes and customs of his own time.

This truth runs like an ornamental design through the whole of the Canterbury Pilgrimage, and especially the Prologue to the Pilgrimage. Sir Walter Scott was accused of antiquarian antics, when he dwelt on the details of badge or baldrick worn by the minor vassals of Marmion. He was accused of being pompously poetical about trifles, merely because they were the trifles of a previous age. But Chaucer has just as much pomp and poetry about the trifles of his own age. He has no difficulty in making poetry out of them, but it is only fair to say that they really are poetical. Everybody who has seen medieval pictures knows how beautiful and balanced a colour scheme can depend on those stiff attitudes or flat perspectives; and the Prologue is, among other things, a medieval picture of exactly that type. We can all see, as clearly as a child sees the figures in a toy theatre, the Yeoman in his green coat and hood and his great silver clasp of St. Christopher, and his quiver of arrows plumed with peacock-feathers; the Wife of Bath with her scarlet stockings and hat as large as a target; the Squire with his long sleeves powdered with a pattern of red and white flowers like a meadow, and hair curled close as in a press; the Shipman with his brown sunburnt face and his dagger hanging round his neck and armpit on a string, whose beard had been shaken in tempests from Hull to Carthage; the Franklin[19] with his sanguine complexion and beard white as a daisy, with his

---

[19] The Franklin was a well-to-do country man who, though of lower-class parentage, still was able to achieve importance in his area. He is one of the main pilgrim characters and is the teller of the "Franklin's Tale".

white silk pouch and prosperous philosophy of Epicurus; the Summoner with the gigantic garland on his head, which seems to give an additional frightfulness to his 'fire-red cherubim's face', of which children were frightened. All this description is in the true sense imaginative. But Chaucer was doing what a great poet does; he was imagining what he saw. Certainly there is no artistic suggestion of his despising what he was. I mean that, in the moral sense, he despised many of the vices of many of the characters; but he did not in an artistic sense despise their emblems and externals, as unsuited to serious art. Above all, he enjoyed them even more as emblems than as externals. And with that we encounter a medieval idea which students of Chaucer must consider with some sympathy, but which is seldom considered with even reasonable justice.

I for one should be the last to wish to see such things as Sumptuary Laws[20] restraining the liberty of the citizen. It is true that the men who suffered the old Sumptuary Laws would have thought their King had gone raving mad, if he had suddenly risen up and forbidden anybody to drink ale, as does the President of the modern American democracy. It is far more of an interference with liberty to veto a man's drink, which he consumes in his private house, than to limit the choice of his dress, in which he walks down the public street. Nevertheless, I should rejoice in being free alike from the medieval rules about dress and the modern rules about drink. Yet I doubt if there is any free-minded and imaginative man, looking at the modern world, who has not sometimes wished that there were some way of ordering the externals of life, so as to make them appropriate; and, above all, so as to make them expressive. The garments and attributes of the Canterbury Pilgrims are expressive. They express what the people are; they express what the poet means. It may be very dreadful that a Knight should bear arms (and we have the assurance of Mrs. Wiffle that

[20] The Sumptuary Laws date back to ancient Greek law, and were designed to regulate the habits of the citizens. Sumtuary Laws were also enacted during the reign of Edward II, with proclamation issued against the "outrageous and excessive multitude of meats and dishes which the great men of the Kingdom had used, and still used, in their castles".

this is the case); it may be very luxurious of the young Squire to have flowers embroidered all over his coat; and Chaucer is obviously chaffing him to some extent, upon his foppishness. But the arms do express the Knight and the flowers do express the Squire. When such flowers were dotted all over the flowered waistcoat of a fat stockbroker in 1860 who read *The Times* and talked about the danger of Puseyites[21] in the Protestant Church of England, the flowers did not express anything at all. They did not make us think that the stockbroker was like a flower; or even, in Chaucer's phrase, that he was like a meadow.

In short, if we ever did want Sumptuary laws, it would not be so much against waste of money as against waste of work; waste of art, waste of effect, waste of colour and design. It is not that we dislike colour, but that we should rather like a language of colours; not that we dislike design, but that we should like designs to appear by design, and not by accident. I confess, though I am as fond of the colour of life as another, I have sometimes had a weird complex of thoughts on seeing a dull dumpy woman, with an expressionless face, approaching me in a hat or coat of flaming crimson like a tremendous Turner[22] sunset. I feel inclined to ask her, as if she were at a masquerade ball, what she is meant to *be*. Perhaps I do her a wrong. Perhaps she glows within with so glorious a charity, that she has a right to robe herself as the Rose of the World. Perhaps she has merely brooded on burning wrongs till she is ready to set fire to London and burn it to ashes. That would be quite a reasonable explanation. But short of that, I have a sort of Sumptuary feeling, that it is a waste of red; a waste of blood and fire; a waste of the most glorious colour God has given to our eyes. Now when those red robes are hung on a Cardinal, or even on a soldier or a judge, they do have this extra glow or intensity of having a meaning. And that is because the custom which clothes such figures is inherited from the old system of symbolism; and that system of symbolism ran through the whole

---

[21] The Puseyites were followers of Edward Pusey (1800–1882), the Anglican theologian associated with J. H. Newman in the Oxford movement.

[22] Joseph Mallord William Turner (1775–1851) is an English painter famous for landscapes.

system of medievalism. Chaucer's coloured figures are all the more coloured, because their colours mean something, as do the colours of heraldry. But that system, of which heraldry was the stamp, is so remote from us that it is necessary to go through all this explanation and argument in order to begin to see what it meant to medieval men. There are different sorts of freedom and even of comfort. And there is such a thing as a coat that fits because it is fitting. A Friar feels freer in a Friar's gown; as a man feels freer in a man's body.

When once we realize that heraldry was not a mummery or even a mystery; but a meaning part of a passion for significance which made all colours, stones, planets, beasts and flowers emblematic to the medieval mind, we may go on to agree that heraldry badly wanted pruning by the time of Edward the Third. If the twelfth century was the medieval spring, and the thirteenth the medieval summer, the fourteenth was a sort of rank and overgrown autumn that was already menaced by the crooked and cruel fifteenth century; in the north at least, very truly, the 'winter of our discontent'. The costumes of the rich, which had already become fanciful, became utterly fantastic; and that with something that was already sinister as well as fantastic. Chaucer's Parson denounces the motley figures of contemporary fops, striped and cut up into patterns, by saying that they look as if they were blasted white or yellow or red by leprosies and loathsome plagues. It was not for nothing that the popular preachers denounced the horned and towering headdresses of great ladies as toppling travesties of the horns of Satan. It is true that the Court looked gay, and also true that there was already something ghastly about its gaiety. Its fine French dances had already something of the Dance of Death, and indeed the Black Death had already led the world a dance. It was in this world, in which the chivalric civilization of the fourteenth century was already passing into the cynicism of the fifteenth, that Geoffrey Chaucer had to live his life, in frequent contact with the Court and complete familiarity with the systems of heraldry and precedence. These things were, in the eyes of many of his contemporaries, by far the chief affairs of his time. They were to that age what Aviation, Breaking the World Record, Swimming the Atlantic, or any use of science for the purpose of speed, are to ours. Some followed them with an excitement quite superficial; others saw them as more or less significant; but they filled the landscape, as Push and Publicity now fill the land and sea and sky. It is only fair to remember that to this period belong many really graceful and worthy stories of dignity and delicacy of behaviour, like that of the Black Prince,[23] when he acted as a servant to his royal captive. It is quite a mistake to suppose that such things were insincere; but it is quite valid to say they were not inconsistent, for instance, with the Black Prince sacking a city in the blind rage of a sick man. What is much more to the point, it may be noted that courtesy and conquest were alike shown in a purely dynastic, that is, a purely family war; a family quarrel dividing the great family of Christendom.

There is one very strange fact, which a few have noticed, about the figure of the Knight in *The Canterbury Tales*. It may be an accident; but, like some other accidents, it is as awful as an omen. The obvious point to be made about the Knight is that he has won great glory in battle; and the poet makes the point quite clear. The obvious example of winning glory in battle, in the poet's own period, was winning glory in the French campaign, on the fields of Crécy and Poictiers. But the poet seems actually to take a detour in order to avoid the fields of Crécy and Poictiers. The poet himself had been distinguished in the contemporary foreign fuss; the tourney between St. Denis and St. George. But the Knight has had nothing to do with pitting St. Denis against St. George. Chaucer goes out of his way to say that his hero has fought for the Cross and not the Crown. He has fought against the heathen in Prussia (which some might indeed call an omen), but anyhow he has only fought against the heathen; and to such a company Prussia was as remote as Palestine. Indeed, it is all very remote; and apparently deliberately remote. The last great war had been between the English and the French. The next great war was to be between the English and the English. But the noblest Pilgrim of the great Pilgrimage has only heard of a war between the Crescent and the Cross. He comes from the ends of the earth; from those ultimate enmities in which Christianity

[23] The Black Prince is an epithet used for Edward, Prince of Wales (1330–1376), the eldest son of King Edward III of England.

is in collision with the things really outside itself. He is the ghost of a grander Europe; of that first De Montfort, with the fixed fanatical eyes, who rode away from the Fourth Crusade because he would not war with Christian men; of that last of the Nine Worthies, who declared that no man must wear a crown of gold, where God had worn a crown of thorns.

Therefore the Knight is of a larger make or framework than the rest; and throws a sort of giant shadow on the coloured crowd; a shadow almost of shame. But the shadow lies also on us and on our children. It is a problem of the present and even more of the future, whether we can make even so large a commonwealth of nations as combined in the Crusade. But if this is true of the significance of the Knights, it is even truer of the Guildsmen or the Burgesses. The point is that, looking into the fog of the future, we may see figures losing their *identity*; as the eventual result of having lost the Crest and the Trade Mark. Here indeed is the vital example of this long and difficult preface; on the need of seeing medieval things as living (or dying) modern things. Blake said that Chaucer numbered the types of men as Linnaeus[24] numbered the plants. But he was a mystic and not a prophet. Most normal men suppose these types to be normal. But in truth the Types are Trades; and the Trades are Guilds. Destroy the Guild and you destroy the natural classification of men. This appears vividly in the great Chaucerian characters. For Chaucer himself was a child of the old Craft and Mystery. And to men today the Mystery is a Mystery indeed.

There exists a misunderstanding rather than a quarrel about medieval and modern ideas; because the two do not meet on the same plane. The medieval world, with all its crimes and crudities, was intensely concerned with ideas as ideas; and not in the least concerned with them as medieval ideas. But the moderns, and especially the modernists, are intensely concerned with the fact that modern ideas are modern. They are sometimes so much excited about it that they neglect to make them anything like ideas. I know some very learned writers on the Middle Ages, whose heads are so constructed

---

[24] Carolus Linnaeus or Carol von Linne (1707-1778) was a Swedish botanist, the first scientist to outline the principles for defining the genera and species of organisms.

as not to permit the entrance even of the idea of an idea. The modern world has immeasurably surpassed the medieval world in organization and the application of such ideas as it has; so that the general improvement in certain kinds of humanity, certain kinds of instruction, and certain kinds of arbitration and order, is not merely an idea, but a material fact. But that does not alter the moral fact; that when we compare medieval ideas with modern ideas, we often find that the modern ideas are comparatively hasty, superficial or unbalanced; or else that the ideas, as ideas, really do not exist at all. There could not be a better example than the comparison between the *idea* of Guilds with the *fact* of Capitalism. The idea of Guilds was worked out very narrowly and imperfectly; and the fact of Capitalism may work out, at least in the opinion of some, more practically and prosperously. But there *was* an idea of Guilds; and there is not and never was any idea in Capitalism. Nobody knew where it came from; nobody especially wanted it to come. Nobody knew where it was going to; and at this moment it appears to be going straight to sheer strangling Monopoly and then to bankruptcy.

Nobody understands the modern world who does not realize this primary truth. The modern world began with the problem of the grocer and the grocer's assistant. It is in fact ending with a vast growth of grocers' assistants and no grocer. It must still be emphasized, obvious as it is, that the grocers' assistants have not *grown* into grocers. They have all remained assistants; only, instead of assisting a humble human grocer, with a soul to be saved, they are assisting the International Stores or the Universal Provision Department. In other words, the servants have not become masters, and will never have the faintest chance of becoming masters. They remain servants; only they are like those slaves that were held to public service in pagan antiquity; they have personal servants over them, but only an impersonal master overall. Now, very broadly, one idea in the Guild is that the grocer's assistant should grow into a grocer. For that purpose, it is obviously necessary to preserve a large number of equal and independent grocers. It is necessary to prevent these grocers from being bought out or sold up by the Stores or the Super-Grocer. With this object the Guild deliberately checked certain forms of competition, protected the weaker brethren; and, preserved the Types that seem eternal in Chaucer's Tales.

Now to anybody who knows an idea when he sees it, it is relatively irrelevant whether the application of this idea be patchy or imperfect, at any particular period. It is not patchy and imperfect, but very nearly non-existent, in our own period. But the point is in the clear comprehension of the idea. It there had been only one Guild, instead of scores and hundreds, it would still have stood for one medieval idea and not for the other modern idea. If its benefits had only been extended to two Guildsmen, they would still have been benefited in a particular way, and according to an idea other than the idea of modern competition or modern monopoly. Chaucer mentions several Master Craftsmen, evidently attached to a Guild, as going on his Canterbury Pilgrimage; he mentions, for instance, a Dyer and a worker in tapestry. If we compare the first with the huge development of the modern Dye Industry, we shall recognize at once the main distinction I mean. More and more people may have come to work in dye factories; more and more processes may have been invented; more marvellous as a matter of science, though often much less marvellous as a matter of art. And although for some time the logic of Capitalism produced worse and worse conditions, the wisdom of Capitalists (following on the courage of Trades Unionists) may now produce (or pretend to produce) better and better conditions. But they produce better and better conditions for servants; they do not attempt to produce a Guild, which is a fraternity of masters. And if we wish to consider the idea itself, clear of all these muddled bickerings about 'medievalism', we cannot do better than take the example of a trade which does still exist today, in something resembling the guise and function which it had in the days of Chaucer.

There rode in the cavalcade to Canterbury, along with the Dyer, the more conspicuous figure of the Doctor. He is conspicuous even in a literary sense; for he is picked out in colours that are still clear and fresh; a striking and almost startling example of Chaucer's power of describing a complete and even complex personality in a few lines. His combination of rich and impressive dress with cautious and hygienic diet is a calculation from two angles finding the exact point of a personality. He was particular that his food should be nourishing and digestible, but took it in small quantities; and though he did not talk about proteids and vitamins, he probably talked in some similar terms from the same learned language. The moment we know this, we know that it is true that he was irreligious; sceptical and anti-clerical in a rather negative way. He was dignified; but not averse from fees. That sort of man still exists; and his general sense of status, his social position and his professional etiquette, are still very much the same. The doctor, in short, still exists as a roughly recognizable figure. The Dyer has totally disappeared; his hand is not subdued to what it works in, but his whole body and soul dissolved in his own dye-vat. He has become a liquid; a flowing stream of tendency; an impersonal element in the economics of the dyeworks. He is not a Master-Dyer; he is at the most a Master of Dyers. But, in plain truth, he is not really a master, but only a paymaster. With every day that passes there is less importance in the mastery and more importance in the pay. The reason why the Doctor is recognizable, and the Dyer is unrecognizable, is perfectly simple. It is that the Doctors not only were, but still are, organized on the *idea* of a Medieval Guild.

In the modern doctor we can see and study the medieval idea. We shall not, even if we are medievalists, think it an infallible or impeccable idea. The Guild is capable of pedantry; it is sometimes capable of tyranny. The British Medical Council, which is the council of a Guild, sometimes condemns men harshly for very pardonable breaches of professional law; it sometimes excludes outsiders from membership who might well have been members. But it does do what a Guild was supposed to do. It keeps the doctors going; it keeps the doctors alive; and it does prevent one popular quack from eating all his brethren out of house and home. It sets limits to competition; it prevents the growth of monopoly. It does not allow a fashionable physician in Harley Street to destroy the livelihood of four general practitioners in Hoxton. It does not permit one professional man to buy up all the practices, as one grocer can buy up all the grocers' shops. And it does permit us to study, in a clear modern example, outside all the medieval controversies, religious and other, what is really to be said for and against this system of economic combination, and what it is that can really be criticized, and can really be valued, in the idea of a guild.

The Physician of Chaucer has changed, it may be said, in every other character except his economic relation to the Guild, which is still founded on medieval economics. As a matter of fact, the story is more comic than the common story of evolution. He has changed so often that he has very nearly changed back to what he was before. It is true that he no longer regards the art of healing as founded on Astrology; though he sometimes founds it on the yet more ancient superstition of Divination by Dreams. But though we have not yet gone far enough for eager young scientists to be dealing in Astrology, there is something curious and almost creepy about their dealings with Alchemy. Many of the most modern specualtions are a great deal nearer to the medieval notion of the transmutation of metals, than they are to the intervering materialist's dogmas of elemental and indestructible fixity. We may yet see the chemist turn into an alchemist, even if there is no immediate prospect of the astronomer turning into an astrologer. There is a typical piece of Chaucerian irony in the passage referring to the Doctor's purely scientific interest in gold:

> For gold in physic is a cordial
> Therefore he loved gold in special.

But nobody will say that this very special love of economic values is merely medieval, and cannot be admitted as modern. If avarice counted from something in alchemy, it has not been entirely absent from the services which modern science has offered to chemical combines and the discovery of mines. It is an amusing fact, by the way, that the quaint old legend, which Protestant prejudice set afloat some sixty years ago, to the effect that the Pope once condemned the study of Chemistry, really referred to this very fact; the fact that medieval religion did attempt to restrain medieval avarice. What the Pope did condemn was the practice of certain quack astrologers and alchemists, who used to go round to the houses of poor people and take away all their pots and pans with a promise of turning them all into gold.

Against this great step in scientific progress the Pope did indeed set his face with ferocious medieval bigotry. If any modern moral authority were to condemn the somewhat similar students of the Art of Salesmanship, who go round tempting poor people to run into debt for all sorts of furniture and appliances for which they cannot ultimately pay, I for one should welcome such an outburst of Papal persecution. But I have no doubt that the progressive historian would give a simple summary of the incident; by saying that it was made a mortal sin to have any chairs and tables.

Anyhow, the Guild principle has in fact saved the Doctor; and left him standing as a separate social figure in any crowd going to Wembley or Wimbledon, as he did in the crowd going to Canterbury. But it is the tendency of all the separate social figures, falling into modern monopolist and impersonal tendencies, to disappear altogether. Standardization lowers the standard of personality and independence in all the types and trades. Under that tendency, we no longer see the Ploughman but the new methods of the Steam-Plough; we no longer recognize the Miller but only a particular machinery of mills; and the current tendency, even of gossip, is to discuss not so much cooks as cookery and not so much clerks as clerking. A certain decline in the Comic Characters, conceived in relation to common trades, once so typical of English literature, is probably due to the decline in the idea of men who were Masters of their trade; and the substitution of numberless servants who had less pride in their professions. And this is relevant; for it may be the end of that long procession of English figures of fun, which undoubtedly began with Chaucer.

True, this is masked by the fact that the moderns can find phrases which they call quite modern, when they mean that they are quite human. Chaucer's unsleeping eye on human nature did indeed spot any number of small but amusing facts, that were true in his time and are true in ours. This could be illustrated even in the examples which I have mentioned and contrasted; the examples of the Doctor and the Dyer. A modern reader gives something like a start of amusement, when he reads of the relation between the Doctor and the Chemist; how 'each of them made other for to win', that is, the

Apothecary recommended the Physician and the Physician ordered the drugs from the Apothecary. That is the sort of social relation that might go on forever, and can certainly go on to-day. On the other hand, Chaucer does not tell us much about the Dyer or his friends, and it is possible that they were an afterthought, inserted for some special reason, as were (in all probability) the three Priests who appear and disappear after the mention of the Second Nun. But he does tell us one thing in connexion with these worthy Guildsmen or Livery Men of City Companies, which is an excellent example of what men say is quite modern, when they mean that it is very ancient. He says that the Dyer, and the other Masters of their respective Mysteries, were quite in the way of becoming Aldermen.[25] He throws a delicate veil, in his own indescribable way, over the question of whether they deserved to be Aldermen, or even wanted to be Aldermen. But he adds that, anyhow, their wives were all in favour of it; and that it is very pleasant to be distinguished from other women by being called 'Madame'. That is a drawing-room comedy that is modern enough, in that sense, and has a present and practical relation to the Honours List and the Sale of Peerages. There is many a knighthood given to-day, not so much because Mr. Biggs wishes to be Sir Benjamin Biggs, as because a more astute person has calculated that when she is Lady Biggs, it will sound quite as good as Lady Beauchamp or Lady Salisbury. The whole of Chaucer's book is dotted with details of this lively and accurate sort, to such an extent that a man might easily suppose that society had hardly changed at all, between the fourteenth and the twentieth centuries. The historic process of change is partly covered by certain comic antics of human nature, which can indeed occur in any age and are instantly recognized across the ages.

But we must not allow this to mislead us to the extent of underrating the change there has really been. Even in the instances I have given, there is sufficient evidence of what has changed and what has not. It is so with the Doctor and the Chemist. The Doctor, who is still the member of a living and real Guild, remains the same. The Chemist, who is not the member of a real Guild, is already changing.

[25] In the Anglo-Saxon history, an Alderman governed a territory as a viceroy.

It is no longer a case of the private physician calling on a private apothecary, living at the corner of the street. He has to deal already with vast commercial combines, with multiple and identical shops, in which all the chemists are servants and none of the chemists are masters. The name of one apothecary is now written in a hundred towns. And we owe it to the survival of a true medieval Guild, that the name of a single physician is not written on a hundred brass plates.

In the same way, while men have ambitions in every age, and women change from age to age even less than men, there really is a difference between the Alderman and Livery in Chaucer's time and in ours. The old Dyers' Company was still concerned only, or mainly, with the defence of Dyers; not only with defense of unsuccessful Dyers, but also, in the long run, with attack on successful Dyers. I know not if there is still a Dyers' Company; if there is, it is doubtless charitable in all manner of ways, but not in that way. It does not exist to bar and break the International Chemical Dyeworks Combine; it does not perceptibly try to do it, and it certainly does not do it. This may be partly explained by the fact that a considerable number of Dyers are aged colonels and clergymen, who have never dreamed of dyeing anything, except possibly their hair.

This example of the Dyer and the Doctor and the Guild is the supreme example of what was meant, at the beginning of this chapter, by saying that we cannot understand the past life of the fourteenth century, until we have begun to look a little even into the future of the twentieth. We are now in the middle of movements that may distort or dissolve all those distinctive and independent types which Chaucer distinguished by trades. In short, we may yet find, in the long run, that the loss of Arms and Heraldry has killed the Gentleman: the loss of Guilds and Mysteries has killed the Citizen. We cannot strike a right balance of judgement about the medieval attempt to organize trades and traders, without considering, not merely that it is now lost, but where the loss of it may ultimately lead. We must not judge by that later but intermediary phase, in which England could be called a nation of shopkeepers, with the implication that each man must keep his shop. If a man wanted to keep his shop, he would have been wiser to keep his guild. Where we have lost the guild principle, we have collapsed into a totally different sort of collectivist plutocracy. For that is what it is; whether we put it in revolutionary terms, by saying that one man keeps a hundred shops, or put it in humanitarian terms, by saying that one shop keeps a hundred men. One vital distinction is that in such a system the organizer can only be an organizer; he must deal with the abstractions and the materials of the trade; with pen and ink and not with dye-vats or wine-barrels.

Now Chaucer came of a line of men that did deal directly with wine-barrels. They dealt as masters and not as servants, at least in the last two generations. But they dealt with a wine-barrel and not with a wine-list; with facts and not merely with figures. For them was natural magic and the world's desire stored in positive pots; solid as those that poured for Christ the incredible wine. He came of people who had dealt with the stuff and substance of things, and in his case, with a highly appropriate sort of thing. If we were to look for an allegory about him who dealt so often in allegories, we could hardly find for his birthplace a more appropriate House of Fame. Forth from among those vats of more than purple dye, forth from among the mighty vats of the vine, brought by the Shipman from the lands of Froissart and Petrarch, he came to walk the world; who went singing all his days as if wine were in his very veins, and hidden in his northern blood, the very secret of the sun.

III

PUBLIC AND PRIVATE LIFE

The name of Chaucer seems to have been quite common in medieval times, and is practically unknown in modern times. This alone strikes me as rather curious and unique. Almost all other famous names reappear in some fashion; there storms across the stage of relatively recent history somebody with the remarkable name of Sir Julius Caesar. We have accepted unstartled a worthy dissenting minister as the Rev. Mr. Shakespeare, and admired a brilliant stage-player with the Puritan name of Milton. But we look in vain for Mr. Chaucer, in Bohemia or Belgravia or the suburbs; nor in 'the Street', nor up the Strand is he. The surname has not even appeared as a florid alias, or alternative title, among those who periodically alter their own pedigree and, like the wanton lapwing, get themselves another crest. Curiously enough, the latter course was actually adopted, in the reverse direction, in the original Chaucer family, if certain historians are correct. According to this theory, the son of Chaucer did really abandon his father's crest and coat-armour in favour of that of the De Roets, his maternal ancestors, supposing, heaven help us (such is the simplicity of snobs) that it would aggrandize Chaucer to be turned into Roet. But nowadays, when the Roets are forgotten, it does not even seem likely that Roet would be turned into Chaucer. Not even the most glittering, shifting and opalescent Opalstein, changing his name for the tenth time, ever seems to change it to Chaucer. I suspect that there is in this fact some faint shadow of something already noted here; something that is not exactly neglect, but is in a sense negligence. I mean that vague popular feeling that poor old Chaucer is a joke; that he is a funny, snuffy old man, like an antiquary or a small bookseller selling black-letter and broadsheets. An odd association of ideas about him, who sang in courts and had the confidence of kings: but I believe a very real one, among those who only know his name; and possibly a partial reason for their failure to claim or cling to his name. As I have said, somehow or other, it does not yet sound quite like a serious name: but, whatever be the reason, it is now at least a very rare name. And though it is very likely that a hundred Chaucers will leap out of dark corners or remote colonies, and write me long letters about this rash statement, it is a fact, at this actual moment by the clock, that I have never seen or heard of any living person bearing the once widespread name of the greatest Englishman of the Middle Ages.

Oddly enough, we may say that it was Chaucer who abolished the name of Chaucer. He did a number of rather remarkable things, including, for all practical purposes, tossing off a little trifle called The English Language. The name of Chaucer, or Chausseur, the maker of footwear, was once a common name because it described a common trade. A man was called Shoemaker as another man was called Tailor or Baker or Butler or Gardener; only he was called Shoemaker in French. For that matter, of course, the terms for tailoring and butlering and other things were of Norman and not Saxon origin; but that is another discussion, and a very tiresome one. The really important fact to be seized is this: that it was rather an unexpected, belated and almost reactionary accident, that the glorious English language came into existence at all. It was one of those lucky things that are not likely to happen and do happen; and often nearly happen too late. The whole trend of progress or organic growth was towards France and England growing together, under the common captaincy of a French-speaking nobility and chivalry. If a serious sociologist, mapping out the evolution of mankind, had existed in the earlier Middle Ages (and they had many other plagues and pestilences), that scientific prophet would most certainly have said that England was destined to become as French-speaking as France. The cultured class generally has an unfair advantage over the uncultured; and the whole culture had originally been a Latin culture. The Plantagenet attempts to make France a part of England were really a half-confession that England was a part of France. Then something happened at the last moment, of the sort that confounds scientific politics; something dimly resembling the combined instinctive movements of a populace and a poet. There was a faint trail of Anglo-Saxon traditions and various dialects like Middle

English; but left to itself the trail would have led nowhere. Then a great genius saw that he could Frenchify it enough to make it English. That is about as nearly as we can define the process. Chaucer Europeanized English; he brought it into the current of culture, by setting it to foreign tunes and mixing it with foreign terms. But Chaucer destroyed the domination of pure French; he destroyed all sorts of incidental terms, titles and conventions that went along with it; and, while he was about it, he destroyed his own name.

It would seem that the poet's grandfather was a certain Robert le Chaucer, who had some post in the Customs connected with the imports of wine from Aquitane; so the connexion with the wine trade can be traced at least as far as that. The creator of The Wife of Bath, the great professional widow of literature, seems to have come of a household somewhat haunted by widows; to an extent to alarm Mr. Tony Weller. His grandmother was married at least twice; his mother was apparently married three times; and, touching later developments, it would seem that his sister-in-law was at least once a widow, before she became the third wife of that determined and untiring widower, John of Gaunt. It is a trivial coincidence, and yet not wholly uninforming; for many earnest students have missed the point about medieval life by not noticing that a thing was often derided as comic and yet was very common; was derided as comic because it was very common. Similarly, when we find medieval moralists indignantly denouncing something, we can generally deduce that it was a very medieval thing. Widowhood was really tragic, which is why kings and knights swore specially to defend the widow and orphan; but remarriage was none the less comic because it was obviously convenient. Anyhow, the way in which these rather entangled relations affected Chaucer is roughly this. His grandmother, Mary le Chaucer, who was probably born a Stace and previously married to a Heyroun, had a son named John Chaucer. After the death of her husband, Robert le Chaucer, she married a certain Richard le Chaucer; having apparently a taste in Chaucers. Richard was certainly a vintner and lived in London, in a part called Cordwaners-strete. There is a curious episode about some people called Stace, probably kinsmen, trying to kidnap young John Chaucer and marry him for monetary purposes; the youth being rescued by his stepfather. The stepfather died in 1349; and John himself went on vintnering with increasing success; as he deputized for the King's Butler in Southampton and even seems to have gone abroad in the train of the King. It seems likely that the Chaucers had for some time been, so to speak, among the camp-followers of the Court; but first in lowlier and afterwards in loftier stations or offices. John married Agnes, daughter of John Copton, of a family connected with the Mint, and lived in Thames Street. When he died, the widow was married again to another vintner, bearing the pleasing name of Bartholemew atte Chapel. So that a certain child named Geoffrey Chaucer, who is presumed to be her son, was provided with a stepfather, as his father had been; and may have received in childhood that impression of a transformation-scene of marrying and remarrying, which he extended into vistas of somewhat unscrupulous exaggeration in the career of The Wife of Bath. There are many other complicated controversies about the Chaucer family; but they may be left, first because they cannot be settled; and second because the Chaucer family is not so interesting as Chaucer.

The life of Chaucer, in the somewhat limited sense of the biography of Chaucer, consists of a very few facts and an incredible crowd of fancies. Perhaps it would be fairer to say a crowd of conjectures; for part of the difficulty lies in the plausibility or probability of some of the conjectures, which come near the ground but never quite settle on it. At the very outset, the writer of a sketch of this poet has to decide whether he will confine himself to what he knows to be true, or speculate at length on many things which he can see to be possible, or even probable, but which may, after all (especially in the light of later research), be entirely misleading. I have here decided to dwell definitely only on the definite facts, and to reserve speculation for what must in any case be speculative: the spiritual and philosophical and literary meaning of the story. My reason is that the ramifications of the mere conjectures of the learned have been so vast, and, in some cases, so vain. They are liable to be pursued patiently, or impatiently, through thousands and thousands of words, and then brought to a stop with a few words. In one case I remember, Chaucer went on the wildest adventures in connexion with the revolt of the citizens of London concerning John of Northampton; a story in which the poet fled to Holland, was flung into the Tower, was released by the personal intervention of Anne of Bohemia, was put to thrilling tests involving the betrayal of his fellow-conspirators, before he could reappear in the light of day. To the whole of which story a subsequent biographer put a full stop of scepticism, by saying it was rather odd that through all these changes Chaucer regularly received his pension with his own hands, quite quietly, in his home in London. I am not going to erect towers of tentative theory which can be so rapidly ruined. The romance called 'The Possible Life of Geoffrey Chaucer, Gentleman', would be a most fascinating and spirited work; 'The Black Prince's Treasure'; 'in the House of Wat Tyler'; 'The Rescue of Laura'; 'What Became of Dante's Beatrice?'; or the great mystery story: 'Why Was Chaucer Robbed Twice in One Day?'—as he really was. Doubtless it was mixed up with the Pope or Wycliffe or someone; for the time was picturesque almost to excess: and the great men he may have met would need a volume apiece. But this volume is only about Chaucer; and this chapter is only about the ascertained facts about Chaucer. The trouble is that they are not only few, but they are not even always the few facts that make up the most rudimentary biography.

A good example, to begin with, is the question about the date of his birth. It is largely calculated from the evidence which he gave in the affair of Scrope and Grosvenor; a lawsuit in which he is officially recorded as being 'forty and upwards, and armed twenty-seven years'. This lawsuit was certainly in 1386, so that presuming that Chaucer was then about forty-five, he was probably born about 1341. But it has always struck me as quaintly typical of the time, as well as the oddity of the Chaucerian problem, that the Court records should be so very exact about the period during which he had borne arms and possessed armorial bearings, and so very vague about the period during which he had been alive. It is possible that Chaucer was himself rather vague, possibly out of natural vagueness, possibly out of natural vanity; but it seems clear that the legal authorities did not trouble to pin him down about his age, when once they were certain about his status of Armiger.[26] That double information, certain on the smaller point and uncertain on the larger, is typical of all the information about Chaucer. There are rather interesting possibilities in such matters, to which I shall refer elsewhere; here I only note in passing that the very date of his birth is doubtful, though the date of his admission into the system of chivalry is clear. The problem of his parentage is in the same lopsided state. It has been traditionally, and apparently truly said (indeed it is substantially certain) that he was the son of a vintner of the City of London; but we do not know this even, so well as we know that he appears later in totally different positions: often the last positions where one would expect the vintner's son to be.

One disadvantage of seeing the same figure in a series of flashes of lightning is that we cannot always be quite certain that it is the same figure. The fact that we have only disjointed bits and snippets of the biography of Geoffrey Chaucer involves the occasional possibility that in the words of the ancient jest about a more ancient poet, it is not the biography of Geoffrey Chaucer, but of somebody else of the same name. In this connexion we cannot forget what we have already noted: that it was then a fairly common name. Nevertheless, there is a series of such glimpses of what would appear to be a continuous historical personality; though some of them seem to me less certainly, and others quite certainly, the personality of the poet. But whether they are certain or uncertain, they are none of them continuous; they are isolated impressions which can only be treated like separate pictures. The searchlight of criticism can only fall here and there, like a spotlight, upon a particular spot; and that so briefly that we cannot always be equally sure that the human figure which we see is part of the human story which we study.

Thus, the very first figure we see is that of a boy in a short cloak with a pair of black and red breeches, who is hanging about in some more or less menial capacity in the house of the Countess of Ulster, who married Lionel of Clarence, one of the sons of Edward the Third. There is also an entry showing that he received a small sum

---

[26] An Armiger was a squire who was allowed to bear heraldic arms.

'for necessaries at Christmas'; and we will hope that the Countess of Ulster had proper ideas about what a boy's necessaries at Christmas are. But the whole thing was on a small scale, and seems to be suited to quite a subordinate position, and we cannot be absolutely certain that the boy in black and red breeches was father to the man with whom we deal.

Next, we have a much brighter glimpse, in much broader daylight, of a very sharp-eyed and observant young man, probably clad as a *scutifer* or subordinate and assistant of some knight, walking about among the tents and painted palisades of a medieval camp, gay with heraldry; noticing especially the blazonry of one particular pavilion, and falling into talk with old soldiers or heralds' followers on the subject. The young man was about twenty years old; the time was the year 1359; and the place was the northern plains of France, stretching from the poplars of Picardy to the vines of Champagne, somewhere near the place where the road goes up to the holy towers of Rheims. There is no doubt whatever that this young man is that Galfridus Chaucer who filled up the chinks in his chivalric or bureaucratic duties with a few little literary exercises, admittedly not without merit. The military campaign, in which he was thus serving as a soldier, was one of the last efforts made by Edward the Third in his later years to repeat the success, or recover the crown of glory, which he had won at Crécy long before. About it, as about much of that dying medieval glory, there was an atmosphere of doom. It was probably felt by all that the first English triumphs could not be recovered; though John of Gaunt's grandson was to make yet another very gallant throw for it at Agincourt. Anyhow, it ended in defeat, and Chaucer, fighting in the defeated army, was taken prisoner.

Here, however, we have the first really important light on the level of life, so to speak, on which he was by this time living. He was not only ransomed, but ransomed by a pretty large sum personally advanced by the King. It is clear that he was already a person of some distinction; or at least a person of some promise; and it is most probable that he was connected with the king by the tie of some task or commission, in which his own personality counted. He was still only a young squire, at most; but the Government was certainly employing the young squire on some particular business. In fact, it was a matter of what may be called (in every sense) Intelligence. It was as important then as now to have in the Intelligence Department at least one person of Intelligence. Such a man is valued, and efforts will be made to rescue or to ransom him. It seems clear at least that about the year 1360 and onwards, Chaucer, young as he was, was acting as some sort of King's Messenger or bearer of dispatches between France and England.

In one of these foreign journeys, later on, he became a friend of Froissart; and Froissart is the type of that time and task in his life. Froissart is the historian who really did know everything about chivalry; except the most important thing: that what had turned into a Tournament had once been a Crusade. Courtesy was stooping to courtliness: chivalry was entangled in heraldry; but much of it was still worth learning; and anyhow these were the things the young poet had to learn. I have already said something of that flamboyant background of heraldry against which he stands. It is the vividness of heraldry in those days, and its vagueness in these days, which gives its amusing moral to the little incident that has often been quoted; one of the few living incidents in which the figure of Chaucer can be seen for a moment walking alive in the daylight. It happened, as noted, much later in his life; but it recalls the romantic youth here in question. The fashionable world, as we should put it, was divided into enthusiastic factions over a quarrel which had arisen about the legitimacy of a coat of arms, which then seemed almost as thrilling as the legitimacy of a child or a last will and testament. The arms borne by the great Border family of Scrope, in popular language a blue shield with a gold band across it (I can say 'azure a bend-or' quite as prettily as anybody else) was found to have been also adopted by a certain Sir Thomas Grosvenor, then presumably the newer name of the two. The trial was conducted with all the voluminous detail and seething excitement of a Society divorce case; reams and rolls of it, for all I know, remain, in the records of the heraldic office, for anybody to read if he likes; though I have my doubts even about garter King-at-Arms. But somewhere in that pile of records there is one little paragraph, for which alone, perhaps, the world would now turn them over at all. It merely states that among a long list of witnesses, one 'Geoffrey Chaucer, gentleman, armed twenty-seven years', had testified that he saw the Golden Bend displayed before Scrope's tent in the battlefield of France; and that long afterwards, he had stopped some people in the streets of London and pointed to the same escutcheon displayed as a tavern sign; whereon they had told him that it was not the coat of Scrope but of Grosvenor. This, he said, was the first time he had ever heard tell of the Grosvenors. Such small flashes of fact are so provocative, that I can almost fancy he smiled as he said the last words.

Perhaps the chief interest of the incident is the reversal of the relations between the witness and the trial; and indeed between the witness and the world. Chaucer at that moment was only of importance because he offered testimony about Scrope and Grosvenor. Scrope and Grosvenor at this moment are only of importance because they elicited testimony from Chaucer. It is an old moral, and obvious enough, that the fashion of this world passes away; yet we often find it hard to believe about the fashion of this age. All that world of the heraldic and the emblematic, full of many very noble meanings as well as many very idle mummeries, has long been rolled away like a scroll and vanished like a cloud; and we cannot conceive that the world once thought all that nonsense necessary. Yet we are not always eager to realize that all which we call necessary may some day be called nonsense. It is amusing to reflect that some day the apocalyptic newspaper files, with their huge headlines about The First Man Who Flew Round The World, or the American professor who thinks we can send wireless waves to Mars, will all seem to our descendants a dust of indescribably dreary triviality; and that nobody will ever look at the long-lost records, except to find a paragraph in a corner, in which Mr. Laurence Binyon or Mr. T. S. Eliot gave evidence about a motor-car collision.

In dealing with all such incidents in Chaucer's life, it is unavoidable that we should have a very little fact to a great deal of theory or hypothesis; because it is impossible to recover the details of his life, but not altogether impossible to recover a good many of the details of his time. His appearance at the great Scrope and Grosvenor inquiry is entirely typical of all we know about him; of his footing among the gentry, which was yet not quite that of a conventional hereditary gentleman; of the confidence that was undoubtedly placed in his word and wisdom, in more important matters than this; of the good sense and clearness which marked all his modes of expression, and would in any case have made him an excellent witness; and even of a certain cheerful curiosity about common things, which made him stop in the street to find out the truth about the new public-house sign. But, on the whole, the difficulty of dealing with the life of Chaucer is that there are so very few of these flashes of daylight, in which the man himself can be seen and snapshotted, moving about on his personal affairs. Almost all we know of him comes from legal documents and official actions; not, as is the case with so many later poets, from contemporary memoirs or personal letters. No man is more personal in his work and more impersonal in his biography. So that, while we can see through his own eyes, with almost startling clearness, the Miller, blind and bloated and roaring with drink, thrusting aside the Monk and making sure of the second place in the series, or the Canon's Yeoman overtaking the cavalcade at a rush, with the foam on his horse's bridle, there was no one present to snapshot the figure of Chaucer himself, as he stood, sharp and observant, outside the blazoned tent in France or the painted tavern in London.

But we do at least know that the rulers observed his observation, and were sharp enough to note his sharpness. He was trusted with diplomatic missions of great dignity, and with some which were, perhaps, too important to be dignified. In other words, it looks as if some of his foreign commissions had been of the nature of what we call Secret Service; and anyhow there is no doubt that he was deep in the secrets of two, if not three Kings. What we know of him publicly through his offices is entirely consonant with what we know of him personally through his poems. If there is one thing that we could have guessed for ourselves, about the personality of the poet, it is that he would have made a perfectly admirable diplomatist. The diplomatist of fiction and drama, especially the diplomatist of melodrama, seems extraordinarily unfitted for diplomacy. He is represented as a rigid and sinister person, with a perpetual sneer, and a background of assassins and the Third Degree. What is wanted in diplomacy is the careful cultivation of the exact contrary of all this; and the exact contrary of all this was Chaucer. The unshaken good temper which was combined with his wide knowledge of the world, his ready realization of the variety of human character, his perfectly genuine geniality towards most people combined with an equally genuine knowledge of the weaknesses of most people, were exactly the qualities most wanted in that time of tangled feudal claims and touchy semidependent vassals. No man ever understood better that it takes all sorts to make a world, or even to make a pilgrimage. No man suffered fools more gladly, for he did actually suffer them gladly; getting any amount of gladness or gaiety out of his private observation of their folly. He was a polished adept in the dangerous diplomatic art of really getting some fun out of funny people.

I shall deal on another page with the details of his political fortunes, the later part of which is admittedly covered with some obscurity. We are not certain of his personal attitude to the palace revolution which replaced the true Plantagenet by the ambitious son of John of Gaunt. We know that John of Gaunt had been in a general sense a patron of Chaucer, as of others; but it is difficult to deduce from this all his individual views about rather unforeseen changes in the next generation. For the purpose of the present problem, it is enough to say that he never ceased to receive a certain amount of reward and protection from the Court; though in his later years he was somewhat poorer and less frequently in public employment. He was not the kind of man to quarrel if he could help it, and, even in those quarrelsome days, none of the rulers seems to have finally or seriously quarrelled with him. The end of their own increasing quarrelsomeness he did not see, but carried with him to the last something of the calmer splendour of the victorious age of Edward. He died before the Wars of the Roses.

I have summarized this chapter under the title of public and private life; and the difficulty is that the poet had a public life that was very much of a private life. Nay, in one sense, it was more private than his private life. We are not in fact told very much about the personal affairs of Geoffrey Chaucer; but what we are told we are told quite frankly. The biography of Chaucer is lost; but it is not hidden. When he does happen to talk about himself, he describes himself quite as vividly as he describes everybody else. He makes fun of himself as he does of everybody else. The description is incomplete, merely because there is not very much of it; and, like most light descriptions of the sort, it does not deal with the most serious matters. But though there is not enough of it to describe a complete person, it does not shrink from being personal, in the sense in which we now speak (generally with grave disapproval) about personalities. Chaucer has told us that he was fat, that he was reluctant to get out of bed, that he was content on occasion to look very much of a fool, that he was thought to neglect his neighbours for his craze for books; and many other things that are quite private and confidential as far as they go. But he has told us nothing of what was really private and confidential: and that was his work in the public service. He was practically by profession a diplomatist; and *his* diplomacy was a very secret diplomacy. In all his maze of multitudinous words, in all his wandering paths of narrative and meditation, in all the thousand things that he touches on as a poet, a philosopher, a moralist and a humorist, he has not left one single word, I think, which throws any light on those political missions which the King his master trusted him to conduct with the princes of France or the great merchants of Italy. His silence is entirely creditable to him; it was doubtless part of his code of honour as a public servant, especially as a feudal servant; but it is not very helpful to his biographers. A little is known, merely because it was generally known, about the object of some of his journeys abroad; but there are others that seem to me to have been of the Secret Service that is really secret. But this contrast between his ease and gaiety on the subject of himself, and his sobriety and silence on the subject of his business, is very characteristic of the man; and strikes that note of balance, or the power of keeping two different considerations in the mind, which will later be found a clue to deeper things. Chaucer (as has been said) was not so simple as he looked. It would be quite false to say, in modern English, that his simplicity was doubled by duplicity. But it would be quite true to say, in the older Latin, that he was duplex; that is, that he could think about two things at once. This sort of noble and honourable duplicity will later be found relevant to his philosophy and his religion.

But the practical matter, for the moment, is that even his public life was a private life. It is only recorded in a few official entries, and we have to depend upon these, or upon things equally meagre, for much of our speculation about all that was really more private, in the sense of more personal. Perhaps this is most notably the case in the matter of the dates of his poems; a difficult matter which is somewhat doubtfully tested by the foreign influences brought in by his foreign travels. Thus, his work was at one time divided into a French and an Italian period; just as his diplomatic career was divided into a French and an Italian plan of movements. Later discussion has shown a tendency rather to turn on a distinction between the two Italian visits; many believing that it was not until the second that he received anything like the full Italian influence. These matters will be dealt with later, not indeed in detail; for there is little that can be called detail; but with reference to the real differences between his French and English and Italian elements. Here it is sufficient to fix the main facts as they concern a biography, even if it be a literary biography. Chaucer began his career as an envoy in foreign parts with certain negotiations in France, referring probably to the peace after the disastrous war and to other things. In 1367, we find him receiving a pension under the particular title of *valettus*: a Court office which, quaintly enough, is sometimes translated as Valet and sometimes as Yeoman. It would be hard to find two words which have strayed farther from each other in their subsequent significance. Anyhow, the next glimpse we have of the poet is that of a ceremonial functionary, carrying a torch or lifting a curtain, in the ordinary small rituals that surround royalty. But it is plain that this was only a sort of interlude, and his missions to France were soon followed by the first of his missions to Italy. It involved his going abroad, apparently alone, with a little money and some letters of exchange; and its full object perhaps will never be known. In 1372 he went to parley with two citizens of Genoa about a port in England suitable to the Genoese trade. It is much debated, among Chaucerian critics, whether the great enthusiasm he certainly showed later for Italian literature came to him through this first visit; but the best authorities now seem to think that all the really valuable 'Italianate' work was done after the second visit in 1378. Anyhow, his first important work, which is not Italianate at all, was the lament over the Duchess who was the wife of John of Gaunt: and the question of his relation to the House of Lancaster would suffice to bring us back to more practical and personal elements in his own life.

Among the very scrappy scraps that historians have had to piece together, there is mention in the year 1366 of a certain Philippa Chaucer being one of the attendants of the Queen. She was granted a pension, and later on we find the pension being paid through her husband Geoffrey Chaucer. This has given rise to endless disputes and difficulties; ranging from the suggestion that Geoffrey had revived the family fancy for Chaucers marrying Chaucers, and married a cousin of the same surname, to a deep and delicate dispute about whether he could possibly have been married in 1366, when a poem written about that year expresses the sentiments of a disappointed lover. Leaving the latter point for a moment, we may note that the theory of any close cousinship involves a non-existent dispensation from Rome, and in any case does not seem necessary. The alternative theory favoured is that he married Philippa de Roet; and if he did, a really interesting situation arises.

If he did, it would seem that two strides, both almost accidental, really took him into a world far above his own. For it so happened, merely by chance, that Philippa de Roet's sister was engaged in John of Gaunt's family as a governess; it seems too probable that she became John of Gaunt's mistress; and it is quite certain that she eventually became his wife. She was his third wife; and men at that stage have often something a little senile about their sentiment. But something seems to tell us that she must have been rather a remarkable woman, whether in a pleasant or an unpleasant fashion; and it seems not altogether unlikely that some remarkable qualities ran in the family. Perhaps there was also something remarkable about her sister Philippa, that attracted the attention of the most subtle judge of character in that age. But beyond that, there seems very little material for judgment. What is much more to the point is, however, that if this identification be true, Chaucer had one wild leap of luck apart from all his services. By a sort of *mésalliance*[27] nobody could have foreseen, the vintner's son became something very like a brother-in-law of the Blood Royal.

The present writer is prayerfully conscious that he was never meant to be a biographer; not having that eye for detail which can trace a tenable theory among many doubts. On the other hand, if unlearned in the more recondite documents, he has in his time studied about one thousand detective-stories, and is often struck by the resemblance between the ingenuity of their authors and the ingenuity of the learned biographers. The true biographer hunts down a hero as the romantic detective hunts down a villain; tracking him, so to speak, by lost buttons and cigarette-ends; deducing his designs from his slightest scribbles or scraps of paper; drawing hints from eavesdropping on his most casual conversational remarks. Unfortunately, there is a fallacy in transferring these talents to the task of biography. A decent detective story is itself a selected bundle of clues, with a few blinds as carefully selected as the clues. If therefore the reader, or his romantic detective, finds that somebody has made a note of the late train to Market Harborough, or observes somebody else wave his hat towards a particular window with a striped green blind, he knows that these things have some connexion, however obscure or remote, with the great problem of who hanged Admiral Bundleton with his own bootlaces. But when we are dealing with the whole life a real human being, and trying to trace its outstanding events, it is not in the least necessary, it is not in the least likely, that all the trivial incidents or allusions will refer to outstanding events. Many of them will refer to things that nobody can possibly discover, after five hundred years; many to things that were next to nothing even at the time; some actually to nothing at all. But some of the illustrious Chaucerian scholars, to whom the world

---

[27] A *Mésalliance* is a marriage beneath one's social standing.

owes such everlasting thanks for elucidating the text and many of the true facts, sometimes seem to be unable to realize this reality. They cannot believe that they are not sleuths, following a trail that was laid for them and cunningly darting upon clues that they were meant to see. Whatever Chaucer does or says, however idly or carelessly, can be taken down and used in evidence against him. Everything that could be an expression of his private feelings is supposed to refer to his private life. Anything, that could be twisted into the expression of an intention, must be an intention that he seriously entertained; anything like an intention that he seriously entertained must be an intention that he actually carried out. If he says anything, anywhere, in any connexion, referring to marriage, he must be referring to his own marriage. If he says, after writing a tragedy, that he would rather like to write a comedy, it must be some comedy that he actually wrote. If he should happen to say, or even happen to make one of his characters say, that he does not like the subject of some story, it must mean that he does not like a particular rival poet, who happens to have told the story. If he makes one of his characters claim to have gone somewhere where he himself actually went, then the fictitious character must be meant for a portrait of himself. This sort of hunting for hints is wonderfully exciting and very profitable and edifying—in murder-stories. But it is not human: and it has no relation to real human life. And when they come to what is in fact the very foggiest and most fanciful phase of human nature, young love and sentiment about the other sex, they become all the more ruthlessly like policemen on the pounce.

Chaucer wrote a poem, apparently an early poem, called 'An Exclamation of the Death of Pity'. It is all about a young gentlman being in love with a young lady, and talking about her to various other people, allegorical and otherwise, in the medieval manner; and complaining especially that pity is dead and there is no hope of the fulfilment of his dream; which certainly seems a rather dreamy sort of dream. But the most elaborate scaffolding of scientific dates and details has been erected on this chance metrical exercise of Chaucer; calculations about when he was married; about whether it could have been written after he was married; about whether, in that case, it proves that he was unhappily married; calculations about the date of his falling in love, the date of his falling out of love, and (of course) the exact identity of the only possible lady whom he could ever have loved. I may be very irresponsible, but all this seems to me to be extraordinarily wide of the mark, touching a man's actual life in this vale of tears. I should imagine that there never was a man, not actually convinced of a vocation of virginity somewhere about the age of seven, who had not had enough in the way of day-dreams and dallyings to have written such sentimental verse by the age of seventeen. Sentimental verse of that sort has been written about a total stranger; about a face seen in a crowd; about a person who did not exist at all. Yet all this subjective side of youthful poetry seems to be entirely forgotten, because we are trying to make an objective biography of Chaucer out of any objects lying about; as the buttons and cigarettes lie about in the murder-story.

Now the fact is that youthful brooding is so subjective that it hardly even needs a subject. Certainly its literary self-expression can often be quite easily transferred to another subject. The poet preserves what the lover has forgotten; and many a famous love-poem may have been begun about one lady and finished about another. The time at which it was published is no clue to the time at which it was written. The time at which it was written is no clue to the theme that it was written about. Save in a few very vivid and personal examples, the theme may have even begun and ended in thought. And it seems to me very unfair to Mrs. Geoffrey Chaucer to deduce, in a detective manner, that her husband was unhappy with her; or that her husband was unfaithful to her; or indeed that there was anything whatever the matter with either of them, from anything so flimsy as the fact that her husband is the author of some rather artificial love-verses, that he might have written to anybody at any time, or touched up at any time, or decided to publish at any time.

Some of the other evidences that have been found before now, by detectives hovering round the Chaucer household, are much more ridiculous than this. Somebody found a confession of domestic tragedy in the fact that Chaucer confessed that he was a little liable to be cross with the voice that woke him up too early in the morning.

This may have been a tribute to his dreams, though more probably to his taste for dreamless sleep; but it can hardly be regarded as a very definite and detailed criticism of his daily or domestic life. As to the hundred and one jests and jeers that are thrown throughout his works at women or wives or marriage, they do not differ from the ordinary conventional joke of Mrs. Caudle's Curtain Lectures, or the picture of any hen-pecked husband in *Punch*, except in being much more refined. For the author of the Miller's Tale was refined. That is, he could be refined; and a good many modern writers are most coarse and clumsy when they intend to be refined. These jokes certainly prove nothing either way about the happiness of his marriage. Such jokes have been made by hundreds and thousands of happy and unhappy husbands, and fill all the libraries of the world. The people who write them think they are funny; they write them because they think they are funny; not because they describe exactly the facts of their own private lives. There seems, in short, to be a curious oblivion of the purely literary reasons for literature. Poetry generally comes out of the poet's life, as distinct from his biography; not out of what he did, but of what he thought when he was doing nothing; not out of the self that he expressed in working or wiving or flirting, but of the self that he could only express in writing. Certainly he does not sit down and keep a diary in verse, with all the details relevant and realistic. That is not the way poetry is written. But it seems to be the way biography is written.

I therefore delicately deprecate the idea of biographers thus appearing as detectives; especially as that not very superior sort of detective employed to collect evidence for a divorce between Mr. and Mrs. Chaucer, five hundred years after their death. I do not know whether Mr. and Mrs. Chaucer were happy or unhappy. Apparently it has not occurred to our bright psychologists that they were probably both. There seems to be a certain lack of vividness in envisaging what marriage is like, as well as what poetry is like. But, as Professor Pollard has justly said, what evidence there is rather points to Chaucer having been both happier and more religious and respectable while his wife was alive than afterwards. It is more to the point that he was apparently poorer afterwards. Which may be rather a compliment to the wife.

I have said that I attach very little importance to the merely exclamatory or flippant phrases, on which the theory of the poet's conjugal tragedy has been based. It is a good rough rule with Chaucer to translate him into modern English, or a parallel modern passage. The passage about his wife waking him up might be rendered more or less correctly thus: 'A voice woke me up, rather as somebody I needn't mention very often *does* wake me up; but then, you see, the voice was very mild or gentle, so I knew it wasn't my wife.' That remark might pass in the patter of any comedian, or the half-impersonal confessions of any comic writer, without being supposed to throw any very blazing or blasting light on the actual misery of his actual marriage. And this is perhaps the most positive and pointed of the purely literary allusions that have been used for this purpose. But it is only right to add that there is one piece of actual record, that is not merely a piece of literature or a lark, which can be interpreted in the sense that the poet had been practically misbehaving himself. It is a rather mysterious legal document in which a young woman named Cecilia de Chaumpaigne releases a Geoffrey Chaucer from his legal liability in some charge of abducting or eloping. It is quite possible, of course, that the matter was concerned with some real wrong, though this does not fully explain it. The woman presumably had some reason for having once involved Chaucer (if it was Chaucer) in the affair. It is equally true, on that argument, that she presumably had some reason for releasing him from it. The best Chaucerian authorities seem to think that it was not exactly a personal matter, but part of one of those curious family conspiracies for getting hold of people and marrying them to other selected people, which were rather a recurrent scandal in those times; in one case of which Chaucer's own father had been the victim. Quite apart from morality, in which any man may fail, it was not at all typical of Chaucer's temperament to engage in any personal or isolated violence or lawlessness; and it is certainly the only mark of the sort against his name. It is possible that he might play something like the part of Pandarus[28] to some Troilus in his own

---

[28] Pandarus was a Trojan leader in the *Iliad* (Book IV) who at the instigation of Athena breaks the truce and wounds Menelaus. He is eventually killed by Diomedes. Modern English usage of the word is to designate a procurer, or a panderer, derived from Chaucer's representation of Pander in *Troilus and Criseyde* as a "go-between" for the lovers.

marrying and remarrying family; it seems more probable that he would play the part of mentor or moderator; hence, possibly the special pardon to himself. There may have been almost any sort of complicated comedy of relations; there may have been simply a bad break and nothing else. The incident forms the most thrilling and entertaining chapter in that Possible Life of Geoffrey Chaucer, which I am not writing and do not intend to write.

We have seen that Chaucer's first Italian mission was to Genoa; it has been conjectured that he went from there to Padua, where it would have been possible for him to meet, as he certainly would have wished to meet, the most famous and in one sense the first poet of the age. Petrarch was in Padua at the end of 1372; and there is certainly something at least like a coincidence in the fact that he was then turning into Latin the same story of Griselda which Chaucer later turned into English. This (if one may say so) seems to me a good example of the difference between reasonable and unreasonable deduction from our fragmentary documents. There is a real objective concrete coincidence or convergence of facts, or at any rate approximation of facts, in Chaucer, Genoa, Padua, Petrarch and Griselda, *plus* the fact that the Clerk of Oxford, in telling the tale of Griselda, actually mentions Petrarch and Padua. Any of these things might happen without any connexion; but it is odd that they were all connected. But when people pass from this to saying that Chaucer must have meant the Clerk of Oxford for himself, or rather a double of himself (seeing that he already happened to be present in his own person), and when they mix up Chaucer's gossiping greediness for all sorts of books with the concentration on Aristotle which is a part of the character of the Oxford Schoolman and philosopher, they go a great deal too fast and indulge in fancy. No two Canterbury Pilgrims can ever be confused for a moment; and the Clerk of Oxford is the Clerk of Oxford, and Chaucer is very emphatically Chaucer. Nevertheless Chaucer *was* interested in philosophy; besides being, in a really natural sense, a natural philosopher.

It is very possible therefore that Chaucer did here enter for the first time into that golden air of the Roman culture that was soon to be the golden air of the Renaissance; at the gates of which, crowned with laurel, stood great Petrarch clad in gold. That was how he seemed, at least, to his contemporaries to stand; and Chaucer certainly did not fail to admire him, however soon or late he began to imitate him; but he seems to have admired Dante more, though he could hardly be expected to imitate him better. Whether there be any connexion or no between the two turns of his fate, it is certain that the mission to Italy was like a golden gate for the practical prosperity of Chaucer. His real period of wealth, public importance and (it is fair to add) public industry, stretches from that St. George's Day in 1374, when the great English poet received from the English King the highly symbolic pitcher of wine (which he afterwards turned into a pension), right away past the death of King Edward in 1377 to the time of the revolt of Gloucester in the councils of his grandson. In the summer of the same year he became Comptroller of the Customs and Subsidy of Wools, Skins and Tanned Hides in the Port of London, and his salary seems to have been augmented by a variety of other payments, in a rather patchwork fashion; by a pension from John of Gaunt; two wardships which carried remuneration, and a special grant from the King on some wool forfeited for non-payment of duty. He then went on another foreign mission to Flanders, of a smaller and secret sort, and we find that in such cases he was allowed to appoint deputies for his official work. But, in the ordinary way, he was a good hard-working official. It is apparent in everything, from such details as we know about the work itself to the particular tone of the relief he expresses at having balanced his ledgers and gone back to his books. In that way he was a good business man; though perhaps rather of the type that is a better business man for his employers than for himself. It is a type not uncommon among good-tempered, abstracted, secretly imaginative men; the type that goes on for years as an excellent Government Office clerk, but when once it is superannuated and at leisure, is not always wise in dealing with its own hobbies or investments. There has been much talk about whether the breakdown in Chaucer's fortunes, and the relative poverty that fell upon him, was entirely due to the later political accident which turned him for a time out of office. It has been suggested, for instance, that a hobby of Astrology, accompanied by a more expensive hobby of Alchemy, ran away with a great deal of his money. In this connexion only two facts can be noted in a mere skeleton of facts like the present. First, Chaucer seems to have had a son named Lewis; presumably by Philippa Chaucer, who is thought to have died about 1387. Chaucer wrote for his son a little treatise on the Astrolabe, treating that scientific instrument very much as a toy, and definitely stating that, whatever there may be in astronomy, there is precious little in astrology. This has been held to refer to a grievance against such medieval experiments. But it seems to me quite sufficiently explained by the fact that Chaucer was a Christian and a Catholic, with plenty of common sense and an acquiescence in the Church's protest against the superstitions of fatalism and doom. Even if he had not been sensible enough to be orthodox on that subject, a man of his nature would certainly be specially orthodox when writing something for his own child. That might not have prevented him playing the fool with sham sciences himself; but the thing is quite unproved. The other proof offered is the very violent explosion against the fraud and rascality of Alchemy in the Canon's Yeoman's Tale, which sounds to some good critics like the real recital of a real wrong. We cannot tell whether Chaucer had this experience; we can be quite certain that he had this conviction.

His second Italian mission first arrests the attention by bringing in certain figures who counted for a good deal, either in life or literature. We find here certainly, for the first time, that he was a close friend of his famous contemporary, the poet Gower; for he left Gower as a deputy to look after his affairs. Here we have another of these typical fancies, that have hardened into theories; the theory of the broken friendship and subsequent quarrel of the two medieval poets. Their relation is of some historical interest, but this sort of guesswork is very unhistorical. We can only speculate on the friendship. Chaucer was a man for whom the world teemed with quiet fun, as it says in the comic opera; and I have often wondered whether he felt the full irony of the patronage to which men such as he are subject. I do not mean the royal or feudal patronage, which was simply a part of the social order of the time, which a sensible man of his type would probably accept as we accept policemen or postmen. It was considered part of the province of a prince to support artists and such odd people; and, though the thing had obvious abuses, there was something to be said for it, if we compare it in all aspects with the problem of the best-seller or the man who starves in Fleet Street. But I mean that more subtle patronage that is extended to poets by poets, and not by patrons. There is always something a little quaint in that relation of the rich artist and the poor artist; or the old artist and the young artist; or the successful artist and the other who is not as yet successful. It is recorded with rather savage irony in Mr. Belloc's sketch of 'The Good Poet and the Bad Poet'. Remember that Hayley as a poet, and not merely Hayley as a squire, was in a position to patronize Blake. There is a grim humour in the fact that a man like Swift felt bound to mention a man like Temple[29] as a literary leader, and not merely as a social protector. The practical patrons of Chaucer did not, so far as I know, appear also as the rivals of Chaucer. At least I never heard of John of Gaunt dropping into poetry; or Henry of Bolingbroke capping *The Canterbury Tales* with a little thing of his own. But the thing has more subtle forms when it comes from the seniors of the school of letters; from those who are, for any reason, considered more established, or more learned, or more in the official limelight, than a mere stray genius. I have always felt that there was a touch of this in the attitude of Ben Jonson to Shakespeare. I am pretty sure there was a touch of it in the attitude of Gower to Chaucer.

John Gower seems to have had a vaguely national or official function, which was never entirely accorded to Chaucer, for all his laureateship and his butt of sack. Shakespeare, following some tradition of tragedy, and more especially of morality, uses the name for the funereal figure appearing before the curtain as a Prologue or prophet of woe and wisdom, to draw all the proper morals from the historical plays; as if it were the name of the licensed and labelled moralist of English literature. Chaucer addresses him as, 'O moral Gower', distinguishing him, in a departmental manner, from 'the philosophical Strode', whose province was presumably philosophy. But the

[29] Sir William Temple (1628–1699) was an English diplomat, statesman, and author. Jonathan Swift was a relative and lived in Temple's home and worked as his secretary almost continually from 1689 to 1699.

delicate difference of tone appears when we pass from what Chaucer said to Gower to what Gower said to Chaucer. Gower was thoroughly friendly; entirely affable. He says that Chaucer is his poet; but he also says that Chaucer is his disciple and even 'his own clerk', who has taken down many of his thoughts, perhaps in somewhat lighter language. And in his doubtless sincere compliment to Chaucer's verse, we have exactly the same suggestion as that made by many graver poets about Shakespeare and his warbling of wood-notes:

> Of dytees and of songes glade
> The whiche he for my sake made.

One would not say that the graver poets disapprove of cheerfulness in the minor poets; but they mention it. Chaucer, like Matthew Arnold in Max's caricature, was not at all times wholly serious. Without claiming to have read every line and word of the moral Gower, which would be a boast of no little hardihood, I suspect that he was, for the most part, wholly serious. When I hint that it is barely possible that Chaucer saw some humour in all this, I do not mean to discredit the view that the two poets were friends. They were both, in their way, men of good will, and one of them was conspicuously a man of good humour. That sort of friendship need not go wrong, unless both the friends treat it wrongly. Blake abused Hayley like a pickpocket; but then Blake was as hard to please as Hayley was tactless in pleasing. Chaucer was not at all hard to please. It is written all over his work that he was very easy to please. George Macdonald finely said that God is easy to please and hard to satisfy; and there is something of that in many great men. I can believe that Chaucer was pleased with Gower's patronage, though I rather doubt if he was satisfied with Gower's poetry.

These being the human and rather humorous probabilities of the case, the ingenious melodrama of the mortal quarrel of the poets has apparently been made up merely out of one chance remark in *The Canterbury Tales*. It is the characteristic remark of Chaucer that he dislikes stories of which the subject is some horrible perversion or monstrosity; he mentions one such legend, which does happen to have been dealt with by Gower. We can only say that this might conceivably have led to a quarrel; but I can find no direct evidence that it ever did. To say it could only have been written *because* of a quarrel seems to me simple nonsense. For the rest, Gower's place in the biography is that of the friend whom Chaucer left to represent him when he went to Italy for the second time: that second visit which introduced him to other historical persons of importance; notably to Bernabo Visconti of Milan, whose tragedy attracted the sympathy of Chaucer, as remains recorded in the Monk's Tale. He was not long in Italy this time, but most critics hold that he saw more books and manuscripts and received then his real introduction to Italian letters. There seems to follow an expanding leisure and importance at home; he was given a new Comptrollership; he was able to appoint a permanent deputy for his old Comptrollership, and in the same year, 1385, he was made a Justice of the Peace for Kent, and in the following year a Member of Parliament, as King of the Shire for Kent. Thus he seems to settle down and spread himself in that very English landscape through which he and his great company will ride forever; when there came the sharp turn in his destiny and something even like disaster.

Richard the Second, the grandson of the old King, had come to the throne as a mere boy; though a rather remarkable boy, to judge by the presence of mind and instinct, at once princely and popular with which in his boyhood he faced and pacified the Peasant Rising. But he naturally suffered from uncles; generally either from John of Gaunt, the Duke of Lancaster, or from his other uncle, the Duke of Gloucester. Lancaster went abroad, leaving his protégés unprotected; Gloucester seized the power and almost the person of the young King, and in the overturn Mr. Geoffrey Chaucer lost all his comfortable jobs, which were given to the Gloucester party. There follow clear indications that he had fallen on evil days. He obtains protection for a year against being sued for debts; he sells some of his pensions for cash down. Relatively to his previous prosperity, his comparative poverty seems to have continued till his death. But relatively to these first pressing years of poverty, immediately after Gloucester's palace revolution, he makes a very considerable recovery; and seems to have received royal help once more, whenever he really required it. For Richard the Second, a year after he had become a man, determined to become a King. He suddenly rent the rod of office from Gloucester; summoned back John of Gaunt, and resumed that sort of rule which Victorian historians always called despotic, especially when it was slightly democratic. The effects of this, and of his ultimate fall, on English history were very great and have been considered elsewhere. But the effects on Geoffrey Chaucer were very practical and consoling; for he was appointed Clerk of the Works in the repairing of the greatest public buildings: the tower of London and the Palace of Westminster, and St. George's Chapel at Windsor. He was later made a commissioner for the repair of high-roads, and though these jobs did not last indefinitely, he was never entirely neglected after the return of John of Gaunt. Richard the Second gave him a new pension in 1394, and later a tun of wine. Fortunately, also, even the fall of King Richard, which changed so many things, did not change this partial recovery of Chaucer's more moderate prosperity. Whatever else Henry Bolingbroke was, he was John of Gaunt's son, and had no quarrel with his father's old poet. He sent him a fresh pension in response to the humorous melancholy of the poet's 'Complaint to his Purse'; and with this Chaucer passed his last days in peace. But his last days had come. He died just after he had moved into a house near St. Mary's Chapel, from which he is said to have looked out in his last hours on the gardens and the great roof of the Abbey.

More than one portrait of Chaucer remains to give a general idea of his appearance, though that was the time of the first beginnings of the portraiture in paint, at least in this country, as Chaucer himself may be called the beginning of portrait-painting in literature. The pictures we have represent him as he was in later life, when the Host of the Tabard chaffed him on his stoutness. It would be interesting to have an earlier impression, touching the days when he was light on his feet, and knew fighting and foreign travel, yet had already what was called his elvish face and the pleasant shyness that covered so much sharpness. The best existing portrait is that published by the poet Occleve, to illustrate one of his own poems. It shows the head in a black hood against a green ground; two tufts of grey beard and a wisp of whitish hair rather recall, at least to modern associations, the elvish comparison; but the face is sober and benevolent, not without something of that sleepiness touched with slyness, that is the mood of much of his later work. Red cords on his dress support writing materials and he appears to be carrying a rosary; at least, as it is certainly a string of beads, it seems most likely that it is a rosary. For I cannot suppose that Chaucer's quarrel with the Friar even if it went to the point of assault and battery, would have prevented him from carrying what has been called the Layman's Breviary, devoted to the Virgin to whom he had so much devotion, merely because the instrument happens to have been invented by St. Dominic. However that may be, the portrait is unmistakably a portrait; the person unmistakably a person. And it is easy to imagine the old man, in much that habit and condition, pottering about the Gothic lanes of Westminster, until he died, almost to a day (it is conjectured), coincidently with the death of the flamboyant, toppling and tottering fourteenth century.

He was buried, as we all know, in Westminster Abbey; the first of the poets to lie in Poets' Corner. There have been differences about the tomb, of late Gothic design, that still covers his bones; but it is certainly so far a genuinely Gothic thing, that it is the only thing in that Corner that suggests the idea of a corner. The more modern monuments do not suggest the sort of persons who would be content in any case to remain in corners. Even if it were erected much later, and not in the best medieval manner, it is so far medieval that it does suggest that the buried man is buried; not that he is impatiently and prematurely resurrected before the Resurrection. Even here we feel something of that *communis sententia*, or medieval common sense; which was so much less rhetorical, and therefore so much more really rational, than the rational eighteenth century. Few will deny that the figures which fill the Abbey to-day, mostly the relics of the eighteenth century, are in their nature rather rhetorical. I do not mind such rhetoric in its place; but I doubt if its place is a Gothic church, and I think it is made to look rather silly by the silent presence of the Gothic tomb. The latter seems to say, in the language of a simpler time, that Galfridus Chaucer had lived his life, and this monument commemorated his death; and that, *salva fide*, there was an end of it. He has swaggered a little in his day, and that cheerfully and pleasantly; but he does not swagger solemnly in his death. He had served in arms, and been among swords and soldiers; but he does not stand wildly waving a sabre and bestriding a cannon, like General Sir Peveril Potts, whose services in the campaign before the Peace of Utrecht will leap to all our memories. He had done his best for his country in diplomatic negotiations with foreigners, and settled several questions of royal ransoms or marriages of considerable importance in their day; but he does not stand grasping a scroll or pointing to a map like the Right Hon. Benjamin Buffle, whose patriotic virtues have boiled over from his tomb in billows of bloated marble. He had written a little thing or two that some have admired; but he does not lean elegantly on an urn or look up at a laurel or invoke an invisible Muse, as does the immortal Timmins, whose works were so widely read by the fashionable world in the Age of Reason. He does not strike any attitude as do the varied representatives of that remarkable company; including, I believe, five or six professional politicians and one butler; probably the most respectable person present. He does not offer any remarks, by means of post-mortem pantomime or sculptured signal or gesticulation. He lies prostrate as when death struck him down; in the last dark instant when he cried upon Christ.

IV

THE GARDEN OF ROMANCE

Chaucer advances into the light of literary history out of a forest of tangles traditions, translations, imitations, partial imitations and patchwork collaborations, like a figure emerging from that chequered and glimmering forest of dreams in which such medieval figures so often walk; in which a half-human figure will carry two faces under a hood of allegory, and haunting half-recognizable voices speak from behind the golden masks of the gods. Most people realize more or less the curious sort of communism in culture that prevailed in those days. Some, however, hardly realize that there were two sides to it. Many medieval translators really were inventing, even while they were translating—or stealing. While the modern egoist has the rather petty prudence of Polonius, and will neither a borrower nor a lender be, the medieval traditional translator would often lend as well as borrow. We first find a poem and read it as if it were an original; and then are surprised to find that it is a rather close translation. Then we read it as a translation, and are surprised again to find that it contains a great deal that is purely original. It is hard to say which of the two would seem the stranger, in the case of any strong and sincere talent to-day. Modern writers are intense individualists, and certainly none more so than the Socialists. If Mr. Bernard Shaw, say, or some more impatient intellect of recent times, had just begun his literary career, he certainly would not begin it by writing laborious English versions of the longest novels of Tolstoy. But still less, if possible, would he add to the length of the works of Tolstoy long passages entirely invented by Bernard Shaw. We should not find the whole dramatic story of Candida somehow embedded in the story of Anna Karenina. We should not find all the best speeches in *Arms and the Man* put into the mouths of moujiks, in the retreat from Moscow described in *War and Peace*. And that is exactly how the medieval translators used to go on. At the first glance, they almost seem to be publishing somebody else's book as their own. At the second glance, they seem to be gratuitously giving away their own work to improve somebody else's book. It cannot be understood without calling up a vanished world of the community of thoughts and themes, in which a tale or a topic was in some sense set up like a target; in which a romantic story was rather like a smoking-room story, which can be told over and over again, with variations by different story-tellers. One author did not so much rob the other as enrich the other. These ragged Northern poets may have taken refuge in the ruins of Greek temples or Italian villas, but not merely in the manner of bats and owls; they repaired the ruins not merely with new stones, but with precious stones. They often wore second-hand clothes; but they patched the old garment, not only with new cloth, but with cloth of gold.

It is necessary, to start with, to make this point clear about the spontaneity and sincerity of the translator. In this, even more than other things, the modern change has chilled the sense of scale or grandeur in Chaucer. There exists a fine French ballade, addressed to Chaucer by a contemporary in France; lauding his work up to the skies with a warmth it would be impossible to doubt; and it has for a refrain, like a burst of boisterous salutation: 'Grant translateur! noble Geffroy Chaucier.' Some English critics have been a little sniffy (I can use no other word) in receiving this fervent foreign compliment; because it appears to describe Chaucer merely as a translator. On the other hand, a brilliant French critic, who does full justice to the poet otherwise, has in this matter also a faint suggestion of sniffness (I apologize to the academy of pure English), in so far as he seems to insist that Chaucer *was* merely a translator; touching certain works of which much has been made. Chaucer was a translator; but his French critic seems to me to miss his countryman's full meaning in speaking of a *great* translator. It is not easy nowadays to think of the thing on quite that scale; partly because it is badly paid; partly because it is badly done. Talking of 'a great translator' sounds like talking of 'a great scrivener', or 'a great stenographer'. But this is to leave out that vital medieval virtue; the enthusiasm of the translator, his primary motive of admiration; sometimes admiration for the author; sometimes simply admiration for the subject. It will be necessary to note, in another connexion, that it is indeed impossible to translate poetry, in the sense of finding a precise equivalent to poetical language. But it is none the less possible to be inspired to write fine native verse by the inspiration of fine foreign verse; or sometimes, even, of slight foreign verse. Indeed, I am disposed to suspect that a translation is always either much greater or much smaller than the original. Now some of Chaucer's translations were much greater than the original. All of them were, in a rather curious sense, more original than the original. All of them seem to move quite naturally in English poetry; though English poetry, in a manner of speaking, had only just begun to move. Indeed translations of this old natural sort do seem to find it easy to get naturalized. 'Drink to me only with thine eyes', is not less a lyric essentially English because it is taken, almost line by line, from the Greek. 'When lovely woman stoops to folly', is none the less an English poem because it was taken, almost word for word, from the French. But in the case of Chaucer we are dealing with something much deeper than the eighteenth-century sentiment of Goldsmith or the robust pedantry of Ben Jonson. He was often dealing with those profound intellectual passions that concern themselves with the ultimates of the universe; with the philosophy that is even prior to poetry. He was moved to translate the original, he was moved to make the translation greater than the original, not by personal rivalry, or even by personal admiration, but by what he himself would call the *primum mobile*, or Great Mover of all hearts and heads; by a direct appeal, not to the original, but to the origin.

Those who do not happen to understand these emotions are at a disadvantage in the matter. This appears very clearly, for instance, in a composition which is generally placed by scholars among Chaucer's early works, and is certainly among his traditional works. I mean the alphabetical address to the Blessed Virgin, commonly called Chaucer's A B C. The French critic, to whom I have referred, pins the matter down to the single point that this poem is undoubtedly a copy of a similar French prayer, written by a French priest. He seems to make everything turn on the fact that the French priest wrote the poem in short lines, and the English poet was wise enough to widen them into long lines. In other words, while admitting the artistic effect, he tends to insinuate that it is an artificial effect. He congratulates Chaucer as an artist or artificer; but he congratulates him upon having selected a more ingenious form of verse, or made an experiment in metre. But this sort of technicality is not tenable in the presence of the poem itself. At least, it is not enough to satisfy any one with a strong sense of poetry. The original French poem is an honest but somewhat bald statement in very short lines; the first line being 'A toy du monde le refui'. Chaucer merely turns his mind to the same subject, and bursts out, 'Almighty and all-merciable Queen!' You do not produce that sort of line by counting the syllables.

Chaucer is not expanding his metre; he is expanding himself. He is expanding his lungs and his heart, like a man stretching out his arms in the pattern of the cross. He only breaks out of the framework of the French metre, because there was not room in it to stretch his arms. The mere words, as they stand, call up the image of a man so standing; and making some such wide gesture of worship. Of course, having once created his lyric metre, by merely breaking into his lyric cry, he has to sustain it throughout the poem, like any other poet; and sometimes sustains it with some difficulty, or (what is worse) with too great ingenuity; also like any other poet. But the poem is not a piece of ingenuity; certainly not a piece of metrical ingenuity. It is an original poem, in the sense that the emotions have their origin in the poet, and not merely in the other poet whose work he had read. I know that; as I know when a love-song is a love-song; or whether a drinking song could really be sung in chorus. Luckily or unluckily, as the case may be, this is a curious kind of love-song. The writer quoted above, remarks, in a tone not uncommon also among some of the English writers on the subject: 'The learned critic Ten Brink, basing his opinion on this prayer as well as some other effusions addressed to the Virgin Mary, which are to be found in Chaucer's work, concluded that he must have passed through a period of intense devotion, more especially towards the Virgin Mary. That is possible.'

It is. It does occur from time to time. I do not quite understand why Chaucer must have 'passed through' this fit of devotion; as if he had Mariolatry like the measles. Even an amateur who has encountered the malady may be allowed to testify that it does not usually visit its victim for a brief 'period'; it is generally chronic and (in some sad cases I have known) quite incurable. And as Chaucer's work, practically beginning with translations like the A B C, practically ends with the almost excessive devotionalism of the Parson's Tale, and has any number of devotional declarations scattered between the two, I cannot understand why his very normal European religion should only be allowed to him during one peculiar period of delirium. But in any case, the point that concerns us here is that Chaucer wrote a poem as well as a translation. It is a poetical poem, not because of its relation to its original, but because of its relation to its subject. It is full of lines that have a certain large and liberal majesty, because they are filled with the greatness of the occasion: 'Glorious maid and mother, which that never were bitter, neither in the earth nor sea'—'O very light of eyen that ben blind, O very lust of labour and distress'—'And bringest him out of the crooked street; whoso thee loveth, he shall not love in vain.' If this were a translation of a heathen hymn to the sun, it would still be the sort which a man only writes by staring at the sun. If this were a Scandinavian song of the sea, it would be one which a man writes by knowing the sea and not merely by knowing the Scandinavian song-book. And the purely literary moral, apart from any moral moral, of all this passage in the poet's life, is that he was already emphatically a poet, even if he was still a translator. He is a poet because he sings; because he opens his lungs and liberates his soul by a resounding and rhythmic utterance, the expression of love or admiration or passionate amazement. It is a primary and not secondary expression; as would be proved in answering the question: 'But what is he admiring?' Is he singing out in admiration of Guillaume de Deguileville, of Chalis, the original singer of the French A B C? No; not at the moment. He is singing to the singer of the Magnificat.

I have begun with this example, not because it is chronologically the first, or perhaps even one of the first, examples of that dependence on tradition in which Chaucer's work begins; but because it is a clear and compact case of the way in which a man may easily be expressing the most positive and even passionate feelings of his own, and yet be technically a traditional type of translator. This double truth runs through the whole of the work of Chaucer, the whole work rightly or wrongly attributed to Chaucer, and indeed through the whole of the works of his contemporaries, which are not by Chaucer at all. The disputes about the actual chronology of Chaucer's first writings are such that the most learned are those, confessedly, who know that they know nothing. The controversy is extraordinarily complex, because of this communal character in medieval literature which I have already mentioned. When he was ostensibly writing an original poem, he thought nothing of quoting at enormous length from anybody who happened to interest him, for any reason. When he was avowedly writing a translation, of a recognized Latin or French original, he thought nothing of putting in chunks of Chaucer which are not in the original at all. But this part of the problem presents itself first, on fairly clear grounds, in the case of the two longer and more important works, with which Chaucer certainly dealt among his earliest experiments; and in which he appears as a true translator, without any particular doubt or disguise about the matter. The first example is his translation of *The Romance of the Rose*; if I may frankly translate the title as the poet did the poem. The other was his translation of Boethius on *The Consolations of Philosophy*.

The Romance of the Rose is rather like the Briar Rose of Pre-Raphaelite legend. It is very beautiful and rather difficult to get through. It is a long allegorical French poem, which was written in two parts by two distinct and indeed very different poets. If we compare it to the Briar Rose, we may say that the first half contains most of the roses and the second half most of the thorns. That is, the first four thousand lines were written by one Guilaume de Lorris, and are a grave and graceful allegory of the kind that can be traced like a tapestry in the background of the medieval mind; the description of a dream, a magical garden inhabited by Virtues and other valuable abstractions; much healthier company than many real persons in fact or fiction, but not very stimulating to a modern taste. The rest of the poem was added nearly half a century afterwards by the satirist Jean de Meung. He seems to have declined to accept the medieval convention that everything in the garden was lovely; with the result that everything in the garden became considerably more lively. Like Chaucer and Langland and the best men of the time, Jean de Meung was perfectly orthodox so far as theology was concerned; but, like them, and perhaps much more that they, he was critical of the growing corruptions and abuses of the Church. His satire was enormously fashionable, especially as some ecclesiastics had condemned it; just as if it were a modern improper novel. In any case, he was a man of ideas, over and above the one idea of the conventional though beautiful allegory; and he probably had a great deal of intellectual influence on Chaucer. But exactly how he and Chaucer stand to each other in connexion with the documents, it is very difficult to decide. It is enough to say here that a very long and continuous English version of the French poem does exist, and is apparently, or at least partially, by Chaucer; but that Chaucer himself (in the medieval manner of which I have spoken) is said to have confused the question further by putting in long passages that do not come either from his original or from himself, but are simply things that happened to please him in all sorts of other authors; chiefly ancient or classical authors. Possibly he may have thought that when something so luxuriant and unlimited as the Briar Rose had once begun to grow, there could not be too much of it. But this was in his early days, and I fancy that by the time he had developed the thrifty and cutting critical quality of *The Canterbury Tales*, he would have admitted that the beautiful entanglement of the Briar Rose was a bit too thick. Nevertheless, his work was never cut in two quite in the style of the work he translated; and in him the blossom and bramble remained a fairly recurrent design. There was always something courteous about him that would not obtrude a thorn without covering it with a rose; and something malicious about him which would not offer a rose without hiding a thorn.

Beyond this, the only gerneral effect of *The Romance of the Rose* on his life is, as has been said, rather the effect of a decorative background. It was all this sort of thing that a poet meant by poetry, in the fourteenth century; as distinct from his own personal experiments or curiosities in poetry; which eventually became much more curious and experimental in Chaucer than they did in any of his contempories. But this is the starting-point of his poetical journey. This is the tradition which he took at first for granted as the tradition of his trade; this is the education as distinct from the evolution of a poet. All the medieval poets began with this story of a dream. We might say that they all began by walking in their sleep; a company of singing somnambulists. It is curious to think that *he* began so; who came to be, of all poets perhaps, the most conspicuously wide awake.

The business of the translation of Boethius touches a general truth, even at the beginning, which will become more apparent and important towards the end. The relation of medieval men to philosophy, and enlightenment in general, was rather curious; and is not covered by the natural metaphors employed. We used to talk of the Dark Ages; most of us know by now that the true Dark Ages came before the true Middle Ages; and that in many ways the Middle Ages were far from dark. But, following the figure of an age of darkness, we are apt to think of an age of twilight; or perhaps, of grey morning light. But the metaphor itself is misleading. Twilight means an equally diffused light; and the difficulty of medievalism was the difficulty of diffusion. It would be truer to compare even the Dark Ages to a dark room, with certain chinks in the shutters through which particular rays of light could pierce. But the light was daylight, what there was of it; and not even a dull or troubled daylight. It was broad daylight that came through a narrow hole. Or it was like some long narrow ray of a searchlight sent out from a great city and falling like a spotlight on a remote village or a lonely man. And just as any man, however much in darkness, if he looks right down the searchlight, looks into a furnace of white-hot radiance, so any medieval man, who had the luck to hear the right lectures or look at the right manuscript, did not merely 'follow a gleam', a grey glimmer in a mystical forest; but looked straight down the ages into the radiant mind of Aristotle. There was indeed, as I have said, any amount of indirect transmission of light; any amount of reflection—in every sense. But I am not talking of the quantity, but of the quality of the light. Such light as they had came, not only from the broad daylight, but from the brilliant daylight; it was the buried sunlight of the Mediterranean. These men seem to be, and in some ways were, men simple or primitive. But their philosophy was not merely simple or primitive. In some cases it came from a ripe and rounded civilization; in some cases even from an over-ripe, from an autumnal civilization; from an over-civilized civilization. We might compare them to children in some cold and gloomy March, looking at the barns filled with the grain garnered by dead men in a forgotten autumn; but anyhow they fed their wild boyhood on things that were mature, and sometimes more than mature. Hence we have the pardox that a rude and primitive society, in some sense starting afresh, yet had so often for its guides, not merely the writers of the old world, but the writers of the world when it was growing old. All such paradoxes work back to the pardox: that the further we go back to first ages of the modern world, the nearer we are to the last ages of the ancient world: as King Arthur stands in Britain at once as the first of the Britons and last of the Romans. Thus a primitive poem, like Abbo's 'Siege of Paris', stops amid the storm of northern arrows rattling on rude roofs and walls, to make mythological conceits that had been copied from the copyists of Ovid or Virgil for five hundred years. But Ovid and Virgil are not the less civilized poets because barbarians continued to copy them. The men of a new civilization were not the less able to understand the civilized poets, because they had been continually copied. In a word, medieval men were not in the twilight; what they knew they knew. They had not read Homer at all; and (strange as it seems in a literate and enlightened age) did not despise him because they had not read him. They had read Virgil much more fully and thoroughly than we have. Anyone who doubts it may make the experiment of quoting beautiful Virgilian lines in a first-class railway carriage, full of politicians and captains of industry. In a word, though their knowledge of civilized antiquity was in a sense scrappy, though the scraps were not only old scraps but sometimes stale scraps, they had enough of them to understand what the great ancients had meant by wisdom; and, unlike some others, they had the great wisdom truly to try to be wise.

The case of Boethius illustrates specially the second truth; that the spring of medievalism had fed on the autumn of classicism. Boethius was a man who lived very late in the break-up of the Empire, under Theodoric. The period, with its power of amalgating old and new, has been much underrated. Boethius hands on the Stoic memories; but it is not really necessary to deny that he was a Christian or assert that he was a nominal Christian. Many pagan philosophers were converted by Christian philosophy. His work was a sort of distillation of all that had been best in Paganism; small in quantity but good in quality. Thus he served very truly as a guide, philosopher and friend to many Christians; precisely because, while his own times were corrupt, his own culture was complete. Generally speaking, the cultured Mediterranean man had come to play this part towards northern men. His disciples had not read Homer, but he had; they did not remember one kingdom acknowledged from Scotland to Syria, but he did; they did not know in detail what fine shades of feeling or criticism had come with Catullus[30] or Lucian,[31] but he did. Thus (in the special case of Boethius) we find this mirror of maturity still reflecting a lost daylight in the darkest age; and playing a unique part, especially in the development of the English. Boethius, who had been martyred for justice by his barbarian master, wrote in prison a book called 'The Consolations of Philosophy'; in which he summed up all the truth and tradition of antiquity. Alfred of Wessex, the first great man of our own island story, wishing to educate his half-savage Saxons, assumes at once that it can be done best by translating Boethius. He also, like those who followed him, put a great deal into Boethius that is not in Boethius. He may be said to have completed the old Stoic's conversion to Christianity after his death. Chaucer, perhaps the last great Englishman of the same united Christendom, feeling the same need of portable philosophy, instantly turned to the same idea of a translation of Boethius. He also quotes from Boethius, consciously and unconsciously, in any number of his ordinary poems. Boethius was a point of view; it was a calm and cultured and well-balanced point of

---

[30] Gaius Valerius Catullus (87–54 B.C.) was a Roman lyric poet.
[31] Lucian (120–200 B.C.) was a Greek artist.

view; and the essential thing to realize is that a medieval man could have it as a common and normal point of view; and take it quite easily, like Chaucer.

All that we mean, in common talk, by 'taking things philosophically' was possible to a medieval man like Chaucer, even if we mean no more by philosophy than his whistling or shrugging his shoulders. The possibility is worth recalling, because it is generally rather left out of sight, both by those prasing medievalism and those reviling it; by those who most admire its mysticism and those who rage most fanatically at its fanaticism. These elements, bad and good, did exist; but there were other elements; other fragments of the old Roman pavement of the world; other bits of the broken Christian empire of Constantine, that a man could pick up here and there. One of them was this Christian stoicism, or what would now be called manliness; and Chaucer was much attracted to it. We may mention here the handful of small poems in which the influence appears; though the dates of all of them seem to be rather doubtful. It stiffens the very virile and spirited little ballade with its familiar lines:

> Hold the hye wey, and lat thy gost thee lede:
> And trouthe shall delivere, hit is no drede.

Somewhat of the same sort is the moral appeal he addressed to Richard the Second on Steadfastness, decidedly a Stoic as well as a Christian idea. The remarkable poem, commonly called 'Gentilesse', in which he appeals to Christian equality against feudal inequality, might be said to savour of that remote concept of citizenship, which had once been left in the code of Justinian as the legacy of the Christian Caesars; anyhow, it suggests an aspect not always considered in the conventional conceptions of heraldry and chivalry. The poem called 'Fortune' opens with a self-sufficing defiance quite in the way of the ancients, and invokes the great name of Socrates: though Chaucer's sense of humour (a very Christian thing) leads him to let Fortune, as a lady, have the last word. The poem called 'The Former Age', a sort of Earthly Paradise, is almost altogether a paraphrase from Boethius.

Anyhow, as has been noted, he did deal thus with Boethius and *The Romance of the Rose.* These two translations were translations, whenever they were written or whatever was written along with them. When we come to the original poems of Chaucer, we come to much disputed matters, especially in the matter of chronology. We have very little to guide us except Chaucer's own references in his own writing, which are generally very amusing and rather disparaging references. We have also the dates of some historical events more or less clearly connected with the poems. Thus we know that by the time he wrote *The Legend of Good Women*, whenever that time was, he had already written the poem on the death of the Duchess, the wife of John of Gaunt; *The House of Fame*; *The Parlement of Foules*, and *Troilus and Criseyde*. For in the *Legend* he makes Love complain that Chaucer has mocked lovers in translating *The Romance of the Rose* and depressed their spirits with the tragedy of Troilus. But the leading lady, representing Woman, pleads for the poet, saying that although 'he can nat wel endyte' (that is, although this writer is unfortunately unable to write), yet he has done his best, by producing various very proper works in her praise; and the remainder of the list is given as above. As we shall note presently, it contains other matter; but it is not certainly a complete list. Many hold that these very early writings included the Legend of St. Cicely, as afterwards inserted in *The Canterbury Tales*; also perhaps the story, or a story, of Griselda,[32] and some fragments of the Monk's Tale. There is also a group, of very doubtful date; *The Complaint of Mars*; *The Complaint of Venus*; *The Complaint to his Lady*; and similar things, all very complaining. On the whole, however, the list in the *Legend* is the important one. It is suggested by some that the passage in *Troilus*, in which the poet expresses the hope of writing a 'comedy', refers to *The House of Fame*, meaning that that vision is divided in three on the model of *The Divine Comedy*. It is possible, and we know that Chaucer venerated the epic. It seems much more probable to me that the promise of a comedy refers to the intention to write *The Canterbury Tales*, or perhaps the Knight's Tale as originally

---

[32] Griselda is the heroine of Boccaccio's *Decameron*.

separate from *The Canterbury Tales*; or, most likely of all (for those who admit literary men to be human beings), some perfectly vague and general intention to off and have a jolly time, after all that weeping; a hazy hope of writing something simply human and funny, such as was afterwards largely satisfied in *The Canterbury Tales*. Strictly speaking, indeed, the list is more enlightening about the life of Chaucer than about the argument of Love; for the poet slips into the list, not only the translation of Boethius, but a theological work by Origen on St. Mary Magdalene and a pronouncement of the great Pope Innocent III, about the miseries of the poor, which hardly seem at first sight to advance the cause of Lovely Woman in pleading before Cupid. For that very reason we may take it as certain that Chaucer had written these religious paraphrases, along with certain roundels and virelays, presumably lost.

On the whole, it seems most probable that he began his creative career by writing *The Death of Blanche the Duchess*, a sort of family service, almost a feudal service, to his patron John of Gaunt; that at some time later he wrote *The Parlement of Foules*, followed by the larger and more ambitious enterprise of *Troilus and Criseyde*, and then *The Legend of Good Women*. The Duchess Blanche actually died in 1369, which gives us one of the few definite points in the chronology. On our own calculations Chaucer would be about twenty-eight, and likely enough to be given a sort of minor laureateship to the Lancaster branch of royalty. There is a more shadowy possiblity of dating *The Parlement of Foules*, because it involves a veiled and tactful allusion to proposals of marriage between Richard the Second and Anne of Bohemia: similar allusions to certain stages of this Royal courtship have been found in *The House of Fame* and in *Trouilus*. But *The Parlement of Foules* is practically concerned only with these proposals, though in a highly allegorical fashion. Richard was actually married to Anne of Bohemia in 1382, but the preliminary proposals and suggestions began in 1380. Short of entering indefinitely, not only into details but into disputed details, this is about all that can be said with certainty of the time and order of these poems; save indeed for one separate problem, which arises out of several references to a poem called *Palamon and Arcyte* and an actually existing poem called *Anelida and Arcyte*. Some suppose the former to be simply the story afterwards incorporated in *The Canterbury Tales* as 'The Knight's Tale'; others an earlier experiment which is lost. The latter is a rather unconvincing fragment full of the laments of some lady whom Arcyte has deserted, but linked with the other by the presence of that very English gentleman, Theseus, Duke of Athens, destined to play so breezy a part in English letters from the *Anelida* to *The Midsummer Nights' Dream*. Those who deal in labels for literature may be suprised to be told that the official ode, the feudal family duty, of a lament over the loss of John of Gaunt's wife, is in fact a very touching poem. First of all, it seems quite incredibly likely that John of Gaunt was really very fond of his wife, and that Chaucer was very sympathetic with so deplorably sentimental a state of mind. It contains a very noble description of love in marriage; of a deep comradeship that has never lost the last intimate veil of courtesy. The point is worthy of remark, because those hostile to such normal things have made a great hash of history, in their version of the medieval view of marriage. Because marriage was made merciless fun of, as it is still; and because love outside marriage, or even against marriage, was often pardoned as romantic or sympathetic, as it is still; above all, because certain fantastic fashions allowed of the public proclamations of the sort of beauty-worship and intellectual flirtation that exists still—because of all this, those who understand neither the fantastic nor the normal have pretended that all medieval men and women saw love and marriage merely as rivals to each other; accepted no marriage except as a dull duty; and enjoyed no love except as an illicit enjoyment. But this is all nonsense; not only to anybody who knows a little of human nature, but to anybody who knows even a little of medieval literature. The truisms remain true, however much fun people may get out of the paradoxes; the cynical paradoxes of satire, or the romantic paradoxes of adventure. A man imagines a happy marriage as a marriage of love; even if he makes fun of marriages that are without love, or feels sorry for lovers who are without marriage. That Chaucer was normal in this, as in nearly everything else, is abundantly proved by his own printed words. It is true that his printed

THE GARDEN OF ROMANCE

words were poetical words, and will be less perfectly understood by those who can only read them as prosaic words. But even these can hardly misread them altogether. And anybody who can read poetry as poetry knows perfectly well when a poet is weighing his words, in a truly weighty fashion, and means exactly what he says. There is something in the sound and measure of the words, as of the tolling and swaying of a great bell; and it sounds unmistakably when the great Theseus lays before the lovers the Christian majesty of the mystery of marriage:

> The first Mover of the Cause above,
> When He first made the faire chain of Love,
> Great was the effect and high was his intent
> Well wist He why, and what thereof He meant.

Any man who really understands it does not see a Greek king sitting on an ivory throne, nor a feudal lord sitting on a faldstool; but God standing in a primordial garden, granting the most gigantic of the joys of the children of men. Poetry of this kind is not written by accident; it does not write itself. The poet who writes it takes a tone as unmistakable as a change in the human voice. Few will say that in this Chacuer was flattering the Duke of Lancaster. Fewer still, I imagine, will say he was flattering the Duke of Athens. He did not write that sort of thing in his sleep, or in a fit of absence of mind. 'Well wist he why, and what thereof he meant.'

The mixture of nonsense and normality in a healthy man, and the particular sort of nonsense which went to make up a medieval man, is very well illustrated, in the same connexion, in the case of *The Legend of Good Women*. At first sight they seem a very extraordinary exhibition of Good Women. They are selected according to a rather pedantic fantasy, which prevailed in the Middle Ages, concerning heroes and heroines who had died for love, as a sort of religion. Chaucer himself calls them the Saints of Cupid; the martyrs of romance who were to be a sort of decorative pendant or parallel to the martyrs of religion. Of the deeper meaning of this historic mood there may be something said elsewhere. But the modern reader may possibly be slightly amused, when Cleopatra makes her positively first appearance in the character of a Good Woman. He will be wise, however, in every sense, if he does not fix his eyes only on Cleopatra. He will be very unwise if he interprets the whole legend in the light, or shadow, of Cleopatra. I mean that he will be wildly wrong if he fancies it to be a Swinburnian hymn of harlotry; or supposes that the Legend of Good Women is really a Legend of Bad Women. Cleopatra finds herself among the saints, because she is credited with what would be called the final perseverence of the saints; with constancy, as distinct from inconstancy. But the poem itself proves that Chaucer did not think that constancy was necessarily the wild constancy of Cleopatra and Anthony, or even of Guinevere and Lancelot. For the great queen, the grand heroine, the perfect woman who rules the rest and leads them and speaks for them, the lady who is set up as the supreme lover, is neither Guinevere nor Francesca[33] nor Iseult[34]. She is Alcestis, the long-married woman who went down to Tartarus to deliver her husband. She is alone enough to show that Chaucer and his age did not merely separate love and marriage. She is obviously put first among the Saints of Cupid because she is one of the Saints of Hymen: and is called a Good Woman because she is a Good Wife.

The Parlement of Foules, presumed to come in between *The Death of the Duchess* and *The Legend of Good Women*, does not indeed give such scope to such sentiments. It is all about proposals for a marriage but it hardly allows of any such serious emotion about the ideal of being married. It is a particularly graceful excerise in that sort of stately levity, which is suitable for compliments paid at court, by men who are rather more than courtiers. In form it is a fable about an assembly of birds, before whom three rival eagles advance their claim to the bird most desired as a bride; presumably a reference to the imperial princes who might have married Anne of Bohemia. It is not so easy to enter into the darker and more delicate psychology of a large bird of prey as of a bereaved husband, with whom you happen

---

[33] Francesca Da Rimini was the daughter of Dante's friend and host during the latter years of his life. She was married to the deformed Gianciotto Da Rimini but fell in love with his handsome younger brother, Paola. "Paola and Francesca" is an episode in Dante's *Inferno*.

[34] Iseult was the lover of Tristan, who like Lancelot was the ideal of high and heroic chivalry. They appear in the medieval cycle *Tristan and Iseult*.

to be personally aquainted. Chaucer had not yet developed that divine impudence, which enabled him to make a cock in a farm-yard talk like Aristotle and Aquinas about the mysteries of the supreme Will and Wisdom. In short, it is a charming parable; but we all feel that the Parliament of Fowls would have had a livelier session, if the Cock had been returned as a member. With *The Legend of Good Women* (leaving *Troilus* for fuller treatment) we pass to matters more purely Chaucerian, as being more personal and peculiar to Chaucer. In the prologue to this poem appears the picturesque and vivid, though quite light and unpretentious, personal sketch of the poet. In the livelier and more telling manner of his later tales, he tells us something of his own habits and humours; how he delights in books; how he is criticized for neglecting his neighbours for the companionship of books; how, when he has done his day's work with the accounts and ledgers of his various public offices, he does not want to go on a holiday but only to sit down with a book. Having worked the description up to this point, he gets the full effect out of the one exception, and makes quite a dramatic entrance for the Daisy. He owns that, when spring first comes on the fields, he suddenly flings away his books and goes down into the daisy-meadows to drink of a deeper delight.

The special feeling of Chaucer for the daisy, among the flowers of the field, has often been remarked, and both the personal taste and the popular tradition illustrate a sound instinct in medieval symbolism. A man might really learn more of the special spirit of Chaucer, by looking at daisies, than by reading a good many annotations by dons and doctors of literature. If he did toil laboriously in the long tangles of the Romance of the Rose, it is true to say that he opposed to it something fresh that might be called the Romance of the Daisy. We might even carry the figurative parallel further, and say that at one end or extreme of poetry is all that Walt Whitman meant by *Leaves of Grass*, the acceptance of the common even in the sense of the chaotic or incomplete, and at the other extreme the symbolic and almost heraldic Rose of the medieval allegorists; and that between that garden and that grass the exquisite and temperate medium or transition was really expressed in the daisy, or the first fresh realism of Chaucer. I am not denying the worth of any of the three types of poetry, from the wildest to the tamest; and I offer every apology to the grass. But when we talk of wild poetry, we sometimes forget the parallel of wild flowers. They exist to show that a thing may be more modest and delicate for being wild. And that atmosphere is exactly the atmosphere of Chaucer and of daisies. Certainly some of Gower's garden roses were tolerably tame flowers. But this is not meant in the modern 'ruthless' realistic spirit. When we say that Chaucer's flowers were wild flowers, we do not mean that they went on like wild beasts. We mean that there is a certain freshness and freedom about their very slightness or subordination, and it is this sort of unmistakable air that comes to us in Chaucer, like a cool wind across a meadow.

I am aware, of course, that some industrious critics have suggested that all this was not only formal but even fictitious, and that Chaucer intended some elaborate compliment to some lady whose name was Marguerite. This is quite possible, as advanced by the best Chaucerian scholars, but there is a type of student who advances it to lay waste the whole daisy-meadow. He has a curious subconscious itch in the presence of poetry; an itch for explaining it, in the hope of explaining it away. But this sort of critic is in any case unreliable, because, in dealing with a poem, he cannot distinguish between its occasion and its origin. He is the sort of commentator who, listening to the enchanted voice of Oberon[35] telling of mermaids and meteors and the purple flower, is chiefly anxious to assure us that the imperial votaress was certainly Queen Elizabeth, and that there actually was a pageant at Nobbin Castle, for a wedding in the Fitznobbin family, in which a cupid and a mermaid figured in such a manner as completely to explain William Shakespeare's remarks — and almost explain William Shakespeare. It is all quite probable; it is all quite true: by all means, let us be gravely grateful for the information. There were doubtless a good many pageants and a good many parades of Cupid and Dian; and I dare say a great many mermaids on a great many dolphins' backs. But, by an odd chance, only one of them ever, in the whole history of the world, uttered such dulcet and harmonious breath that

---

[35] In medieval legend, the king of the fairies was Oberon.

the rude sea grew civil at her song, and certain stars shot madly from their spheres to hear the sea-maid's music. That is the kind of thing that has rather a way of only happening once. And if we really must find out where it came from, or why it came, we shall be wise to guess that it had a good deal less to do with the Mermaid at Nobbin Castle than with that other Mermaid at which Mr. William Shakespeare of Stratford sometimes took a little more wine than was good for him. In the same way, any appreciator of poetry as poetry knows that the medieval poet had a real kinship or sympathy with daisies and what they stand for, quite apart from whether or no he used them for personal purposes on particular occasions. It is quite possible that Chaucer took pleasure in the pun about the daisy when he was in love with some lady called Marguerite. It is much more probable that he had to pay some conventional compliment to a lady called Marguerite, and jumped at the chance of using a little thing he had already written about daisies. But anyhow it was he who wrote it, and it was about daisies that he wrote; and anybody who cannot see that cannot see that Walt Whitman liked grass because it is rank and ragged or that William Morris liked roses because they are symmetrical and symbolic. The whole picture he contrives to suggest, of his rising at the faint call of May, and leaving his books, and going forth like a shadow to find the green meadows under the grey dawn, is full of a certain kind of cool and colourless intoxication which would call up a crowd of daisies in any imaginative mind, even if he had never mentioned them. If he knew anybody called Marguerite (and shared with the professors that profound scholarship, of the school of Stratford-atte-Bow, which reveals that Marguerite is the French for daisy), he would very probably mention that. It has been similarly ascertained that a lady named Rose has sometimes been compared to a rose, and, I presume, a lady called Rhoda to a rhododendron. But a poet, and his particular kind of poetry, are really to be judged by the fact that he prefers to talk most of roses, or rhododendrons, or sunflowers, or poisonous-looking orchids, or daisies in the fields of morning. His selection of such things strikes the note which he wishes to strike, and lets us realize the things of which he likes to dream. In this sense the selection and use of the daisy is

Chaucerian; individually and unmistakably Chaucerian; it is one of the clues to Chaucer. It may be remarked that whenever he uses the word elsewhere, though in a casual connexion, it has the same sort of freshness and filicity. Among those splendid and spirited sketches in the Prologue of *The Canterbury Tales*, slashed in with a few strokes as verbally fastidious as Stevenson, we are told that the jolly red-faced Franklin, or country squire, in whose house 'it snowed meat and drink', had a beard 'as white as a daisy'. There could hardly be a better example of Chaucer's brilliant brevity of description. If he had said white as frost or snow, it would have been banal and suggested some senile decay. As it is, he conveys that even the blanching of the man's beard seemed to make him look more lusty and lively. Finally, as a last lesson from the daisy, it seems probable that the poet was quietly aware, so to speak, of the rather large and daring significance of the derivation of daisy from the eye of day; which gives to that small object something apocalyptic like the sunrise, and a sort of claim to be the eye of the whole earth. It is notable, because it connotes that something, which was kept rather quietly in the background, but which I have called elsewhere the greatness of Chaucer.

Anyhow, the personal preface of *The Legend of Good Women* naturally rather overshadows the legend itself; but even in the latter the interest is not altogether impersonal. Chaucer is chaffing himself, more or less, upon an imaginary charge of being a misogynist, and represents Love as charging him with having done great wrong to lovers, and notably to ladies. This, as has been said, seems to refer chiefly to *The Romance of the Rose*, which seems a little unfair; it is hard if a man, who has had the toil of copying out and translating such an interminable poem, should have also the burden of defending all its sentiments. But it is notable that the poet sets himself politely but decisively to the task of disproving his hatred of women. He does it all the more energetically because it was a very unnecessary task. Chaucer certainly did not hate women, let alone lovers; he did not hate anybody. At any rate, whether it be a strength or a weakness in him, he did not hate anybody much. All his talents were on the side of sympathy, even when they seem to take the form of satire. That is where he really does differ, for instance, from Dante; and there is something rather national about the difference. But indeed Chaucer had written or was about to write a more complete answer to the charge than is found in *The Legend of Good Women*. So far from thinking ill of women whom he was expected to admire, he managed to think well, or at least to think kindly, of a woman whom the whole world expected him to deride and despise. In the *Legend* he praised each woman in turn, for being a faithful lover. But he could not bring himself to curse a woman, even for being a false lover. The curious way in which this corner is turned, with a curve rather than an angle, is one of the most singular and individual qualities in the poem that probably he wrote most carefully and seriously, and intended to be the outstanding creation of his career.

There is nowhere a more whimsical, or even weird historical product than the story of Troilus and Criseyde. To begin with, it is a myth made out of a mistake; or what would now be a misprint. There never was any person called Criseyde, even in the sense in which there was a person called Helen. She is only the corruption of the name of somebody else, who was entirely different. And yet this walking misquotation walks the world as a more living creature than most legendary figures quoted on the highest authority; this talking typographical error not only talks to us, in an animated manner, in an unmistakably human voice; but also with a new voice that strikes a new note in human history. The tale of Troilus and Criseyde is an anachronism, an anomaly; in some sense a prodigy and a portent. It is a Homeric story of which Homer had never even dreamed. It is a posthumous Pagan myth belatedly born centuries after the death of Pagan mythology. It is a medieval romance, invented by medieval men, who seem to have managed to revere it as a part of pagan Antiquity, and to have practically forgotten that they had made it up out of their own heads. Finally, it is a Christian story entirely about Pagans; it is full of the particular sort of moral sensitiveness and sense of spiritual freedom which alone makes possible certain sorts of criticism; and especially of self-criticism. Criseyde is a Christian creation because she is a Minx; and a Minx is a product of the culture of Christendom.

Many even among educated readers may be aware that the name of Criseyde is all that the Dark Ages had left of that very harmless person Briseis, the beautiful slave whom Achilles and Agamemnon each claimed as part of the spoil of war. It illustrates the difference between the two atmospheres, that the former lady is a passive instrument of fate, while the latter lady is a very active example of the abuse of free will. Briseis is blameless because she is blind. Cressida[36] is even false, in order to show that she is free. Because Briseis was beautiful, the dogs tore on the Trojan plain the limbs of mighty chieftains: 'Such was the sovereign doom and such the will of Jove'. But because Cressida was something more than beautiful, was something of what men have come to call romantic; because she was wilful and mysterious and incalculable, Diomed is wounded and Troilus is slain; and bards lament, reproaching, not Jove, but Criseyde. Nobody had ever thought of reproaching Briseis. With this extraordinary medieval postscript to the Iliad, we come upon an entirely new world of curious and even complicated feeling; produced by the overflowing of medieval mysticism into the old jests and tragedies of love and lust. It is seen at its finest in Chaucer's version of the tale, because Chaucer was perhaps the man with the finest feelings in that age. It is a basic blunder to suppose that he was superficial, merely because he had a light touch. A light touch is a mark of strength and not weakness, in spiritual as in bodily things; and (in those days especially) to be in that sense superficial was a way of avoiding being intolerably sentimental.

It is a commonplace that this tale was treated both by Chaucer and Shakespeare; and it is rather a misfortune that we generally think first of the version that was written last. Anyhow, it illustrates a certain difference (of which there will be more to say later) to note that the Renaissance version, compared with the medieval version, is certainly livelier, and certainly not happier. It is the liveliness of the second fermentation; and what in Chaucer was still wine, in Shakespeare is very like vinegar. The chalice of Chaucer does indeed contain the dark wine of tragedy and the lamentation of lovers. But he laments

---

[36] Cressida is a form of "Criseyde".

chiefly for true lovers, and even when he implies the existence of false lovers, he never begins to imply that all love is false. Indeed his simplicity contains a subtlety that is not always justly valued, and can hardly be too carefully considered. When I say it is a new note, I do not mean of course that there was anything new either about jeering at lovers or raving at false lovers. I mean that there was something new in the particular way in which Chaucer balanced both so as to produce neither; the way in which Chaucer did not jeer and did not rave; but jested without jeering and reproached without raving. The charity of Chaucer towards Cressida is one of the most beautiful things in human literature; but its particular blend belongs entirely to Christian literature. Pagans had felt the agony and anomaly of true love given to the false lover; but the mixture was never a blend like this. Catullus, the most subtle and (as some would say) the most modern of the ancients, had reached the paralysing paradox of 'I hate and I love'. But the particular Chaucerian tone cannot be translated as 'I hate and I love'; it is something more like a combination of 'I adore and I pity', with 'I pity and I condemn'. Again we feel, if only for a moment, that it was not quite so absurd to talk of putting 'Daunt' into English; for many have felt the same fine shade in the feeling of Dante about Francesca.

But even apart from the more merciful view taken by Chaucer—even in the case of the rather merciless view taken by Shakespeare (which was indeed the view originally taken by Boccaccio)—there was a mystical medieval element in all this tragedy, or bitter comedy, about false love. It might almost be translated into theological language as a sense of the insecurity of the souls of others; though the theologians, to do them justice, generally urged us to begin with a sense of the insecurity of our own. I know of course that Chaucer does once, in a sort of noble weakness, snatch at a sort of fatalism as an excuse for his heroine; chiefly because he really cannot think of any other excuse. He is heart-broken about it: but this does not alter the new universal tone of *moralizing* about love. It is not fanciful to see something of a new spirit, even in the spiritual sense, in this closer vigilance touching the problems of the weak and wavering human will. It is really, for reasons on which we shall remark later, a sort of shadow thrown by a mystical and metaphysical cloud upon the classic and flowery fields of pure poesy. The medieval world did incessantly talk about true lovers and false lovers, where the classical world would often have been content to talk about lovers. And though there are many false lovers in classic fable, it is interesting to note that their falsehood does not really discredit them; and the false lover is the true hero. Theseus is not less the Athenian hero because he deserts Ariadne; nor Aeneas less the pious Aeneas because he deserts Dido. But a new note has crept into laments like that of Anelida and Arcyte; a suggestion that the false lover is the false knight, and has broken some bond of chivalry. All this atmosphere, heavier with moral responsibility and self-determination, was not unconnected with the special social ideals of feudalism; and the notion of a wandering knight still owning dependence on a distant lord. But it was also deeply affected by that religious idea, which denied doom and substituted damnation or salvation determined by the will; the spirit that made Dante acclaim freedom as the first of divine gifts, or made Chaucer contradict Calvin, centuries before he was born, in the very first words of the Parson's Tale. In the very centre of that Christian cosmos, everything pivoted on the idea that the human heart could be given to God or withheld from him. The highest affections of the soul could turn this way or that, to the divine or the diabolic; and the supreme charity was valued because it was not enforced. It is rather a grim joke that the main tenet of the most orthodox creed might be summed up as Free Love.

Another new step, or rather a new stride, is taken in literary progress with the publication of Chaucer's version of Troilus. It concerns the character of Pandarus; and Pandarus really is a character. With him we have the first full appearance of Chaucer as a humorist; that is, of Chaucer at his broadest and best as a benefactor of humanity. The character of Pandarus does indeed sprawl through that very lengthy poem rather lazily, like the limbs of a giant where they have room to stretch themselves. The author has not yet achieved that brilliant brevity, that power of dashing in a whole personal description in a few strokes, which he developed later in *The Canterbury*

Tales. The humour of Pandarus is not quite so humane as the humour in *The Canterbury Tales*; it is sometimes deliberately unpleasant; but it is the humour of a humorist. It is also important, in the matter of the general literary transition, to notice the points in which Chaucer changes the tale as he had read it in older versions. It is very significant of his independent craving for character that he turns Pandarus from a young cousin to an elderly uncle. Bernard Shaw said somewhere, very truly, that the vigour and virility of Rembrandt are best shown in his preference for painting old women rather than young ones. There is the same sort of clean and interested love of character in Chaucer's excellent descriptions of elderly men; such as the Franklin and the Knight. It must not be forgotten in relation to this change in the romance of Troilus. As has been noted already, the whole story has a very eccentric evolution from its Greek origin, and had already gone through curious changes. Criseyde was once Briseis; and Pandarus was not always a pandar. It seems to have begun with the usual graceful friendship of two youths, Troilus and Pandarus; pretty much like Damon and Pythias or Pylades and Orestes. But Pandarus had to take on, more or less, what was known in later theatrical circles as the part of Charles's Friend.[37] And it was an almost inevitable implication, even in modern theatricals, that Charles's Friend was rather more cynical than Charles. Anyhow, Troilus's Friend became very cynical indeed; and the part he has to play, of bringing the lovers secretly together, lent itself easily to the less-pleasing jocularity of medieval and Renaissance literature. Thus, by the time of Chaucer, Pandarus has become a funny old man; and, by the time of Shakespeare, he has become a decidedly nasty old man. But, for the moment of medieval transition, the point is that Chaucer made the young man old, because he wished to make the character at once more ripe and more quaint, more experienced and more fixed. In that sense the character of Criseyde's uncle takes the new road as the first of the Canterbury Pilgrims; the first of that great and gay procession of the English comic characters, which has not ended with Falstaff or with Pickwick. We must not

---

[37] Charles's Friend is possibly a reference to the character Orlando, who defeats Charles in a wrestling match in Shakespeare's *As You Like It*.

exaggerate the proportions of the change; the Chaucerian art is still mainly dominated by the serious romance of medievalism; with decoration for its form and sentiment for its substance. Only the less serious passages which are filled by Pandarus suggest the beginning of that new and powerful use of the comic, which seems sometimes almost more tremendous than the tragic.

I do not know whether it is one of Chaucer's jokes (and I am sure he made many jokes that nobody knows) when he appends to this apparently interminable poem, consisting of no less than eight thousand, two hundred and forty-six lines, the cheerful comment, 'Go, little book; go, my little tragedy.' But in any case it is profoundly significant that he adds to this the remark that he hopes some day to be able to write, 'Some comedy.' This has been variously interpreted; even in the sense that he meant *The House of Fame* to resemble *The Divine Comedy*. But it seems to me more likely that he had found the one comic character in his tragedy so amusing a study that he hoped to produce some more; or, in other words, that he found Sir Pandarus such good fun that he had already guessed, perhaps, that his greatest talent pointed towards such achievements as the Wife of Bath or the Nun's Priest's Tale.

On the whole, we may say that in *Troilus* we find that Chaucer, who was already a good poet, is beginning to be a great poet. There were depths and delicacies of regret, when the heroine entirely declined to be heroic, which were not possible in anything like *The Legend of Good Women*; where the heroines stood in a row, all being resolutely heroic. There could be a directness, even an excessive directness, about the jokes of Pandarus, which was not to be expected in the indirect diplomatic discussion of an international alliance, as explained by eagles. Chaucer has become Chaucerian, and emerges as a man of genius distinct from the many men of talent, who could then be counted on (if officially required) to go to sleep and dream of a house of gold or a garden of lilies. But when all this is allowed for, it will be well to realize also that all Chaucer's work, up to *Troilus* and including *Troilus*, come under a certain general description, that hardly applies to *The Canterbury Tales*, and are conducted within a framework of conventions, from which he afterwards broke away. In other words, the great poem of *Troilus and Criseyde* is possibly the last and certainly the best of the series of works written primarily under the power and magic of that special sort of Romance which turned love as it exists between lovers first into a sort of philosophy and then into a sort of religion; a thing that had both its grammar and its gospel; both its science and its asceticism. It is true that it would affect many robust rationalists as merely amounting to sentimentalism. But there was much more in it than that; as there was much more in Rossetti or Swinburne than appeared to the satirists of aestheticism in *Patience*[38] or *Punch*.

Indeed that wood of wandering lovers, with their figured garments and burning pallor, and insistence on the kinship of desire and death, is a very easy thing to make fun of. A modern man may legitimately smile at the curious convention, by which it appears to be necessary for anybody in love with a young lady to collect a large number of other young ladies, and tell them all about it, and elaborately thank them for their gracious sympathy and their highly exemplary patience; yet the man with the superior smile may not realize that he is being superior to Dante. He may think himself much more robust than the medieval lover who swoons when the conversation takes a discouraging turn; or the poet who weeps over the death of an abstract person called Pity, because his young woman (in more robust language) has turned him down. Yet it may be questioned whether the modern man really is more robust than Chaucer; or even half so robust. Nor would he find it easy to laugh at Chaucer very long, without beginning to have a dark suspicion that Chaucer was laughing at him. The truth is that Chaucer included this phase of romantic and visionary passion, and many other things as well. But he included it because God had given him a remarkable talent for seeing what good there was in things; and there was a great deal of good in this. A man vowed to this religion of romance may appear to us very effeminate in his emotions; but he might easily need to be very virile in his experiences. He could be

[38] Patience is a reference to *Patience of Bunthorne's Bride*, an opera by Gilbert and Sullivan.

called upon to fight; to die; and, what is worse, to wait. Professor Pollard, who certainly has no medieval battle-axe to grind, remarks in his excellent study of Chaucer that the discipline of such lovers was rather severe and noble than merely weak and self-indulgent. The really important point, as a point of biography and history, is that, however stale we may find it now, it seemed at that time fresh, because it really was fresh. The *Vita Nuova* really was the New Life; there had been nothing exactly like it before, in all the history of love.

Romance was a strange by-product of Religion; all the more so because Religion, through some of its representatives, may have regretted having produced it. But it is quite obviously the transfer of the tragic responsibilities of the Faith to the field of almost pagan passion. It is sometimes said that Christianity has been weak and ineffectual. The truth is that it has been so powerful and effective that it coloured even the things it had not hoped to influence; and changed its enemies as well as its friends. Even worldliness, when it did not become otherworldliness, became another sort of worldliness. Even the Church, as imperfectly represented on its human side, continued to inspire even what it had denounced, and transformed even what it had abandoned. Anyone who judges by living facts, and not by dead details, can see the Christian ideal remodelling even the Pagan image in its own image. In a word, Chaucer was right (as he generally was) when he talked, with pleasant blasphemy, about the Saints of Cupid. They were in one sense saints; because they were in one sense martyrs. He could talk about martyrs of love more reasonably than modern rationalists talk about martyrs of science. But both are in this sense rational; that a martyr really means a witness. And these two types are indeed witnesses. They are witnesses to the necessity, which forces irreligion to borrow the terms of religion.

In short, whether or no this or that Christian may choose to oppose romance or chivalry, it is quite certain that without the Christians there would never have been any romance or chivalry to oppose. It is also perfectly true that there was a great deal of romance and chivalry which it would have been quite sensible to oppose. The period during which Chaucer lingered in this literary garden, extends from his first official poem on the Death of the Duchess[39] to the completion of *Troilus and Criseyde*. But it includes one or two less pivotal poems, of more doubtful date, in which this sort of garden had perhaps rather run to seed. One is the work called *The Death of Pity*, to which I have already referred; another is *The Complaint of Mars*, and perhaps *The Complaint of Venus*; and *The Complaint to His Lady*, apparently a continuation of the former. These things are more shadowy and have a more shadowy relation to Chaucer; but they obviously have a relation to this contemporary Romance. Whether they are by the poet or no, they belong to this period of poetry; and it is well that this period should be understood. In the final phase of *Troilus and Criseyde* it can be fully understood; and Chaucer fully understood it, in its limits as well as its liberties.

This religion of romantic love had till lately all the advantages, and has now all the disadvantages, of having been revived by the Victorians. 'Love Is Enough', which was the title of one of William Morris's plays, might have been the motto of all William Morris's period. Rossetti and Browning, as well as Tennyson and Mrs. Browning, wrote always with this implication, right or wrong, of identifying the ideal morality with the higher sentiment of sex. We were all more or less brought up in that tradition, which contains a real truth; but we all know that there has been of late a reaction against it; rather an excessive reaction, beginning with Mr. Bernard Shaw and ending with Mr. Aldous Huxley. There are only two considerations in this connexion which affect a fair judgment of its earlier appearance in the age of Chaucer. The first is this; that, for all the advance of rationalism and science, the medieval romanticist was much more of a realist than the modern romanticist. The medieval poet did not deny that love-stories could end badly; it was the Victorian novelist who invented the idea that they must always end well. The medieval man may sometimes have been a sentimentalist; but, to do him justice, he was not an optimist. He did not pretend that this particular kind of emotion, healthily popular as it is, and eternally

---

[39] The "Death of the Dutchess" is a reference to Chaucer's *Book of the Dutchess* (1370), the first important extant poem by Chaucer. It is an elegy for John of Gaunt's first wife, Blanche of Lancaster, who died in 1369.

attractive as it is, has only brought happiness and never unhappiness to human beings. The true lover was often tragic; the inspiriting thing about him was simply that he was true. Whatever therefore may be justly urged against the mere cushioned comfort or upholstered respectability of Victorianism, certainly cannot be urged against the thorny thickets and visionary vigils of medievalism. The second fact to remember is even simpler and more to the point. It is that Chaucer, having paid a magnificent tribute in *Troilus and Criseyde* to all that is really generous and humane in the worship of a highly medievalized and almost Christianized Cupid, does finally give his judgment; and his judgment is not in favour of the cult of Cupid but against it. In a series of verses of great beauty and power, as Professor Pollard has noted, he gives his ultimate decision that happiness is not to be found by dancing after any heathen god of love; but by looking up, as he bids all the 'young fresh folks' to look up, to where a more terrible but a more tender god of love hangs, not on Olympus but on Calvary. Thus, in relation to the whole of this business, of the medieval ideal of True Lovers, which Chaucer every bit as much as Browning can treat at its very truest, we may say that Chaucer was large enough to be delighted by the vision; but too large to be deceived by it. His claim to greatness gains on both sides; and he will not suffer by any cynical phsychological discoveries, which the latest sceptics may imagine they have made about the falsity of Romance. If the nineteenth century deified Romance, if the twentieth century deserts Romance, the great medieval Maker is equally master of that vision; four hundred years ahead in seeing it; and five hundred years ahead in seeing through it.

V

THE CANTERBURY TALES

To watch the unfolding of the genius of Chaucer is to watch a pattern changing into a picture; or into a series of pictures. It is something like the illusion of a sick or sleepy child, staring at a wallpaper, for whom the flat plants seem to branch and blossom, or figures to begin to move among the formal trees. His work begins with the purely rhythmic decorative style that possessed medieval prose and verse, even more than medieval painting and carving. It ends with something more than the realism of Renaissance pictures; with something suggestive of the realism of modern novels. There is even a sort of paradox in it; that in his vigorous and adventurous youth he was formal; in his comparatively crippled and limited old age he was free. When he was a young soldier, fighting sword in hand against the spears of France, or a young traveller and political agent, dealing with delicate crises in the cities of Italy, his style of writing was still as rigid a pattern as the prison-bars that enclosed Palamon and Arcite.[40] When he was something more like a shabby old pensioner, stout of body and lean of purse, limited, as it were, to the view from his own lattice looking towards the Abbey and his own future grave, he broke out into a dance of lively and dramatic detail that reminds us rather of Dickens or of Balzac. We see him gradually breaking those flowery chains of his youth, and then living to sow such very wonderful wild oats in his old age. It is in itself an inspiriting sight, and the outline of a gallant story. But, for all that, we must not exaggerate one side of the matter, or imagine that he merely escaped from a prison to free hostelry and highway, when he fled from the House of Fame to the Tabard in Southwark.

For instance, it is well to remember that the purely medieval Chaucer has been an inspiration, even more, if possible, than the

---

[40] Chesterton is referring to the bars that imprisoned the two heroes Paloman and Arcite of the "Knight's Tale".

purely personal Chaucer. Art critics are now everywhere returning to that medieval sense of rhythm in art, and many literary men, long before, returned to it in literature. William Morris was a Socialist and in his time a typically modern man; what is very much more important, he was a typically manly man. He was eminently sane, hearty and healthy; and his broad face and leonine beard were in a sort of symbolic way felt as types of freedom and fraternity. But the Chaucer who inspired Morris was the Chaucer of the long elaborate pageants and allegories; even more than the Chaucer of the last brief excursion into the coarse comedies of daily life. A man wandering through the coloured corridors and labyrinths of the long decorative tales of The Earthly Paradise does sometimes feel a little like a fly crawling across a wall-paper. But that paper is a fly-paper that has attracted a good many flies. A Cambridge professor of chemistry whom I knew, a man whose whole main business was material modern science, had for his whole conception of a hobby or a holiday an endless journey in those realms of gold from the Glittering Plain to The Wood At The End Of The World. Mr. George Moore, who still manages to be a modern man of our time as well as his own, delights above all things in the decorative poetry of Morris; especially in the most meaningless parts of it, like the recurrent emblem of 'two red roses across the moon'. Now nearly all this inspiration was drawn, not only from Chaucer, but from the early romantic Chaucer as distinct from the later realistic Chaucer. If the hero of *Troilus and Criseyde* seems to be an unconscionable long time dying, the hero of *The Life and Death of Jason* also seems a little leisurely in his life and slow in getting to his death.

The moral is obvious enough; that what we call the length and even the monotony of medieval literature is a human pleasure and a human need, in certain moods and moments of mankind. It lay like an infinite inviting sea in the background of the fourteenth century. It returned like a refreshing and copious flood to the dry and dusty respectability of the nineteenth century. And, in the case of Chaucer, our very admiration for his later discoveries may make us exaggerate the futility of the traditions he inherited. Sir Topas may create a false perspective, rather as Don Quixote creates a partly unjust retrospect. Readers infer from the novel of Cervantes that the old romances were all rubbish; though Cervantes goes out of his way to explain that they were not. Readers may remember the name of Sir Topas[41] as a satire on chivalry, though in fact it follows on a very noble exaltation of chivalry in the person of the real Knight; the Knight who is without a name. Something of the same irony may even be found in the lives of the two men of genius. For Chaucer, who travesties Topas, had figured in armour and armorial bearings in the most florid period of the wars of chivalry; the terrible tourney of the Leopards against the Lilies. And Cervantes, credited with despising and destroying romance, had himself lived one of the most wildly romantic lives in history; escaping from slavery among the Paynims of Africa,[42] and wielding a sword and losing a hand in the deathless death-grip of Lepanto.

There is, then, something to be said for the long poetical allegories eventually abandoned by Chaucer; as for the long prose romances ultimately satirized by Cervantes. Their very extention and expanse satisfied a psychological need now perhaps only felt by children and poor people, who like to have a very big book for their money. Yet there are few cultivated moderns who have not felt something of the pleasure of being able to lose themselves in the longest books of Dickens or Trollope. But there is more in it than that; for man lives by his devouring appetite for morality. The chivalric romance does really represent the Christian conception of life, which is at once a Quest, a Test and an Adventure. And the decorative allegories, that seem so dead to us, were once alive like a dance with the balanced morality of the Middle Ages.

Dante makes the very heavens dance, in the last pages of the Paradiso; sweeping the sky with swaying and spinning ballets of angels and spirits; and the symbol is very appropriate to the philosophy. It is appropriate; not because the dance stands for disorder, but because it stands for order. The dance is in its nature a rhythmic and recurrent

[41] Sir Topas is the main character of the tale "Rhyme of Sir Topas". An effeminate, cowardly hero with decidedly middle-class values, he sets off searching for an elf queen. Chaucer assigned himself as the teller of Sir Topas' Tale.

[42] Paynims of Africa is a reference to the pagans of Africa, especially the Muslims.

thing, returning upon itself; and was therefore a perfectly correct and orthodox type of medieval moral theology. This, by the way, will be noted by the intelligent as correcting the exaggerated solemnity, with which some scholars have taken the tirades of fanatical friars, and other people, against the use or abuse of dancing. Doubtless there was much that was really pagan left in popular dancing, and doubtless there were plenty of donkeys in holy orders who found paganism in what was not really pagan. But in face of a fact like Dante's vision of the celestial dance, it is not tenable that the medieval mind thought of dancing merely as immorality or indecency. Nobody would describe people as doing in heaven what he had a deep and indignant horror of their doing on earth. Mahomet would not describe his Paradise as a place where the faithful were incessantly occupied in carving and worshipping idols. The Pacifist would not point happily to a future life in which everybody would be always waving sabres and firing off guns; the Prohibitionist would not picture heaven as a state of perfection in which the blessed could drink rum and gin for ever and ever. And Dante would not have filled the skies with dancing, if he had instinctively thought of the dance as degrading. The truth is, of course, that he instinctively thought of the dance as decorative and rhythmic, and therefore corresponding to a certain character in his whole conception of life. Indeed, it marks the whole difference between medieval life and modern life.

A certain break or sharp change in history can hardly be sketched more sharply, than by saying that up to a certain time life was conceived as a Dance, and after that time life was conceived as a Race. Medieval morality was full of the idea that one thing must balance another, that each stood on one side or the other of something that was in the middle, and something that remained in the middle. There might be any amount of movement, but it was movement round this central thing; perpetually altering the attitudes, but perpetually preserving the balance. The Virtues were like children going round the Mulberry Bush, only the Mulberry Bush was that Burning Bush which they made symbolical of the Incarnation; that flamboyant bush in which the Virgin and Child appear in the picture, with René of Provence[43] and his beloved wife kneeling on either side. Now since that break in history, whatever we call it or whatever we think of it, the Dance has turned into a Race. That is, the dancers lose their balance and only recover it by running towards some object, or alleged object; not an object within their circle or their possession, but an object which they do not yet possess. It is a flying object; a disappearing object; and, as some hold, a disappointing object. But I am not concerned with condemning or commending either the religion of the Race or the religion of the Dance. I am only pointing out that this is the fundamental difference between them. One is rhythmic and recurrent movement, because there is a known centre; while the other is precipitate or progressive movement, because there is an unknown goal. The latter has produced all that we call Progress; the former produced what the medievals meant by Order; but it was the lively order of a dance.

When we understand this dance, we understand the order or pattern of the early poems of Chaucer; and above all why he does not seem to be in any hurry to finish them. Judged by our higher standards of hustle and pep, the Canterbury Pilgrims do not seem to be in a very great hurry to get to Canterbury. But they are like American tourists in the pace they observe, in getting to the pilgrims' goal, compared with the pace of Pandarus or Phoebus[44] in getting to the point. But this leisurely quality is bound up in the very nature of the work, or play. A dance is a thing enjoyable in itself, and given such a dance of gods and heroes, it can go on for ever. A journey, if it is enjoyable on account of its object, is not equally enjoyable if it goes on for ever. I know that some moderns have tried to confuse at once the metaphor and the mind, by pretending that the joy of the journey is in something that can never be enjoyed. But this is a confusion. If they could express themselves clearly, they would either say that the journey is itself the goal, or else that the journey is hopeless and only an illusion makes it hopeful. Otherwise, they are

---

[43] René of Provence is a reference to René le bon roi (the good king), (1408–80) the son of King Louis II.

[44] Phoebus is an epithet of the god Apollo, the sun personified.

out on a tramp that has no end, to find and inn that has no existence. The more reasonable progressives profess to envisage an end of some kind, and when praising the goal naturally tend to foreshorten the journey. These are the authors of Utopias and plans of perfect social reform. But the poet, who is describing a dance of virtues, or a pageant of beauty, has naturally no particular impatience that this should itself end. And something of this lingering love of his own day-dream unduly prolongs his own description. It has the effect, especially for modern readers, of making much of such medieval writing dull. But even if we find it dull, let us not suppose it was the product of dullness, when it was the product of delight.

Of course, even these early works of Chaucer, on the old medieval model, are of very varying merit. *The Book of the Duchess* is a very affecting, because a relatively young and innocent, version of human grief; *The Parlement of Foules* has already more of the freedom of the fable about cocks and hens; *The Legend of Good Women* has moments in which it almost turns into a graver though certainly not greater *Canterbury Tales*; and the tale of Troilus and Criseyde, though to us inordinately long, has high and magnificent passages that are worth the toil of reading anything ten times longer. The point here, however, is that there is a sort of break in the story of Chaucer's style, and that the break came comparatively late in his story. He probably regarded the tale of Troilus as his supreme work, and the Canterbury Pilgrimage as a more casual postscript. His masterpiece is a kind of afterthought.

It might be maintained that, in the very act of leading his coloured crowd out of the Tabard and the town, and along the open road, Chaucer symbolized something of the change from the medieval balance to the modern march; from the philosophy of the Dance to the Philosophy of the Race. Few modern racing men, fewer still among modern racing motorists, will regard the journey as much of a sporting event. Few journeys have a greater air of leisure; and nobody, certainly, will suggest that it was a race in which the best man was meant to win. The fact that the Reeve always rode at the tail of the procession will be sufficiently balanced by the fact that the Miller apparently rode at the head of it. Here at least the medieval poet can have meant no allegory of spiritual superiority. But there is also a serious element in the idea of the Canterbury Pilgrimage which makes the Pilgrims' Way something more than merely the open road. So far as having a definite purpose is concerned, the Pilgrim of Chaucer is as genuine as the Pilgrim of Bunyan. He is not in such a hurry because he is not in such a horrible fright; and there is no question of the Franklin or the Squire putting his fingers in his ears and fleeing from London as from a City of Destruction. But he is none the less really fleeing to Canterbury as a City of Salvation. Anyhow, he is not merely wishing to escape into the wilderness and leave all cities behind. I shall discuss in a moment the really new element which the poet half consciously introduced into his long comedy of travel; the element of delay, or what a medieval man would have called dalliance. But though he admits a good many things besides pilgrimage and piety on this side of Canterbury, he does not admit anything beyond Canterbury. His scheme of travel is still dominated by the idea of a definite purpose, and the fresh forces which entered literature at this stage were more subtle, more subconscious, and more difficult to judge with delicacy, than a mere procession or progress into the void.

I know it was commonly said, both in medieval times and modern times, that the pilgrimage had become a mockery, by which it seems to be meant merely that it had become a holiday. But it was because it had been a popular shrine that it became a popular holiday. That this involved all the revelry, buffoonery, drunkenness and incidental swinishness of all sorts that belonged and still belong to a popular holiday, we could learn easily enough from Chaucer's own description, if we had not already learned it from our own common sense and experience. But Chaucer himself is very careful to put first the solid fact that a great many people, at least, did really wish to render thanks to St. Thomas of Canterbury for help in their past sickness; a good proportion of his own pilgrims are certainly religious people acting from religious motives. The truth is that, in this matter, I am again haunted, I might almost say tormented, by that little query which I put in the first pages of this book; the query that runs, 'But what of to-day—and what of to-morrow?' If it was a scandal to have religion mixed with riot or profanity, has it been such a complete cure to have riot and profanity unmixed with religion? If it was superstition to venerate the bones of a great man killed by a tyrant, is it any more intelligent that millions of clerks should go down and merely gape at the Sea, without having even the sense to worship Neptune? Is it more dignified that bankers should give us a St. Lubbock's Day on which nobody thinks of St. Lubbock; not even to the point of adoring colossal images of ants and bees? Simon of Sudbury, Bishop of London, had denounced the popular profanation of the pilgrimage. The Wycliffite tradition, and afterwards the Puritan tradition, has treated him as a hero. He may have been a hero, but he was not a prophet. He did not know what was going to happen to popular religion, when it had lost the Canterbury Pilgrimage. The truth is that anybody who tries to look at Simon of Sudbury's problem from both sides, from front and behind, will realize its real difficulty; but will incline to a simple if slightly impatient conclusion. He will be tempted to say that human beings are not to be trusted with a religion. But are they therefore to be trusted the more without a religion?

Chaucer died and left his last great work unfinished; his most perfect achievement still imperfect. Though he lived a long and busy life, he, more than any other great writer, died young. He had only come to the beginning when he came to the end. He was already old when his work became suddenly and entirely new. There have been cases of men trying a new trick or experiment and breaking down in the middle of it, as did Dickens in the detective-story of Drood. But the experiment was a small one; which he might have made at any time, and one which many others had already made. There are cases of an author in his last days writing something rather separate and unique, like a last confession or farewell; as did Shakespeare with the unearthly loveliness of *The Tempest*; or, in another way, Ibsen in the rather incomprehensible outbreak of *When We Dead Awaken*. But these were things not to be developed or extended further, even by their authors, let alone by anybody else. For good or evil, they were not things that could be done twice. Nobody could write another play like *The Tempest*; nobody, I should imagine, wants to write a play like *When We Dead Awaken*. But *The Canterbury Tales*, the last unfinished work of Chaucer, is in quite another sense unfinished and finished. It is not only a new scheme, but a new style. It is not only a new style, but potentially a new school. It is as if he had been an architect, who through a long and successful life had planned out the round arches of the Romanesque and the squat pillars of the Norman churches, and then, almost on his death-bed, had dreamed of and designed the first Gothic cathedral. For indeed *The Canterbury Tales* do remain rather like a huge, hollow, unfinished Gothic cathedral with some of the niches empty and some filled with statues, and some part of the large plan traced only in lines upon the ground.

Just as in such a case, the arches would stand up more strongly than the statues, or the walls be made first and more firmly than the ornament, so in Chaucer's work the framework is finer than the stories which correspond to the statues. The prolonged comedy which we call the Prologue, though it includes many interludes and something like an epilogue, is made of much stronger material than the tales which it carries; the narrative is quite superior to the narratives. The Wife of Bath's Tale is not so good as the Wife of Bath; the Reeve's Tale is not so vivid as the Reeve; we are not so much interested in the Summoner's story as in the Summoner, and care less about Griselda than about the Clerk of Oxford. The Miller does not prove even his own rather brutal energy, by telling a broad and rather brutal story, half so well as the poet conveys it in those curt and strong lines about his breaking a door by butting it with his red-bristled head. And the whole conception and cult of Chivalry is no better set forth, in all the seventy pages that unfold the Knight's Tale, than in the first few lines that describe the Knight. It is impossible to say for certain, of course, whether Chaucer realized how much more real and original were the passages which concern the Pilgrims than those which concern their imaginary heroes or martyrs. It is possible that, like many another great original genius, he did not know which parts of his own work were really original, still less which were really great. It is likely enough that Shakespeare attached more importance to some laboured conceit, in the manner of the Euphuists,[45] than to such stabs of staccato speech as 'Kill Claudio!' or 'Undo this button'. It may be that Chaucer really did regard the Prologue as a mere frame, in the sense of a picture-frame. In that case, we can only say he invented a new kind of picture-gallery, in which the picture-frames are much better than the pictures. Still, a word must be said for the understanding of the pictures, even when he had boldly stolen them out of other people's picture-frames. In other words, we must understand something about stories as stories, before we even open this medieval story-book.

I have taken too much notice, perhaps, of those who are still so childish as to talk about the childishness of Chaucer. I mean in the sense of bearing with him, as if he talked broken English. It would be truer to say he talked the unbroken English, which we have since broken up into bits and snippets of American slang or jaded journalese. There is rather more sense of a rounded whole, in expressing the religious sentiment in words like 'Almighty and almerciable Queen', than in saying, 'Up-to-date scientists admit worth-while qualities in religious urge'. I leave it to the most modern critic to decide which sounds like English and which like Pidgin English. I have pointed out that the poet was not in fact infantile or immature in any comtemptible connotation of the words; but in many ways an experienced and even a polished person. He was an artist who picked perfect words to produce his exact effect; he was a diplomatist who was probably himself picked out for his power of picking his words tactfully and persuasively; he was a philosopher who drew theoretical distinctions, along the lines of contemporary thought, with almost the delicacy of a theologian; he was a well-read man, who could collect stories of all shapes and colours from the ends of the earth; whose fancy could follow the mazy mythology of Ovid, and whose intellectual imagination could measure the starry stature of Dante. But I confess that there is a real element which might rightly be called childishness, if the term be used in a healthier sense, for something that may or may not have grown up, but has not grown

---

[45] Euphuists is a reference to literati in the Elizabethan period who used high flown diction or an elegant literary style noted for excessive use of balance and alliteration and frequent use of similes drawn from mythology and nature.

old. There is a quality in Chaucer, and in the whole civilization that produced Chaucer, which men of rather wearier civilizations must make a certain effort to understand. It is something that moderns have mainly praised in childhood; because moderns have not preserved it in manhood. It is gusto; it is zest; it is a certain appetite for things as they actually are, and because they actually are; for a stone because it is a stone, or a story because it is a story. If that is merely simplicity, he was simple. If that is merely stupidity, he was stupid. That is, if we would appreciate him or his age, we must go back to something that stirred in us when we first found that the door of a doll's-house would open; or when we first found that the end of a story could be the point of a story, as in the surprise that ends the admirable story of Puss in Boots. Chaucer and his friends were really capable of reacting to those surprises; of waiting patiently for the point of those stories; of treating the whole narrative process as a pleasure in itself. Most modern people cannot really do this; they have read too many novels. They have forgotten the very verbal meaning, by which novels once meant news. They have lost the positive pleasure in a double fashion; partly because they have been bewildered by too many plots; partly because they have been even more bewildered by the newer sort of novels, which have not got any plots.

Now when we talk of Chaucer, or for that matter of Shakespeare and many others, as borrowing plots, or copying plots, or repeating plots, we must always remember that the age was really simpler in the sense that there were fewer plots; and that a plot was a very precious thing. It was really prized, unlike many other precious things. It was prized because it had a point, and people were normal enough in their nervous system to start at the prick of the point; instead of having their dead minds punctured all over with old pricks, like the diseased arm of a drug-fiend. A mere anecdote was thought worthy of careful presentation, as a relic was worthy of a casket of jewels. The medieval man spent, or wasted, music and ornament and developed detail upon a pointed story; just as the more subtle modern novelist wastes them upon a pointless story. The point to seize is that the people involved were really so far simple, or (as I should say) so far receptive, as to regard a mere story as something rich and rare; something that was a gift; something that was a good in itself. Most of *The Canterbury Tales*, and especially the first and most finished of them, are good in themselves. I mean they are good even apart from the way in which this particular man of genius presented them. We may say, if we like, that Chaucer's stories are excellent, only they are not Chaucer's. But we must realize that Chaucer thought they were excellent, and enjoyed them as much as if he had invented them. We must not leave out the love of mere naked narrative in the men of medieval times. Every one knows, for instance, the outline of the Knight's Tale; how two friends quarrelled for the same lady-love and were condemned to settle it by combat; how one knight prayed to Mars to give him the victory, but the other knight prayed to Venus to give him the lady. It is a good story; it would make a good play; if a play were still a thing with a plot. Everybody knows, I suppose, the plot of the pardoner's Tale, which is a plot in the precise sense; of how three thieves went to find Death to slay him, and found only a heap of gold; and how one was sent to fetch food and wine, which he poisoned, while the others plotted to stab him and did so; so that they all found Death on their heap of gold. That is a good story, and contains a grim crescendo of dramatic action. This element of mere pleasure in narrative must be allowed for, in all accounts of the atmosphere of the age. For instance, the story of Griselda, as a moral story, must be balanced with a great mass of medieval jokes and satires about the woman ruling the roost, and the grey mare being the better horse. But the story of Griselda, as a story, is simply one of the numberless legends and fables about a person passing successfully through a series of tests or trials; like the weird tasks of Michael Scott[46] or the Twelve labours of Hercules. Men listen to it, as children would listen to it, merely to see how the person passed through his or her misfortunes to the end. If this sort of innocent intensity be called childishness, it is true that the age of Chaucer was childish. But we must recover something of the spirit in order to understand the age; we must sink back into that barbaric past, and

---

[46] Michael Scott (1789-1835) was a Scottish novelist.

far beyond it into dark depths of primitive instinct, and even endure to hear some cry out of prehistoric savagery commanding us to become like little children.

Nevertheless, there is another side; and an aspect in which the pictures are extremely picturesque. It is a commonplace of the critics that the actual stock of stories, which fill up the framework of *The Canterbury Tales*, is a borrowed stock from all sorts of sources, like the plots of the plays of Shakespeare. But the narrative poet had at least one opportunity of showing dramatic talent which was denied to the dramatist. Shakespeare did not have to offer each of his comedies as the creation of one of his characters. We only know that Hamlet liked a particular play about Hecuba[47] and that Theseus could put up with a particular play about Pyramus and Thisbe.[48] We are unilluminated touching the theatrical tastes of King Lear or Macbeth. But Chaucer had a collection of characters almost as diverse in dignity or indignity, and had to select a story for each. The stories are chosen with admirable art; with much more aptitude than some speeches in some dramas. Nothing could be more fitting than the sustained nobility of the Knight's Tale; a tapestry of heroes clad in gold, except perhaps the ragged and rending contrast that tears it at the end. When the monk is just about to begin his dignified recital of the deaths of kings, and the drunken Miller roars him down with his cataract of coarse, not to say foul narrative; an admirably managed collision of comedy; as if the ruffian had thrown a pail of slops over the statelier story-teller. But other examples, which are less well known, illustrate the same persistent neatness of impersonation. What could be more apt than making the dignified anti-clerical Doctor careful to narrate, not a Christian or even romantic story, but a story of the stoic virtue of heathen Rome; the story of Virginius,[49] precisely the sort of hero whom such secularists have always preferred

---

[47] Hecuba is the wife of Priam and mother of Hector in Homer's *Illiad*.

[48] Pyramus and Thisbe are lovers in the Babylonian classic story of Ovid's *Metamorphoses*.

[49] Virginius is the Roman plebian who, upon learning that his daughter Virginia was to be handed over to Appius Claudius to be his slave, grabbed a butcher's knife and stabbed her crying, "There is no way but this to keep thee free."

to the saint. How right it is that the chivalric romance of the young Squire should differ from that of the old Knight, in having a touch of the Arabian Nights about it; a more irresponsible and fabulous flight, upon a winged horse, into the golden horizons of Tartary. Equally delicate is the instinct which makes the Prioress, the refined and charming spinster, tell the beautiful legend of the child singing down the street on his way to the crown of martyrdom; or the Father Confessor of the nuns, a comfortable humorist of the type rather common as the male adviser of devout females, tell a sort of playful parable, full of nods and winks, in which the weaknesses of humanity are courteously covered by the feathered costume of cocks and hens. It is more generally recognized that the quarrel between the Summoner and the Friar is vigorously illustrated in their respective narratives, and the same sort of interplay of tales occurs in many places throughout the whole. Perhaps nothing is more characteristic of the Wife of Bath's Tale than the enormous and inordinate length of the Wife of Bath's prologue. One is momentarily reminded of the proportions between one of Mr. Bernard Shaw's plays and one of Mr. Bernard Shaw's prefaces. Nobody will say that the Wife of Bath bears a marked resemblance to Mr. Shaw; for of all the Pilgrims she was possibly the least Puritan. But her glorious and garrulous egotism, her unfathomable and inexhaustible vitality, are quite admirably hit off in the mere fact that she talks about things in general at such interminable, if not intolerable length, long before she gets to the beginning of her story at all. Chaucer, with his typical shrewdness, has not supplied any such long personal preface to any of the other stories. There are, of course, any number of other minor examples of the same aptitude; indeed there are very few of the stories that are in themselves entirely impersonal, or could have been shifted to any other person. It is not for nothing that the comfortable and prosperous Merchant tells a tale that is rather naughty, in the manner of a French farce, but not gross in the manner of the Miller's Tale. I will not debate the case of the Cook's Tale, specially called 'Gamelyn', because I know its authenticity is very doubtful. Finally, there is the supreme example that I have already given, of the irony of the rhyme of Sir Topas. I mean the fact that the poet's own story is the only unpoetical story. The tales are always appropriate; and the inappropriate is the most appropriate of all. Chaucer has distributed caps to fit the heads of the whole company; and when he reserves the dunce's cap for himself, it is all the more fitting because it does not fit.

If, then, we regard the stories in a dramatic light, as connected with the characters and quarrels of the story-tellers, we can stretch our minds to take in a general conception of the work which Chaucer was doing, whether he knew he was doing it or not. The whole work takes on the character of a Novel, the first true Novel in history. In it the fundamental logic of most previous story-telling is already reversed. The story-tellers do not merely exist to tell the stories; the stories exist to tell us something about the story-tellers. The novel of character has appeared, and the novel of character is something rather even from the epic, let alone the allegory or anecdote or story with a point. For though the great epic poets, Homer above all, have sometimes a very strong sense of character, still their ultimate motive is a true movement towards a crisis or an act; a turning-point of time illustrative of fate of man or the will of God. Homer has made a real character of Hector, but the subject of the Illiad is not the character of Hector, or even the life of Hector; it is the death of Hector, and the death of Hector is the doom of Adam. It is quite different with that more modern form of art for art's sake, which may be called character for character's sake. We could not expect to have Hector talking for ever in his tent; as we should like to have Falstaff talking for ever in his tavern. One could not go wandering aimlessly with Orlando and Ruggiero as one could with Don Quixote and Sancho Panza, or with Mr. Pickwick and Sam Weller. There would have to be a Quest of some kind, that is, an ultimate epic action; the epic is always a *chanson de geste*.[50] And in the same way, nobody perhaps would have been more surprised than Chaucer to be told that he had added or discovered something that is not to be found in Virgil. Yet it is true that we might be interested in a Knight who never got to Canterbury, as we could hardly be interested in a Trojan hero who never got to Rome. In the novel of character, characters are

---

[50] *Chanson de geste* is the type of several old French epic poems of the eleventh to thirteenth century.

companions; and *The Canterbury Tales* is the grand original of all such works, because they appear in companionship.

Indeed I rather wonder nobody has tried to turn it into a novel. Many have made a paraphrase; including some cases in which it might rather be called parody. But, oddly enough, the experiment which would be the most frivolous seems to me the most fascinating; and I am rather surprised that it has never been tried. There have been renderings of the medieval poet into modern verse, and renderings into a sort of medieval prose. There have also been renderings into a more or less modern prose. But I have never seen what I may call a rendering into modern fiction. I wonder that somebody, especially among the novelists, has not tried his hand, merely as an experiment or a joke, at turning the Prologue and framework of *The Canterbury Tales* into the form of a modern novel. The thing might be done, of course, in very different degrees of seriousness or silliness or pure satire. It would be quite unhistorical to turn the medieval crowd into modern crowd; for in a thousand things all the characters are really medieval. But, like many anachronisms, it would be a great joke. It would be amusing to see how far we could really get along with the Host as a modern hotel-proprietor, the Knight as a retired Colonel knighted for his military services, the Clerk of Oxford as an Oxford don, the Franklin as an ordinary country gentleman with a good estate, the Doctor as a modern doctor, the Parson as a modern parson, and so on. It would be historically illuminating to see what could be done; still more historically illuminating to note what could not be done. For the moment, however, I do not mention this imaginary modern novel with any wild intention of attempting to write it. I mention it as the shortest and sharpest way of conveying, to the modern reader, what seems to me the amazing genius of Geoffrey Chaucer as a novelist.

It is not a question of the broad comedy of farce which is most commonly mentioned by the critics, as in the unedifying quarrels of the Summoner or the Miller. It is a thread of thoroughly sound and thoughtful psychology that runs through almost all the interchanges, rather especially in the passages that are comparatively quiet. I will take only one example to illustrate what I mean. It is an example that I have never seen noticed, though doubtless some of the very able Chaucerian students have noticed it. But I rather fancy most people have not noticed it, because it is not anything in the way of an insult, but is rather a compliment. Only it is exactly the compliment that would be paid by that particular sort of person, to the other particular sort of person, at that particular time and place. I mean the passage in which the Franklin, the hoary but hearty old squire, with the big appetite and the beaming geniality, listens to the tale told by the other or medieval sort of Squire, the young gallant who is the son and attendant of the Knight. This young gentleman has pleasing manners, and I suspect a certain modest self-complacency, but he has been taught to treat his elders with respect, and to mingle such courtesy with his natural high spirits. He tells a tale which is of the nature of a fairy-tale, as compared with many of the others; a fine fantastic fable about a king who had a magic ring and a magic horse; there is nothing else noteable about it, except that he evidently tells it with fluency and gusto and makes himself, more or less consciously, rather a fine figure in the company. At the end of his story comes one of those minor humours which reveal the real novelist's grip on human nature. The old Franklin, who has been listening, I imagine, with a slightly gaping gravity, impressed by the continuity rather that the content or precise meaning of the monologue, seems to shake himself, assumes an air of massive and venerable solemnity, and ponderously compliments the young man on having said his little piece. He informs the youth (if we may so translate him) that he is a credit to his family and upbringing; that he has perfomed his duties in an eminently satisfactory manner, and generally that he is almost a model to his generation. Then the thought behind all this begins to shape itself, and the old gentleman introduces the lamentable subject of his own son, who is (it would seem) a most prodigal and unprofitable social character; quite unlikely to go out of his way to entertain the company by telling, or even leaving half-told, the story of Cambuscan [51] bold. The rest of

---

[51] Cambuscan refers to "The Squire's Tale".

the old squire's speech consists entirely of regrets and gloomy prophecies about his own absent and unpresentable offspring. Now that is a living incident that leaps at the eye; a story that comes straight out of the things that really happen. It is as quiet and as real as Jane Austen. It has only to be translated into the language of a modern novel, and it would be as vivid even to the modern novel-reader. He would instantly see the poor old gentleman shaking his head and saying (entirely irrelevantly, because some other young man had just finished a recitation), 'Ah, I only wish *my* boy could be made to understand, &c., &c.' It reminds one of that situation which Stevenson truly said would make an excellent comedy; in which two grumbling old fathers had each a sort of half-jealous, half-argumentative, admiration for the son of the other.

Now there are any number of little lively scenes like that, in the intercourse of the characters in *The Canterbury Tales*. They are filled with that truth that is especially the truth of fiction. I mean that Chaucer knew exactly what sort of person he meant by the Franklin and exactly what sort of person he meant by the Squire; and therefore knew exactly what they would say to each other, even in a contingency that he had not yet especially considered. The characters have been already built up by innumerable small touches, and, inprobable as it may sound in such a connexion, nearly all the seemingly accidental touches are actually used, or do actually tell, in the full development of the comedy. There would not be that particular touch of comic pathos, about the poor old Franklin's disapproval of his son, if the Franklin himself had been primarily a moralist or a model of austerity and abnegation. The fact that we know the old man to be himself rather a jolly old heathen, enormously fond of food and drink, gives him somehow all the human helplessness of a very normal father. Similarly, it was not for nothing that we were told of the young Squire, long before he began to tell the Squire's Tale, that, with all his gaiety, he was meek and serviceable, and carved before his father at the table. It was exactly that touch of deference in the young dandy, that probably produced the vague but vastly favourable impression which moved the Franklin to speech. We can imagine the young man anywhere, even in a modern novel. He would be the sort of young man from Oxford, who is very careful to address an older man as 'Sir'.

And all this was done when the world had never so much as dreamed of a novel, in the modern sense of a mere study of the fine shades of fictitious character. This was done in an age of rigid religious allegories, of flat and decorative romances of chivalry, of stories having indeed a hundred merits of harmonious pattern or verbal melody, of spiritual idealism or intellectual symbolism; but hardly as yet even the beginnings of what we now call the psychological element in narrative. Chaucer did it alone; he did it almost by accident; he did it by sheer moral imagination, in a style of which there were as yet no models to emulate and no rules even to break. It was like the first portrait drawn in a world that had known nothing but patterns. Beautiful patterns indeed, and ingenious and intellectual patterns, and patterns showing a profound knowledge of mathematics and their relation to metaphysics; but with never a line or a curve in them calculated to teach anybody how to begin the particular picture of a face. It may be said that this is too sweeping a description of the world of literature to which Chaucer had access, and so in a sense it is; but it will be found, I think, that the exceptions really prove the rule. Dante, for instance, most certainly had a profound sense of a human character, in the deeper sense of a human soul. I think it probable that it was this sense of individuality in Dante that so profoundly attracted Chaucer; and made Chaucer, with an insight remarkable at the time, prefer the bitter exile of Ravenna to the resplendent Loureate of Rome. But even the case of Dante does not meet the particular point I mean. The reason is not merely that Dante could not, by the very nature of his work and plan, develop the delicate and light comedy in consideration here. Nobody would expect to find the joke about the Franklin and the Squire cheerfully introduced into the Circle of Ice[52] or mentioned in passing by St. Bernard when discoursing on the Beatific Vision. But the reason is deeper than that. It is the reason given, with great insight and wisdom by Mr. W. B. Yeats, when he said that tragedy swamps character while comedy consists in character. Dante deals with those

[52] The Circle of Ice is also known in Dante's *Inferno* as the "Ninth Circle" in Hell. This was the "home" of Satan and the traitors Brutus, Cassius and Judas Iscariot.

huge and heroic passions which are simply human or superhuman; but in any case overwhelm the small differentiations that make all the fun of comic fiction. The Franklin is essentially one particular father grumbling over one particular son, in one particular set of highly amusing social circumstances. But the cry of the father in Dante, as it comes out of the Tower of Hunger, is simply the cry of fatherhood. I am not claiming for Chaucer the very highest power of tragic or typical expression, which is not so much the voice of men as of man. But I do claim for him that his comedy of character was of the finest; but above all, that it was the first.

Nevertheless, if we are to understand the medieval world, but still more if we are to understand the modern world, we must recure to the real limit or term set to the long-drawn-out comedy of the Canterbury Pilgrims; the limit which is Canterbury. It is true, as I have said, that this original and astonishing adventure in literature does bring in all that we value most of the fiction of the present; but it also brings us to a certain blank or doubt about the fiction of the future. The Novel was a speciality of the nineteenth century; precisely because it did seem, in the lull of the liberal enlightenment, possible to study mere individuality or idiosyncrasy; and to study it in a world of eternal leisure. It was not for nothing that the three-volume novel was found in the seaside library. There was a sort of suggestion of an endless holiday, in that study of character for character's sake. I do not mean that it was not, or is not, or will not always be, a normal and even noble intellectual interest. I mean that the age of the great novelists took the holiday for granted: assumed that the basis of the human brotherhood could never be broken up. The real trouble is this; that after a certain point of intellectual differentiation, the brotherhood is broken up. In revolution, men will not stand still to be studied. In a fundamental philosophical disagreement, men will not even agree about what is worth studying. This modern division is masked by the mildness of modern manners. The Conservative clerk and the Socialist clerk do not bawl and bellow at each other as did the Miller and the Reeve; but they disagree with each other much more than did the Miller and the Reeve. And when the Socialist actually acts as the Communist, even the mildness has been known to be modified. It is also masked by a modern mysticism, which leads many to feel quite honestly that they can do without the definite goal of the journey. But while this may mean for some a growth of sympathy, it means for most a break-up of sympathies. There is nothing to keep the Pilgrims on the same Pilgrimage.

The truth is that the broad religion creates the narrow clique. It is what is called the religion of dogmas, that is of facts (or alleged facts), that creates a broader brotherhood and brings men of all kinds together. This is called a paradox; but it will be obvious to anyone who considers the nature of a fact. All men share in a fact, if they believe it to be a fact. Only a few men commonly share a feeling, when it is only a feeling. If there is a deep and delicate and intangible feeling, detached from all statements, but reaching to a wordless worship of beauty, wafted in a sweet savour from the woods of Kent or the spires of Canterbury, then we may be tolerably certain that the Miller will not have it. The Miller can only become the Pilgrim, if he recognizes that God is in the heavens as he recognizes that the sun is in the sky. If he does recognize it, he can share the dogma just as he can share the day-light. But he cannot be expected to share all the shades of fine intellectual mysticism that might exist in the mind of the Prioress or the Parson. I can understand that argument being turned in an anti-democratic as well as an anti-dogmatic direction; but anyhow the individualistic mystics must either do without the mysticism or do without the Miller. To some refined persons the loss of the latter would be no very insupportable laceration of the feelings. But I am not a refined person and I am not merely thinking about feelings. I am even so antiquated as to be thinking about rights; about the rights of men, which are extended even to millers. Among those rights is a certain rough working respect and consideration, which is at the basis of comradeship. And I say that if the comradeship is to include the Miller at all, it must be based on the recognition of something as really true, and not merely as ideally beautiful. It is easy to imagine the Knight and the Prioress riding to Canterbury and talking in the most elegant and cultivated strain, exchanging graceful fictions about knights and ladies for equally graceful legends about virgins and saints. But that sort of sympathy, especially when it reaches the point of subtlety, is not a way of uniting, or even collecting, all the Canterbury Pilgrims. The Knight and the Prioress would be the founders of a clique; as they probably were already the representatives of a class. I am not concerned here with whether the modern mind prefers its pretensions to popular breadth or its claims to creedless spirituality. I am only pointing out that it cannot have both at once; that if religion is an intuition, it must be an individual intuition and not a social institution; and that it is much easier to build a social institution on something that is regarded as a solid fact. Now, however strange it may seem, the men of the Middle Ages did regard the miracles of St. Thomas of Canterbury, and the help given them from heaven by his intercession 'when that they were sick', as examples of a solid fact. There was any amount of human historical evidence for such miracles; and they were too ignorant and primitive to have learnt to prefer determinist theory to historical evidence. And as all men desire health, and as even the worst men may ask heaven for help in ill-health, and as few except the very worst would refuse altogether to be thankful for being healthy, the whole purpose and attitude of the Pilgrimage rested on a reality recognized by all sorts of people, good, bad and indifferent. A religion of miracles turned all this crowd of incongruous people into one company. A religion of moods would never have brought them together at the tavern, far less sent them trotting laboriously to the tomb.

That is perhaps the deepest difference between medieval and modern life, and the difference is so great that many never imagine it, because it is impossible to describe it. We may even say that the modern world is more religious, in that the religious are more religious. Anyhow, there is nothing to prevent a modern mystic being as mystical as St. John of the Cross; and doubtless many students of St. John of the Cross are even now approaching his sanctity. But we may be practically certain that if there is a modern man like the Miller or the Reeve, he has not got any religion at all. He certainly would not go on a religious pilgrimage, or perform any religious duty at all. One of the quarrels in *The Canterbury Tales* sounds exactly like a quarrel in a public-house to-day, between a boisterous bookie and a surly north-country groom. It is still possible to find two such persons in a public-house; it might be possible to find them in a public conveyance going down to the Derby. But how are we to stretch our minds so as to imagine the bookie and the groom deliberately going together to Glastonbury, soley to inquire into the recent psychic phenomena supposed (by some) to be connected with the Holy Grail? That is the measure of the difference between Chaucer's Age and our own. That is the measure of the difference between an objective religion, worshipped as an object by the whole people, and a subjective religion, studied as a subject only by the religious. There is something much more dramatic and challenging than the disagreement of the Summoner and the Friar: and that is the agreement of the Summoner and the Friar. They would never even have come together to quarrel, except in a social system that fundamentally assumed them to agree.

Thus, the Canterbury Pilgrimage takes on a very symbolic social character, and is indeed the progress which emerged out of the medieval into the modern world. All modern critics can take pleasure in the almost modern realism of the portraiture; in the variety of the types and the vigour of the quarrels. But the modern problem is more and more the problem of keeping the company together at all; and the company was kept together because it was going to Canterbury. It will be another business, if the variety of companions discovers a variety of aims. It will raise a new problem if the Miller, with his appetite for more vulgar noises, refuses after all to go to Canterbury and insists on going off to Ramsgate; possibly the scene of sports in which he bore away the Ram. It will be a different thing, if the Merchant firmly refuses to ride beyond Chatham, because all his interests are limited to the progressive industry of that wealthy and dirty town. Darker days will come, when the Prioress, not content with pitying mice, will withdraw to a Vegetarian Hostel on the hills of Westerham, inhabited by cranks; while the now aged Knight, swearing that the Service is going to the dogs, and that these damned pacifists haven't a damned patriotic instinct left, shall devote himself furiously to the fortifications of Dover. As their conterparts stand to-day, it is easier to imagine the Wife of

Bath wanting to go sunbathing at Margate, or the Clerk instantly returning, with refined disgust, to Oxford, than to imagine either of them wanting to toil on together to a particular tomb in Canterbury. For the moment, this division of heart is masked by a certain heartiness, in the modern pursuit of mere games and pleasure; but you cannot make a complete social system out of games and pleasures. You cannot, in some dark hour of peril, ask thousands to die for the Derby, or even to be taxed to death for the International Golf Championship. A nation that has nothing but its amusements will not be amused for very long. Moreover, the amusements are at least as narrow as the devotions and dedications. You will not persuade the Clerk of Oxford to go to Ramsgate, merely to see the Miller win the Ram. You will not persuade the Miller to go to Oxford, which might well have been named, at that time, after the Dumb Ox of Philosophy: St. Thomas of Aquin. But they were both ready to go together to the shrine of St. Thomas of Canterbury. The real modern problem is — what pilgrimage have we on which these two different men will ride together? I mean, of course, one on which they will ride together and remain different. There are many forces making for a superficial sameness in modern life; far too many. There is standardization and the stunts of journalism and the various forms of conscription and coercion rather peculiar to our time; such as Prohibition. But you do not re-consecrate the Cathedral by shutting up the tabard; or make men want to go on a pilgrimage by forbidding them to go to a public-house. There are many modern forces, commercial or scientific, tending to make men look or talk the same. But the Clerk and the Miller did not look and talk the same. They had nothing in common but their purpose; but they had a purpose. It is very puzzling to look at the real society around us at this moment, and consider whether it has a purpose. For the present, at least, there is no Canterbury in sight for the Canterbury Pilgrims. The coloured cavalcade is halted somewhere in the suburbs, and suffering the bewilderment dating from that day, when sectarians and journalists and jerry-builders between them decided that every man should live in the same villa and every man in a different universe.

Some of these conclusions are inevitably coloured with my own convictions; but I do not think that those most opposed to them will differ greatly about the contemporary facts. Few will deny that a certain kind of straight-forward story, with a plot and a point, but adorned with vivid portraits of different persons, began to enter the world in Chaucer's time. Not many will deny that the developments of that straight-forward story is doubtful and perplexed in our own time. It is possible, of course, that somebody will make something out of it; something that is another story; something that is not a story. Something may be done with the subconsciousness of the Miller or the dual personality of the Wife of Bath. But I doubt whether it will be what we have known as a readable romance, if it cannot hold together the Wife of Bath as one person or the Canterbury Pilgrimage as one party. I am not alone in thinking that we are likely to see the breakup of the particular culture made by the Renaissance, at least as much as Chaucer was in a position to see the break-up of the particular culture of the Middle Ages. Nor am I alone, I fancy, in suspecting that this special creation called the modern Novel, which began with him, may end with us.

At least, in this lighter and (dare I say) lesser matter of letters, may we who are burdened with conclusions, or even convictions, be suffered to entertain a suspicion? A suspicion that in the secret matter of happiness (not prosperity, or efficiency, or even equality, but happiness) men do not merely progress indefinitely, but rather pass a flashing moment of maturity; pass it, for instance, when they drink just too much good wine at the Tabard and fall under the table, or progress beyond Canterbury and fall into the sea. That there is an instant of radiant ripeness which the drunkard does not recover, and to which neither does the dead return; and that this crisis of perfection, in literature and the love of literature, comes when what is old and simple can still mingle with what is new and strange. When men can still listen to a story like children, but can already savour the humours of men like men; when men can still be surprised at the logical turn of fate that swings round and strikes down the victorious Arcite, but can already be ironically entertained by the torrent of self-expression from the Wife of Bath, who exults in sheer egotism for pages before she gets to any story at all; when they were still so unsophisticated as to be moved by the mountainous yet ever mounting crescendo of magnanimity in the generous rivalries of the Franklin's Tale; and yet have gained enough of culture to appreciate some verbal felicities in the telling, as in the Dantesque touch of the woman's wild prayer that all the high black rocks be sunken into hell; when a man could yet weep like the Host (that sentimentalist!) over the mere death of a simple maid, and yet roar down a bore or a bully with the joyful contempt of Rabelais;[53] when they could find a melodious pleasure in the mere flow of a narrative and yet remain sufficiently wide-awake to react when it ended with the point of an anecdote; when the world was young enough to be capable of hero-worship and old enough to be capable of humour; and that this flame of the highest happiness flashed for a moment in the mirror of the genius of Chaucer; like the noonday sun upon a naked sword.

[53] François Rabelais (c.1483–1553), French scholar, humanist, satirist and author.

VI

CHAUCER AS AN ENGLISHMAN

We have heard much of late of something called Emergent Evolution; a phrase which, like many scientific phrases, we may find rather useful so long as we do not use it scientifically. Evolution as explanation, as an ultimate philosophy of the cause of living things, is still faced with the problem of producing rabbits out of an empty hat; a process commonly involving some hint of Design. But evolution, and especially emergence, as a convenient and compact description of a sort of relative growth we can all see for ourselves, is very useful in many connexions, and especially in connexion with the problem of England in the later Middle Ages. The Englishman, as a national figure now fully nationalized, stands in the modern world for certain associations or impressions, true or false, but anyhow fairly familiar. We could hardly say simply that, in Chaucer's time, the Englishman was non-existent. We cannot exactly say that the Englishman was existent. We can say that the Englishman was emergent. But it is necessary to state more exactly the stage of his emergence, and the true proportions in which he was like and unlike ourselves.

The nineteenth-century version of the Englishman would be entirely false in the fourteenth century. It may be urged in answer (by curious and restless minds) that the nineteenth-century version was entirely false in the nineteenth century. It is easy enough to point out contrasts and inconsistencies that might seem to make the whole ordinary English legend a lie. The normal Englishman was supposed to be a sturdy and stoical figure, who hated to show his feelings for fear of seeming flashy; or making anything so theatrical as 'a scene'. And his most popular novelist was Dickens and his most fashionable statesman was Disraeli. But though it is obvious that he was much more romantic than he thought he was, it is true that his romance about himself was the romance of being unromantic. That is, it was the romance of being practical; even the romance of being prosaic. There was a multitudinous English type made on that model, and they really were more national as well as more normal than the quacks or geniuses whom they admired. It is obvious that the 'unpatriotic' Cobden[54] was a hundred times more of an Englishman than the patriotic Lord Beaconsfield; and perhaps the humdrum Trollope more representative than the dazzling Dickens. When all allowances are made, it is true that a type had appeared, by about the end of the eighteenth century, which was commonly regarded as the English type and is even now only partially transformed; a type compared with which most foreigners appeared volatile or violent or exuberantly vivacious. Its story had been one of two or three centuries. Its foundation, like every foundation, was religious: its first basis had been Puritanism; on this was erected all the ugly opulence of Industrialism; and then there had matured another influence, most modern but perhaps most fascinating and fashionable of all; what may be called the genteel stoicism of the Public Schools. The gentlemen who governed England, the gentlemen who *were* England, received their two great commandments. They must play the game and they must not play at it. Above all, they must not play at it playfully. A singular seriousness must be directed towards the sports that most other people think merely sportive; and they must be made the rites of a religion of patriotism. With this went all the kindred things: the pride in evading emotion; the contented confession of a certain ignorance of music or foreign refinements; the hazy identification of the vices of industrialism with the virtue of industry. This Englishman did exist; at any rate he did try to exist. And there is a sense in which the ideal is more important than the real. The real is only useful to realistic novelists. It is the ideal, or in a better language the god, who really leads the masses of men and turns the corners of history.

When we have firmly and clearly modelled the image of what the whole modern world has meant by an Englishman, we must instantly and utterly destroy it. When we have once vividly understood what was really meant by the national ideal in the nineteenth century, we must utterly sweep it away from the whole field of the fourteenth

---

[54] Richard Cobden (1804–65) was an English statesman and publicist.

century. Nothing whatever resembling that conscious ideal of common sense, or cold virility, existed for Chaucer and his contemporary countrymen. Indeed, so far as there was a general atmosphere and attitude, it was all the other way. If the Victorians could have actually had a vision of Chaucerian England, they would have thought the Englishman was a Frenchman. All the jokes against the Frenchman would be jokes against the fourteenth-century Englishman. All the emotions and expressions of emotions were there, especially those considered most un-English. If Jules and Jacques kissed each other, it would seem altogether absurd to Thackeray. If Palamon and Arcite kissed each other, it would not seem in the least absurd to Chaucer. That men should on occasion weep, and even weep in public, seemed no more unnatural to the writers of the older England than it did to the writers of the Old Testament or the Iliad. But the contrast is even plainer in the gesture of joy than the gesture of grief. The tag about Merry England is not unhistorical; for many historic witnesses did regard it as rather merrier than the neighbouring nations. The Victorian Englishman was rather prone to regard a damned fiddler as a damned foreigner. The medieval visitor to England described it as full of fiddling; as especially addicted to music and minstrelsy and dance and song. From the Victorian point of view, in so far as England did differ from France, it was in being rather more French than France. And indeed the Victorian, or the man who finds virtue only in the modern Public School ideal, must frankly face the fact that in the fourteenth century what he has called England did not exist. Not only was there another nation, but it was in a sense a Franco-English nation. It was partly because France and England were so nearly one nation, that the kings struggled so long to make them one kingdom. Anybody can see in history how near were the national types to each other then, and how far apart they are now. The Black Prince and Bertrand du Guesclin[55] understood each other much better, as enemies, than French[56] and Foch[57] could understand each other as allies. Behind

---

[55] Bertrand de Guesclin (1320-80) was a constable of France and a soldier.

[56] John Denton Pinkstone French (1852-1925) was the First Earl of Ypres and a British field marshall.

[57] Chesterton is referring to Ferdinand Foch (1851-1929) who was a French marshall.

all was the great unity of Christendom, more than twelve hundred years old, which the later insular Englishman had never even heard of. Such was the condition when the first cracks appeared in that Continent. France and England did not unite; and the great English nation was founded, very largely by Joan of Arc.

Now it is when we have frankly and fully realized this that the fun begins. It is when we have cleared our minds of the last lingering notion that the proverbial practical Englishman existed then, as he exists now, that we can begin to consider what is meant by saying that he was not existent; but he was emergent. Geoffrey Chaucer no more regarded himself as John Bull than a prehistoric Red Indian regarded himself as a Regular Guy. He no more prided himself on being a plain blunt Englishman, with a Bible under one arm and a business ledger under the other, than a Cossack of the twelfth century prided himself on being a Communist of the twentieth. It was an utterly different world, the old world of Christendom which had once been the Christian Roman Empire; a world in which the local loyalties were still feudal; the larger loyalties still often imperial; and the ultimate loyalty entirely religious and long centred in Rome. Nine-tenths of the mind of a man like Chaucer were busy with things that have entirely vanished from the world, as seen by an English patriot to-day. The vast, if shadowy, suzerainty of the Emperor that had reared itself against the supremacy of the Pope; the assumption at the back of every Christian mind that the Crusades ought really to be continued, though they had already been practically abandoned; the serious juridical argument about the Plantagenet claim to the French throne; the vast and crowded ways of medieval travel, which followed so largely the great roads to the great shrines of the Continent. It can all be summed up by saying that Chaucer would have thought it quite as natural to go on a pilgrimage to Compostella as on a pilgrimage to Canterbury. It is also worth remarking that, if he had gone on a pilgrimage to Compostella, or to any Christian shrine in Hungary of Poland or the other end of Europe, he would very probably have seen a statue of St. Thomas of Canterbury looking down on him in a strange land.

But the point is this; that while nine-tenths of his mind made him a citizen of the old empire of Christendom, there was another tenth of his mind; and it was beginning to tell. Canterbury would not suggest to him anything resembling what we mean now by a cathedral city or an Archbishop of Canterbury. It would be more likely to suggest the Pope who had avenged St. Thomas on the tyrant who had him slain. But he was beginning to feel, with a part of his mind, that Canterbury was Canterbury and not Compostella: that it had a Kentish and not a Spanish smell about it; that, while it was an international shrine, it was a point of pride to have an international shrine inside one's own nation; and that, while it was only one of the holy places, it was convenient and comfortable to have a holy place so near home. We may say, if we like, that his subconsciousness was more national than his consciousness; I suspect that it was as yet only a corner of his subconsciousness; but it was growing; it was evolving; it was emergent. And it is really a subtle and fascinating study, far more fascinating than anything offered by a cheap simplification, modernization or nationalization of the Chaucerian phase, to trace out the first faint beginnings of the separate national character that exists to-day; the real roots of the difference that afterwards, in its later exaggeration, divided England from Europe.

There are several very curious, and even mysterious, things about Chaucer, which do already mark him out as a man somewhat different from the same sort of man in the France or Italy of his day. There are moments when we can truly say that the medieval Englishman is already beginning to be the modern Englishman. Something, often something oddly negative (as is often the case with the quaint qualities of the English), has begun to appear, in such a way that we can say now, though it is doubtful if we could have said then, 'This man is beginning to look devilish like an English Gentleman', or, 'If he does not look out, this will end in being a Good Sport'. Not that I would imply any lack of sympathy with these modern ideals, in moderation; I merely mean that, in this time of transition in which Chaucer lived, we sometimes suddenly see them looming far ahead; things not perhaps inevitable, but certainly unmistakable. These possibilities already existed; they need not eventually have been so much exaggerated; above all, they need not have been so much isolated. Anyhow, Chaucer could already boast of being distinguished from his fellow-Christians; though he could not yet boast of being divided from them.

I will take first one very strange example; the position of the poet in relation to fame and fashion. He was not an unsuccessful man. For the greater part of his life he was a successful man and a poet; and yet we cannot say exactly that he was a successful poet. That is, he was not successful as a poet in the way in which some of his contemporaries were successful as poets: praised and applauded as poets; crowned and enthroned as poets. In this respect there is a curious parallel between the mystery of Chaucer and the mystery of Shakespeare. They were neither of them failures or outcasts; they both seem to have had a good deal of solid success, though Shakespeare was wealthiest in later life and Chaucer in middle life. But they were more successful than famous; and more famous than glorious. The odd obscurity of Shakespeare, in some aspects, which has been the negative opportunity of so many cranks and quacks, is a real fact so far as it goes; and it can best be measured if we compare it, for instance, with the flamboyant fame of Ronsard[58] a few years before in France. Some say that Shakespeare's death was disreputable; it is a far more creepy and uncanny fact that his life was respectable. He lived and died, not like a first-rate failure, but like a fourth-rate success. He lived and died a proper provincial burgess, a few years after Ronsard had gathered round his gorgeous death-bed that great assembly of nobles and princes in the robes of religion, and proclaimed to all Europe as with a trumpet that no man born had known so much glory as he, and that he was weary of it and thirsty for the glory of God. The obscure death of Shakespeare is almost as startling a contrast, whether it was disreputable or respectable.

Now Chaucer moves in almost exactly the same manner, on what may be called a lower level of moderate success. As we can compare the respectability of Shakespeare with the public glory of Ronsard,

---

[58] Pierre de Ronsard (1524-85) was a French poet.

so we can compare the respectability of Chaucer with the towering splendour of Petrarch. Petrarch was not, I fancy, a much greater poet than Chaucer; certainly not so original a poet as Chaucer. Petrarch had a public triumph like the triumph of Julius Caesar; like the triumph of an Emperor who had conquered the world. He passed through the streets of Rome with an army of banners and trumpets, to where he was crowned with laurel, the eternal crown, upon the high rock of the Capitol, and went to Mass like a king in state, to leave his wreath on the altar of St. Peter's. And all this time we find the English poet, greater or at least as great, moving about busily, but entirely lost in the crowd; noticed by nobody in particular except the few people who sent him on his rather mysterious errands; apparently having a good deal to do, but always of the sort that rather involved his avoiding observation than obtaining fame. He seems to be all over the place; but he is always under the surface. Nobody says, 'I met old Chaucer in Westminster'; nobody writes, 'I had the honour to meet no less a person than Mr. Chaucer when I was in Italy'. He was in Italy when the radiant and resplendent Petrarch was there; certainly in the same country, probably in the same town. It is highly probable, though by no means certain, that they met. The question has been debated down to the last detail by men much more learned than I. But a much more important point, as I should consider it, is this: that in any case people would have said that Chaucer had managed to meet Petrarch; not that Petrarch had managed to meet Chaucer.

Now we may easily note this, to begin with, with the somewhat melancholy moral, 'That is about as much as England will do for literature and literary men'. Probably it was true then, as it is certainly true now, that France and Italy would lend themselves more naturally to a great popular enthusiasm for a poet as such; to a great national and even political pageant in honour of pure Beauty. It is also true that they have preserved, perhaps by their more direct hold on pagan antiquity, more of the ancient idea of an *officium* or official status of the Bard or the Orator; a sort of sacred position like that of the Priest or the Sibyl. Compared with that, we may say that in England all authors are amateurs. Many of them were primarily what used to be called humorists; that is, many of them were characters and some of them pretty queer characters. Even as early as Chaucer's time, it would seem, there was something of this aversion to the public carnival for the crowning of a poor literary gent. But, unless I am mistaken, there was something else in it, much more deep and subtle. Mr. Geoffrey Chaucer, with his unobtrusive way of going off on Government business, his taste for being trustworthy and not conspicuous, his carrying of important dispatches and trying to look like anybody else, has something extraordinarily English about him. We almost feel that he has given 'his man' a holiday and quietly packed his suit-case at the club. Already, in the fourteenth century, there is faintly foreshadowed that indescribable tone of the English gentleman on such a job. He is the unofficial official. He has the official obscurity of numberless gentlemen in Government offices. He has even a touch of the strong silent hero, who goes on Secret Service in the novels of Sapper[59] and Le Queux.[60] All this, of course, is a wild exaggeration like the novels in question; for, as I have said, the thing had only just faintly begun to be a tendency and had not yet ended in a type. Still, we cannot dismiss a dim impression of that sort of gentlemanly understanding, of that sort of impersonal personal mission, when we compare the sort of success that was allowed to Chaucer with the sort of success that was allowed to Petrarch. We have, perhaps, a hint of the sort of man who really, in his heart, thinks it more important to share a secret with his country's rulers than to be acclaimed like a god by all the crowds of his countrymen. Anyhow, it seems to me that there is already a subtly national note in this odd use of a man of genius; and this concentration on public affairs as private affairs. Chaucer was not in the least like a modern Englishman; but he was the beginning of something of which the modern Englishman was the end. The point here is that it had already begun.

Second, there is something symbolic in his social rank. There is even something symbolic in the doubts about his social rank.

[59] Sapper is the pseudonym of Herman Cyril McNeile (1888–1937), an English writer of crime and adventure.
[60] William Tufnell LeQueux (1864–1927) was an English novelist.

Something was already growing, and was especially developed in England, which was not quite explained by the logical system of ranks and guilds in the Middle Ages. For logic (or what reasonable people call reason) was almost the very soul of the Middle Ages. Yet something more indeterminate is already detaching itself; and in England it has become most detached. It is symbolized, as I say, in the very fact that one aspect or tradition of Chaucer shows him as the child of a common vintner selling barrels of wine to ruffians like the Shipman; while another shows him not so much a courtier as almost a cousin of some great prince like John of Gaunt. Something individualistic in English development made this really true of individuals, though not of classes. It must not be confused with that lifting of men from the lowest to the highest estate, which was a common action of medieval monarchy, as of all genuine monarchy. King Henry could raise the butcher's son as King Cophetua[61] could raise the beggar-maid; that true personal authority often had a touch that seemed like magic. The thing I mean concerned the way in which the upper middle class abutted upon the upper class; and how particular people could cross the line in a particular way, especially in this particular country. Nor must it be confused with that opportunity often offered to the poorest to rise by the ladder of learning, and the assistance of the Church, which was the peculiar glory of the Middle Ages. This matter I mention now is more of a social accident; it would always be rather a chance for the richest than for the poorest; but they probably had more of a chance here than elsewhere. One way of putting it would be to say that the system of nobility was no longer mere nepotism; but it was still mere favouritism. Another way of putting it would be to say that the vintner's son, in the words of the comic opera, was appointed by a job; and a good job too.

Our England has been an aristocracy which denied that it was aristocratic. In this queer inverted pride there has often been hypocrisy, but often only inconsistency; the desire to combine limited privileges with liberal sentiments. Anyhow, its story for the last

---

[61] King Cophetua is a mythical king of Africa who fell in love with a beggar girl and married her.

century or two has been that of a governing class which pretended not to govern. Now nothing of that last phase was possible to the philosophy of the Middle Ages. Princes they knew and citizens they knew, and the authority of superiors and the equality of brethren; but accepting social superiority as an atmosphere, while not asserting it as an institution, would have seemed to them mere nonsense. A medieval man would have thought it simply a mad paradox for anybody to give a man a coronet and a coat of arms to make him admirable, and then call people snobs for admiring him. When they crowned a man king, they made him king; and would have thought it silly to crown him, if he were only what we now call a constitutional king. Sometimes they preferred a republic; occasionally it degenerated into an aristocratic republic. But they did not explain that aristocracy is more democratic than democracy. All this singular way of talking is entirely modern, and we must not look for anything like that in the social position of Chaucer. Nevertheless, there is already something distinctively English in the social position. There is something private and occasional in his way of slipping into the social class above his own. We can almost hear the County, or the Club, saying that after all he is a damned good fellow; not without the implication of a damned useful fellow. But the point of the admission was, as it continued to be at least until very lately, that the exception was exceptional. It was exceptional even if it became pretty frequent or general. It was exceptional because it was personal. The word went forth that the vintner should be accepted; not that the vintners should be. So, until lately, the whole object of English aristocratic diplomacy was to admit the green-grocer without admitting the greengrocers; to admit the pork-butcher without admitting the pork-butchers; and especially of late, to admit the pawnbroker and the money-lender on the same principles and in even larger numbers. With the last phase of all (which has begun to happen in our time), in which the gentleman no longer patronizes the pawnbroker, because the pawnbroker patronizes the gentleman, we are not here concerned.

Thus, though the social status of the poet was only a sort of far-off signal, that might hint to historians that a long historical process had begun, there is something satisfactory and almost soothing in its embodiment in so great and so magnanimous a man. For it is not fair to forget the good side of this curious opportunist aristocracy adopted by the English. It has certainly proved the only human and workable way of preserving aristocracy, which has really not been preserved at all, as a method of government, by anybody except the English. Everywhere where aristocracy was logical, that is, where nobility and heredity and heraldry went together in a consistent scheme, that nobility has ceased to govern the nation. It has always been elbowed aside either by democracy or by despotism. The working of the English method does really require a certain kind of geniality and good humour; a certain spirit which, if we wish to see it at its very best, we could hardly find more vividly embodied than in the personal character of Chaucer.

I do not think it fanciful to find in Chaucer's work, not only the first faint outline of the English Gentleman, but also the first faint outline of the English Lady. There is no doubt that the Prioress in *The Canterbury Tales* is a Lady; but she seems to me to be an exceedingly English Lady. The considerable social importance of her little dogs would alone strike the special note. She was a spinster with exactly the right amount of sentiment; as exhibited in the motto on her brooch or clasp. She was particular about manners at table. She did not like to see a mouse caught in a trap. And indeed we may once more indulge our fancy, in finding one of these ancestral adumbrations; the suggestion of the whole temperamental tendency expressed in the special kind of kindness to animals so much valued by the English gentry to-day. It is a special kind; and some critics might even find it a paradoxical kind. The Prioress was more logical than many a modern lady, whose favourite cat (if he is anything of a logician) must be profoundly puzzled at being allowed to kill mice but not to kill birds. The same critic (if he were in a mood to be merely critical) might possibly describe the gentry of England as a nation of fox-hunters perpetually boasting that they are not bullfighters. But the critic would be too critical, if he implied that the inconsistency was an insincerity. There really is a particular kind of affection for animals, which is very marked among the modern English; and in some indefinable but very vivid fashion, it does rise up before us in the presence of this medieval English lady. Somehow, she does waft across the ages a delicately mingled atmosphere of refinement and fuss. It is indeed an error to suppose that our ancestors were merely barbarous and benighted to a man, about difficult questions like our relation the the lower animals; or that the notion of avoiding cruelty is merely new or modern. It is not even true, as some more sympathetic people imagine, that tenderness to wild animals was the isolated individual discovery of the great St. Francis of Assisi; original as he was in many ways. There are any number of old medieval stories about hermits and holy men who protected animals from the hunters, for instance; and might not have been so popular after all with the North Blankshire Hunt. It was a characteristic of St. Anselm a century before St. Francis. The truer way of stating the case is that men have always been pretty patchy and inconsistent in their attitude to animals, and that we ourselves are pretty patchy and inconsistent still. In every age there are a few who are very careful and many who are very careless, and a modern lady with a devotion to mice might find herself almost as much in a minority at a modern tea-table as did the Prioress at the Tabard.

I only mention the matter here, however, as another example of that almost creepy unconscious fashion, in which we can feel the mind of Chaucer beginning to work towards the things that afterwards went to make up the peculiar modern mood of the English nation. As I have suggested that there was something, so to speak, of pre-natal nationality about Chaucer's way of going about his business, I may add that there is an even more unmistakable social savour about Chaucer on a holiday. In all his remarks about his companions, as well as in his few remarks about himself, there is all that particular sort of self-effacing sociability which has really, when all cant is disposed of, made the English gentleman the best companion in the world. It has been complicated by all sorts of inconsistencies, and by many that have arisen since Chaucer's time. It has been often narrowed by aristocracy and sometimes soured by Puritanism, but it is there still; and in the Catholic Canterbury pilgrimage it is there already. It is marked off from the same kind of courtesy among

Frenchman or Italians by two unmistakable marks, which still exist; a certain casualness and flippancy, especially to fill up silences, and a certain half-conscious policy of avoiding deep disagreement on matters that really matter. Chaucer is all for letting sleeping dogs lie, including the greyhounds of the Prioress. He is not fond of fuss. He rather evades the questions asked of him, and does not mind looking more of a fool than he is. It is when I consider the man at this particular moment, in this particular aspect, in the hour of holiday when he was most himself, that a vague notion occurs to me that may be the explanation of the difficult problem of his politics.

Chaucer lived in a time that was the turning-point of English history; more truly the turning-point, I think, than even the time of Shakespeare. Being, like Chaucer, made free of a free religion, I do not admit that men or societies are bound to any inevitable doom. So I will not say that after what happened in the England of Chaucer, nobody could have avoided what happened in the England of Shakespeare. But I will say that in the time of Chaucer a turn was taken and a road was partly travelled, which it would have been necessary to retrace in order to avoid the destruction or transformation that lay ahead. What happened in Chaucer's time was that the Nobles broke the King, and could actually set up a new man to call himself King, though he was no more than a Noble. These things always happen by stages; and this could not have happened so early, except that the Noble was the nearest to the royal blood. But he was almost admittedly a usurper, and his success stood for the breakdown of many medieval principles that nobody before had ventured to break. What Chaucer himself thought of the political position we have no certain means of knowing. The catastrophe occurred late in his life, when he was probably willing enough to receive occasional help from the Court he had known in his youth, without interfering further in its quarrels. It has sometimes struck me as rather curious and interesting that when he addressed to the new King his humorous ballade about the emptiness of his purse, he accompanied that very broad hint with an Envoi which might have more meanings than one. It begins, 'O conqueror of Brutus' Albion' and, though he hastened to add more formal salutations, this might possibly be read as a reference to the violent and untraditional origin of the reign. Something of the same oddity has always struck me in Andrew Marvell's admirable Horatian Ode on Cromwell, which is supposed to be a compliment to Cromwell, but sounds to me like a prolonged sneer at him. The long parenthesis on the dignified and courageous death of Charles the First can hardly have been very cosy reading for Cromwell. And the last lines, about 'the same arts that did gain a power must it maintain', sound to me uncommonly like saying, 'You've got everything by brute force, and you'll jolly well have to hang on to it'. However this may be, I do not pretend that there is even this amount of criticism necessarily implied in Chaucer's action, when he addresses Henry of Bolingbroke as a Conqueror rather than a King. Still, it is one of those half-shades that seem faintly suggestive where all is shadowy; and I think it likely enough that Chaucer's mind was somewhat divided on the matter. On the one hand, he had been of the party and group of poets whose patron was John of Gaunt, the father of the usurper; on the other hand there is nothing to prove that John of Gaunt himself, let alone all his poets and protégés, would have approved entirely of the usurpation. Then, again, the tone of Chaucer's previous poem, addressed to the dethroned King before his dethronement, lends some support to the idea that he thought that prince was reckless or almost riding for a fall. He continually repeats, in no very courtly tone, that what the realm needs everywhere is Steadfastness; with the possible inference that its ruler was not sufficiently steadfast. This was certainly a charge made against Richard the Second, both in his own time and in ours, but here again the inference is very insufficient. To take another parallel from the age of Marvell; there were many Cavaliers who continually reproached Charles the First with his errors in the earlier stages, but who supported him at the last and to the last, from Wentworth who died for him on the scaffold to Falkland who died for him on the battlefield. I think, therefore, that there is very little that can be inferred from the fragmentary evidences of Chaucer's political attitude. He had been a diplomatist, but not a politician, and the common desire of almost every intelligent diplomatist is to keep as far as possible out of politics. He had been ready to represent the country and the court among foreigners, but it does not follow that he had any particular partisan interest in the quarrels of native factions among themselves. With the question of whether there was any political significance in his disappearance from office, and interlude of obscurity, I deal elsewhere.

In any case, all such speculations are conditioned by the great historical limitation called human life; the fact, too often forgotten, that such a man never saw the sequel that we see. Shakespeare, who on the whole upholds the legend of a lack of steadfastness in Richard the Second, could see far too much of what followed to think that steadfastness was secured by the accession of Henry the Fourth. Though Shakespeare seems on the whole Lancastrian in his sympathies, he was much more conscious of the inevitable perils of pitting Lancaster against York. He looked back at his princely but pathetic Richard, the last pure Plantagenet, across a valley of dry bones, of death and futile destruction; of which Chaucer could never have had a hint. There was no way in which the old court poet, brought up in the splendid court of the victorious Edward, could guess the ghastly evisceration of England by feudal rebels up to the exhausted peace of Bosworth.[62] Chaucer was brought up in a time when the Lilies could be triumphantly quartered with the Leopards, as if France and England had become one country. He never knew that the time was coming when England would become two countries, or perhaps three or four countries, and her shield be quartered in a very different sense. Yet that disruption of England in the Wars of the Roses was of some curious concern to Chaucer, as a poet as well as a patriot. For I cannot but suppose that the desolation of that dynastic war was the explanation of something that needs not a little explaining; the comparative barrenness of the Chaucerian tradition in literature after his death. He had, if ever man did in the world, started a new impulse; yet it seemed to have stopped almost as soon as it started. It would be an exaggeration to say that we had no medieval poets before Chaucer and precious few after him. But there was nothing like the poetic progeny or dynasty we had every right to

---

[62] The Bosworth Field was a battle in the War of the Roses. (August 22, 1485).

expect, until long afterwards when the Renaissance came to England. And I suspect it was due to the conqueror of Brutus' Albion,[63] who did more by his example to encourage potential conquerors than to encourage potential poets. If Chaucer did expect steadfastness from the Lancastrian usurpation, he suffered a post-mortem punishment for his mistake.

Thus the readiness of Chaucer to support the party of the son of John of Gaunt, though regarded by good historians as probable, is certainly not proved. But I confess that I come to regard it as more probable, when I contemplate, as I am doing here, his curiously casual English attitude as expressed in the comedy of *The Canterbury Tales*. With so much about him of what has made the English glorious or generous or genial, there was something also of what has made them gullible and indifferent and too much controlled by events. Chaucer was not a snob, but he was something of what they call in America a regular guy or in England a clubable fellow or a man's man. I could easily believe that he was never so much in revolt against the success of Bolingbroke as Shakespeare was against the success of Burleigh; for Shakespeare was a tragic poet with a touch in him of the revolt of Timon.[64] It is a possible fancy, where all is fanciful, that the greatest Englishman of that age did not rebel against the tragic turn of the age, because he was too English to be a rebel. He may even have been duped by that dull cynicism that talks about the need of practical politics, and then gives itself up to be plundered by practical politicians. He may have been so far infected by such opportunism as to accept Henry of Bolingbroke as a practical politician. He would not be the less English for having joined in the biggest blunder of English history. But I repeat that there is no proof of the fact; it is little more than a possibility, and it is a possibility

---

[63] "Brutus' Albion" comes from Geoffrey of Monmouth's *History of the Kings of Britain*. Brutus is a mythical ancestor of the British, and Albion is the ancient name for Britain.

[64] The Revolt of Timon refers to Shakespeare's play *Timon of Athens*. Timon, a generous man, finds himself in financial difficulties and discovers that the friends whom he had helped during their trials and difficulties, now refuse to help him. As a revenge, Timon orders his men to show charity to no one.

that only interests me here because it goes along with all the other hints that there was already something in the medieval Englishman pointing towards the particular idiosyncrasies of the modern Englishman. It had nothing to do with the higher part of his mind and work, which was concerned with that everlasting light in which all things stand bright and solid; but on the lower level it is likely enough that he may have let things slide like sand. He may have let sleeping dogs lie; little knowing, like many another opportunist, that what he really did was to let slip the dogs of war.

There is one comment which may well be added at this point. It is agreed that in the modern sense of novelty, the production of new nostrums and notions, to be worked into systems like Socialism or Christian Science, Chaucer was not a man who troubled about ideas being new. It was quite enough for him, strange to say, that they were true. He was in many ways really conservative and even his talents did not lie in the direction of new definitions or demands. A critic might put it in the form of saying that Chaucer was a true son of the feudal system, in that he was even proud of being a dependent. He was, as we have seen, proud of being a dependent of the poet Ovid, a dependent of the philosopher Aristotle, a dependent of the theologian Aquinas. All this is true, and it is a truth that disposes at a blow of all the dreary attempts that have lately been made to represent medieval society as utterly servile or brutal or bigoted. Every man who has ever opened a book of Chaucer, every man who has ever opened the doors of Chaucer's mind, and world, knows all that to be nonsense, even when it is nonsense supported by detailed or laborious learning. Chaucer was a great poet; he was a great man; but he was not a great revolutionist, not even in that sense a great reformer; certainly not a great iconoclast or heretic. He was not a man to hurl Bolshevist opinions like bombs into the crowd of conventional people with whom he lived so courteously and contentedly; he did not have them to throw, and he would not have thought them worth throwing; certainly not worth the explosion. If anybody thinks this sort of 'taking the world as he found it' a proof of littleness, such a person cannot be expected to accept my view of

Chaucer's largeness. But the critic, in withdrawing the compliment from Chaucer, must withdraw the slander from the Middle Ages. It is quite certain that the reader of Chaucer instantly breathes an atmosphere of breezy and cordial brotherhood, of charity towards all sorts of men, of a sense of the worthlessness of rank and wealth in comparison with worth, of a sense of fundamental freedom and fraternity in the commonwealth of Christian men. These notions must have been normal medieval notions, or a man like Chaucer would never have had them, or bothered about them. He was not the sort to go digging for abnormal notions. There is that amount of truth in calling him a conservative or even a courtier. They must have been ideas that a man could casually express; or Chaucer would not have remained a court favourite all his life, when he was always expressing them so casually. If that is what is meant by denying originality to Chaucer, the charge is true. There was nothing of the New Morality about him; there was nothing of the man who wears no clothes in Hampstead or cannot keep cats because they are carnivorous. It was not so that he held the view that men of rank should be rebuked or that gentility was not mere ancestry. If these liberal sentiments had been fads in that sense, to the medieval mind, nobody with a notion of personal character can think that Geoffrey Chaucer would have joined the faddists. Some may hold, but I do not hold, that a man cannot be really original who has this huge appetite for what is normal. Anyhow, Chaucer had it, and he was so native to his age and country that his attitude must have seemed tolerably normal to them.

So far we have seen in faint outline a figure very familiar to us in modern literature and to some extent in modern life. He minds his own business; he does not talk shop; he is even content to remain under the mystical cloud of being Something in the City; he does not make scenes, and has a particular kind of limited politeness to servants; he is rather silent and yet somehow sociable, in the sense of being able to get on with other fellows at the club or (it is right to add) in the camp; he is manly; he is modest, at least in external manners; he is well-bred; he is well-groomed; he is solid and reasonable and reliable; but he has his good points, for all that. And the greatest of these is something that neither Puritanism nor the Public School has contrived to kill; he is generally fond of a joke. His great national contribution to the culture of Christendom has been that quality. It is the English sense of humour, like the Spanish sense of honour or the French sense of right reason. It is true that a certain sort of pompous ass like Sir Willoughly Patterne or Mr. Dombey has been exhibited as an Englishman; but he has generally been exhibited by Englishmen. Podsnap would not have been so absurdly English, if Dickens had not been an Englishman. True, there is only one Dickens, but there are a million Dickensians; a great many more Dickensians than there are Podsnaps. On the whole, the prevailing spirit of the English is an appreciation of this sort of fun, especially when it broadens into farce. Indeed, when it is properly understood, there is something in it that breaks out beyond the limits of mere farce, and becomes a sort of poetry of pantomime; a climax of anticlimax. Dickens is full of wild images that would be nothing if they were not funny. They would be not merely nonsensical but non-existent, if they were not (I say with some firmness) so damned funny. Mrs. Todgers's wooden leg; Mr. Swiveller's gazelle who married a market-gardener; the toothpick of the gentleman next door, which if sent to the Commander-in-Chief would produce such marked results; the effect of Henry the Eighth's little peepy eyes on Mrs. Skewton's view of history; these are things that would simply cease to exist in a really rational universe. They are not symbolic; they are not really satiric. They are upheld by an invisible power and lifted without support upon the wings of laughter; by a power more unanswerable and more irresponsible than pure beauty.

Now compared with the fun of Dickens, there is certainly something altogether shrewd, sensible and solid about the humour of Chaucer. He was, as has been said already, only the seed of that separate growth; but it was growing separate and was soon to be growing wild. We shall note elsewhere the way in which the medieval common sense of Chaucer differs from the almost maniac laughter we sometimes hear from the Elizabethans, even from Shakespeare. But for all that a frontier had been crossed, and there is already in Chaucer an element of irrational humour, which is not the same as the old rational humour. The old humour had been a form of satire. Chaucer often sounds satirical; yet Chaucer was not strictly a satirist. Perhaps the shortest way of putting it is to say that he already inhabits a world of comicality that is not a world of controversy. He makes fun of people, in the exact sense of getting fun out of them for himself. He does not make game of them, in the actual sense of hunting them down and killing them like wild vermin or public pests. He does not want the Friar and the Wife of Bath to perish; one would sometimes suspect that he does not really want them to change. Anyhow, a softening element of this sort has got into his satire, even if he really meant it for satire. But, with this step, he is already on the road to the Dickensian lunatic-asylum of laughter; because he is valuing his fools and knaves and almost wishing (as it were) to preserve them in spirits—in high spirits. In a hundred other ways his humour is English, and not least in this, that he often uses flippancy to avoid an argument and not to provoke it.

For I have so far confined myself strictly to considering what (unfortunately) a great mass of modern Englishmen mean by an Englishman. I have taken the matter from this end, so to speak, and started with the strictly national type produced by Protestantism and the modern division of nations. And I have pointed out that, even in terms of this familiar type, Chaucer is readily recognizable as English: that he contains the seeds of some of the things that have since become even extravagantly English. But I apologize to England for talking as if these things alone were English; and to Chaucer for supposing that he did not know and love an England that was relatively free from all these things. There is matter much larger than these little social tricks in the real heritage of the English; and Chaucer was the true trustee of that heritage; above all of the great national heritage of humour. It is the custom to boast that it is more than wit, but the really interesting truth is that it is more even than humour. It is not merely a critical quality; in a sense it is even a creative quality; a sort of crooked creation that is called the fantastic or the topsy-turvy. Here again it is possible to quote things from Chaucer that seem to have come into the world centuries too early, and to be of the type of the nursery nonsense of to-day. That this wild spirit runs through all English literature can be proved by a single quotation from Lear. I do not mean the comic Lear but the tragic Lear; who was almost equally nonsensical. There was never a crazy touch in the crack-brained style done better than that of Shakespeare's fool, when he says:

'This prophecy Merlin shall make; for I live before his time.'

This poetry also Mr. Lewis Carroll shall make; but Chaucer lives before his time. Even in the Father of English Poetry that far-off cry of pure folly can be heard, perhaps for the first time in human history.

There is in English humour something that can not only be compared to art for art's sake, but might more truly be described as adventure for adventure's sake. It is not unconnected with the sense in which the more honourable part of English conquest and colonization was adventure for adventure's sake. I mean that it was not really directed towards a consistent policy of rule. Grave historians have expressed a mild astonishment that the British were so long unconscious of the British Empire. It is a possible explanation, to suppose that they were unconscious of it because it did not exist. It was not an empire in the logical sense of an *imperium*; a scheme for extending a type of civilization over countries that had not got it; as other empires wished to extend the Roman Law or the Spanish religion. It had first the practical purpose of trade; but after that its purpose might more truly be descibed as fun; the satisfaction of seeing strange places—and leaving them strange. If we like to put it so, the adventurer had something nobler than greed; which was curiosity. Now that curiosity always delighted in curiosities. They were like the curios that sailors brought home from the strange seas; parrots and monkeys and tropical shells. But there was even more interest in the curiosities the sailor could not exactly bring home to his landlady; such as Cannibal Kings or Chinese temples or Arctic whales. There runs through the English adventure the vague desire that these funny things should *remain* funny. He does not specially wish to convert the yellow men in the temple; though he might attempt a constitutional compromise about cannibalism. And there runs through the English humour the same notion of amusing monsters, to be stared at. And Chaucer is at the spring of this spirit; because to him the Wife of Bath is an amusing monster. We do not approve of her; but we do not feel responsible for her, any more than for a whale or a white elephant. There is a wise fool whose eyes are in the ends of the earth; and the English invented that phrase of yet more imaginative folly: 'The other end of nowhere.'

It is a very extraordinary fact, when considered historically, that Chaucer should have been so unmistakably English almost before the existence of England. It is the details of language, like the details of landscape, that give this entirely unique and unmistakable touch. It is an elvish touch, to use a term that was actually used about the poet. It almost suggests that the other name of England is Elfland. Yet it has nothing whatever of the thin ethereal spirit of faerie; as we see it, for instance, in the Celtic myths and the poems of Mr. W. B. Yeats. It is a solid and almost smug sort of goblin market; a real town where the goblins are really marketing. The nearest we can come to a more serious definition is that it is a certain spirit of nonsense even in landscape. We find it in the names of some real English villages, which might have come out of the wild geography books of Mr. Edward Lear. We feel it in some of the impossible places invented by Mr. Edward Lear, which might be the names of real English villages, valleys or downs; such as that typical title, 'The Hills of the Chankly Bore'.

Now this touch is instantly felt in Chaucer. The Pilgrims' Way does not run merely, in the medieval manner, through meadows patterned with flowers or forests dark with enchantment. But neither does it run merely through reasonable and recognizable places like Southwark and Sittingbourne. There is something selective in the eye of Chaucer, which is already open for other and special things. Nobody at home with the nonsense element I mean can read that phrase, in the account of the pilgrimage, about passing a town 'which that i-clepd is Bob-Up-and-Down', without his heart leaping with joy, and bobbing up and down with that buoyant and unconquerable city. I do not know exactly what it means; and there have been all sorts of speculations about it. I do not know whether Chaucer made it up out of his own head, which is quite possible; or whether it was a real English village, which is also quite possible; or whether it was a nickname connected with some local jest, which is perhaps most probable. Some have suggested that it was so called because something in the winding, rising and falling road made it appear to be on different levels at different stages; and that sort of rambling road probably was then, and certainly is now, rather specially characteristic of the English countryside. But the feeling of the curious primeval kinship between England and Chaucer is justified in either case. I do not care whether it was something that England invented and Chaucer glorified; or whether it was something that Chaucer invented and England glorified. The spirit of a man who loves that landscape can sometimes run so close to the land, that it invents something that exists already. I remember composing, when I was quite young, the first rough form of a song about the round hills and rolling, almost revolving roads, of which a man dreams after a day in Sussex. In that song I invented an entirely imaginary town of Roundabout as the mystic centre of this rotatory landscape. And it was some time afterwards that I discovered that there really is a town in Sussex called Roundabout, because the men of Sussex had seen the same scenes and dreamed the same dream.

Therefore there is, it seems, something primitive about this poet, because he is as large as the land and as old as the nation. There was little enough in him of the mystic, in the narrow or special sense; yet it is impossible not to feel something mystical about his magnitude as an emblem of England. He had somehow got into his head and into his note-book a certain national quality, centuries before the nation attempted to understand or describe its own quality. He had, for instance, the humour that is at once broadened and blunted by good humour. He had the particular *sort* of soft-heartedness that can be seen in the English; sometimes an incomplete and illogical sort; but not far removed from that of Chaucer's Prioress, who might have been frightened of a mouse, but wept over its being in a trap. He had the English type of tolerance and in some things the English type of irresponsible individualism; there is that amount of truth in Matthew Arnold's view that he was lacking in 'seriousness'. He was not the stuff of which Reformers are made. He took things as they came, and the world as he found it, and men as God had made them, or even as they had made themselves. He had a curious sort of abstract liberality underlying concrete conservatism, which was very national, and can be seen in many Tories who are devoted to a Monarchy and explain that it is just as republican as a Republic. In all this he is the First of The English; and his figure has therefore this quality of a type and even an archetype. That figure is seen in the sunlight of history walking among the gay pavilions and palaces of French kings and French-speaking knights and nobles; negotiating war and peace in what was practically a French quarrel about a French pedigree; he is seen learning a thousand things from the sonneteers of Italy and the troubadours of Provence; but within him something is born, and it is the name by which we live. He may or may not have made the somewhat dreary attempt to translate *Le Roman de la Rose* into English. But nobody could possibly translate *The Canterbury Tales* into French.

There is something personal about England. Rome or France or Bolshevist Russia or Republican America, each in its own way, is a principle; but England is a person. And it is very like the very indescribable sort of person this book has to describe. I will not be so daring as to define what William Blake meant by The Giant Albion; but we may agree that if the country called by poets Albion could be conceived as a single figure, it would be giant. And when I think of Chaucer in this primary and general fashion, I do not think of a Court poet receiving a laurel from the King or a Flagon from the King's butler, nor even of a stout and genial gentleman with a forked beard setting forth from the Tabard upon the Canterbury road; but of some such elemental and emblematic giant, alive at our beginnings and made out of the very elements of the land. Perhaps if we were caught up by that eagle that whirled away the poet to the gates of The House of Fame, we might begin to see spread out beneath us the titanic outlines of such a prehistoric or primordial Anak or Adam, with our native hills for his bones and our native forests for his beard; and see for an instant a single figure outlined against the sea and a great face staring at the sky.

VII

CHAUCER AND THE RENAISSANCE

It will be noted that many quotations from Chaucer in these pages are recast in a manner that may well distress Chaucerians; though it is done with the hope of increasing the number of Chaucerians in the world. I can only say that I am acutely sensitive to all that can be said against what I am doing. To say that I have modernized Chaucer has a very ugly sound, and might stand for a very ugly thing. The first difficulty about disturbing any ancient language, that is good of its kind, is that the man who turns it into new language may turn it into pretty thoroughly bad language; in the sense of something worse than slang. There is also this paradoxical but practical fact: that the very examples in which the meaning of a word has changed are the examples in which we know what it means. If we substitute a very modern word, we may find that everybody uses it and nobody knows what it means. It marked the use of an old phrase, of which the meaning has changed, when the Prayer-Book said, 'Prevent us, O Lord, in all our doings'. But nobody does imagine that the vicar, who reads it out in the parish church, means that he wants to be tripped up with boobytraps and butter-slides in everything he attempts. The dead word, like the dead language, does in a sense remain sacred. 'Prevent' is a Latin word and still makes sense in Latin. But there is always the peril that turning it into modern English might mean turning it into more modern American; and ghastly possibilities open before us, of some future reformer altering 'prevent us' to 'put us wise'. Or, to take another example, it is now extremely archaic English to talk about the Holy Ghost. But it is perfectly intelligible English, although it is archaic English. It stands for a certain idea which was strong when the language was made, and it stands exactly where it did. Whereas, even so reasonable a change as that of 'ghost' to 'spirit', may bring in a nuance of change, owing to modern uses of the word 'spiritual' and the looming spectre of Spiritualism. Similarly, it is archaic to talk about ghostly counsel or ghostly consolation. But nobody does in fact imagine that ghostly consolation means consoling people by telling them ghost-stories. Whereas, if we begin to think of what does give spiritual consolation, or appear to give it, to a great many modern people, the most horrid possibilities begin to close in upon us. We may end by altering old English to something that is not English at all; and talking about an Uplift or (heaven defend us) about an Urge.

Therefore, while I believe in occasionally changing the Chaucerian speech or spelling, I believe in changing it as little as possible, and indeed only where the original is utterly unintelligible to an ordinary modern reader; or where (what is far worse) the accidental look of ugly unintelligible words makes a passage appear undignified, which in fact is full of dignity. Several excellent attempts have been made to modernize Chaucer; nor is the idea itself confined to the times we call modern. It strongly possessed the great critical imagination of Dryden; a poet whose greatness, humanity and English breadth were in many ways very Chaucerian, but who was persistently underrated in the nineteenth century, merely because he had voted Blue instead of Buff in the party quarrels of the seventeenth century. It would be truer, of course, to admit that the prejudice had real roots; and that Dryden's crime was his lack of enthusiasm for the establishment of plutocracy and his Catholic dislike of the Puritans. Anyhow, he had every right to recur to the great English tradition of the medieval poet; and he did admirable work in paraphrasing and popularizing whole sections of the Canterbury Tales. His version shows very clearly the particular limitations of his age, and we may be absolutely certain that all our versions will show posterity the very obvious limitations of ours. But it is on the whole much better than many experiments of the sort in our own time. A modernized version of four of the Canterbury Tales has recently come from America. It is ingenious and intelligent; but is shows very clearly the danger of needless modernization of what is merely medieval, without being, for any reader, in the least meaningless. What is wanted is not the reconstruction of every line of Chaucer so as to make it fit metrically and grammatically into a modern line.

What is wanted is a careful preservation of the old construction of every line, except where it is quite impossible to keep the construction and yet put the right construction on it.

For there is another objection, far deeper that the first I mentioned. It is really true to say that the best guide for doing this job is to remember that it is impossible to do it. After all, by trying to do it at all, we are treating medieval English as a foreign language, and there never was, is not, and never will be, a translation of a poem from a foreign language. There have been some beautiful poems written in one language, more or less parallel to beautiful poems in the other. There have been reasonable translations into the one language, which were good enough to goad people into really learning the other language. There have even been great poems, which professed to be only translations of small poems. But no man has ever reproduced the atmosphere and magic of one single word by the use of another word. Nobody could put the exact equivalent of 'revisit thus the glimpses of the moon' into any other English words; and he certainly could not put it into German or Russian or Chinese words. It is this separation that makes necessary such intermediate explanations as these; it may be that the Tower of Babel was indeed the chief tragedy of mankind. But anyhow, it is strictly true that we can translate anything in reason. We cannot translate anything that is beyond reason; like the way in which mere sound and spelling can be a spell. The American edition, of which I have spoken, does really translate everything in reason. It explains the ordinary sense of Chaucer's narrative with sustained and competent clearness, but it works on the assumption that everything must be translated from the foreign language called Chaucerian into the other language called English — or perhaps American. The consequence is that while the style and the story go forward energetically, something has gone out of the story and the style; and what has vanished is the song. Thus, to take the test case of a passage so often quoted, the dying speech of Arcite, I should think it quite satisfactory to leave the lines substantially as they stand:

> What is this world? What asken man to have?
> Now with his love, now in his coldë grave,
> Alone withouten any company.

But the conscientious transatlantic translator thinks it his duty to make it scan in modern grammar by saying:

> What is this world? What asketh man to have?
> Now with his love, now cold within his grave,
> Alone, alone, with none for company.

Now somehow or other, with the best intentions, he has broken the backbone of the tragic line with a load of repetition, like the repetitions that fill up bad blank verse; while the original simple line 'alone withouten any company' is like a desolate yet living cry, echoing in a vault of stone. That is the intangible trick that we call poetry. And that is the paradox of dealing with the present problem of Chaucer. The same thing that convinces us that he must be translated convinces us that he cannot be translated.

In my own citations, therefore, I have adopted the principle of altering the lilt or accent or form of the line as little as possible, and only altering the words where they are in actual fact foreign words. But I am quite conscious that even by doing this I lose a great deal, and can only say that there are readers who could hardly get anything, if this were not lost. If I criticize other experiments, I would accompany the criticism with a profound groan of gratitude, to St. Thomas of Canterbury or my patron saint, that I have not got the job of carrying out my own principles of interpretation through a complete translation of Chaucer's works. The thing is so stupendously difficult that even to do it decently is to do it admirably. I for one (if I may excuse myself in the polite manner of the poet among the story-tellers) do not propose to do it at all. But it seems only right, since I have quoted the poetry in a particular form, according to my own taste and fancy, that I should insert here this brief note upon the practical rules I have observed. For the rest, I am quite sure that the translator need not avoid slight variations of speech, such as are no longer used but are still understood. On the contrary, I think he should preserve them rather carefully, for they very often have a unique quality lost in the later development of the language. The old word can actually strike a new note. We have all observed the fine touch of distinction given in Shakespeare or Milton by the mere shifting of the accent on a familiar word, or the variation of a customary termination; the pleasure there is in realizing that Hamlet says 'I'll wipe away all trivial fond recòrds', merely because we always say 'récords'; or in repeating Milton's ending, 'And summons given, the dread consult began'. I hope no American will translate Milton into English and turn it into a consultation — the common consultation one has with a doctor or a dentist or a trustee. There is not a little of this pleasure, among the many pleasures of reading Chaucer. Aristotle, the teacher of medieval men, said very truly that the language of poetry has a perpetual slight novelty. It is none the less so, when the slight novelty is a slight antiquity.

In my own unscrupulous experiment, I should aim at two things; first, as far as possible preserving the original word; and second, preserving the originality of the original word. Now in some cases we cannot keep the force of the word, if we keep the form of the word. Men cannot think a strange word striking if they do not know what it means; but short of that, it may be all the more striking because it is more strange. There has been very little recognition of the possibility of such an intermediate course. Chaucer is either copied in a style that is not popular, or translated into a style that is not Chaucer.

There was never a better criticism of Chaucer than that written within a hundred years of his death by old Caxton[65] the printer; nor has this particular aptitude with words been expressed in words so apt. The medieval master printer's estimate is worth libraries of the patronizing pedantry, that has been written in the four hundred years that followed. 'For he writeth no void words; but all his matter is full of high and quick sentence'; that is, sense; *sententia*. The melodious but monotonous etiquette of much medieval poetry was a perpetual temptation to write void words; like the void words of modern journalese; except that the medieval words at least were graceful and the modern words base.

Very tentatively, therefore, and with all the mingled tact and terror

[65] William Caxton (c. 1422-91) was the first English printer and an important translator of Chaucer and Marlowe.

proper to an amateur in a field where so many scholars must have speculated, I am in favour of doing for Chaucer something like what has already been done for Shakespeare. I mean publishing a popularized version, in so far as this can be done by the mere simplification of spelling or clarification of common words, where the difference is a difficulty; and nowhere else. I do not mean modernizing Chaucer, in the sense of making him appear modern; I mean only elucidating him just enough to permit him to appear medieval. I imagine that a multitude of medieval things have already, in fact, been treated in this way; Malory and the Paston Letters and any number of Border Ballads, especially those in the original Scots. It is unfortunate that Chaucer happens historically to stand, as if he were a Borderer himself, on the exact frontier between writing in a foreign language that is translated and writing only in an old-fashioned language that needs only to be brought up to date. This makes the thing much more difficult to do; but not the less worth doing.

Broadly, my principle would be this; that no reader minds meeting an old word, but is only bothered when he meets a new word. I mean, of course, a word that is new to him; a word that is old enough to be new. He does not dislike, but likes, any ancient medieval monument as such, so long as it does not block the road, and hold up the ride to Canterbury. For instance, in the famous line I have quoted from the Knight's Tale, what in the world is the use of altering the word 'withouten'? If there be any human being who can read the line, 'Alone withouten any company', who does not know at once that 'withouten' means 'without', I should imagine he must be a very rare and isolated sort of reader; withouten any company and certainly withouten any common sense. But when, in another passage I have also quoted, the poet lamenting over Troilus speaks of 'this false world's brotelness', then I should boldly alter it in the modern version to 'brittleness', precisely because it would be quite natural to suppose that it meant 'brutalness'. Where there is an ambiguity of that sort, for a modern reader, I would not give the word a modern meaning, but merely give it back its own medieval meaning. I admit that the task would be terribly delicate, and I have not the faintest intention of trying to do it myself. It would be a matter of tireless and sustained tact, every touch of which would look like caprice. It would have to turn perpetually to different solutions for different problems; sometimes alteration, sometimes accentuation, sometimes annotation. Anyone rushing lightly upon it may well be checked at the very start; for I think the very first line of *The Canterbury Tales* presents the greatest difficulty of all. Many a modern reader may have been induced to try Chaucer, as merely a rather old-fashioned English writer, and found, 'Whan that Aprille with his schowres swoote,' a slight obstacle at the start. Merely to show what I mean by using different methods, I should be frankly inconsistent in dealing with the difficulties of that line. I should leave 'Whan' (who would be such a fool as not to know that it meant 'when'?) but I might in compassion alter 'schowres' to 'showers', lest the consonants be really misleading, and because the syllabification is just the same. I should put an accent on the second syllable of 'Aprille', and the mark showing that the 'e' is not mute. Finally, if I could not change 'swoote' to sweet' (because, curse it, it has to rhyme to root), I would put a foot-note to say that it is meant for sweet and pronounced more like 'sooty'. I see a vast and varied task open before me; from which I cheerfully turn away.

Now my only excuse for dwelling on this literary possibility is that I do think it a matter of vital importance to open up the English past at least as far as Chaucer, in the sense that it has been opened up as far as Shakespeare. As I shall try to point out here, the great river of the national culture and character did in some sense grow narrower as well as swifter and stronger, at the moment when it came over the rocks in the cataract of the Elizabethan Renaissance. But, anyhow, it falsifies everything to suppose that, because all modern intellectual life still moves with the impetus of that mighty fall, therefore the fall is the same as the fountain. A man does not understand England who has read Shakespeare and not Chaucer, any more than a man understands Italy who has read Tasso and not Dante, or a man understands France who has read Ronsard and not Villon. Anybody can see that these ancient inspirations are constantly coming to the surface again, sometimes much later than the later fashions; that much cynical French writing derives rather from Villon than from

Ronsard, or that the new vision of Italy may find more in the imperialism of Dante than in the ornamental chivalry of Tasso. So there are all sorts of things in Chaucer, or for that matter, in Langland, which should come out in a complete consciousness of the English destiny; and which happened, by historical acccident, to be more or less out of sight for the very greatest of the Elizabethans. In a word, the ordinary modern Englishman will considerably enlarge his mind by reading Chaucer; and it is my humble desire that he should to some extent be able to read Chaucer, even if he is unable to read Middle English or Anglo-Saxon or Norman-French; or if he is, by mere sloth and moral weakness, unable to read the learned books in which the structure of these various languages is set forth. I do believe, as Dryden did, that it would be a good thing to make Chaucer an ordinary possession of ordinary Englishmen; and I should not think the thing thrown away, even if, like Dryden's experiment, it had to be done over again about three hundred years hence. In the future, for all I know, men will say that our culture began with Dryden. In that case our culture will stop short with Dryden. Even at present, as I do know, many men talk as if our culture began with Shakespeare. In that case their culture stops short with Shakespeare. And, as I propose to suggest in this chapter, there really are matters in which even Shakespeare stops short of Chaucer.

But in these opening words I only claim to maintain that Chaucer is readable, or can readily be made readable by ignorant people like myself; I am not in the least concerned to conceal my ignorance. It will be noted that nowhere in this book have I made any pretence of pronouncing upon the purely philological or grammatical or metrical problems, with which the study of Chaucer, for the students of Chaucer, teems on every side. There is a whole labyrinth for grammarians and the scientific students of language in the development of the medieval English dialects, and the degree of their absorption in the French-English of Chaucer. There is world of inquiry, and very interesting and important inquiry, in the matter of his adoption of Continental metres or schemes of scansion, and the order in which he adopted them. But it is the whole point of this book that Chaucer is literature and not linguistic study for the learned; that it needs very little to make him popular in the sense that literature can be popular; and that learning is a totally different thing. I have learned some rudiments of Chaucerian problems at school, or rather neglected to learn them at school, and I have read and forgotten a good many facts on the same subject since. But I should no more think of setting up to be an authority on Chaucer than an authority on Punch and Judy; or Pickwick; or the Christmas pantomime. These things are not studied, but appreciated. What little I remember of earlier instruction leads me to think that it has changed a great deal, and that some parts of it were always rather crabbed and perverse. I remember that the jokes of Chaucer were the subject of specially serious discussion. Doubtless there does exist this second class of Chaucerian difficulties, but I doubt whether I am particularly suited to overcome them.

There is something faintly irritating in the fact that so many popularizers of Chaucer have described his humour as 'sly'. And yet there is something in it; or something to be got out of the right understanding of it. Doubtless it is partly due to a more or less external and technical trick of expression; he is very fond of laughing in a parenthetical manner, like the aside of a comic actor; so that even when the joke itself is jolly and obvious enough, it has the grammatical shape of a broad grin in brackets. This is common enough; perhaps the best example is that charming passage in the charming fable of the Cock and Hen, in which the former bitterly exclaims in Latin, *mulier est hominis confusio*,[66] and Chaucer gravely adds the explanation:

> 'Madame, the sentence of this Latin is
> Woman is mannës joy and mannës bliss.'

When the critic calls this sly, we can see what he means; but in fact the effect is produced not so much by being secretive as by being simply impudent. Anyhow, the general effect is produced by being large and simple and all of a piece. Chaucer's humour is spread over

---

[66] *Mulier est hominis confusio* is Latin for "woman is [the source of] man's confusion".

so wide a surface of himself that it is always partially present, when he seems most serious and especially when he seems most simple. But there is a third accidental aspect in which Chaucer may truly in some sense be congratulated on his slyness. I suspect that he has made a good many jokes that his critics and commentators cannot see; and one or two which the commentators have sat down grimly and resolutely to prove not to be jokes at all. True, their serious explanations change. I remember how a schoolmaster explained to me with desperate seriousness, in the days of my youth, that Chaucer's remark about the French language, as spoken by the Prioress, was pure and unstained by any adulteration of amusement. Chaucer says that the Prioress spoke French very well according to the school of Stratford-at-Bow: 'For French of Paris was to her unknown.' The authority then proceeded to prove, with academic passion, that French, so long the language of the English court and aristocracy, really was talked correctly at Stratford; and therefore Chaucer can be acquitted of the grave charge of flippancy, when he said she was unacquainted with the French of France. I fancy that the smile of Chaucer, as he left the court without a stain on his character, might truly be described as a little sly. For it might occur to simpler souls than the academic, and intelligences more in touch with Chaucerian simplicity, that even if correct French is talked by foreigners, there is still something a little funny about pitting it against that national tongue as talked by the natives. If I were to say, 'Professor Hiram Q. Hike spoke the most correct and cultivated English that Boston can produce, though he ignored some nuances adopted in London, England', I think it barely possible that I might be suspected of irony. And the charge would not be answered by saying that the people of Boston do talk English, or something they have a right to call English; that they talk much better English than the people of Bison City, Texas; and that Boston is justly proud of a great tradition of English scholars and critics. There would still remain the faint possibility that critics even more English might be found in England. If somebody said, 'Our Guatemalan guide talked a vivid and picturesque Spanish, which would have considerably puzzled the inhabitants of Spain', it would not entirely extract the sting to say that Spanish is the official language of Guatemala. And so, when even a poor medieval poet goes out of his way to compare the French talked by an English lady with the French talked by a Frenchmen, I am, and was even as a boy, disposed darkly to suspect that he saw the fun of it. Of course this individual authority may have been only an individual and not an authority. I only know that the criticism was confidently imposed on me in my schooldays. But what amuses me most is to discover that a totally opposite criticism has been confidently imposed since. Later on, I discovered that the serious commentators were saying (at another stage) that the passage about the Prioress means, not that she spoke French well, but that she did not speak French at all. And they quote certain phrases two hundred years later, which suggest that knowledge acquired in Stratford-at-Bow had become a proverb for total ignorance. This seems much the more plausible dogma of the two; but even of this I am daring enough to have may doubts. Saluting in all seriousness men better informed than myself, and being myself in every way a citizen of Stratford-at-Bow in the matter of ignorance, I still think that the emphasis of such expressions varies much from age to age; that a suggestion might be positive under Elizabeth which was relative under Edward III; and that the nuance of Shakespeare's language might be different from the nuance of Chaucer. I still think that the best way of finding the nuance of Chaucer is to look for it in Chaucer. Given the character and the context, I think it most likely that Chaucer meant the Prioress to speak French as an English school-mistress speaks it, stiffly and imperfectly but not altogether without pretension. The joke against this sort of *parly-vooing* might easily have been broadened and blunted until it came to mean common insular ignorance. But I may be quite wrong; and I do not attach much importance to the question of being right. I only note that if the learned are now right, some of the earlier learned were very wrong.

A somewhat more serious reason, however, led me a few paragraphs back to bring into consideration the attempt of Dryden to popularize or modernize Chaucer in his own day. For the whole of this business of the modern translation of Chaucer, or the medieval difficulties of Chaucer, is bound up with the general destiny of literature and language after his death. He was indeed saluted after his death in tones of very noble loyalty and gratitude by the few fine English poets that were at all worthy to praise him; by Occleve[67] and by Lydgate.[68] But we hardly have that impression of a literary dynasty that we might have expected as following such a king and conqueror in the world of culture. Curiously enough, as many acute critics have pointed out, the richer and more romantic quality of Chaucer's tradition was carried on rather more continuously in Scotland than in England. The Wars of the Roses, I suppose, had something to do with it. Anyhow, when a full poetic inspiration came to England, it came as the influence of de Meung or Petrarch had come to Chaucer; direct from foreign lands, but from lands now in the full noonday of the Renaissance. Everybody can see the sense in which that noonday sun was brighter even than the brightest star in the medieval night of the north. But there is something more to be said about the comparison, which has never, as it seems to me, been said sufficiently clearly. And as the matter arises directly out of an attempt like that of Dryden, and the suggestion that it should be repeated, I will deal with it here.

To many in the nineteenth century the notion of Dryden paraphrasing Chaucer was very like their notion about Pope translating Homer. It was the notion of a primitive giant being introduced by a dwarf who was also a dandy. They thought that Pope had done nothing but provide the golden-haired Apollo with a gilded peruke, or the swift-footed Achilles with a pair of high-heeled shoes; giving a new irony to the weaknes of the heel of Achilles. They exalted Chapman's Homer against Pope's (as did Keats, the greatest of the Romantics) merely because Chapman was full of the particular Elizabethan type of fire and fancy. Only, as Arnold and others eventually hinted, there was something to be said on the other side. Pope was not very like Homer; but he is so far like Homer that he talks like a sane man; and the great Elizabethans did not always do so; neither indeed did the great Romantics.

[67] Thomas Occleve (c. 1369–1450) was an English poet.
[68] John Lydgate (c. 1360–1451) was an English poet and priest.

In the same way, the critics of the more romantic nineteenth century felt sure that Dryden could do nothing in the red-rose thicket or daisied lawn of the medieval poet, except clip the hedges with the extravagant trimness of topiary; or turn a Dantesque forest into a Dutch garden. It was owning to the particular angle at which they stood at that moment to historical research and political theory. They exaggerated very much the antiquity and simplicity of Chaucer; they also exaggerated very much the artificiality and decadence of Dryden. They did not understand the many respects in which Dryden stood much nearer to Chaucer than they did themselves. And we may repeat, with all respect to them, that one of these was the same as in the other case; that Chaucer and Dryden both talked sense. There was indeed, as I have suggested before and shall more fully explain later, a sense in which Chaucer talked nonsense; and a somewhat different sense in which Shakespeare talked nonsense. But they did not talk nonsense with that high seriousness, that earnest belief in effort, that faith in the utmost for the highest, which was sometimes the special glory of the Victorian era. There was even a quality of objective rationality, which separated them in some degree from the imaginative ambitions of the Elizabethan era. Chaucer may be a very ancient well of English undefiled; and Dryden may be only a seventeenth-century specimen of an artificial lake, not to say an ornamental pond. But both the well and the pond have this in common; that they are still waters that may possibly run deep, and do at any rate reflect calmly the real objects of earth and sky. Whereas the torrent of the Renaissance in the sixteenth century, and the torrent of the Romantics in the nineteenth century, are much too splendid and inspiring as torrents to be useful for any sort of reflection. In other words, we need to look a little more carefully into the real merits of these various phases of literary history, and to note especially what there was about Chaucer that does in some ways separate him from Shakespeare; and may even in some ways unite him to Dryden. I think the quickest way of approaching it is through something in the particular nature of his humour, even though it is so elusive as to have caused disturbance among the learned, some of whom call it sly, some of whom refuse with dignity to see any humour at all.

However, this particular sort of slyness, and its distinction from a darker kind, does give us a key to certain very vital changes following on the Chaucerian simplicity. I know that commentators, or those critics who chiefly shine as commentators, are often gravely anxious to clear great men of the charge of talking nonsense. They apply it to Shakespeare; who has whole passages in which he talks nothing but nonsense. When Hamlet says, 'I am but mad north-north-west: when the wind is southerly, I know a hawk from a hand-saw,' the remark strikes his critics as one eminently suitable for scientific and rationalizing treatment; some hastily amending it to 'I know a hawk from a heronshaw,' and the other, I think, inventing some new tool or utensil called a hawk. I know nothing of these things; they may be right. But seeing that the man was a fantastic humorist in any case, and pretending to be a lunatic at that, and seeing he starts the very same sentence by saying he is mad, it seems to me, as a humble fellow-habitant of Hanwell, that he probably meant to say, 'a hawk from a hand-saw', as he might have said, 'a bishop from a blunderbuss', or, 'a postman from a pickle-jar'. Now this sort of wild fantasticality is Shakespearian but not Chaucerian. Chaucer has in the background too much of that logic which was the backbone of the Middle Ages. The Renaissance was, as much as anything, a revolt from the logic of the Middle Ages. We speak of the Renaissance as the birth of rationalism; it was in many ways the birth of irrationalism. It is true that the medieval School-men, who had produced the finest logic that the world has ever seen, had in later years produced more logic than the world can ever be expected to stand. They had loaded and lumbered up the world with libraries of mere logic; and some effort was bound to be made to free it from such endless chains of deduction. Therefore, there was in the Renaissance a wild touch of revolt, not against religion but against reason. Thus one of the very greatest of the sixteenth-century giants was almost as much of a nonsense writer as Edward Lear: Rabelais. So another of the very greatest wrote an Orlando Furioso[69] which might sometimes be called Ariosto Furioso.

[69] Orlando Furioso (*Roland the Mad*) is a romantic epic by Lodovico Ariosto, published in 1516.

So, in the same way, the narration of Raphael Hythloday is a wild jest. But there are some who still believe, quite literally, that Thomas More's Utopia describes the Utopia of Thomas More. For all I know, there may be some who believe that his friend Erasmus wrote *The Praise of Folly* because he thought that all fools were truly deserving of praise. As the Latin exercise-book said, there are some who laugh; and there are some who apparently don't, under the most extreme provocation. There may be some, for all I know, who would quote the anti-feminist observation of Chaucer's cock, with its cowardly parenthesis, as solid and scientific proof that a dead language was used to keep the people in ignorance; and that woman was oppressed by refusing her the benefits of education.

In any case, the truth in this suggestion of slyness is that it is a suggestion of sense. Chaucer was a man much more prudent, and in some ways much more balanced, than the great men of the Renaissance who came after him. Just as it was not in his temper, so it was not in his tradition, to let a joke run away with him, or to indulge a fantasy at the expense of everything else. It was the essence of the medieval philosophy that there is danger in all directions, just as there is good in all directions. That is the meaning of that balanced scheme of Mortal Sins, of Pride and Sloth and Avarice and the rest, with which Chaucer actually concludes and crowns the whole huge design of *The Canterbury Tales;* and of which Mrs. Haldane,[70] the wife of the professor, recently remarked mysteriously that they are all 'quite out of date'. Whether she really meant that nobody nowadays runs after money, or neglects any of his duties, or thinks too much of himself, I do not know. But what the medievals meant, by thus dividing and labelling the vices, was that a man might fall into one of these vices even when fleeing too far from another. A man who neglects his business may fall into sloth; a man who pursues his business may fall into avarice. And what the wreckers of the medieval system really did, practically and in the long run, was to let loose some of the vices on the excuse of exterminating the others.

---

[70] Chesterton is either making a reference to John Burdon Sanderson Haldane (1892–?) a British biologist or to John Scott Haldane (1860–1936) a British physiologist.

After the Renaissance, the Pagans went in for unlimited lust and the Puritans for unlimited avarice; on the excuse that at least neither of them was being guilty of sloth.

The poets, who take the tone of the time, had often a touch of this lawlessness, and of something that can be worse than lawlessness; concentration. That is, the time tended sometimes to be not only maniac but monomaniac. Chaucer inherited the tradition of a Church which had condemned heresies on the right hand and the left; and always claimed to stand for the truth as a whole and not for concentration on a part. He came indeed in days when that tradition was not at its best, and was beginning to degenerate into bitterness and abnormality; but he is himself a living embodiment of what that tradition had really been. *Communis sententia*; the phrase is Latin and very medieval. It marks the real effects of 'the vulgar tongue' that everybody knew what it meant while it was in Latin, and nobody notices what it means now it is in English. A modern man using the term does not even notice the word 'common' and means the very contrary of 'common'. He means private judgement; his own personal incommunicable sense. But Chaucer was very medieval and he was pickled in common sense.

The point is worthy of note, because it is one of the points in which his greatness has been rather unfairly overshadowed by the greatness of Shakespeare. When all is said, there was in the very greatest of the sixteenth-century men of genius a slight slip or failure upon the point of common sense. That is what Voltaire meant when he called Shakespeare an inspired barbarian; and there is something to be said for Voltaire as well as for Shakespeare. Let it be agreed, on the one hand, that the Renaissance poets had in one sense obtained a wider as well as a wilder range. But though they juggled with worlds, they had less real sense of how to balance a world. I am sorry that Chaucer 'left half-told the story of Cambuscan bold', and I can imagine that that flying horse might have carried the hero into very golden skies of Greek or Asiatic romance; but I am prepared to agree that he would never have beaten Ariosto in anything like a voyage to the moon. On the other hand, even in Ariosto there is something symbolic, if only accidentally symbolic, in the fact that his poem is less tragic but more frantic than 'The Song of Roland'; and deals not with Roland Dead but with Roland Mad. Anyhow, what is here only accidental becomes in the Elizabethans rather anarchical. When all is said, there is something a little sinister in the number of mad people there are in Shakespeare. We say that he uses his fools to brighten the dark background of tragedy; I think he sometimes uses them to darken it. Somewhere on that highest of all human towers there is a tile loose. There is something that rattles rather crazily in the high wind of the highest of mortal tragedies. What is felt faintly even in Shakespeare is felt far more intensely in the other Elizabethan and Jacobean dramatists; they seem to go in for dancing ballets of lunatics and choruses of idiots, until sanity is the exception rather than the rule. In some ways Chaucer's age was even harsher than Shakespeare's; but even its ferocity was rational. Chaucer describes a whole crowd of many-coloured personalities, of all possible types and tendencies. But I do not remember that, in the whole five volumes of Chaucer, there is such a thing as a madman.

In other words, the medieval mind did not really believe that the truth was to be found by going to extremes. And the Elizabethan mind had already had a sort of hint that it might be found there; at the extreme edges of existence and precipices of the human imagination. That is why there followed in theology and thought, after the Renaissance, such extremes of Speculation as the Calvinist or the Antinomian. I am concerned here to point out a difference rather than a preference; my own preferences are pretty obvious, but they are not the obvious truth involved here. The point is that even those who see the change as bringing more liberty may admit that it brought less sanity. Chaucer was not on the edge of a precipice, but in the middle of a solid meadow of daisies. And he not only was sure of his own common sense; he was also sure that the sense was really common.

Somebody said, and eventually everybody said, something about 'the spacious days of Queen Elizabeth'. I fancy it has falsified history more than any other popular quotation. If they had said, 'the spacious days of King Richard the Second', it would, in some ways, have been much more true; that is, in the sense of a consciousness of the whole problem of the whole people, of community with other countries and the Continent as a whole, or the vision of life in the light of a general philosophy. The Elizabethan epoch was of intense interest; of intensive intelligence; of piercing sharpness and delicacy in certain new forms of diplomacy and domestic policy, and the arts of the ambassador and the courtier; and, especially in one or two great men, of vivid and concentrated genius in the study of certain particular problems of character. But it was not spacious. If there was one thing it did not possess, it was that particular sort of fresh air that blows over the daisied meadows of Chaucer. Its special and specialist studies involved men in almost everything except fresh air. I have used the word 'involved' by accident; but it is applicable as well as accidental. Everything, even the great poetry of Elizabethan times, was a little too much involved. In literature it was the age of conceits. In politics it was the age of conspiracies. In those conspiracies there is a curious absence of the fresh popular spirit that often blew like a wind even through the heresies and horrors of the Middle Ages. None of it was in the same world with Peasants' Rising. The age of Richard the Second was an age of revolutions. The age of Elizabeth was an age of plots. And we all know that this was mirrored more or less even in the mightiest minds of that epoch. It is almost in a double sense that we talk about Shakespeare's 'plots'. In almost every case, it is a plot about a plot. He has even a sort of restlessness vaguely connected with the sixteenth-century sense of the importance and the insecurity of princes. 'Uneasy lies the head that wears a crown'; and also the head that has crowns on the brain.

That Shakespeare is the English giant, all but alone in his stature among the sons of men, is a truth that does not really diminish with distance. But it is a truth with two aspects; a shield with two sides; a sword with two edges. It is exactly because Shakespeare is an English giant that he blocks up the perspective of English history. He is as disproportionate to his own age as to every age; but he throws a misleading limelight on his own age and throws a gigantic shadow back on the other ages. For this reason many will not even know what I mean, when I talk about the greater spaciousness around the medieval poet. If the matter were pushed to a challenge, however, I could perhaps illustrate my meaning even better with another medieval poet. It is vaguely implied that Shakespeare was always jolly and Dante always gloomy. But, in a philosophical sense, it is almost the other way. It is notably so if, so to speak, we actually bring Shakespeare to the test of Dante. Do we not know in our hearts that Shakespeare could have dealt with Dante's Hell but hardly with Dante's Heaven? In so far as it is possible to be greater than anything that is really great, the man who wrote of Romeo and Juliet might have made something even more poignant out of Paolo and Francesca. The man who uttered that pulverizing 'He has no children,' over the butchery in the house of Macduff, might have picked out yet more awful and telling words for the father's cry out of the Tower of Hunger. But the Tower of Hunger is not spacious. And when Dante is really dealing with the dance of the liberated virtues in the vasty heights of heaven, he is spacious. He is spacious when he talks of Liberty; he is spacious when he talks of Love. It is so in the famous words at the end about Love driving the sun and stars; it is the same in the far less famous and far finer passage, in which he hails the huge magnanimity of God in giving to the human spirit the one gift worth having; which is Liberty. Nobody but a fool will say that Shakespeare was a pessimist; but we may, in this limited sense, say that he was a pagan; in so far that he is at his greatest in describing great spirits in chains. In that sense, his most serious plays are an Inferno. Anyhow, they are certainly not a Paradiso.

I only use Shakespeare here as a parallel, and I will not continue it indefinitely as a parenthesis. Otherwise I should, of course, qualify the word paganism by well-known facts about his life, as well as by the whole tone of his literature. That Shakepeare was a Catholic is a thing that every Catholic feels by every sort of convergent common sense to be true. It is supported by the few external and political facts we know; it is utterly unmistakable in the general spirit and atmosphere; and in nothing more than in the scepticism, which appears in some aspects to be paganism. But I am not talking about the various kinds of Catholic; I am talking about the atmosphere of the sixteenth century as compared with the fourteenth century. And I say that while the former was more refined, it was in certain special ways more restricted, or properly speaking, more concentrated. Shakespeare is more concentrated on Hamlet than Dante is upon Hell; for the very reason that Dante's mind is full of the larger plan of which this is merely a part. But, it may reasonably be said, I have no right to take the case of Dante in order to make out a case for Chaucer. I am not likely to pretend that Chaucer absorbed every detail of the Thomist theology and purely theoretical ethics of the Divine Comedy. What, it may be asked, has Chaucer to do with Dante; what did he actually inherit from Dante? I answer, the spaciousness. The general sense of not being himself in prison; for Chaucer does not himself go to prison with Palamon and Arcite, as Shakespeare does in some sense go to prison with Richard the Second. Nay, to some extent, and in some subtle fashion, Shakespeare seems to identify himself with Hamlet who finds Denmark a prison, or the whole world a prison. We do not have this sense of things closing in upon the soul in Chaucer, with his simple tragedies; one might almost say, his sunny tragedies. In his world misfortunes are misfortunes, like clouds in the sky; but there is a sky. And there is a quite indescribable serenity that comes from security, in the thought that the sky is settled in an accepted order; or, as the medieval men used to put it, that the heavens are incorruptible. This sense, which Chaucer has vaguely and Dante vividly, is in all its variations quite different from the later mood that culminated in Ford[71] and Webster;[72] where the storm has become more than the sky. It appeared in Chaucer in a leisurely and allusive fashion, but it is there all right; and it is the consciousness of a cosmic philosophy at the back of the mind. It is enough to a man of his temperament to joke about it; to say that it can all be found in 'olde bookes'; to feel a sort of satisfaction that somebody somewhere has a hundred books, clothed in black and red, of Aristole and his philosophy. But it is the feeling that was lost at the Renaissance, when so much else was gained; the feeling of a sort of reasonable repose in the common sense of Christian philosophy; especially the colossal common sense of St. Thomas Aquinas.

[71] John Ford (1586–1640) is an English dramatist.
[72] John Webster (1580?–1625) is also an English dramatist.

Thus we have the paradox that the spirit of the Renaissance, at the very moment when it seemed to most men to be emerging into the daylight, was, in another sense, at that very moment plunging into the dark. It was plunging into those dark problems of scepticism with which the world is wrestling still. But it is not a mere question of some calling scepticism an enlightenment and others calling it a benighted gloom. There really was something of mystification and secrecy in the very air which Shakespeare breathed; which remains in the sort of biographical problems which he left behind him. I have said elsewhere that there is a certain parallel between the obscurity of Chaucer and the obscurity of Shakespeare, in a practical or political sense. But the cases are very different in this spiritual or atmospheric sense. The mystery of Chaucer is mainly negative; it simply arises from the fact that we happen to have a few official records and no private memoirs. It is a *hiatus valde deflendus*; but it is not, thank God, a Cipher. Nobody can imagine *The Canterbury Tales* being a Cryptogram. It was only possible to suggest it of Shakespeare because Shakespeare had the bad luck to live in an age of cryptograms. That is, he lived in an age of conspiracies. But in fact, there are real riddles for Shakespearians; quite apart from the mad riddles of Baconians. There is no Mr. W.H. to distract our minds from the poetry of Chaucer. Chaucer's purely personal poems are mostly of the sort that anybody could understand; such as frank and hearty demands for more money. There are problems about his private life, as is noted elsewhere; but they are not presented in a manner at once deliberate, defiant and tantalizing, as are some of the relations adumbrated in the Sonnets. His Dark Lady was never so dark as all that. She is rather, so to speak a wash-out; a figure so faint and pale that we cannot be certain whether she existed, or whether the poet is really writing about her at all. Here again, the obscurity is merely negative; but in the Sonnets there is a positive obscurity, a darkness visible. It was said that Shakespeare unlocked his heart with this key; but it sometimes seems truer to say that he hampered the lock.

It is well to remember that this particular *kind* of perplexity has really come into the world since the breakdown of the medieval order; even though the breakdown was accompanied by brilliant diversions in all other directions. It is true, for instance, that the Renaissance had expanded the exploration of the earth; and in that sense, I have spoken of its artists inhabiting a wider and a wilder world. But in some other respects, they inhabited a world which, though certainly wilder, was not so wide. It was very exciting to discover that there were Red Indians or yellow Chinamen; but it did not increase the old Roman and philosophical sense of the broad brotherhood of the *humanum genus:* the human race. Rather it raised new problems about it; problems which produced all sorts of horrible things, from slavery to anthropology. It was very satisfactory to know that you could pay a visit to mountains made of silver or cities made of gold; but humanity was not in fact so much united by the wealth of Ferdinand[73] as by the poverty of Francis. Nothing, indeed, was destined in the long run to produce such bottomless botheration and bewildering intellectual difficulties, as the relation of the precious metals to the older and more practical economics. Those gallant men, who stormed the gates of the sunset to set up the golden banners of Spain, were fortunately unaware that they were fixing on a peak in Darien the enigmatic ensign that we call the Gold Standard.

What we have to realize, in short (against much of the atmospheric assumptions or allusions of modern literature), is that the older intellectual world was not stupid merely because it was static. Whatever our creed, that is as stupid as calling Confucius stupid because China was static. Chaucer's world was simpler, in the sense that there were fewer unanswered questions. But whether or no we think the questions had been rightly answered, they had certainly been rationally answered. Intelligent men had answered them in an intelligent way; in such a way that an intelligent man like Chaucer could repose in the reasons given. This is simply a fact of history, necessary to the elucidation of biography; it has nothing to do with whether we ourselves accept the theology, or even the philosophy. The point to grasp is that we disagree with it as a philosophy; as we might disagree with the Platonic or the Positivist philosophy; not as

[73] Chesterton is referring to King Ferdinand of Spain (1452–1516) the founder of the Spanish monarchy.

we disagree with a wild savage taboo in Africa or a Prohibitionist prejudice in Alabama.

There are inferences from all this which I shall discuss in the last chapter of this book. For the moment, the point to realize is, not merely that there is something to be said for medievalism against the Renaissance (a view which Ruskin and modern medievalists have sufficiently made clear), but that in some special aspects medievalism could be more rational, or even more rationalistic, than the Renaissance. I am well aware that it is a case not only of complexities, but of contradictions. It is true on the one side that the very reason of medievalism was rooted in religion; it is true on the other side that the very frenzy of the sixteenth century was akin to a thirst for truth. But the distinction I draw is true; and it is of some importance in life and letters. The Renaissance genius was never so much intellectually inspired as when he seemed to be intellectually intoxicated; and his very depression was an exaltation. It would be something to be able even to despair like one of Shakespeare's characters. A dying man might want to live, if he could go on producing such phrases as 'Absent thee from felicity awhile'; he might even continue to absent himself. A murderer might grow cheerful, if he were able to utter his misery in those words about life being a thing 'full of sound and fury, signifying nothing'. But try the experiment of reading a few lines of Aristotle or Aquinas, even as echoed by Chaucer. You will begin to wonder (dare we say it?) whether the great Life of the Renaissance, if it had been a little less full of sound and fury, might not have signified more.

VIII

THE RELIGION OF CHAUCER

It marks something thin and repetitive, about much of the comment on Chaucer, that we can all remember reading twenty times a comparison between Chaucer and Langland. It commonly adds to a description of *The Canterbury Tales* something like the remark: 'A very different picture is given in *Piers Plowman*.' It is indeed a different picture, because it happens to be a different book, written by a different man. But it would be perfectly easy to make the same contrast concerning two descriptions of the same period written by the same man. It would mark a rather wider contrast to describe the scope and spirit of Pickwick, and then add: 'A very different picture is given in *Hard Times*.' For that matter, it would be almost equally effective to take two of the Dickens novels that come next to each other in his earliest period and say: 'A very different picture is given in Oliver Twist.' And in both cases a reasonable critic will answer, somewhat impatiently, that it is indeed a different picture; for the reason that a good painter does not generally paint two pictures at once. But in the case of the medieval authors, there is always a sort of insinuation that one of the two pictures must be false; and that in any case the happier and more humane picture cannot be true. The suggestion is that Chaucer, being a court poet, was a sort of conservative optimist, while Langland, being supposed to be a popular poet, must necessarily have been a pessimist; and pessimists must necessarily be right.

As a matter of fact, all this view is riddled with inaccuracies, even about the actual comparison bewteen Chaucer and Langland. Supposing there were any particular reason to compare them, a real comparison would be considerably more complex. For instance, though Chaucer is called a courtier, it is Chaucer, much more than Langland, who is always saying that true nobility is not in noble birth but in noble behaviour; that men are to be judged by worth rather than rank; and generally that all men are equal in the sight of God and similarly, though Langland is treated as a revolutionary, it is Langland much more than Chaucer who is always saying that up starts have seized power to which their birth does not entitle them; that the claims of family have been disregarded through the insolence of novelty, and that men are bragging and boasting above their station. There is doubtless much to be said for both these views, nor are they really inconsistent with each other. But Chaucer can scarcely have said the first in order to flatter the aristocracy, nor Langland said the second as part of a demand for change. It is also curious that many have missed the point of certain passages in Langland as they have missed the point of so many passages in Chaucer. The author of *Piers Plowman* denounces a vast variety of evils, indeed an almost universal conspectus of evils; because the very form of his book is an account of something very like a Day of Judgement; and not an account of a casual ride of holiday-makers to Canterbury. But in many places he denounces the fourteenth-century conditions, not so much because certain classes have too little as because they have too much. He denounces the riot and excesses that accompanied the economic overturn of his time; but much of it was a condition of high though perilously precarious wages, and a wealth which was not under adequate or responsible control. He sometimes speaks of beggars as if they were bullies, rather than abject creatures; and while he certainly thinks the poor are in danger, it is not his point merely that they are in destitution. His point is rather that they and everybody else are in chaos; and there is much in that sort of lopsided luck that suggests our own time as well as his.

The point is here, however, that Langland was nothing so simple as a man lamenting over a starving people; and certainly Chaucer was nothing so simple as a smug snob or conservative not knowing or caring whether anybody could starve. They were men of very different temperaments, but they did not after all bear such very different testimony. They were both highly intelligent Christians and Catholics living in an extremely bewildering time of transition; in which some things were certainly breaking free, but a good many things appeared to be breaking down. The rather remarkable ballade which Chaucer addressed to Richard the Second might have been written by Langland himself, in his sternest mood of reproach and responsibility. The burden of it, even in the literal sense of the refrain of it, is a repeated insistence that only Steadfastness can save the nation in such a welter of novelties. It is not difficult to imagine that particular personage called Steadfastness walking about for edification in The Field Full of Folk.

It is doubtless true that while Chaucer could sometimes be as severe as Langland, it is not very likely that Langland would be as jocular as Chaucer. But that in itself hardly shows that Chaucer was lacking in popular sympathies. The English lower classes have been known to make jokes, both then and now. As a matter of fact, I fancy Langland would have been much more harsh to the coarse and common people on the Pilgrimage than Chaucer. But the whole comparison arises from the initial ineptitude of not realizing that one kind of man will write one kind of book; and that one kind of book will of its very nature contain one kind of material. We might as well complain that *Everyman* is tragic as complain that *Piers Plowman* is prophetic, in the sense which some call pessimistic. It is by its whole plan and conception a vision of Christ calling all human society to repentance. It is not very likely that Chaucer, considered as an artist, would have attacked that particular literary scheme at all. But if he had attacked it, he would have had exactly the same fundamental ideas about the nature of repentance and the authority of Christ. And, what is perhaps more cogent here, he would have had exactly the same fundamental belief in the sacramental and ecclesiastical system of the Middle Ages. Those who do not realize that fact simply do not know that system; though it did not, curiously enough, disappear with the Middle Ages.

Some critics have vaguely suspected Chaucer of being a Lollard, through a simple ignorance of what is meant by being a Catholic. I am aware that there is a Victorian convention, according to which a literary study should not refer to religion, except when there is an opportunity of a passing sneer at it. But nobody can make head or tail of the fourteenth century without understanding what is meant by being a Catholic; and therefore by being a heretic. A man does not come an inch nearer to being a heretic by being a hundred times a critic. Nor does he do so because his criticisms resemble those of critics who are also heretics. He only becomes a heretic at the precise moment when he prefers his criticism to his Catholicism. That is, at the instant of separation in which he thinks the view peculiar to himself more valuable than the creed that unites him to his fellows. At any given moment the Catholic Church is full of people sympathizing with social movements or moral ideas, which may happen to have representatives outside the Church. For the Church is not a movement or a mood or a direction, but the balance of many movements and moods; and membership of it consists of accepting the ultimate arbitrament which strikes the balance between them, not in refusing to admit any of them into the balance at all. A Catholic does not come any nearer to being a Communist by hating the Capitalist corruptions, any more than he comes any nearer to being a Moslem by hating real idolatry or real excess in wine. He accepts the Church's ruling about the use and abuse of wine and images; and after that it is irrelevant how much he happens to hate the abuse of them. A Catholic did not come any nearer to being a Calvinist by dwelling on the onmiscience of God and the power of Grace, any more than he came any nearer to being an atheist by saying that man possessed reason and freewill. What constituted a Calvinist was that he preferred his Calvinism to his Catholicism. And what constituted his Catholicism was that he accepted the ultimate arbitration which reconciled freewill and grace, and did not exclude either. So a Catholic did not come any nearer to being a Lollard because he criticized the ecclesiastical evils of the fourteenth century, as Leo the Thirteenth or Cardinal Manning criticized the economic evils of the nineteenth century. He said many things which Lollards also said, as the Pope and the Cardinal said many things which Socialists also said. But he was no nearer to being a Lollard; and nobody can begin to suggest that Chaucer was a Lollard, unless he can prove either or both of two propositions about him. First, that he held the only Lollard doctrine that was ever properly defined or denounced; the doctrine that 'dominion is founded on Grace', that is, that nobody but a good Catholic purified by the sacraments has any political rights or powers. And, second, that if he did hold it as a private opinion, he would in the last resort have preferred that private opinion to membership of the Body of Christ. I need not say that there is not the wildest suggestion of a reason for supposing that Chaucer was a Lollard either in one sense or the other.

To me personally, the Lollard is the most sympathetic of all the heretics. I might say, in a figure of speech, that he was the most Catholic of all the heretics. He was, beyond any possible question, the least Protestant of all the heretics. His whole suggestion, so far as there was any clear suggestion beyond a healthy discontent, was the superiority of the Catholic ideals of holy poverty and brotherhood to the ranks and powers of this world. But his thesis as a thesis is not tenable; nobody could live in a society in which practical authority and right were only recognized in holy and innocent persons. The experiment of telephoning to a policeman to stop a murder, and being told that he must call on the priest for confession on his way to the scene of the crime, would be enough to settle the legal practicality of Lollardy. It seems to me enormously unlikely that a man of Chaucer's temperament, which was sensible almost to excess, ever thought anything of the kind. It is quite certain that he never said anything of the kind. It is equally certain that he did say something else of a totally different kind, which Lollards said also; that it was disgraceful for priests and men in authority to be base and unworthy; or, as he put it in a picturesque figure, that it was horrible to see a filthy shepherd and a clean sheep. But there is nothing particularly Lollardish about saying that; thousands of Catholics have said it in every age and are saying it now. It is worthy of remark, perhaps, that Chaucer's very strictures on clerics are rather clerical than anti-clerical. That is, they are based on the notion that the priest is not merely bad when he ought to be good, but bad because he ought to be better. In the same passage he used another figure of speech, which is even more conclusive. 'If gold rust, what shall iron do?' He never doubted that the priest, as a priest, had received something as precious as gold in comparison to iron. But, the ultimate test is even more practical. The question is, even if Chaucer was anti-clerical, would he have allowed it to make him anti-Catholic? Would he have left the Church for the love of a grievance? There is not, and never has been the shadow of a reason to think so.

For the rest, he was unquestionably and even passionately devoted to the particular parts of Catholicism that have been most condemned by Protestantism. He had a devotion to Our Lady perhaps greater than that of Dante; as great as that of St. Bernard in his great oration in Dante. The poem significantly called his A B C , as if it were the first elements of his childlike faith, contains language that goes almost beyond the doctrinal limit in attributing omnipotence and supremacy to Mary. In short, there is no reason for saying that Chaucer was a Lollard; but there is overwhelming reason for saying that he was not a Protestant.

Modern critics have congratulated Chaucer, or congratulated themselves, on the fact that he was so enlightened a reformer as to satirize the Monk and the Friar. Curiously enough, they have neglected to notice what he satirized them for. Rather simple things of this sort do often get overlooked. And the simple truth is that Chaucer satirizes the Monk for not being sufficiently Monastic. He may have been right or wrong; but it is certain that if he was right, the Reformers of the Reformation were wrong; and only on the assumption that they were wrong can we pretend that he was in any sense right. The point is rather practical; because nearly all studies of this period are full of the suggestion that Chaucer, like his contemporary Wycliffe, was a sort of morning star of the Reformation. We can only answer that in that case he was an eccentric star who wanted the sun to move backwards instead of forwards. In the whole of his satirical sketch of the Monk, the point is, not that the Monk is sunk in monkish superstitions, but simply that the Monk is not monkish enough. Protestantism, as it ultimately developed, professed to free monks and nuns from the prison of the cloister. It welcomed runaway monks and nuns to the freedom of the secular world; even when their conduct was rather alarmingly free and somewhat startlingly secular. But all Chaucer's denunciation is directed, not so much at a monk, as at a runaway monk; and that not because he is a monk but because he is a runaway. He jeers at him for coming out of the cloister and partaking of the pleasures of the world. He jeers at him indeed in his own jovial and even genial fashion; making up an imaginary defence for the monk, which is full of a hearty hatred of work and the bother of reading books. Why, he asks, should the jolly fellow do any work at all? Why should he work with his hands, because St. Augustine believed in the Dignity of Labour? Let St. Augustine work if he wants to. But this breezy outburst certainly cannot be taken seriously as an attack on monasticism, unless it is to be take seriously as an attack on manual labor, or labour of any sort. There are doubtless modern critcs who are capable of taking that or anything else seriously. To those troubled in spirit by the divine disturbance of humour, it will be obvious that Chaucer is simply chaffing a monk for his cheek in not being a monk at all. The whole of this passage, taken in an historical and social sense, is simply a protest against the decline of monastic discipline. It is like a patriotic protest against the decline of military discipline. Such a protest would very probably contain an ironical congratulation, on the lines of 'He who fights and runs away will live to fight another day'. But it is scarcely the sort of congratulation that any soldier would be flattered to receive. The fact is that the man who said this sort of thing was the flat contrary of a modern opponent of asceticism. Neither Chaucer, nor anybody who really counted in Chaucer's day, ever dreamed of complaining that monks were monks. They only complained, as Chaucer did, because the monks were not monks.

Chaucer, of course, took for granted the whole Catholic theory about the normal vocation of Marriage and the exceptional vocation of Virginity. He explains it all, in strictly orthodox theological terms; though in one place he puts it, with a twist of his quaint humour, into the mouth of the Wife of Bath. She is the lady who has buried four husbands and explains that, on the whole, Virginity is not her vocation. Here again, if this were a joke against anything, it would not be a joke against the Virgin but against the Wife; or at any rate against the Wife of Bath. Indeed, anyone superficially acquainted with medieval culture and the Chaucerian origins will know that the latter is the more likely of the two. He will know that while such a satirist was ready to satirize both unmarried and married people, he was rather more ready to satirize the married than the unmarried. The references to Theophrastus [74] and his clerical copyists make that clear enough. But he will also know, what is the most important point of all, that whenever the satirist became a serious writer, he accepted quite as naturally the status of the officially unmarried as that of the officially married. He no more dreamed of suggesting that there ought to be no Monasticism than that there ought to be no Marriage. He was bred in the bone and blood of a whole living society, of which one was as much an organic part as the other. He might, like many another medieval writer, deal rather scandalously with the scandal of monks or nuns who broke their vows. He would never, like a modern writer, think it scandalous that they kept their vows.

As a matter of fact, Chaucer deals even with the former scandal less scandalously than most of his great contemporaries. It is a point of some importance, as marking not only the more genial and less militant temper of the English poet and the English people, but as illustrating the point that England was really less anti-clerical than Europe. The English people were the most remote from heresy, when the English rulers were the most near to schism. But there was also an amiable element, not only national but personal. It is suggested, somewhat plausibly I think, that the extremely abrupt introduction of the Second Nun, followed by her equally abrupt dismissal without any description, and with only the mysterious addition of Three Priests (who never appear again and have no stories to contribute), is really a badly botched excision and join, to cover the fact that Chaucer originally wrote something about the Second Nun which he decided not to publish. Nor, I think, need such an act of prudence have been merely prudential. If Chaucer had ever let his mind run along lines of such licence as did Boccaccio, in suggesting the immorality of nuns, I do honestly believe that Chaucer himself would have been ashamed of it. For that matter, it is true that Boccaccio himself ultimatily repented of it. But there was in Chaucer from the first something quite different from the hard scorn and hot

---

[74] Theophrastus (c.372–c.287 B.C.) was a Greek philosopher and the successor to Aristotle in the Peripatetic School.

repentance of the Italian. It was something which, in the legend of Robin Hood, went along with the same English devotion to the Blessed Virgin; so that it was said that the outlaw 'would never hurt a company that any woman was in'. Chaucer merely as a man (if I understand anything at all of the man) would always have felt that he might say things about monks that he must not say about nuns; in which one other English Catholic may be permitted to agree with him.

Anyhow, whether we take the test of the cult of Mary, or of the code of Monasticism, or of any other recognized mark for modern criticism, it is perfectly obvious that Geoffrey Chaucer was an ordinary orthodox medieval Catholic and never dreamed of being anything else. Nor did he ever dream that he was likely to lose that status (to all who held it the most vital thing in life and death) by making fun of fat friars or monks who went hunting instead of working with their hands. But those who, reading history backwards, look for the later type called the Protestant in a medieval man who was not even a Lollard, may find in every sense a more final answer in the final pages of the great poem. It may be suspected that few of them have read as far as those final pages; still less had the heroic tenacity to read through them. Everybody knows the joke about Lord Macaulay; who said of Spenser that few of his readers were in at the death of Blatant Beast;[75] thereby proving that Macaulay at least was not one of the few, or he would have found out that the Blatant Beast does not die after all. Something of the same doubt affects the case of those to whom Chaucer's religion seems not only a simple matter, but merely a religion of simplicity.

They are naturally attached to the beautiful description of the Parson, which sounds in many ways very simple, and which occurs at the beginning of *The Tales* and is therefore easily skimmed even by the superficial. They remark very truly that Chaucer, for some reason or other, evidently preferred the parish priests to the monks and friars; though I know not why there should be supposed to be something vaguely Protestant about preferring one set of Catholic

---

[75] "Blatant Beast" is a character in Spenser's *Faerie Queen* representing infamy or more commonly, slander.

priests to another. There is certainly nothing very Protestant about taking it for granted that one medieval Catholic must have been right in his preferences. Nevertheless, those who imagine that Jesus Christ and the Gospels were first discovered by Martin Luther, and are never mentioned among Catholics, have hinted in a hundred ways that the mention of these things in the first description of the Parson shows him to be a good hearty Protestant Parson, with Muscular Christianity and Morning Service at eleven o'clock. May I inflict on such readers the somewhat heavy medieval penance of reading what is (very deceptively) called 'The Parson's Tale', with which Chaucer deliberately winds up the whole series of tales? It is in fact simply a sermon, and if ever there was a medieval sermon, in the whole range of the Middle Ages, it is that of the simple Parson of Chaucer. It is arranged in the formal and almost decorative scheme of the Seven Deadly Sins, each division having equally formal and doctrinal sub-divisions; and each division and sub-division stating with minute accuracy the exact and distinct Roman Catholic doctrine, as is to this day. There is the need of Confession to a priest, the distiction between mortal and venial sin, and all the rest. There are a hundred points on which it agrees with itself then and now, and differs from everybody else then and now. It is appallingly long and elaborate, but it does not trip on a single term; and there is written all over it in large letters Nihil Obstat and Imprimatur. For those who believe in the change of morals or the innovations of science, it may be amusing to note that the simple Parson indulges in a ferocious, and somewhat ruthlessly realistic, outburst against Birth-Control.

There is one point in this connexion that should be made clear. Nobody understands the nature of man, the nature of medieval man, or above all the nature of the medieval man named Geoffrey Chaucer, who imagines that this sort of long explanation is necessarily a bore. At any rate, it is not necessarily a bore to the writer, even if it is for the reader. All healthy and vigorous minds have great pleasure in explaining anything; and especially in explaining a system. There were so many systems in the Middle Ages, ranging from the gravest to the most trivial matters, from hagiology to heraldry, from the rules of faith to the rules of falconry, from the calculation of planets to the language of colours, that the general effect on the modern mind is that of a complicated and bewildering pattern. But almost all the men expounding these things took a palpable and even passionate pleasure in the pattern. This was not less, but more the case when it was a doctrinal or dogmatic pattern. Chaucer has a huge appetite for theological and ethical explanations; he will often turn aside for them in the most casual and incongruous context. It is thoroughly typical of him that he makes the Wife of Bath pour out a torrent of turbulent, gross and egotistical discourse, as course as a fishwife's and as personal as Margate landlady's; and yet feels it perfectly natural that she should pause to explain the correct Catholic doctrine about Virginity and Counsels of Perfection. It was perfectly natural. It would not only have been perfectly natural to Chaucer. It would probably have been perfectly natural to the Wife of Bath. Here and there, even in modern England, we may find the remnants of that ancient relish, when some tavern talker expounds heavily the whole case for atheism or the Anglo-Israelite theory or the proofs from Apocalypse that the Kaiser was the Beast. But if we wish to find the tradition more truly and directly descended from the Middle Ages, and until lately really moving a whole people as it did in the Middle Ages, we must go, strangely enough, to the Puritans of Scotland. There was found the true medieval passion for logic and the long exposition of a system. The Scot in Stevenson's stories, who 'sits with relish' under a thunderous but entirely theoretical theologian—he had preserved one thread, though only a thin black thread, out of the woven tapestry of the Middle Ages. In that sense, so far as this island was concerned, the Calvinists were the last Catholics.

It is the paradox, but the truth of the matter, that what may be called the dullness of medievalism came from the excitement of medievalism. The vigour and vivacious interest required to follow those interminable arguments, or interminable allegories, were the virtues of a young and virile humanity. An eagerness more inexhaustible than that of a child was needed to carry readers breathlessly through the endless decorative forest of *The Romance of the Rose*. It is a truth of psychology that needs a fuller exposition; for no psychologist has yet written a very necessary book called 'A Defence of Bores'. Perhaps it is the bored rather than the bore that needs defence, but it is true that the bored is the weaker of the two. It is the bore who is joyous and triumphant; the true conqueror of the earth. Or, to put the matter less flippantly, it is true that a living and logical gusto for giving long explanations of everything, though it may be an infliction on the sensitive, is itself an attribute of the strong. To anyone who knows what logic is, the sustained lucidity and consistency of the Parson's Tale is itself sufficient proof that writing it was, for Chaucer, not merely a moral toil, but an intellectual joy. A modern man is quite entitled to say that joy in writing it is one thing and joy in reading it quite another. But the medieval man may have been the more joyful of the two.

In another sense, of course, the question of Chaucer's religion rises into a region that is far above all this controversy. I have already mentioned certain fragments, from his religious poems, which are like flashes of this more serene and enduring light. But if we are to realize what a man like Chaucer meant by that light, and how and why it differed from daylight (the daylight which he of all men loved as he loved the daisy), we must cast back and consider some more general principles which are the explanations of his attitude; not only because they were universally understood as the basis of medieval thought but because they are almost universally misunderstood in the outlook of modern thought. The poet never mentioned them because he started with them, and the critics never mentioned them because they have not reached them as yet.

Perhaps the largest fact about the Middle Ages is that two forces worked and to some extent warred in that time. One was that mystical vision, or whatever we call it, which Catholics call The Faith; the other was the prodigious prestige of Pagan Atiquity. Neo-Pagans of the Swinburnian interlude imagined that Paganism stood merely for light and liberty, and Catholicism merely for superstition and slavery. But the case was much more complex, upon any reading. Some superstitions, such as Astrology, still imposed themselves although they were Pagan; or rather *because* they were Pagan. They seemed to be classic, like Aristotle and Virgil. It is amusing to read the medieval

Catholics on Astrology, and note how much they resemble the modern Catholics on Evolution. Both feel *first* that no science must be allowed to deny the dignity and liberty of the human soul; but the medievals have the same vague respect for all that is labelled Antiquity that we have for all that is labelled Science. Or again, in the matter of liberty, the mere instinctive growth of a Catholic peasantry had already loosened the old slavery, when lawyers insisting on the old Roman Law tried to revive the definition of the slave. The mystical element had its own crimes and cruelties; but the point is that both elements were mixed and that the conflict was very complicated. One truth, however, was fairly constant; that Pagan and Christian conceptions ran parallel; but the Christian *above* the Pagan.

It is wholly typical of our time that the old theologians are commonly blamed for subtle distinctions; because in our time we tend always to superficial resemblances. It is counted the triumph of classification to class everything together; that is, the triumph of classification is to say there are no classes. Imperialism painting the map red and internationalism painting the globe grey are alike in practice; in so far as each will spread the paint very thin, if it can only spread it very far. Almost all forms of popular science shine chiefly by shallow parallels. For instance, the whole business of Comparative Mythology is made up of shallow parallels; that is, of superficial resemblances which cover deep and fundamental divisions. I have legs and a table has legs; if I am large and round, it is also possible for a table to be large and round. Therefore I am the legendary counterpart, or possibly the mythical origin, of the Round Table. But if I modestly advance this claim, it may occur to some that the differences between a man and a table are fundamental; while the resemblances between table-legs and merely human legs are superficial; they are in fact almost metaphorical. A man is alive and walks about; a table seldom does so, save under the moral influence of Sir Arthur Conan Doyle. And the abyss between the organic and the inorganic is too absolute to be bridged by the figure of speech called a wooden leg. So we commonly find in current discussions a pretence of finding things roughly similar when they are radically different; as if a man were accused of splitting hairs because he obstinately distinguished between feathers and ferns.

Thus there are critics so shallow that they cannot see the quite fundamental difference between the Puritanism from which England is emerging at the present time and the Asceticism from which England was emerging in the time of Chaucer. The difference, or rather the contrast, is clear and sharp; and has nothing to do with whether we happen to prefer one or the other. It may be maintained that Puritanism is more practical, or even more concerned with the present world. It may be reasonably alleged that ascetic mysticism was too much concerned with the other world. But the roots are utterly distinct; even when there is in both a renunciation of the things of this world in the name of the other world. And the difference is this; that the older ascetic saw heaven as very bright, and this world as dark in comparison. But the later Puritan saw heaven itself as dark, in the sense of stern and rather stormy; and his genuine imagination exulted in the storm. For him the Lord was in the thunder, much more that in the still small voice; and he was thus at the opposite extreme to even the most extreme ascetic, or excessive ascetic, who wished the sound of lutes and viols to cease, so that the still small voice might be heard. The point is, however, that the old ascetic was looking for joy and beauty, whether we think his vision of joy and beauty impossible or merely invisible. But the true Puritan was not primarily looking for joy and beauty, but for strength and even violence. This can be stated, and for a hundred years has been stated, in a form favourable to the Puritan. He has been called the stalwart and virile Puritan; he is always very much gratified to be called the grim and rugged Puritan. The other religious ideal can as easily be stated in an unfavourable form; suggesting a sentimental and childish attraction to bright colours or costly trinkets. I am not at all concerned with the favourable or unfavourable comments here. But, favourable or unfavourable, they point to a clean-cut contrast between the two things. There is such a contrast between those things; which is why so many modern writers describe them as the same.

The contrast instantly appears in black and white, when the two creeds express themselves in externals. When once the ascetic was assured that certain things were dedicated to divine things, he wanted them to be exceptionally brilliant and gorgeous things. He wanted the vestments of the priest to run through all the colours of the rainbow or the marbles of the shrine to mimic all the sunsets of the world. The Puritan insisted that the preacher should wear a black Geneval gown, instead of any coloured vestment, and that the chapel should be a shed or barn and not a temple shining with marbles; and he was consistent with his fundamental conception. He was not merely stern towards other people's religion or irreligion. He was stern towards his own religion; and was most stern where he was most religious. In his religious picture even the high light was a hard light; the sort of harsh and hueless light that can be seen in the black engravings in the old Family Bibles. It was not a question of preferring light to darkness; it was a question of preferring a colourless light to coloured light. It was not a question of flowers or beautiful raiment, conceived as a vision of heaven rather than of earth; it was a question of being on the side of the storm against the flower or of the stark bones against the garment. As I say, it can be described as a sublime exultation in strength and severity; appealing to sturdy races or to strict family traditions. It can also be described (so far as I am concerned) as a return to heathenism and a howling to the gods of fear. But it is a fact of history, which still plays a part even in politics; that certain people were proud, not of being stern to this or that indulgence; but simply proud of being stern.

Now this note is *never* found in medieval asceticism. Nobody can imagine St. Thomas Aquinas saying, 'I am a grand grim old Dominican, who stands no nonsense; we are a rugged stock, scorning the pleasures of the world.' Nobody can conceive St. Bernard boasting, 'We Burgundians are a harsh, hardy race and like the thunder in our hills more than the pretty flowers of a garden paradise.' These men may have dwelt too much on the supernatural as compared to the natural, according to our own views upon such matters; but they thought the supernatural more beautiful than the natural; not merely more naked or elemental or terrible. M. Reinach, a learned Jew who has an artistic admiration for medievalism certainly quite untinged with Catholicism, has very truly pointed out that the purely medieval artists always represented heavenly beings as gay and happy, and attributed sorrow only to the lost. The insistence even on the Man of Sorrows and the Mater Dolorosa, in artistic expression, belongs to a time after the medieval. It was in the seventeenth century that the two more sombre religious moods appeared in the two religions. In the Catholic world it became in some sense a worship of sorrow; in the Puritan world a worship of severity, and in some cases of savagery. The point here, however, is that we cannot understand medieval men, even the most extreme or extravagant ascetics, unless we understand that to them the contrast was quite clear between the cross and the crown; between the harsh and the angular timber of the cross and the coloured jewels of the crown. A man like Fra Angelico might live a very plain life; but he did not imagine paradise as a penny plain, but very decidedly as twopence coloured. A man like John Knox prided himself on being plain even in his religious conceptions; some might say flippantly that he was too much of a Scot to spare the twopence. From him descends a sort of pride in rudeness, growing more self-conscious with later times; but unknown even to the rudest people in older times. We may think that the earlier saints tried to be saved by an excess of humility; but nobody tried to be admired for an excess of hardness. They did not even excuse themselves for being hard-hearted by calling themselves hard-headed. As a rule, they did not call themselves anything, except miserable sinners.

This is a good example of the subtle contrasts of history; the contrasts which a shallow person will probably see as resemblances. It is much easier to see that Buddhism and Byzantine Christianity both have images or incense or gilded shrines, than to see that their fundamental theories flatly contradict each other. It is much easier to say that Pelagians and Puritans both quarrelled with bishops than to state lucidly their two separate beliefs, which were at opposite extremes of belief. The Lollards of the fifteenth century were in many ways the very reverse of the Lutherans of the sixteenth century. Yet it is found convenient to class them together, because it is now found convenient to class nearly everything and anything together, in a generalization which is obviously sweeping and certainly superficial.

When we have thus firmly grasped that medievalism had a heavenly vision (or illusion) of which the colours were intrinsically beautiful and even gay, we can then follow correctly the curious and interesting process by which the rest of the environment grew somewhat gayer. In other words, the next phase is that in which men like the Troubadours and the Italian poets, and in the present case the English poets, began to give gayer expression to their pleasure in the pagan poets; especially in Ovid. Now this pagan prestige covered, to a great extent, the pranks of the poets; and yet it produced a duality in the medieval mind which often puzzles the modern mind. It is not that the later medieval man is torn, like Tannhäuser, between Venus and the Virgin. He often seems, like Chaucer and Petrarch, to be able to turn with comparative lightness and innocence from the subject of Venus to that of the Virgin. But we shall completely misunderstand him, if we think that his levity means that they are too sympathetic or similar to be contrasted. On the contrary, his levity means that they are too unequal to be compared. There still remains the same contrast between this world and the other, even when this world has allowed itself to grow more worldly. There still remains the contrast between the cross and the crown, even when the cross has been moulded in gold, and jewelled more than all royal crowns.

Perhaps it might be pictured somewhat thus; that for a medieval man, his Paganism was like a wall and his Catholicism was like a window. No discussions of degree or relativity can get over the difference between a wall and a window. It is more even that a difference of dimension or of plane; it is very near to one of negative and positive. Anyhow, just as a very white sheet of paper looks black if held up against the sun, so any wall looks dark against any window. It may be a whitewashed wall, but it will not be as white as the dullest daylight. Now in the early days of medievalism, the wall of the world really was rather grey and grim. There was, as Mr. Belloc has said, something stark about the very strength of the first medieval structure of secular society. The wall was, let us say, of the cold colour of earth, and only the window had the colours of heaven. As medieval civilization progressed, and for a time it progressed very rapidly and well, the wall of this world was painted in brighter colours. When men like Petrarch and Chaucer were almost within sight of the Renaissance, they painted the wall with gorgeous designs in gold and scarlet. They did not hesitate to paint it with highly Pagan designs of gods and nymphs. Considered as mural illuminations, these things were very illuminating. Contrasted with the dull stone of the Dark Ages they were very bright. But, contrasted with the window, they were still dark.

It never really crossed the mind of any typical man of the Middle Ages, or for that matter of any typical man of the Renaissance, that the lightness of his mural decoration could approach anywhere near to the light from heaven. They were still divided by that abstract abyss between a window and a wall, which is like the chasm between light and darkness. If the window were curtained, if the wall were considered in itself, by artificial light, he would go almost any lengths in the enjoyment of its glitter or gaiety of colour; not to mention its sometimes rather excessive gaiety of subject. But he did not make it a rival to reality or the daylight. The moment he put the two into competition, he treated the lesser with contempt. For instance, some of the best Chaucerian authorities profoundly doubt; and I as an amateur, ignorant of all but human experience, also profoundly doubt, the authenticity of that queer postscript to *The Canterbury Tales*, expressing regret for all literary vanities except some poems of religion. It seems an unlikely sort of ending to any work; especially to a work that was not in fact ended. But if it were authentic, I could understand it better than men who are better scholars than I. Even if Chaucer wrote it, it would not mean what a modern poet would mean by being ashamed of his poems. It would not mean that they were something specially bad on their own plane; it would mean they were nothing on his ultimate plane; the plane of death and eternity. If this is inconsistent, his admitted works are inconsistent. Venus and Cupid dance in and out of his long love-poems on a principle of unfailing recurrence. They are a burden in the sense of a refrain; before the end, I fear, they are a burden in the sense of a bore. Of the many minor trades that Chaucer seems to be practising before us, perhaps the one he enjoys most is that of an architect of heathen temples. He never used better his beautiful sense of design than when fitting up those shrines with the ivory statue of Venus or the red metal of Mars. Troilus, the heroic lover, is necessarily in perpetual relation to the god and goddess of love, and many might read whole pages of such a poem and suppose it to be a translation from Ovid or Theocritus.

But when Troilus was actually dead and done with, the poet suddenly turned and spat all these things out of his mouth, as the saint spat the temples of Laodicea.[76] He treats all his graceful gods and goddesses exactly as 'the damned crew' which the Puritan Milton hurled howling from all their hollow fanes.

> Lo, here of pagans' cursed olden rites,
> Lo, here what all their high gods might avail,
> Lo, here this wretched worldës appetites,
> So here the end and guerdon of travail,
> Of Jove, Apollo, of Mars and such rascaille. . . .

. . .or (if we may modernize the language further) of all such rascals. That is what the serious Chaucer said of the serious Paganism. That is what he thought of the painted pictures on the wall, when there was talk of their blocking up the window.

To most modern people, with their notions drawn from the nineteenth century rather than the twentieth, this will seem an inconsistency, and in a sense it is indeed a complexity. But it is a complexity essential to the understanding of what they would call the simplicity of the Middle Ages, and especially the simplicity of 'Dan Chaucer'. There are perhaps three elements in it; one concerned with his time, one with his creed, and a third very specially with himself. The first was a general character of medieval philosophy especially Thomist philosophy, if we compare it with the real rival philosophies of the world; with the Buddhist philosophy or the Calvinist philosophy or the Positivist philosophy. It is the main mark of St. Thomas Aquinas, for instance, as compared with the few sages who are as great. He does lift Faith above Reason; but does not lower Reason. He does put the supernatural higher that the natural; but does not lower the natural. He says that the lower thing is in every sense worthy; except that compared with the higher it is worthless. This

---

[76] Laodicea is a Biblical city where the residents are "lukewarm" or indifferent to religion.

led to a habit of thinking on two levels, or even on three. It was like the medieval theatres which sometimes had three stages, one above the other; so in the poetry influenced by this philosophy, there was the lower stage in which the heathen gods were high, and the higher stage in whch they were low. Secondly it was connected with a character in Catholic morality as distinct from Protestant morality. I do not wish to state the contrast controversially, for it is easy to state it favourably or unfavourably to either side. But the point of Protestantism was that it wiped out *all* a man's sins at once, as if they were all equally sinful. *All* Christian's burden fell from him before the Cross. He did not have to unpack his own luggage in the confessional-box. But Catholicism always tended more to a table of sins, as of different weights and measures, and a real sense that while all are positively heavy, some are relatively light. This accounts for the very varying laxity of medieval and other writers about lighter things. Even when they thought the lover was a sinner, they never thought he was so great a sinner as the traitor. They might have thought Lancelot infinitely inferior to Galahad; but they also thought Modred infinitely inferior to Lancelot. We see these shifting and conflicting crosslights shining or darkening continually on the figure of Troilus. These matters of medieval philosophy and morality made up much of the paradox; but there was a third part of it that was not entirely of any period or system, but came out of the character of Geoffrey Chaucer.

If there is one feature that stands out, we might say sticks out, from the literary personality of Chaucer, it is a curious sort of hilarious half-ironical welcome to people more cynical than himself. He has an impulsive movement to applaud what he does not approve. It is as if their impudence gave him so much pleasure, that he could not withhold a sort of affection based on gratitude. We all remember the extraordinary virtues attributed to the Summoner:

> He was a gentle harlot and a kind,
> A better fellow could men nowhere find:
> For he would suffer for a quart of wine
> A good fellow to have his concubine
> A twelve-month, and exuse him at the full.

Fastidious readers have formed the impression that Chaucer's Summoner must have been about as objectionable a person to go on a pilgrimage with as anybody in the world, even the Miller; yet Chaucer cannot contain himself for gladness at the thought of such sociable eccentricities. His attitude towards the Shipman is more sympathetic than that of Stevenson towards a pirate. And indeed, so far as I can make out, the Shipman was, among other things, a pirate. But Chaucer is not to be shaken out of his geniality by trifles like that.

> And certainly he was a good felawe
> Full many a draught of wine would he draw
> From Bordeaux Ward, while the chapmen sleep;
> Of nice conscience took he no keep.
> If that he fought, and had the higher hand,
> By water he sent them home to every land.

which is said to be a polite way of saying that he made them walk the plank. But while Chaucer is on this level of artistic amusement, a little murder does not trouble him. Yet there were some murders that troubled him very much indeed. When he was once on the higher level, of considering the sufferings of the murdered, and facing the serious question of whether murder is morally advisable, he was rather specially a pathetic, rather than a stoic moralist. It would be hard to count the number of times he repeats the piteousness of the death of this or that person unjustly slain, as in the piercing lines about the boy martyr in the Tale of the Prioress. But he had set up, as part of the structure of his own mind a sort of lower and larger stage, for all mankind, in which anything could happen without seriously hurting anybody; and an upper stage which he kept almost deliberately separate, on which walked the angels of the justice and the mercy and the omniscience of God. This was a sort of cosmic complexity, which was supported by the dual standpoint of his morality and philosophy, but which belonged in any case to his individual temperament. It was a temperament especially English; but it is not quite fair to infer in the usual fashion, that it was therefore merely illogical. At bottom, it was no more illogical than the three dimensions are illogical. It depended on whether he was thinking along one line; or in the flat, as in broad farce; or of the solid images of virtue.

Chaucer did not hate the world; he did not under-value it or despise it; he only distrusted it, as a mellowed and matured old gentleman might distrust a bridge made by larky little boys. His sense of the vanity of earthly fortune and success was the recognition of a fact; not the insurgent rise of a feeling. He did not particularly dislike fate or dislike fortune, any more than he disliked the Shipman or the Wife of Bath; he was simply aware of what they were really made of. In this unruffled and radiant receptivity, he is rather unique among poets, and even among great men. Perhaps it would be true to say that he had the power of liking people whom he did not respect; and that he had extended this sentiment to the Goddess of Fortune and even to the Three Fates. His Christianity warmed and deepened whatever in this was Stoic, nay, whatever in this was Epicurean; but it is the whole point that his creed and culture had digested the dead philosophies; that is, brought them to life in a living organism. But his spiritual sanity showed itself most in this variety of emphasis or pressure; in being able to take at once his heathenism so lightly and his Christianity so weightily; in treating the gods and the grim fates as trifles, and the little relics and holy tokens as if they were larger things.

Thus the personal humour of Chaucer is an indirect, and perhaps distorted, derivative of the moral mood of his age and creed. It had bad by-products and good by-products; and Chaucer's wit was one of the best. But they ramified back to that double root in the rationalism and super-rationalism of the medieval moral philosophy. In short, Geoffrey Chaucer was exactly what 'the gentle Pardoner' was not—he was a gentle Pardoner. But we shall misunderstand all the men of that curious and rather complex society, if we do not realize that in a sense their eccentricities were connected with the same centre. The official venality of the bad Pardoner, and the very unofficial amiability of the good Pardoner, both came from the peculiar temptations and difficult diplomacies of the same religious system. They came because it was not, in the Puritan sense, a simple system. It was accustomed, even in minds much more serious than Chaucer's, to seeing (so to speak) two sides of a sin; to seeing it, now as awful and appalling merely because it was a sin; now as a venial sin utterly and unutterably different in its ultimate direction from a mortal sin. It was out of the abuse of distinctions of that kind that the distortions and corruptions appeared, which are made vivid in the flagrant figure of the Pardoner; the practice of Indulgences which had degenerated from the theory of Indulgences. But it was out of the use of distinctions of that kind that a man like Chaucer had originally reached the sort of balanced and delicate habit of mind, the habit of looking at all sides of the same thing; the power to realize that even an evil has a right to its own place in the hierarchy of evils; to realize, at least, that in the abysmal relativities of Hell and Purgatory, there are even things more unpardonable than the Pardoner.

In any case, this attitude is directly connected with the reality of his religion. Chaucer was more unmistakably orthodox than Langland; not because Chaucer was more superficial, but because he was more fundamental. Langland was troubled about many things, though most of them were worthy things; social order and moral discipline and the economics and ethics sharply needed in his time. But Chaucer had the one thing needful; he had the frame of mind that is the ultimate result of right reason and a universal philosophy; the temper that is the flower and the fruit of all the tillage and the toil of moralists and theologians. He had Charity; that is the heart and not merely the mind of our ancient Christendom; and between the black robes of Gower and the grey gown of Langland, he stands clothed in scarlet like all the household of love; and emblazoned with the Sacred Heart.

IX

THE MORAL OF THE STORY

Those strangely fanatical historians, who would darken the whole medieval landscape, have to give up Chaucer in despair; because he is obviously not despairing. His mere voice hailing us from a distance has the abruptness of a startling whistle or haloo; a blast blowing away all their artificially concocted atmosphere of gas and gloom. It is as if we opened the door of an ogre's oven in which we were told that everybody was being roasted alive, and heard a clear, cheery but educated voice remarking that it was a fine day. It is manifestly and mortally impossible that anybody should write or think as Geoffery Chaucer wrote and thought, in a world so narrow and insane as that which the anti-medievalists laboriously describe. They have no chance, on their own theory and argument, of answering that Chaucer was cheerful because he happened to be lucky in some ways, though unlucky in others; and certainly lived among the rich, though himself, at certain periods, decidedly poor. The whole point of Chaucer is in the fact that he does not retire with lords and ladies, like Boccaccio, to tell his tales. He is enjoying not the walled garden but the world. The world he is enjoying is just as much the world of the Ploughman and the Cook as of the Prioress and the Squire. Moreover, it is vital to the hostile contention that even emperors and princes could be crushed under superstitions that paralysed them like nightmares; and that to all men even the promise of heaven was only the threat of hell. And it is a stark staring fact, of everyday psychology, that a man like Chaucer could not have lived in a world like that. We are placed in a dilemma; but the horns are hardly of equal length. We know that Chaucer did live in the fourteenth century; we cannot be so certain of estimates formed in the twentieth century — or (as a matter of fact) surviving out of the nineteenth century. We know that Chaucer did live; and we are by no means so certain that the modern historians are alive.

In this chapter I would advance a certain general proposition, which I know will be called a paradox. We know the thousand things in Chaucer that converge to make it inconceivable that he should have walked about alive in a merely barbarous or bigoted or benighted epoch. We know, to mention one thing out of the thousand, the gentleness of his controversial manner; the way in which he feels confident that a light touch will tell; his assumption that his companions, gentle and simple, will understand each other. We know that men do not write like that, in an age when nobody could understand them. We know his bottomless bonhomie and good temper; as of one who had certainly never been tortured to exasperation by the alien world. We know his levity; the way in which he can flit from flower to flower even in the garden of heathenism; obviously without any pressing panic about the possibilities of heresy. We know his soaring hilarity and high spirits; never stronger than in his old age and comparitive poverty, when he began to sing of the April day when men took the road of Kent to Canterbury. We know that this did not come out of a dark and twisted superstition of a debased social slavery; and it only remains for us to ask what it did come from.

Now I will here advance the thesis that this cheerfulness or sanity came from theology. I say deliberately, not religion, but theology. It was not *his* theology: it was the theology at the back of the philosophy at the back of his mind. So far as a general religious sentiment goes, that might indeed have given him moods of thankfulness; but it would also have given him moods of melancholy. In so far as he was romantic (and he was); in so far as he was sometimes sentimental (and he was) he would often have become that sick and smitten lover so common in medieval romances. In all that medieval province there was something of Botticelli; even something of Burne-Jones.[77] Nothing is more typical of that time than the fact that its very real valour and virility were nevertheless covered with a veil of merely poetical sentiment, which strikes us as rather affected and lackadaisical; like the iron armour of a knight covered by some embroidered vestment with figured patterns of broken lilies or heartbroken ladies. All the literature of that time is loud with Complaints

---

[77] Sir Edward Coley Burne-Jones (1833-98) was an English painter and designer of the Pre-Raphelite school.

of Lovers and Confessions of Love; and there is a sense in which men like Chaucer did make of it a religion as well as a romance. For instance, we have seen that Chaucer, with very Chaucerian freshness (almost in the slang sense of impudence), calls his collection of Pagan ladies, like Dido or Cleopatra, by the title of 'Cupid's Lives of the Saints', or 'The *Acta Sanctorum* of Cupid'. Romance was a religion; certainly it was all that the modern Romantics mean by a religion. It was even rather more respectable than some of the modern developments that owe their inspiration to Byron or George Sand. It demanded very real virtues; fidelity to the death; patience even in despair; courtesy even in combat. Now if Love had really been a religion to Chaucer and Petrarch, even in the sense in which it was to some extent a religion to Keats or Rossetti, it might well have been in many cases a rather sad religion. Chaucer, however romantic, is quite sufficiently realistic to realize that Cupid can be a tyrant or that jealousy is cruel as the grave. If this sort of poetic sense of beauty is what we mean by religion (and it is what many moderns mean by religion), *that* alone would not have kept Chaucer cheerful. It was his real religion that kept him cheerful. Perhaps it will seem less paradoxical, if I point out that it is exactly parallel to the example of the greatest of Chaucer's contemporaries. You will find precisely that religion of lovers in Dante's *Vita Nuova*; and in *that*, therefore, Beatrice fades away like a fancy and leaves the poet sad. It is only when Beatrice reappears as a Theological Virtue in the *Paradiso*, that things begin to brighten up a bit. They were so paradoxical that they thought brightness came from the sky.

The real trouble of the Middle Ages lay in their rudimentary and relatively bad communications for the handing on of their good things; not in the least in their not having the good things to communicate. We are in a position to appreciate the distinction at the present moment; when we have very good communications and nothing to communicate. The comparative impotence of medievalism to carry out its own plans, whether evil or good, can indeed be best tested by comparing their processes with a practical thing like a large modern news-paper; that loud and regular organ by which our civilization daily proclaims that it has nothing to say. Had it existed in the Middle Ages, it might conceivably have made the philosophers more popular; it would certainly have made the tyrants more tyrannical. No man in the Middle Ages was so rich that he could have sent a herald to every man's house every morning, to challenge with trumpet and tabard any other view than that which this particular rich man wished to promulgate; yet that is exactly the power now possessed by several rich men, much less dignified than any rich man in the fourteenth century. No man was rich enough to nail a proclamation upon every man's door at dawn, as some are now rich enough to place a newspaper upon every man's table at breakfast; in both cases to be taken as unanswerable because it is unanswered. It is amusing to speculate what would have happened if Caxton had come a century earlier and developed all the powers of a few centuries later; and that an engine like the Press had been (as of course it would have been, and indeed still is) in the hands of the governing class of the day. If the King could have made the same statement suddenly and simultaneously to all his subjects, it would doubtless have averted many revolutions founded on rumours; nor would this be the less effective because the rumours were true and the royal explanation was false. Richard the Second could probably have prevented the Peasants' Rising, if he could have posted his promise of reform and offer to be a popular leader, made in the famous speech at Blackheath, to every cottage and hovel in the whole feudal countryside. After that the promise could be broken in due course, as it was then and probably would be now; possibly through the same agency, the pressure of the plutocrats in Parliament. Similarly, if Bolingbroke had been able to send horsemen so swiftly all over England that every squire, yeoman or vassal could hear his side of the case and no other, if he could have done all that in one day on the very day when he deposed Richard the Second, there would probably have been no rising in the North, no Battle of Shrewsbury or legend of the return of Richard. It would certainly have hugely solidified the position of the usurper; and whether that would have been a good thing the reader must be left, on his own general principles, to judge. It is enough to note, as one aspect of the rudeness and delay of medieval communications, that revolutions could occur in one part of the country without the most powerful persons, in another part of the country, having even the power to parley with them. And if, on the other hand, something happened about which any parley was undesirable, there was then no really efficient machinery for keeping the public misinformed on the matter.

But whatever we may think about the halting of political information, there is no doubt that the halting of general information was a defect of the ruder conditions of medieval life. The information existed, and was in many matters very varied and full. Nor was it necessarily regarded as privileged information; it was never impossible for a poor man to obtain instruction in medieval England as it was impossible for a Negro to obtain it in a great part of nineteenth-century America. It was not so much that he was forbidden to get it, as that it was physically difficult to get. All books had to be laboriously transcribed by hand; the possession of a mass of such manuscripts was rare; and they were handed about cautiously, by comparison with all modern caution in the lending of books. Even a cultivated man like Chaucer, with a comfortable salary, seems frequently to get glimpses of the most important books indirectly, or even accidentally. Often he seems never to have seen the very books that we should chiefly expect him to see. After having been long regarded almost as a mere copyist of the Decameron, he is now supposed, by the most recent scholars, never to have seen the Decameron at all. But he did see one story out of the Decameron; not as it was written in Italian by Boccaccio, but as it was translated into Latin by Petrarch. It is possible that he owed even this to the accident of meeting Petrarch. Similarly, while he had certainly read Ovid and Virgil, it is thought improbable that he had ever seen a manuscript of Livy: though he invokes Livy and praises Livy and actually tells a tale out of Livy. Probably he took it from somebody who took it from Livy. There is any amount of this indirect, distorted and scrappy element in the culture; education by haphazard and hearsay. In this sense the opportunities of culture were limited; the communications for conveying culture were limited; the machinery for popularizing culture was limited.

But the culture was not limited. The education that was imparted, the education that was interrupted, was not limited. The books, that were borrowed or copied or translated or mistranslated, were not narrow or limited books. They were books which often conveyed, more completely than the fashionable books of any other epoch, the idea of an enlarged and enlightened philosophy of life; the consideration of both sides of a question; the balancing of one consideration against another; the conception of the whole sublunary world under the light of reason. Consider only one ordinary possibility, which in the case of Chaucer amounts to a probability. Suppose at some time some medieval man had only three medieval books. And suppose those three were, first, some version of the works 'of Aristotle and his philosophy'; second, the Divine Comedy of Dante; and third, the Summa of St. Thomas Aquinas. This is not to possess books but to possess worlds. They are three universes of thoughts and things; or rather three aspects of the same universe; the one positive and rationalist; the other imaginative and pictorial; the third moral and mystical, but still inherently logical. A man might own a whole Circulating Library of modern novels and minor poets, without having anything like such a cosmic conspectus, or complete consideration of all sides of the real world. But the vital point to seize, in connexion with the particular case of Chaucer, is that the philosophy considered as a philosophy, and even the theology considered as a theology, was one which aimed at a certain equilibrium, achieved by giving so much weight to one thing and so much less or more to another. I know all about the harsher side of it, and especially the harsher defence of it, as it affects the humanitarians of our own time; that it believed in devils; that it defended itself by inquisitors. But that has nothing whatever to do with the present point, about the nature of the thing defended. That thing was a poised and proportioned thing; thought out and thrashed out by the comparison of many thoughts; not a single thing or a simple thing, in the sense of the isolation of one thought. And though even a man like Chaucer, through the limits of the medieval machinery, received this culture in a rather fragmentary way, he received enough of its fragments to be filled with its fulness. He was full enough of that fulness not to let his own thought be merely fragmentary; in the sense of thinking one fragment of truth as good as the whole. Still less did he think, as does the true heretic, that the fragment of truth is better than the whole.

External ecclesiasticism had indeed so far degenerated in Chaucer's day that many good and simple people then, like many good and simple people now, had begun to cry out for a simpler religion; for a simplified Christianity. They had that natural yearning, which always begins with a prayer for a single eye and always ends (with painfully exact fulfilment) in winking the other eye, in a one-eyed concentration on a single object. Modern historians often accept it, even now, as the purest form of idealism; but it always means being a man of one idea. It means very precisely fulfilling the proverbial phrase about the man 'who has not two ideas in his head'.

Now the Schoolman always had two ideas in his head; if they were only the Yes and No of his own proposition. The Schoolman was not only the schoolmaster but also the schoolboy; he examined himself; he cross-examined himself; he may be said to have heckled himself for hundreds of pages. Nobody can read St. Thomas's theology without hearing all the arguments against St. Thomas's theology. Therefore, even when that sort of faith produced what many would call ferocity, it always produced what I mean here by fairness; the almost involuntary intellectual fairness of one who cannot help knowing that the universe is a many-sided thing. That is precisely the temper of Chaucer; and that is what I mean when I say that he got his broad-mindedness from his theology; though it was not what is now generally meant by a broad theology. The essential point is that it was not a simple theology. As I have said, many medieval heretics, admired by modern historians, were even then beginning to cry out for a simpler theology. In the time of the Lollards, and in their particular and painful circumstances, it was often pardonable, and certainly ought more often to have been pardoned. In the time of Mr. G. M. Trevelyan,[78] which is somewhat later in history, it is more mystifying. One would suppose that an able

---

[78] George Macaulay Trevelyan (1876–1962) was an eminent English historian.

and cultivated man, who has lived to see the subdivision and suicide of all the sects, would have had enough of such simplifications. But in his interesting book, on the Age of Wycliffe, he makes a comparison equally suicidal. He says that his hero proposed, in the most sweepingly Protestant manner, to free the parish clergy of all control by Popes or Bishops or anybody else; until every parson should be as independent as a Presbyterian minister in Scotland. The example is somewhat unfortunate. Certainly the creed of Calvinism, which all Scottish ministers were forced to teach for two hundred years, was a simple creed. Nothing could be simpler than saying that men go to Hell because God made them on purpose to send them to Hell. But even of that childlike innocence and simplicity a good many people seem to have grown tired at last. Nothing could be simpler than the stark negation of the Scottish Sabbath; for nothing can be simpler than nothing. Yet even of the childlike Scottish Sabbath, it is sometimes said that the children grew a little restless towards the end of the day. Their modern descendants certainly grew as restless towards the end of the nineteenth century as ever the Lollards did towards the end of the fourteenth century. And when among *these* eighteenth-century Presbyterians there arose a Poet, that unfortunate bard was not quite so calm or so contented or so cheerful as Chaucer.

Matthew Arnold coupled Chaucer with Burns, as two fine poets who fell short of 'seriousness'. It is queer that he does not see the very contrast he suggests. Chaucer may or may not be serious, but he is not seriously in revolt against seriousness. He does not resent the Parson or the Clerk of Oxford being wholly serious. He leans back easily against the hundred books of Aristotle; like a man in his own home. Chaucer may be too much at ease in Zion. But Burns is not at all at ease in his Zion. The attitude of Burns to the local and national theology is one of revolt and nothing else. It was simply a dingy provincialism that could only narrow the mind. But for Chaucer his theology was a thing that broadened his mind. It brought him into contact with great minds like Dante and Aquinas; it linked up his country with all Europe; it even referred him backwards to the greatest sages of pagan antiquity. That is the fact that must in fairness be balanced against the slow progress and patchy incompleteness of medieval education. Chaucer, though a courtier and diplomatist, might have only one or two books; little trifles tossed off by Aristotle or Dante. Robert Burns, though a peasant and a poor man, might have a chance of buying a whole load of books of Scottish theology; a small library of Calvinistic sermons. Only he did not want to. He did not like them. He was never moved to say of them, 'On bokës for to rede I me delyte.' Poor Burns never got out of the Puritan fog for one breath of that fresh air and daylight, of quite spontaneous spiritual joy and gratitude, with which the medieval poet stretches out his hands to saints and sages as to his best benefactors and friends. In that larger enlightenment of theological theory, Chaucer could afford to be relatively cheerful and charitable even about the degradations of ecclesiastical practice. Chaucer had more tolerance for the corruptions of Catholicism than Burns had even for the decencies of Calvinism. And it is not hard to see why; because, while Chaucer's mind had been irritated or distressed by the incidental evils of a corrupted Christianity, at least his soul had not been poisoned and blackened and blasted by the monomaniac horrors of a Simple Christianity.

He had not seen all theology shrivel to a single thought; its very thunders of indignation all on one note; or the whole great Christian philosophy hardened into one harsh doctrine. It is that flat featureless inhumanity, that repetition of pattern, that absence of ornament, that made Puritanism to a man like Burns, not a castle of enchantment, not even a false enchantment, but merely a prison. It is that which gives that indescribable irrationality and violence to the cry of Burns; an irrationality that was perhaps the beginning of Romanticism. But Chaucer is never irrational; however much he may be irritated. He feels in a vast if vague fashion that he has Reason behind him; as he has Aristotle and Aquinas and a whole civilization behind him. It was in many ways a decaying civilization; it was (for the time being) even a dying civilization. But it was a dying civilization by which a man might live; and even live merrily. He did not suffer the particular kind of suffocation that comes in the *cul-de-sac* of a single idea, which is called a simple creed. He had the breadth and the blessings of a complicated creed. Its corruptions, as distinct from its complications, often took the form of the most abominable abuses; because the corruption of the best is the worst. But the corruption of the worst is nothing at all; it simply ceases; it does not even continue to corrupt.

As I have already emphasized, I have very considerable sympathy with the Lollards; the particular heretics of the Chaucerian epoch. They were often infamously treated; they were sometimes intuitively right. In so far as they originally set out to reform the practical Catholicism of their day, there were few reputable Catholics then, and there are no reasonable Catholics now, who would deny that Catholicism very much needed it. In so far as they had a desire to purify Catholicism, they may often have been spiritually right even when they were intellectually wrong; and in that sense, may have been better Catholics than the Catholics. But in so far as they had a desire to *simplify* Catholicism, the Catholic Church was ten thousand times right in its desire to defeat and crush them. That notion, in its essence a very negative notion, has never wrought anything but ill to Christendom; and is always returning with a plausibility and a false simplicity to tempt and to betray Christians. Mahomet, centuries before, had tried to create a simplified Christianity, and had created a world of fatalism and stagnation. Calvin, centuries afterwards, tried to create a simplified Christianity, and created a world of pessimism and devilworship. It was of the very life of the ancient civilization, Pagan as well as Christian, from which medievalism drew its deep and strange type of strength, that it was rooted in very varied realities; that it had made a cosmos out of a chaos of experiences; that it knew what was positive and could yet allow for what was really relative; that its Christ was shared by God and Man; that its government was shared by God and Caesar: that its philosophers made a bridge between faith and reason, between freedom and fatalism; and that its moralists warned men alike against presumption and despair. Only by understanding all that ten times complicated sort of complication, can we see how Geoffrey Chaucer could find life so simple.

The meaning of Aquinas is that medievalism was always seeking a centre of gravity. The meaning of Chaucer is that, when found, it was always a centre of gaiety. For very many modern people, even of those who are sympathetic with, or even reverential towards, the religion that prevailed before the Reformation, quite honestly believe that it is solely a mystical ecstasy; and that sincere believers in it must be saints or nothing. In fact, it is exactly the other way round. It was Protestantism that was a mystical ecstasy; especially Protestantism in its pure form of Puritanism. It was the really good and sincere Protestants who were saints or nothing. The political period, that was actually named The Reign of the Saints, meant the Commonwealth that was The Reign of the Puritans. A frivolous Puritan was not a Puritan at all. But it is not true, in the same sense, that a frivolous Catholic is not a Catholic at all. A Catholic may be like (or indeed may actually be) a dancer whose whole business is dancing, a clown who has to be continually thinking about clowning; but may feel all the time that there is solid ground to dance on, in the sort of solid world that his soul inhabits. And this has a way of happening, especially at moments when the world is becoming much less solid, for people who are more serious. When corruption and chaos are disturbing ordinary minds, and many good men are only worried and serious, it has often happened that a great man could apparently be frivolous; and appear in history almost as a great buffoon. One of the sonnets of Mr. Maurice Baring has a haunting line about the souls of lovers blown upon a wind: 'to rest for ever on the unresting air.' In a very different connexion, it can be said that these rare and sane spirits did rest on the unresting air of a revolutionary epoch or a dissolving civilization. And there is always something about them puzzling to those who see their frivolity from the outside and not their faith from the inside. It is not realized that their faith is not a stagnation but an equilibrium. If we take three men as types; Chaucer and Thomas More and Cervantes, we shall note that they were three Catholics whose lives cover the whole story of the breakdown of Catholicism; the first appearing in the earliest disturbances at the end of medievalism; the second at the very crisis of the crash; the third just after the division of Christendom was practically complete. And our first impression will be that they were all three of them humorists, who took things very easily, considering the dreadful days of destruction and transition in which they lived. The only legend left by Sir Thomas More was that he actually died laughing. It is quite true that he died joking, though there was already the beginnings of the Puritan stiffness that would not unbend to jokes; just as his fellow-martyr Kimball died smoking, in spite of the fury which faddists like James the First were to fulminate against tobacco. There is something almost irresponsible in the intellectual ease with which Cervantes feels himself free to chaff chivalry out of existence; when so many greater things, that went with it, had largely ceased to exist. The greatest of all satires on mere medievalism came out of the man and the country most full of what is called the medieval creed. But Catholicism is not medievalism. It is only something that could make medievalism tolerable to a man like Chaucer; just as it could make something more like modernism tolerable to men of the Renaissance like More and Cervantes. The whole story will make no sense, unless we realize that the Catholic philosophy can content a man; rather specially if the man is a philosopher; and not least if he is a laughing philosopher.

In this sense we are quite ready to admit that Chaucer was only a lucky and lonely elf, who found a sunbeam and danced in it. But sunbeams only come from the sun, and the sun is the centre of a solar system. At any rate, his sun was the centre of his solar system. If we are to understand it, we must go back to a very ancient sunrise; nay, to many repeated sunsets. It is *not* true that his daylight spirit belongs only to the day that had not yet dawned; the day of the Renaissance. If we want to trace that light, we must trace it backward through the ages; and, by way of a beginning, as was here recorded at the start, we must go back to Boethius. It does not matter for the moment whether we call that culture Catholicism or the continuity of an ancient Humanism. We must go back to that 'long evening by the Mediterranean', as it has been finely called, when all that was best in a Christian Empire, in the person of Boethius, remembered the Stoics and defied a tyrant and died. There were not two men who died, a Christian and a Stoic; but one man who was already both. That is the heritage that had been handed down to Christian men; and it was not lopsided or bigoted. Why did Alfred throw himself at once upon the translation of Boethius? There were any number of dreary hagiographical legends for him to translate. Why did St. Thomas, at the very top of the Middle Ages, think also of Boethius? Why did he resist the short-sighted panic that condemned Aristotle? Because against a thousand wild and wanton accidents, in the confusion following on the barbarian invasions and the failure of the Roman scheme, the spirit of all that society was making for a balance; a balance like that of the two eyes of a man; or that which gives two scales even to Justice blind. It was holding hard on to civilization and an equal law, and that hold did not fail, even when the civilization failed.

The ancient central civilization from which the Lollards and Lutherans and later Puritans broke away was, or looked like, a dying civilization. So the central civilization from which Mahomet and the Moslems broke away was, or looked like, a dying civilization. Byzantium appeared in the eyes of Mahomet, as Babylon in the visions of Petrarch, as a thing stiff with gold but stiff also with fossilization; a thing visibly sinking under the weight of its own wickedness and wealth. It is not specially surprising that many in the Dark Ages preferred Bagdad to Byzantium, and even called it the superiority of Islam to Christendom. But it has not in the long run meant the superiority of Asia to Europe; or even the absorption of Christendom by the advance of Islam. Similarly, the setting up of sects in the sixteenth and seventeenth centuries has not meant in the long run the absorption of Catholicism by the advance of Puritanism. What Mahomet and Calvin and all those thus breaking away from the dying civilization did not realize, is the curious fact that it is a dying civilization that never dies. It does decline, and has done so any number of times; it does decay; it is always at it. But it does not disappear; and, the end of more or less debased periods, has a way of managing to reappear, when its enemies have in their turn decayed. The moral is, I will venture to think, that it is unwise to desert this perpetually sinking ship, or betray this everlastingly dying creed and culture. It has had another period of final extinction; even since its final extinction at the end of the Middle Ages. It has suffered eclipse in the Enlightenment of the Age of Reason and Revolution; which in their turn begin to look as if they had seen better days. And to-day it stands erect and resurrected; and to right and left of it the Moslems have stagnated and the Puritans starved; starved not only for the art and symbolism normal to men, but now for the faith and conviction once special to themselves. No; it was not wise to leave it, even for the Republic; it will not be wise to leave it, even for the Soviet.

The moral is that no man should desert that civilization. It can cure itself; but those who leave it cannot cure it. Not Nestorius nor Mohamet nor Calvin nor Lenin have cured, nor will cure, the real evils of Christendom; for the severed hand does not heal the whole body. Those outside the body will endure only centuries of separation and then death. Where are the Nestorians? Meanwhile, within the body of the Christian world, there was a perpetual and centripetal tendency towards the discovery of a just balance of all these ideas. All those who broke away were centrifugal and not centripetal; they went away into deserts to develop a solitary doctrine. But medieval philosophy and culture, with all the crimes and errors of its exponents, was always *seeking* equilibrium. It can be seen in every line of its rhythmic and balanced art; in every sentence of its carefully qualified and self-questioning philosophy. It was everywhere in the air, though it affected various people in various degrees now impossible to distinguish. But it was everywhere a movement towards civilization; towards the centre of ideas; whatever might be the wild decentralization of events. And, while there are many proofs of this, there could be no more full or unanswerable proof than the shout that showed that normality had been found. For a great voice was given by God, and a great volume of singing, not to his saints who deserved it much better; not to any of those heroes who had made that clearing in the ancient forest; but only suddenly, and for a season, to the most human of human beings.

The text of this book has been set in Bembo by the Neumann Press of Long Prairie, Minnesota. Printed on Warren's Sebago paper by Thomson Shore, Dexter, Michigan. Bound in Kennet cloth by John H. Dekker & Sons. The cover and jacket design are by Darlene Lawless O'Rourke.